New Museums

New Museums

Catherine Donzel

Telleri

THE ART OF THE HABITAT

Series edited by Olivier Boissière

Front cover
Fondation Beyeler,
Basel, Switzerland.
Architect: Renzo Piano.

Back cover
Guggenheim Museoa,
Bilbao, Spain.
Architect:
Frank O. Gehry.

Preceding page
Shimosuwa Museum,
Nagano, Japan.
Architect: Toyo Ito.

Editorial Director: Jean-François Gonthier
Art Director: Bruno Leprince
Cover design: Daniel Guerrier
Writers: Catherine Donzel with Véronique Donnat and Olivier Boissière
English adaptation: Unity Woodman, Lisa Gardner
Editing: Françoise Derray
Assistant: Sophie-Charlotte Legendre
Composition: Graffic, Paris
Filmsetting: Compo Rive Gauche, Paris
Lithography: Litho Service, T. Zamboni, Verona

ISBN : 2-7450-0036-5
Printed in the European Community

TELLERI - 30, rue de Charonne - F-75011 Paris

Contents

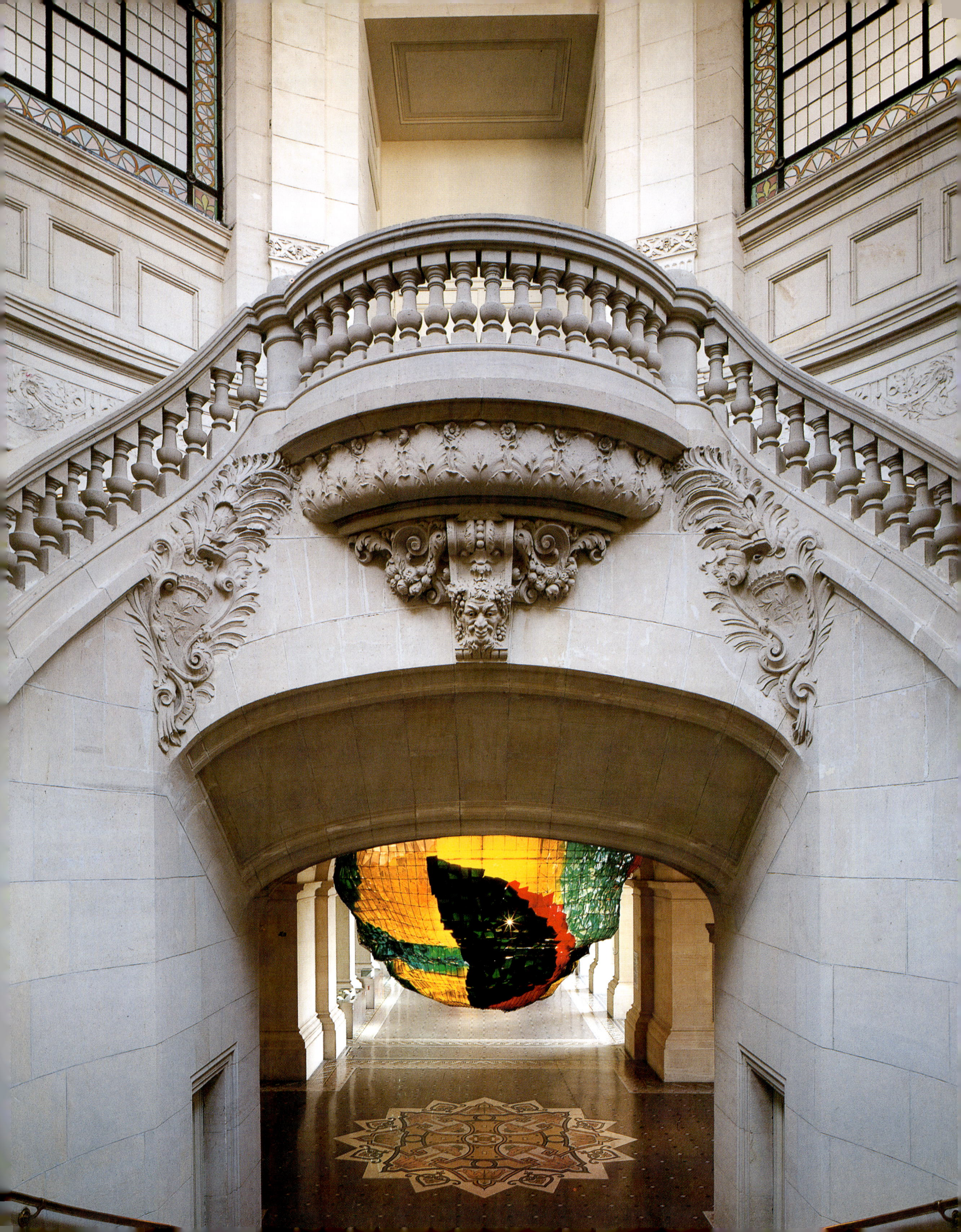

Introduction

Over the last few decades, we have seen a proliferation of new museums. The reasons for this are manifold and often disputed.

Clearly influential, however, have been developments in the conservation and exhibition of artworks, including temperature control, electronic surveillance and lighting. There has also been significant change in how museums acquire contemporary artworks, whereby they tend to short-circuit the traditional gallery/collector channels, buying works of artists at a much earlier stage in their career and at lower prices. These acquisitions naturally call for new approaches to exhibition and storage space. Moreover, large, well-established institutions have had to modernize, often seizing the opportunity to expand.

The rise of new museums also stems from a wider notion of the term "culture": all our activities and every manifestation of our ingenuity are now worthy of consideration. And so it is that museums are springing up that specialize in fashion, agricultural machinery... even cheese.

This growth is coupled with a new rationale: with the "engineering" of culture, administrators and directors can make a profit out of almost any cultural heritage by merchandising with postcards, T-shirts and hot dogs. The museum of yesterday with its exhibition halls and storage rooms, flanked by a few administrative offices is no longer; today it is a pandemonium.

New Museums limits itself to painting and sculpture, whether classical or contemporary. Its aim is to show new aspects belonging to museums of different caliber from the new Getty Museum in Los Angeles, the Guggenheim in Bilbao to the Beyeler Foundation in Basel. These projects have called upon world renowned architects including the Spaniard Rafael Moneo, the Portuguese Alvaro Siza and the Americans Richard Meier and Frank O. Gehry. Museums are, after all, the privileged domain of the most contemporary of architectural expressions.

Palais des Beaux-Arts,
Lille, France.
Architects:
Ibos & Vitart.

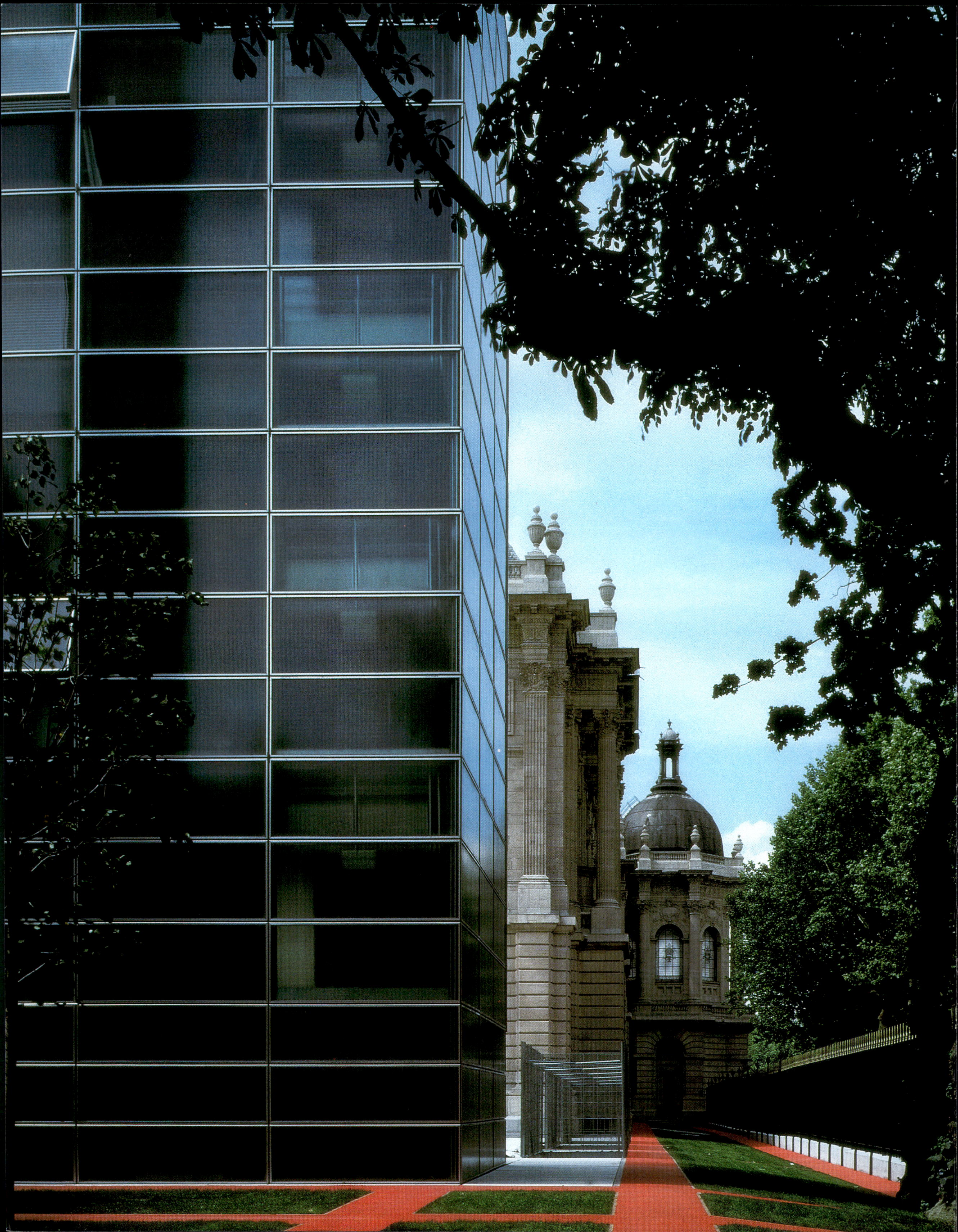

Ibos & Vitart

Palais des Beaux-Arts

Lille, France

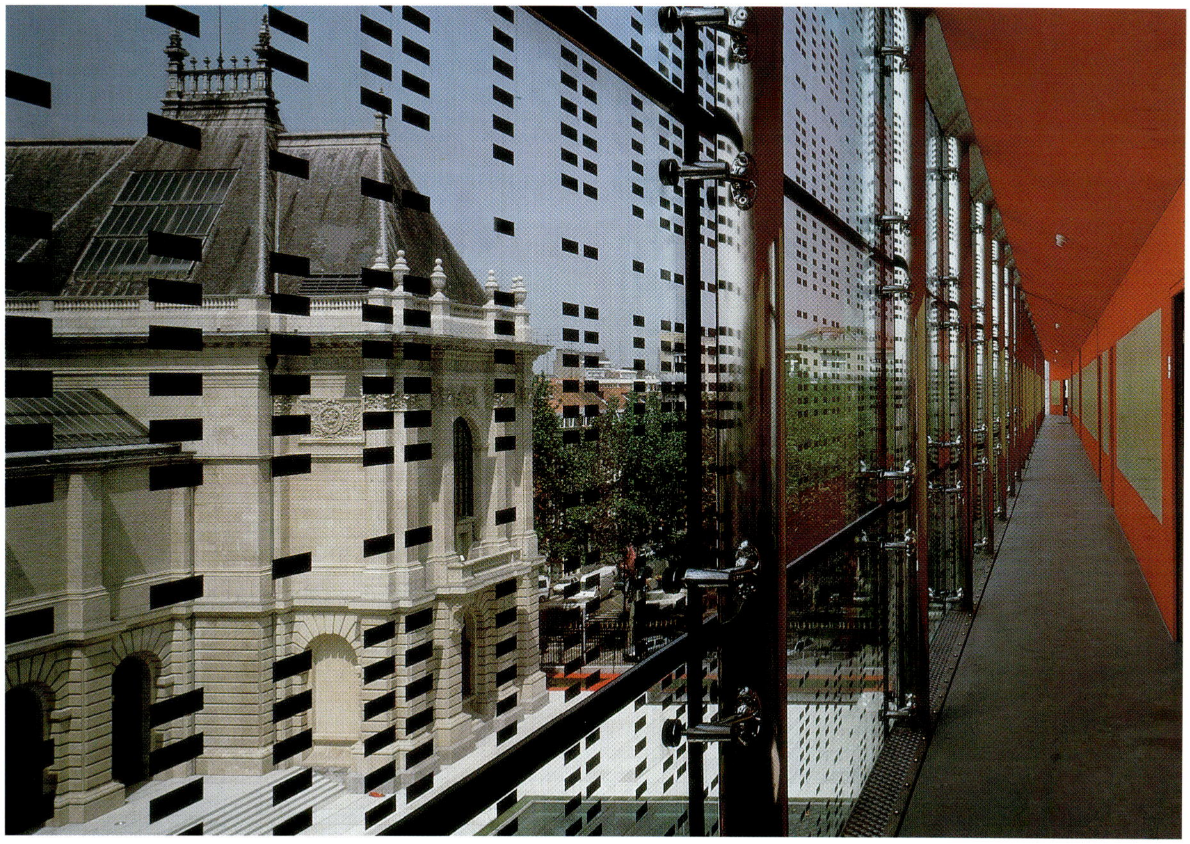

The renovation and extension of the Palace of Fine Arts of Lille is noteworthy not only for the redesigning of the interior of the old building but also for the construction of the extraordinary blade building standing apart from the south facade. This architectural addition has become almost the symbol of the museum, its logo, its distinguishing feature. The "blade" is sheathed in glass, not only reflecting the facade of the 19th-century palace but also defining in transparency a play of gold monochromes on a red backdrop, repeating the interior signboard of the exhibition galleries.

Opposite page
Detail of the back facade of the blade building housing the administrative offices.

It was the 1890's that witnessed the construction of the Museum of the Palace of Fine Arts in the very center of Lille facing the imposing police headquarters: a sumptuous neoclassical monument embodying the privileged status of the northern capital and bringing together some of today's most important French collections.

Besides its two very famous Goyas, the Palace of Fine Arts houses thousands of paintings, drawings, sculptures and art objects, to say nothing of the sixteen relief maps of northern cities which Lille's mayor Pierre Mauroy was able to wrest away from the collections of the Invalides Museum in Paris. In 1990 the difficulty inherent in accommodating these gigantic relief maps was precisely the deciding factor in the renovation and the extension of the Palace of Fine Arts. A palace whose vast spaces had become particularly congested after a century of intentionally accumulative museology. Due to generalized overcrowding, the galleries had been divided lengthwise and mezzanines added; since the 1930's, the atrium was encumbered by a monumental staircase; and a hideous addition had obstructed and disfigured the garden side facade since 1970.

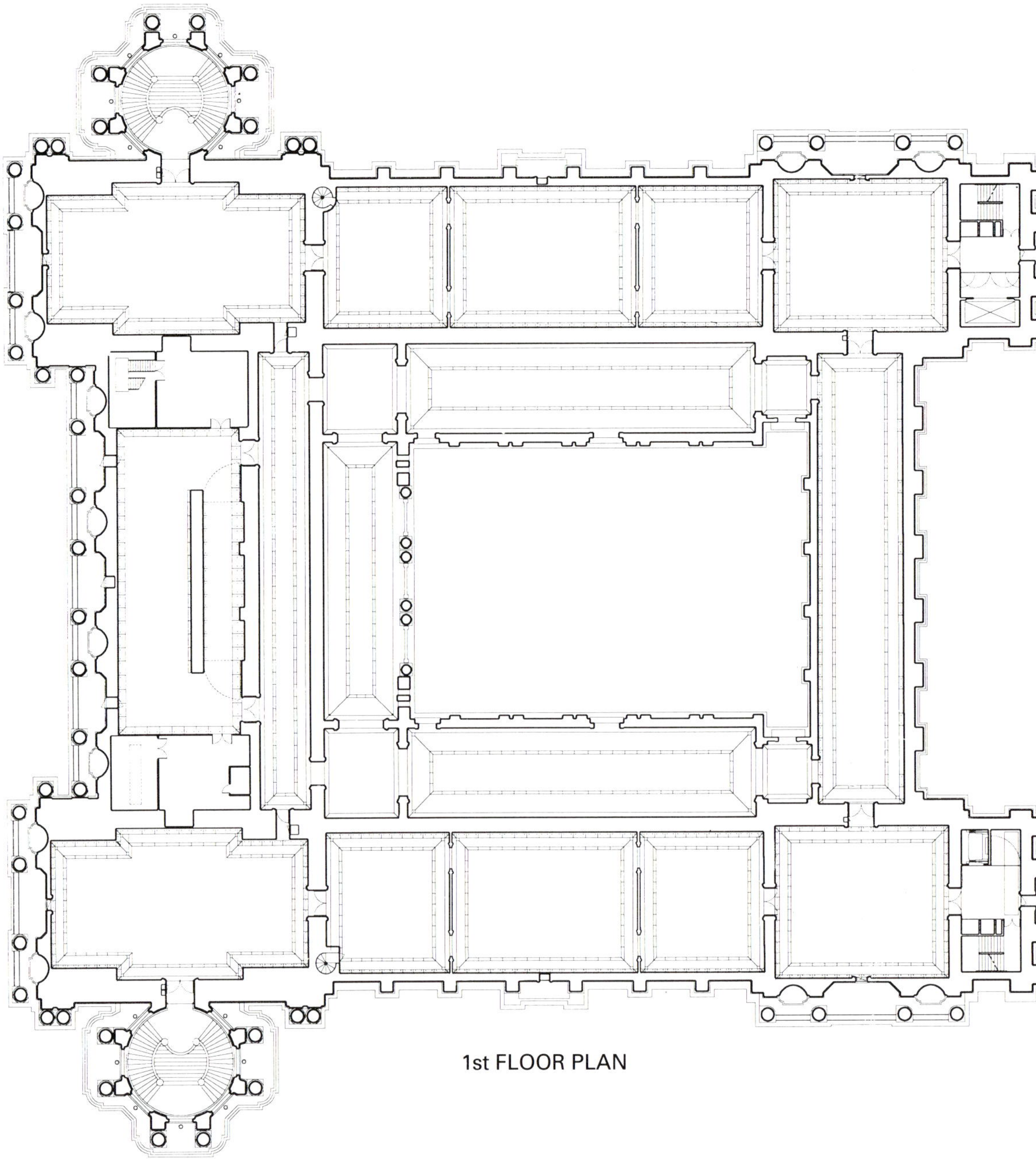

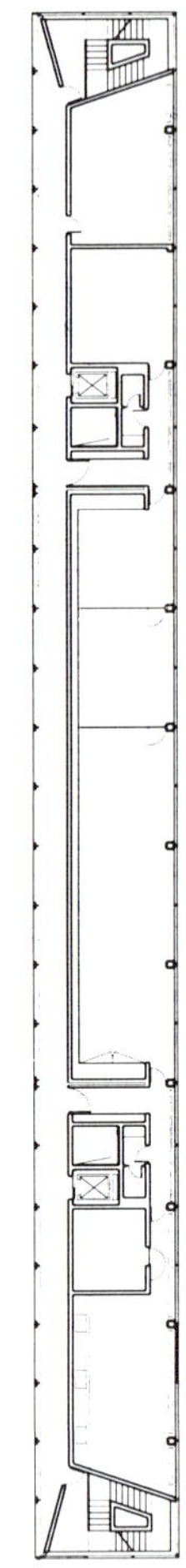

1st FLOOR PLAN

Plans of the Palace of Fine Arts and diurnal and nocturnal views of the museum's south facade reflected in the "mirror" of the blade building.

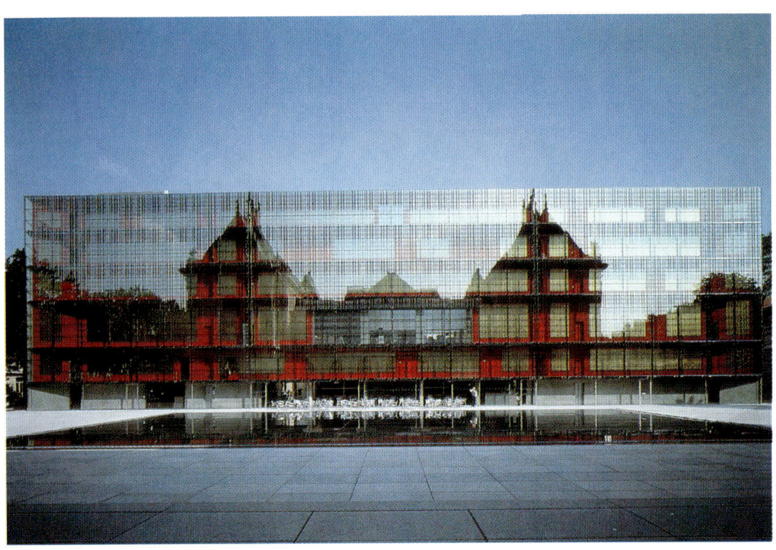

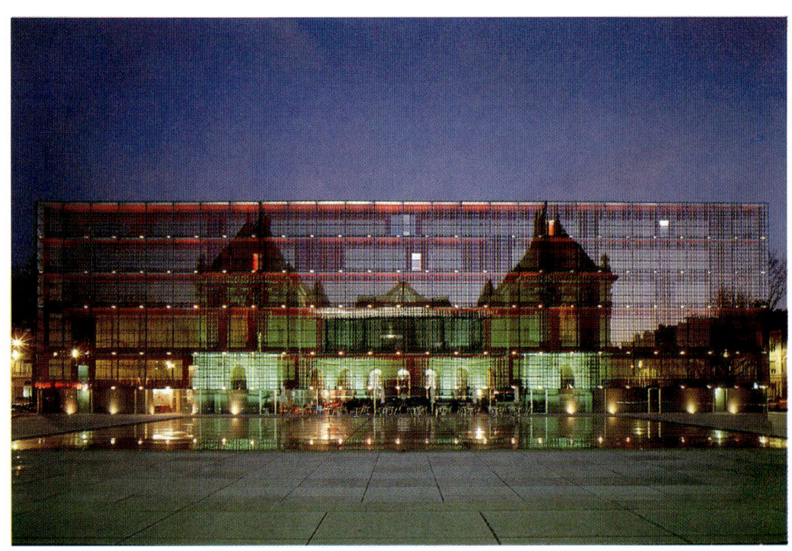

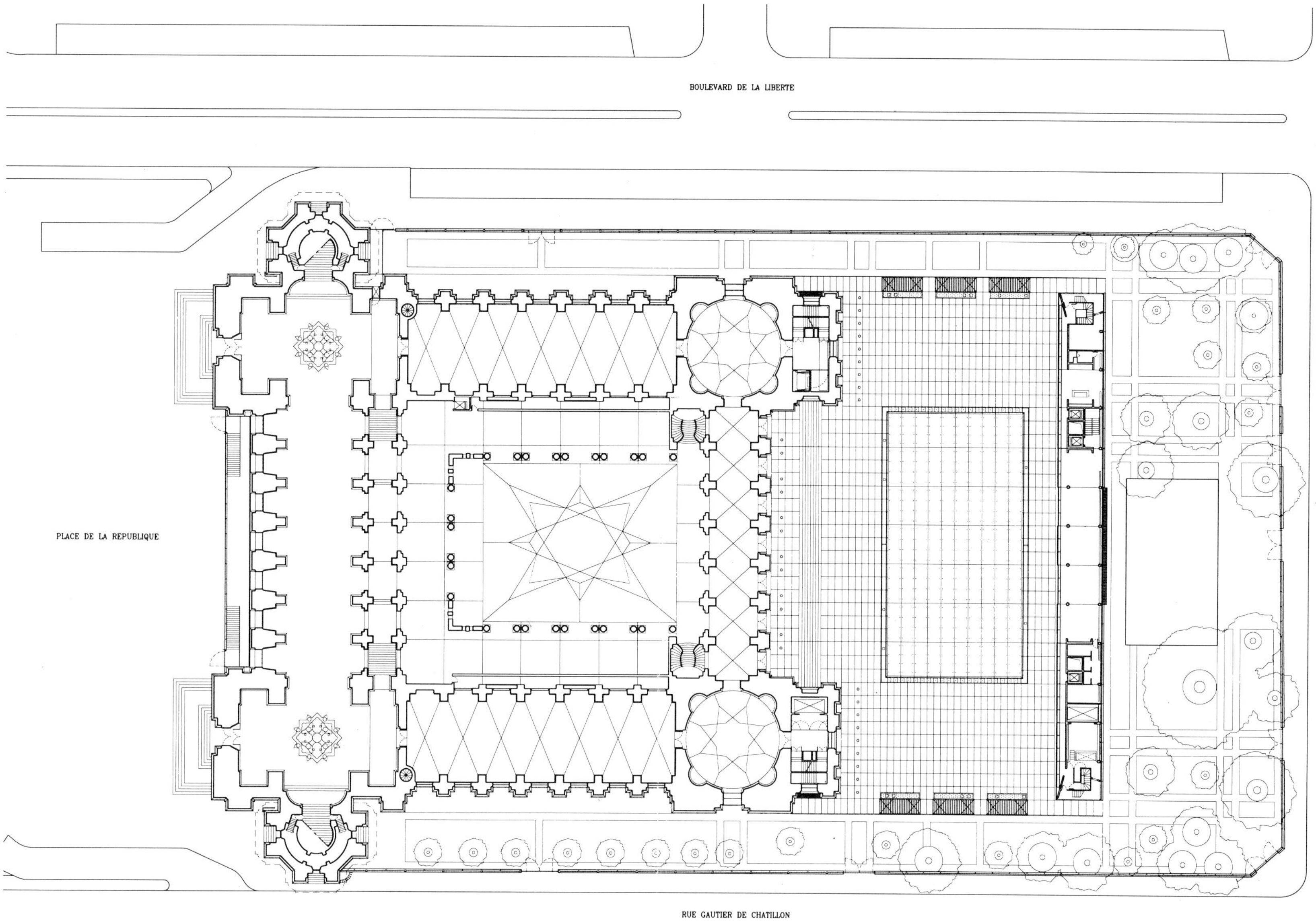

Ground floor plan

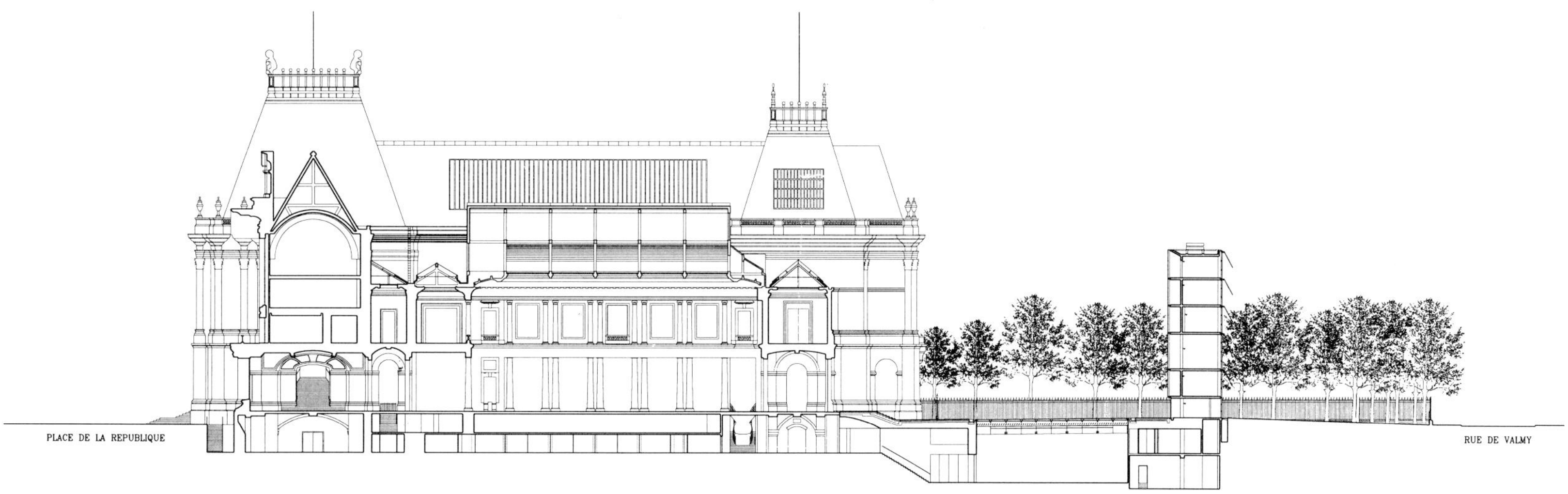

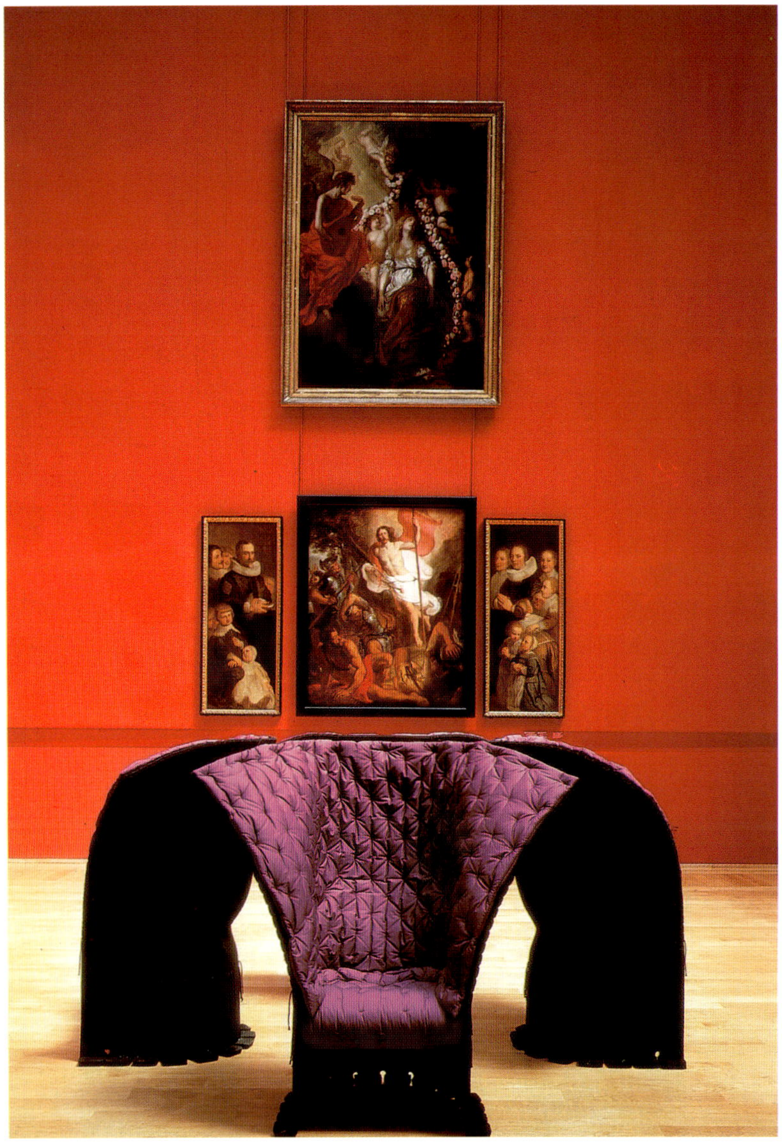

Detail of one of the painting rooms on the second floor whose high galleries are lit with skylights. Pale oak floors, Pompeii red walls, the remaining elements of the decor including the door frames are all painted matt white. To comfort but also to demystify the idea of a painting salon, Gaetano Pesce's sumptuous and amusing armchairs.

It was then that Jean-Marc Ibos and Myrto Vitart, winners of the city's architectural competition, proposed a project which, albeit radical, aimed at the rediscovery of this late 19th-century building whose extraordinary potential they presaged.

Their first undertaking was the colossal job of cleaning and demolition: on the exterior, restoration and clearing of the south facade; on the interior, the rediscovery of the magnificent hewn stone structure and suppression of all obstructions to restore the full dimensions of the atrium, to reveal the majestic volumes and beautiful suites of rooms. For Ibos and Vitart, restoring a sort of fluidity to the space also meant introducing a great freedom of circulation and communication in a museum unbolted and deliberately opened out onto the city.

The two principal extensions obtained on the back garden were designed with this idea in mind: a blade-like building sheathed in glass and standing apart from the south facade to free an outdoor patio which in turn covers the temporary exhibition hall. What this creates is a small plaza which offers Lille residents a pleasant meeting place, rendered even more convivial by the location of a cafeteria on the ground floor of the blade building. Revealing nothing of its functionality, this surprisingly thin structure in fact houses the administrative offices. From the patio its mirror-like facade resembles a huge panoramic screen reflecting the 19th-century building, punctuated in transparency by gold monochromes on the red backdrop of the gangways. This colored signboard sets up an exterior/interior dialogue where the gold is found on the blind panels of the atrium and the red on the walls of the painting galleries.

There is a dominant tendency for rationality which here and there attenuates the fantasy of the decorative details: fiber optic lights create starry constellations under the ground floor arches and center lights – the work of Gaetano Pesce – are suspended like jeweled nets in the entrance hall. Pesce is also the creator of the amusing sofas in the exhibition spaces, very turn-of-the-century stuffed purple upholstery, with the required reinterpretation and respectful distance that predominate in the renovation of the Palace of Fine Arts. □

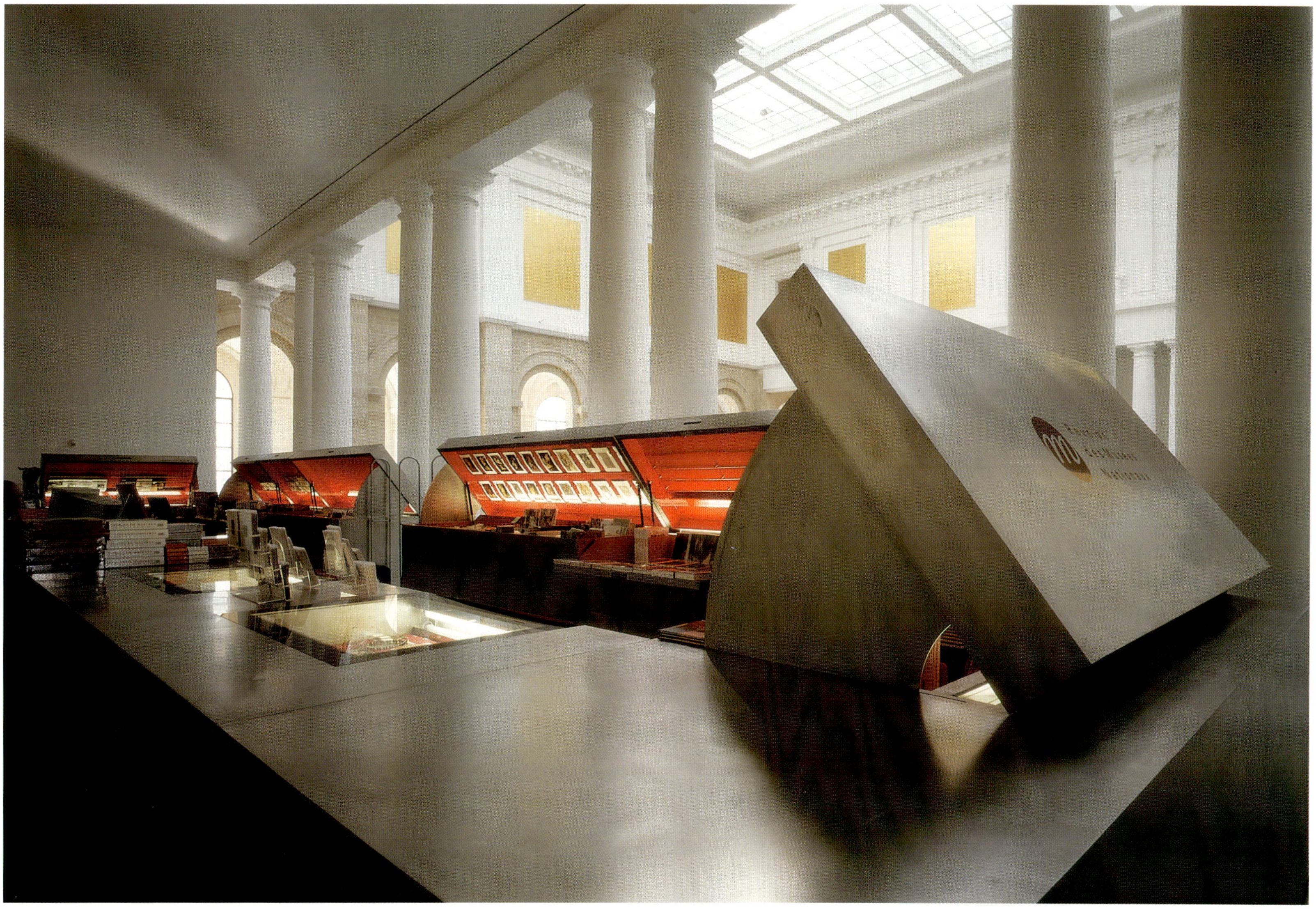

The bookstore installed under the colonnades of the central atrium. The magnificent hall, whose authentic proportions were restored by the removal of the staircase which had encumbered the space since the 1930's, is painted entirely in white with a polished cement floor.

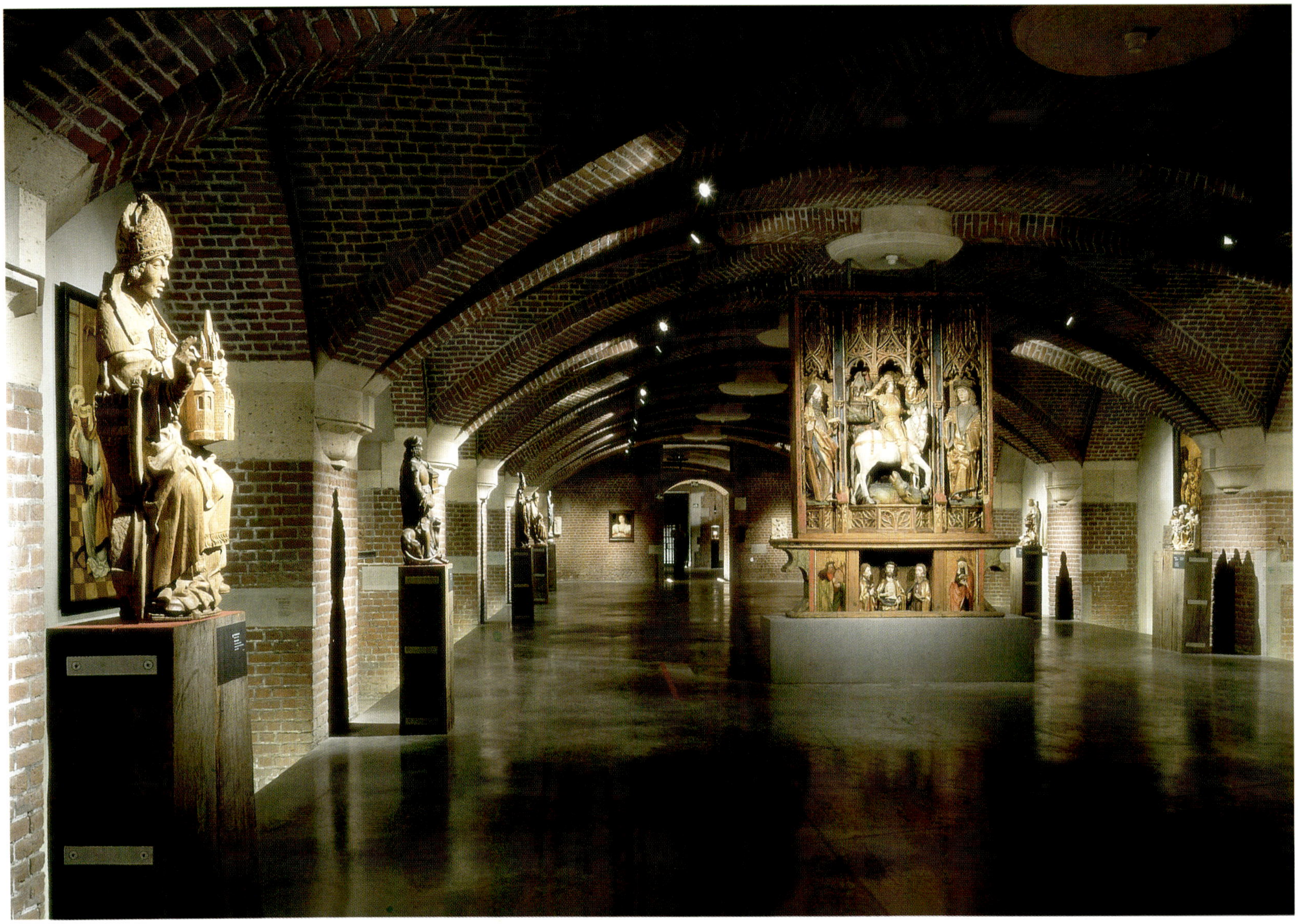

The job of cleaning which allowed the rediscovery of the magnificent hewn-stone structure also revealed the splendid brick vaults of the basement. The Middle Ages and Renaissance collections are exhibited in this beautiful space whose theatrical quality is enhanced by the art objects displayed on the stands.

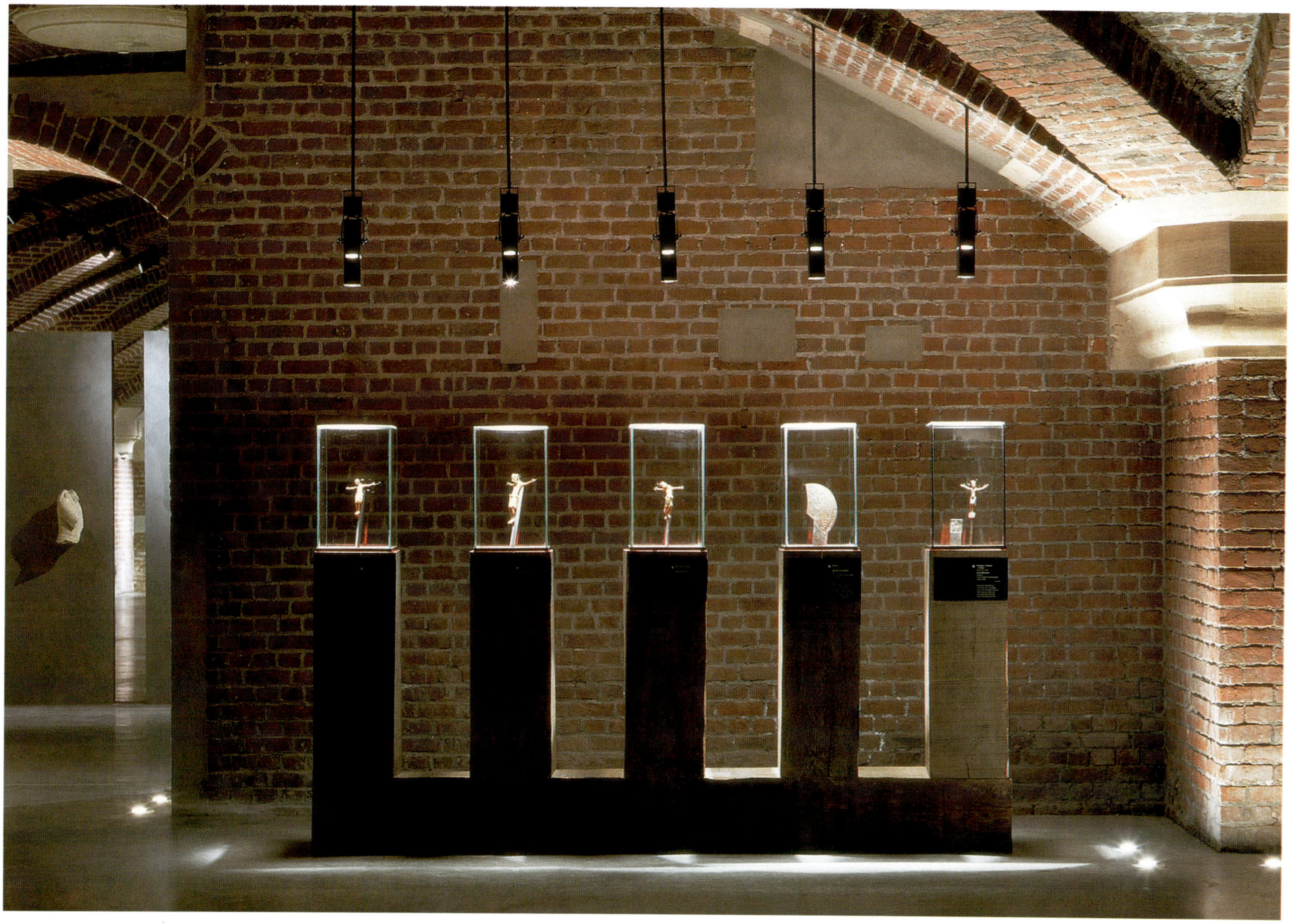

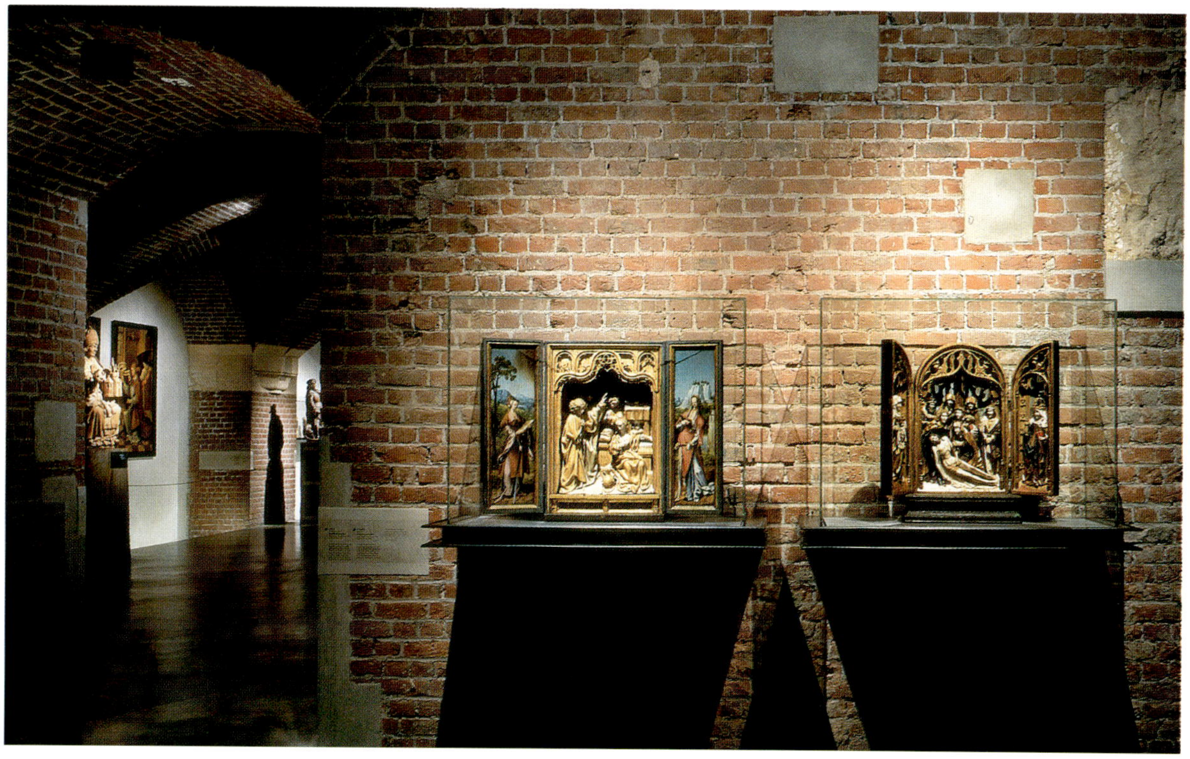

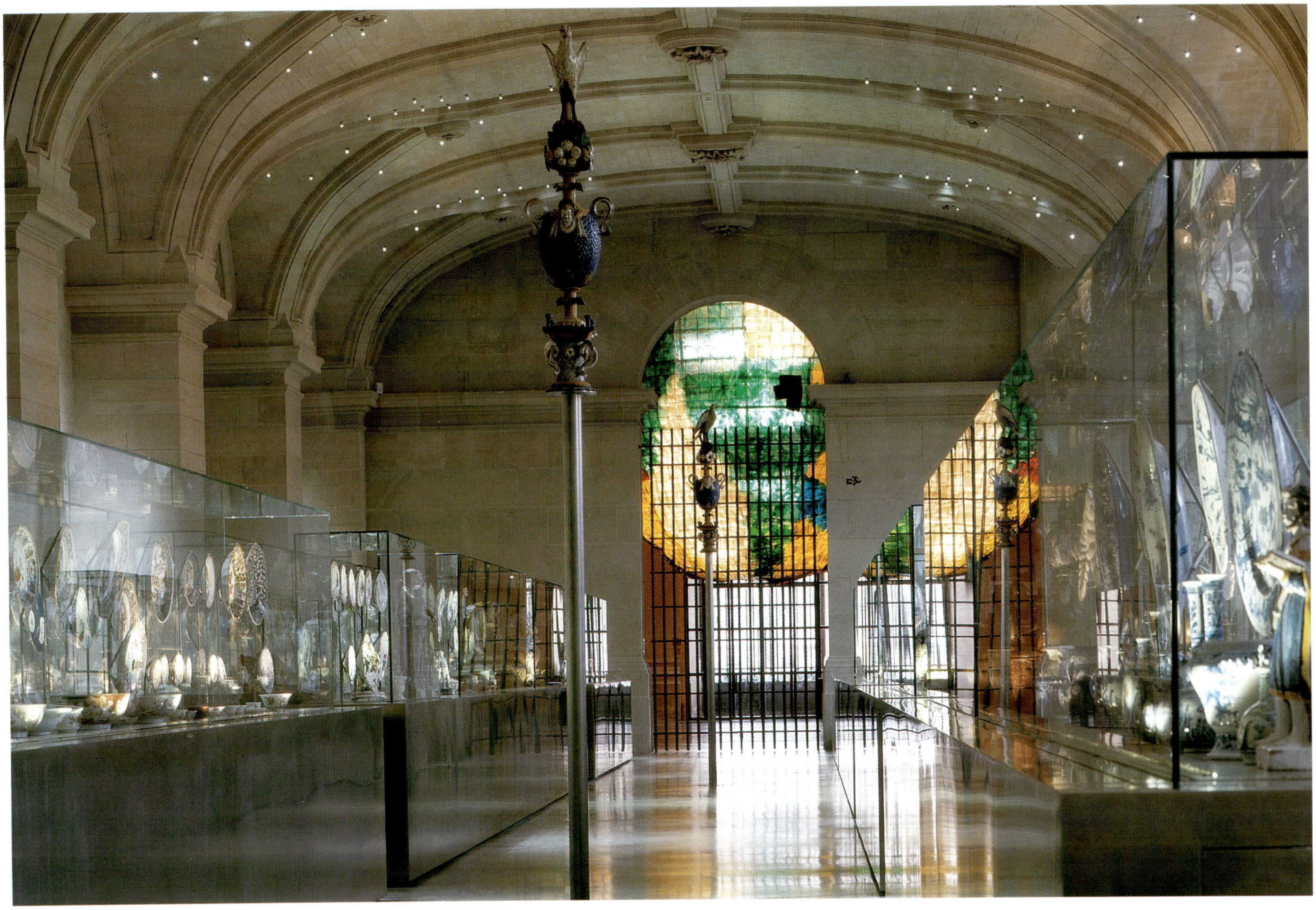

Partial view of the exhibition space reserved for the ceramic collections. The ceramic and sculpture departments are housed in the lateral ground floor galleries.

Opposite page
The brilliant colored focus at the end of the ground floor galleries, whose arches display luminous constellations, are two massive ornamental glass center lights created by Gaetano Pesce.

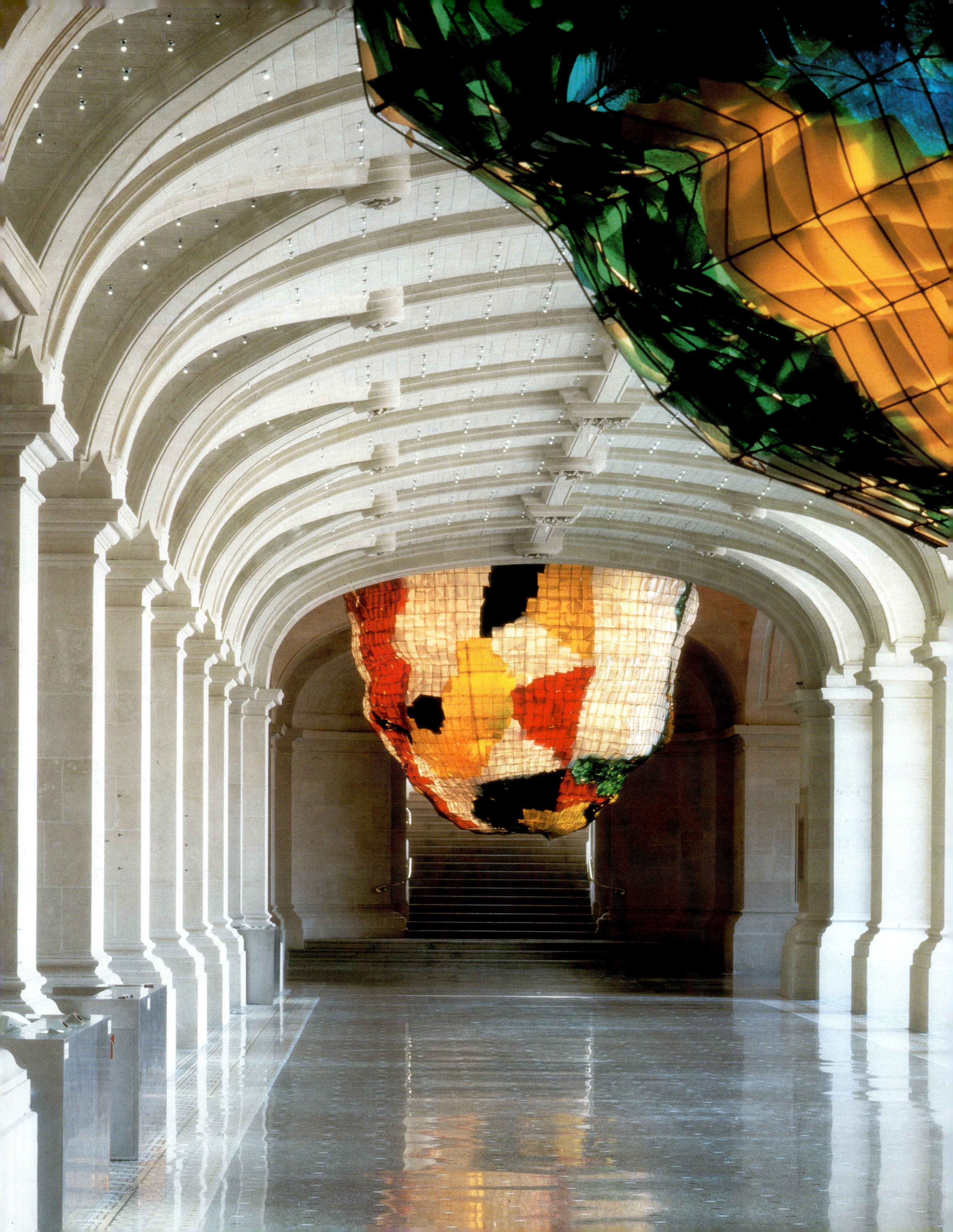

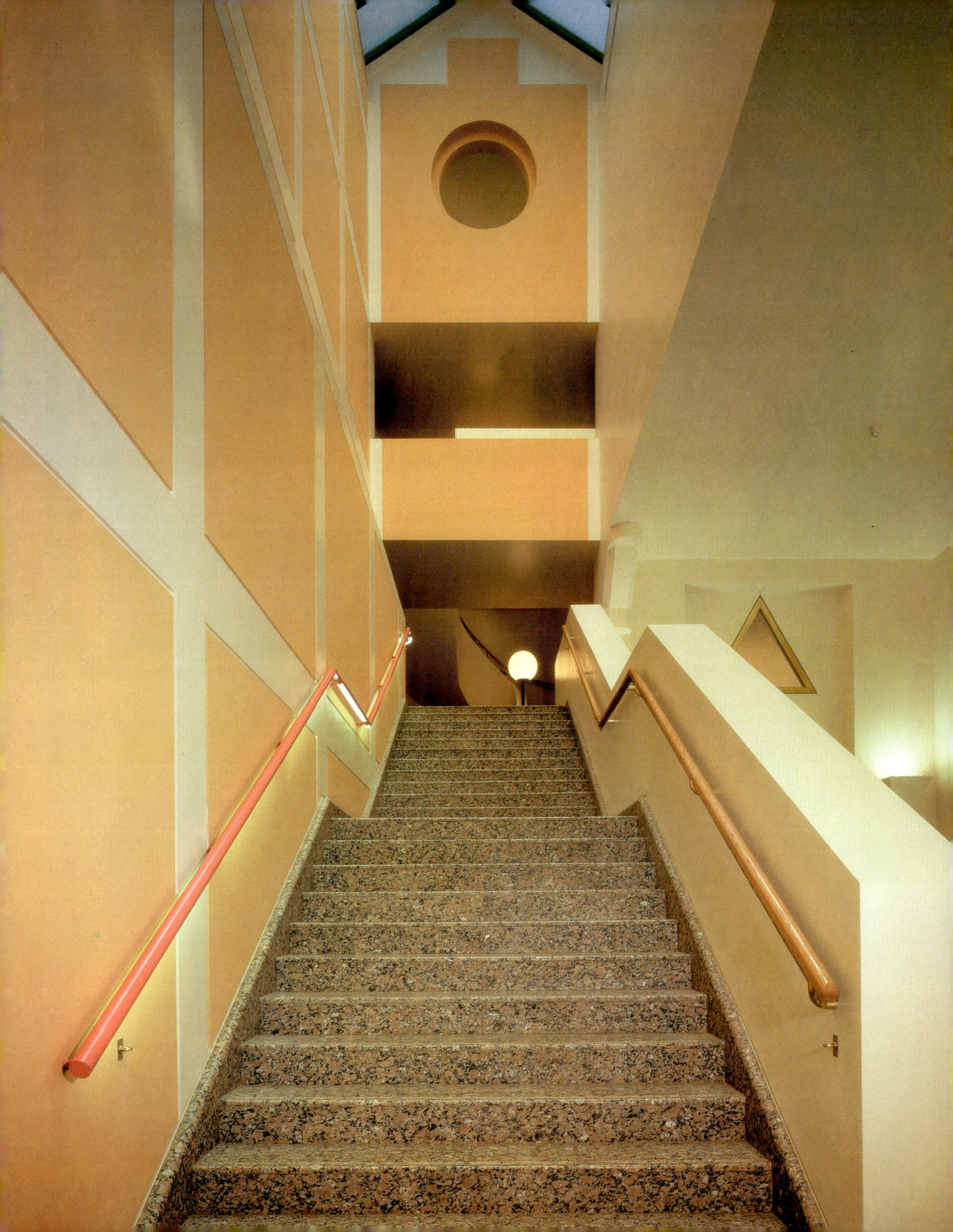

James Stirling and Michael Wilford

Clore Gallery

London, United Kingdom

The extension of the Tate Gallery is deliberately eclectic. Mimetic plurality to integrate the new building into its surroundings and to connect it to the main museum which it joins laterally. Playful heterogeneity as well, reflecting the Clore Gallery's function, especially designed to accomodate groups of school children. The whole resembles an endearing "garden pavillion" attached to the main house, the entry hall opening up like a greenhouse behind the large triangular glass wall divided by bright green slats.

Opposite page
The stairway leading to the exhibition rooms is casual and colorful, deliberately theatrical: like an operetta decor, punctuated at the top by the luminous orb of the banister.

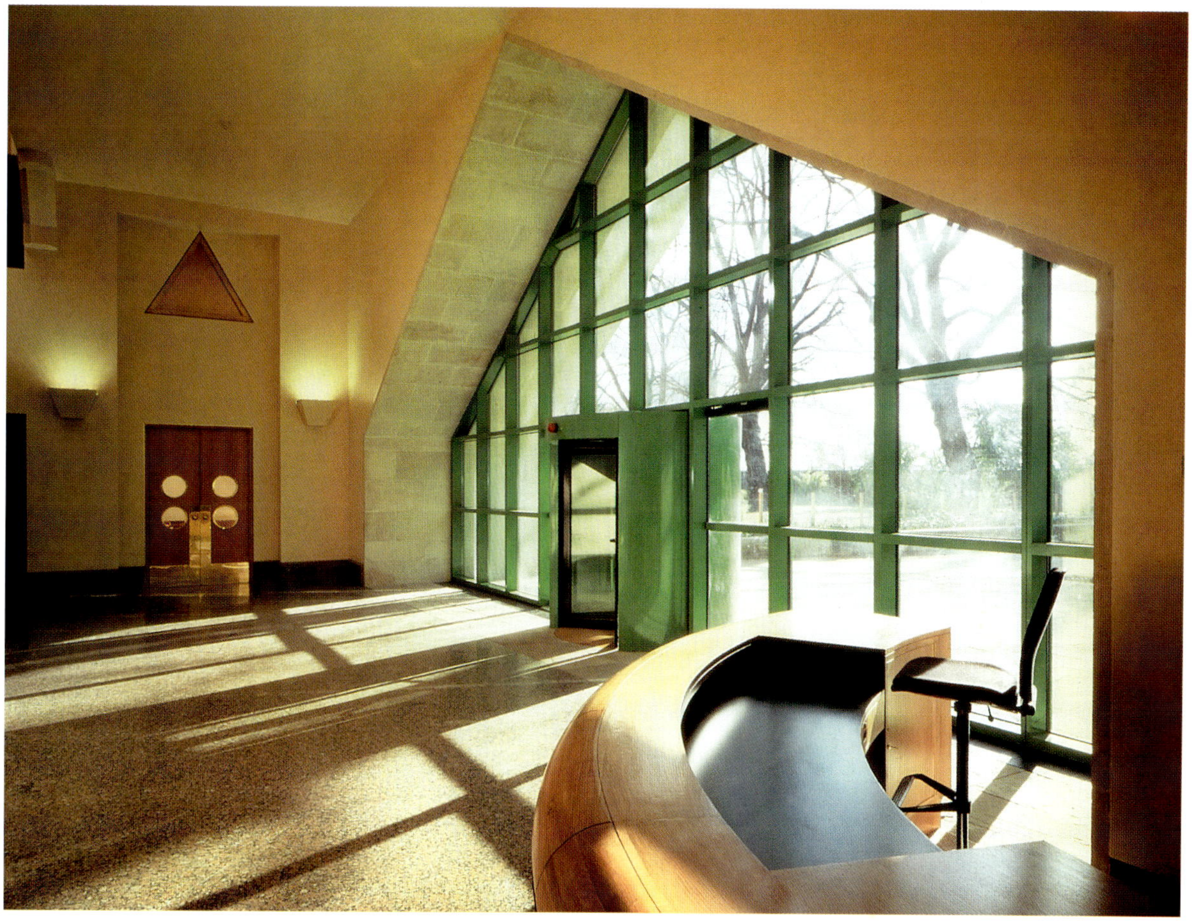

The Tate Gallery was initially founded in 1897 to house the Victorian philanthropist Sir Henry Tate's collection of English painting. Ever since, its collection has continued to grow with the acquisitions of non-British art and in particular Impressionist, Fauvist and Surrealist paintings, including a prestigious sculpture collection.

Having become one of the most important modern art museums, thanks to donations from Henry Moore, Barbara Hepworth and Alistair McAlpine, the Tate Gallery has had to face the inevitable problem of lacking space. For decades now, all the major Western art museums have flocked to offer their expert advice. The extension of the Tate, undertaken as early as the 1970s, was due to be finished by 2001; being wholly dependent on private donations, however, it has been a slow process. The completion of its new wing, the Clore Gallery or Turner Wing, is only the first phase of the project.

This L-shaped extension was built on the grounds of the old Queen Alexandra Hospital, perpendicular to the edifice.

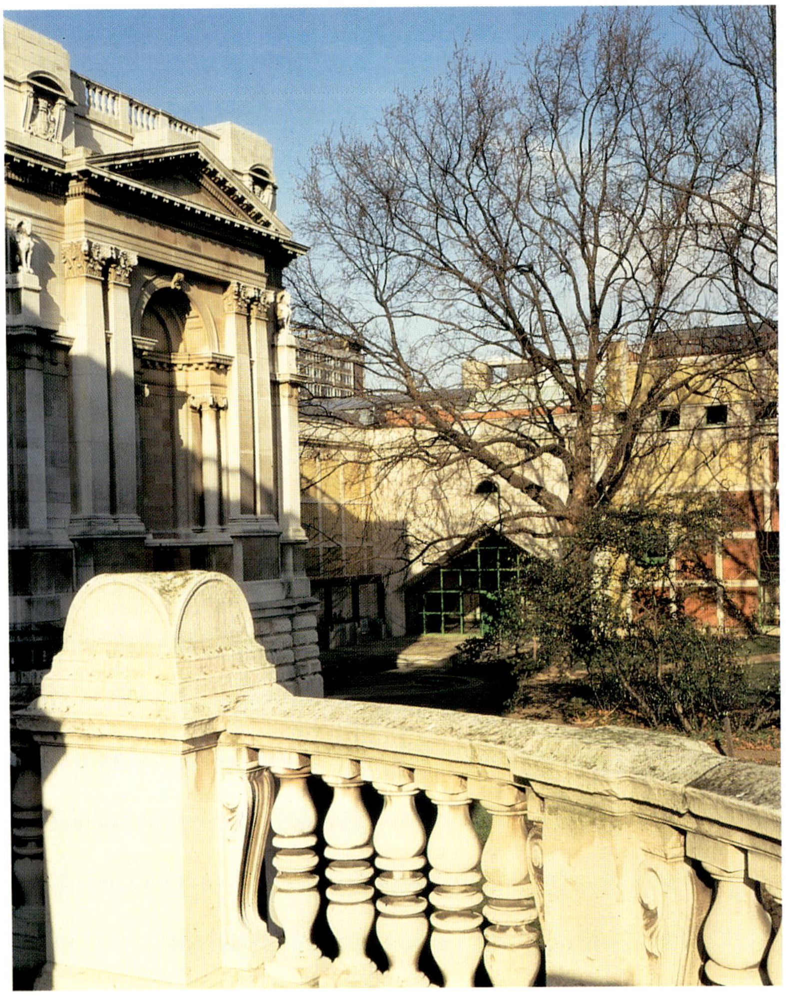

Joining, on either end, the palatial Tate and the brick hospital, the new building had to reconcile itself to two very different constructions. Its architect James Stirling deliberately played with this seemingly irresolvable contradiction by adopting the same ocher tones and cornice of the Edwardian facade and, where the edifice approaches the hospital, ending in red brick. The facade to the service areas, conversely, is wholly functional and ceases all reference.

All these elements interrelate, fuse into one another and integrate into a unified whole with a large grille motif that makes for a possible harmony. Stirling intended this harmony to be dynamic, in other words constantly contested by the discontinuity of its themes and discordant elements: small angular windows jut out suddenly from the facade and the door and window frames are painted in a curious apple green. This astonishingly eclectic building, which Stirling describes as a "garden pavilion," translates the cultural plurality of the Clore Gallery with its daily visits from a diverse public and especially from groups of school children. Then there is its informal side and the endearing, almost overly poetic garden leading to the entrance hall with its little fountain and pergola.

The interior mirrors the same colors, offset harmony and discontinuity as the exterior – or at least on the ground floor shared by the cloakroom, auditorium and hallway. As soon as one heads toward the exhibition halls dedicated to Turner, up the informal stairs lit up from the roof like in a greenhouse, the traditional sober museum environment returns. The walls are smooth and a highly sophisticated lighting system uses both natural and artificial light, creating the same costly comfort of a 19th-century museum. Here, the architectural premise has been to aim for a neutral practicality – yet another facet to this metamorphic building, a building that speaks all sorts of languages. □

The L-shaped building of the Clore Gallery adapts itself to the old building with dissonant harmony. Capturing certain elements of the main edifice – continuing the classical cornice on the lateral facade or repeating the triangular geometry of a pediment – it modifies and incorporates this architectural language.

Opposite page
From the main hall, the play of transparency superimposes the triangle of the entrance over the triangular 19th-century pediment of the old building.

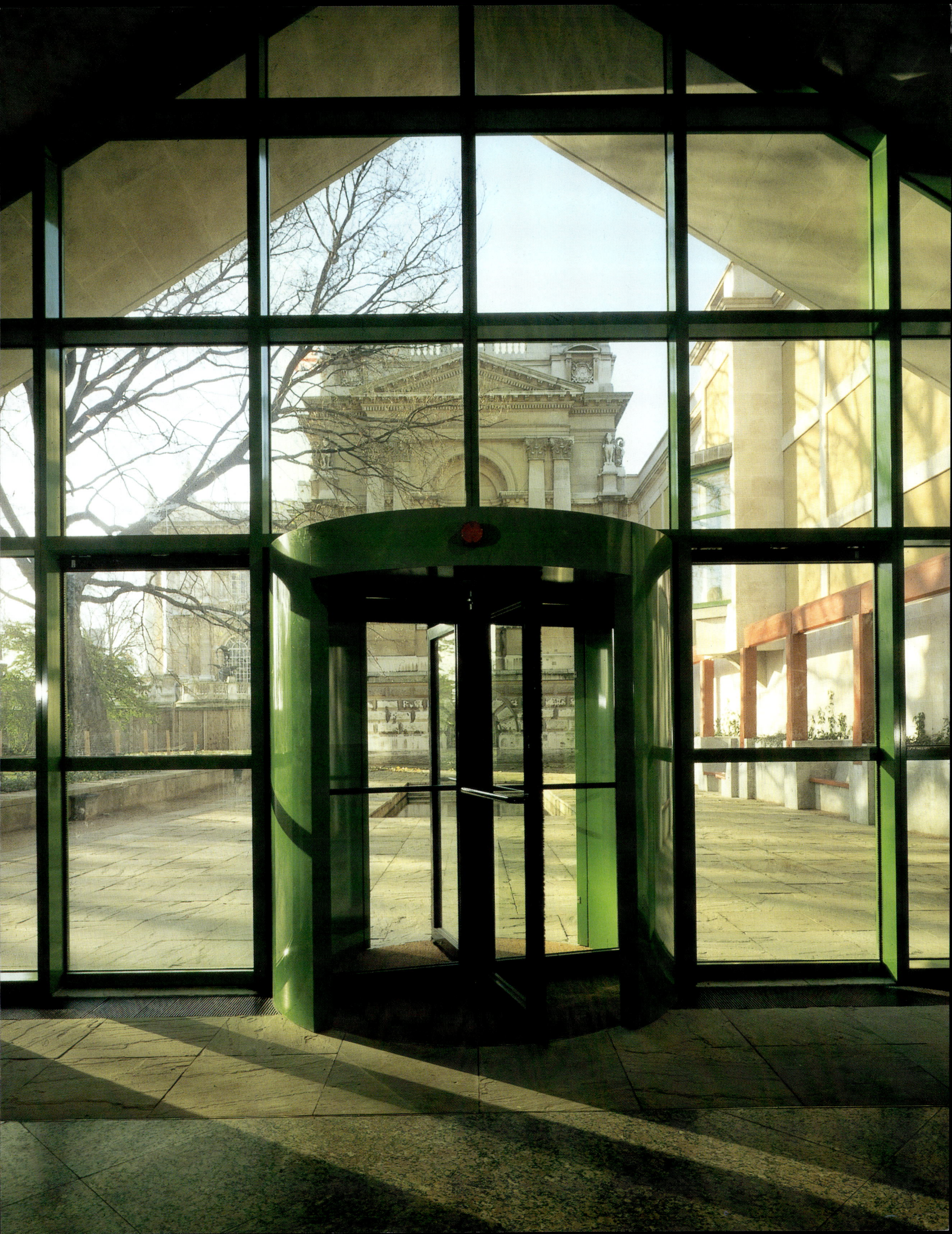

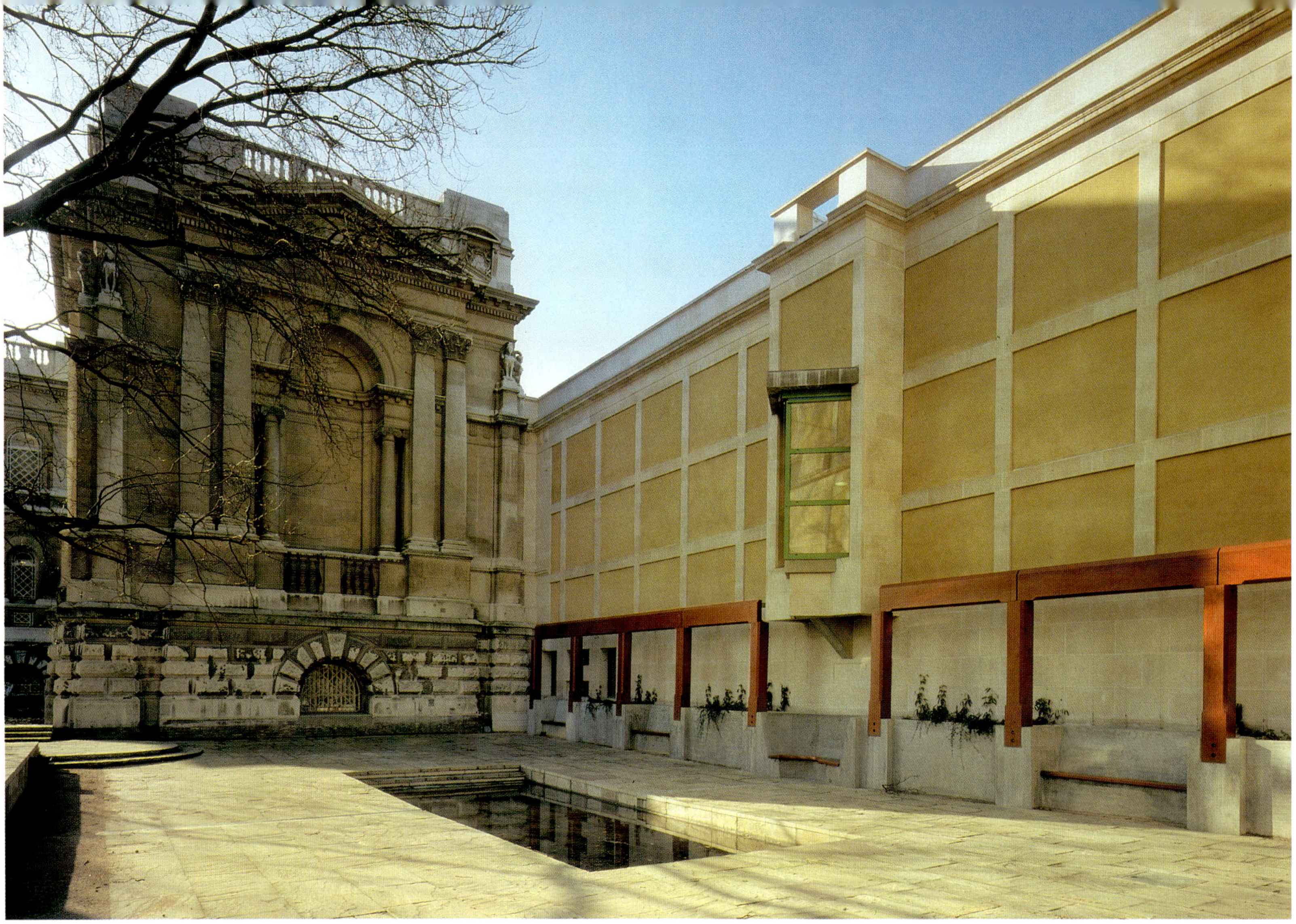

The heterogeneity of the edifice, recaptured in a repetitive grille motif, is modified according to the various settings and functions. Along the length of the patio, the "grille" highlights in red, ocher and white, a bucolic facade underlined by festoons of pergola.

In a progressive and concordant manner the facades go from ocher stucco to red brick, from monumental and public conotations to the strictly functional. The service facade being the ultimate stage in these metamorphoses: simply modern and utilitarian.

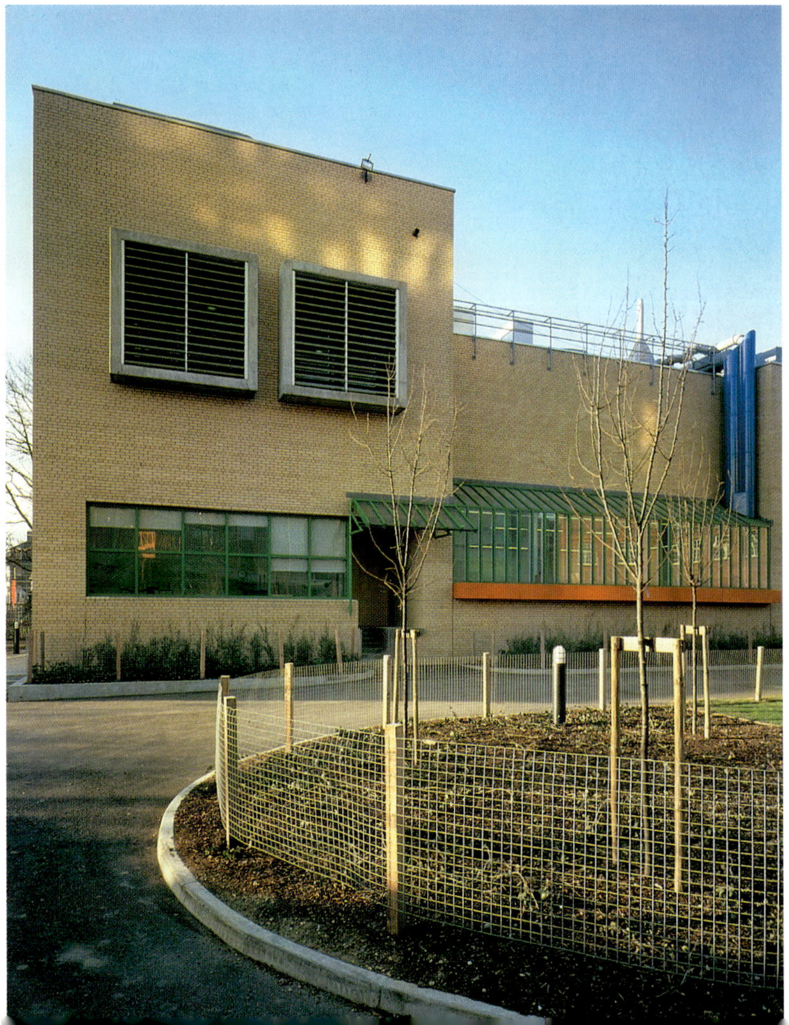

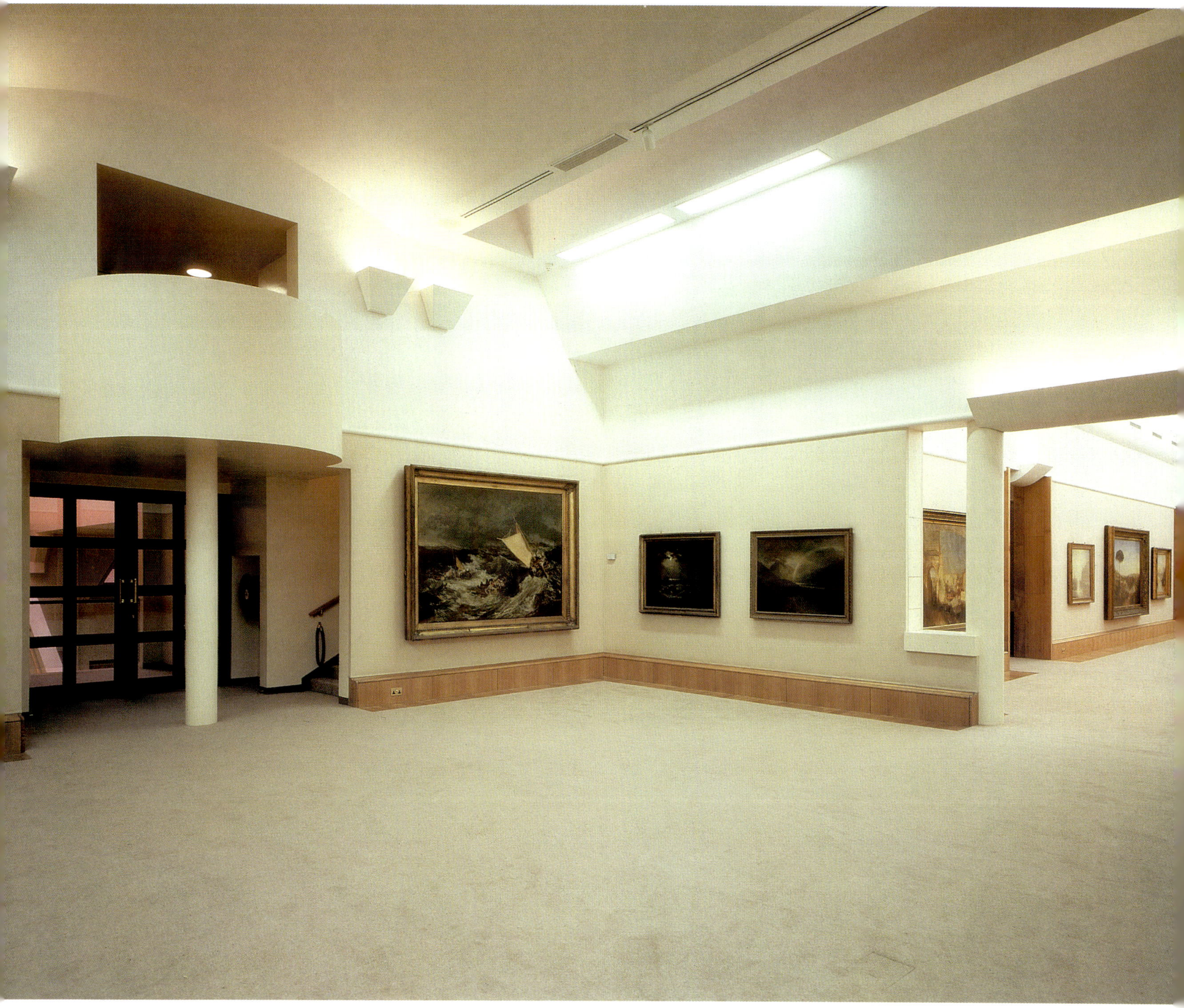

In the exhibition galleries all architectural play is set aside in favor of the most rigorous neutrality: architecture becomes a support, a backdrop for the works exhibited. Apart from the very sophisticated lighting system, one finds here the traditional setting of 19th-century museums and galleries.

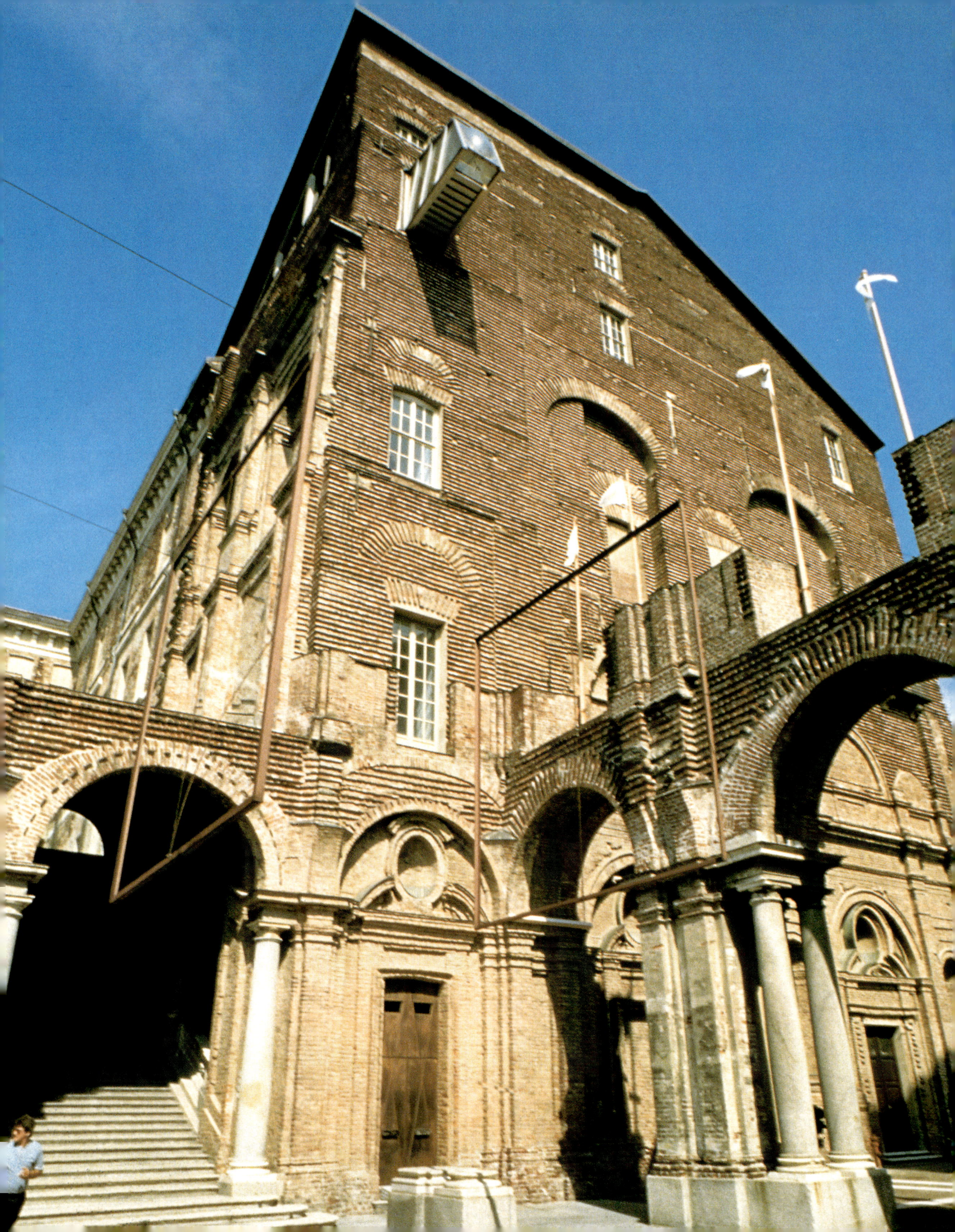

Andrea Bruno

Castello di Rivoli

Turin, Italy

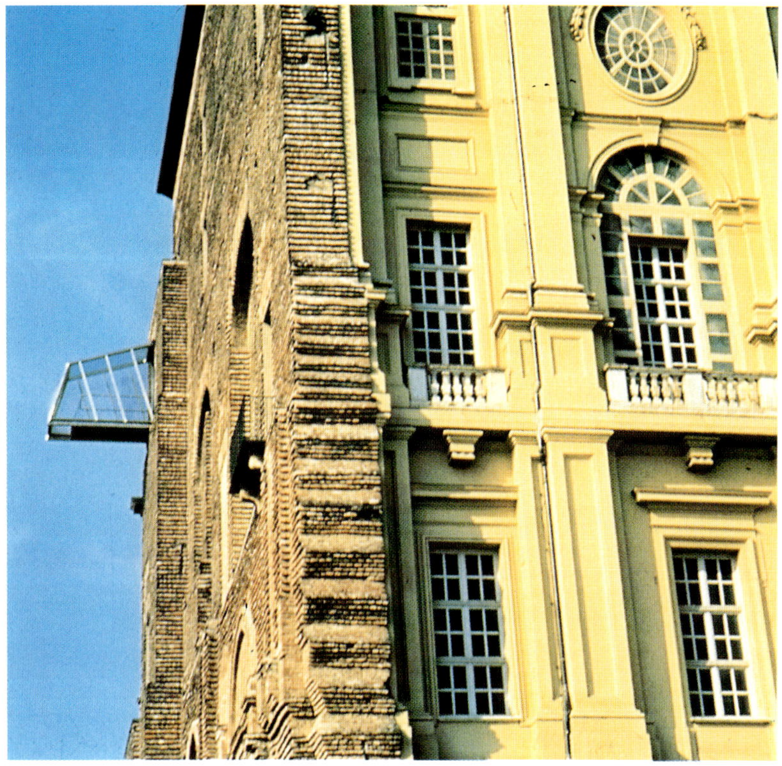

To conserve and restore architectural patrimony as a useful and eloquent testimony was Andrea Bruno's primary concern in his realization of the Rivoli Castle Museum of Contemporary Art. As an architect and a humanist, he reused the work of his predecessors, without destroying either its spirit or form.

Opposite page
Side view of the Juvara building with the beginnings of the colonnades of the unfinished atrium.

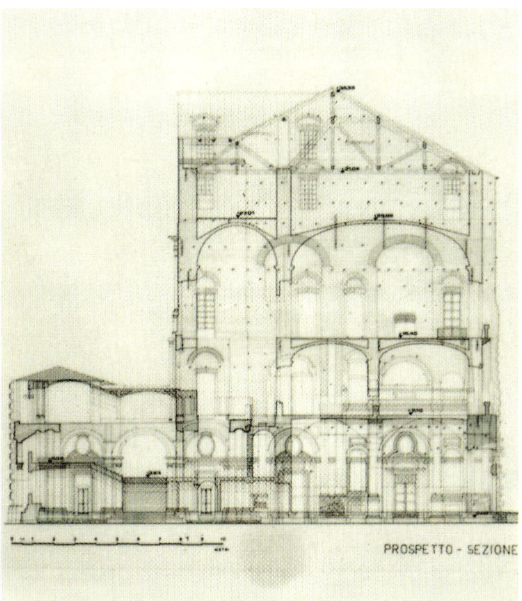

Today's museology is no longer limited to the conservation and exhibition of art objects but also includes the architectural space as an essential protagonist. There is no longer any hierarchy between the contents and the container and the building becomes as important to the visitor as the works exhibited therein. At the Rivoli Castle this idea results in a wonderful historic and artistic paradox: the project of the future Museum of Contemporary Art will finance the restoration of the beautiful Baroque building in which it will be housed, the program including both the restoration of an 18th-century decor and the constitution of a decidedly contemporary collection.

Begun in 1718, the building of this palatial residence was one of the splendid projects which Victor Amadeus II, Duke of Savoy and King of Sicily and Sardinia, had foreseen for his northern capital, Turin. The Rivoli Castle was created as a grandiose edifice erected upon the vestiges of a 17th-century palace. Work stopped abruptly in 1727 before completion of the main structure: a central atrium for which only a few arcades were built. It is this unfinished quality which architect Andrea Bruno wished to authentically restore when work started in 1979. Above all it was necessary to rid the monument of all extraneous,

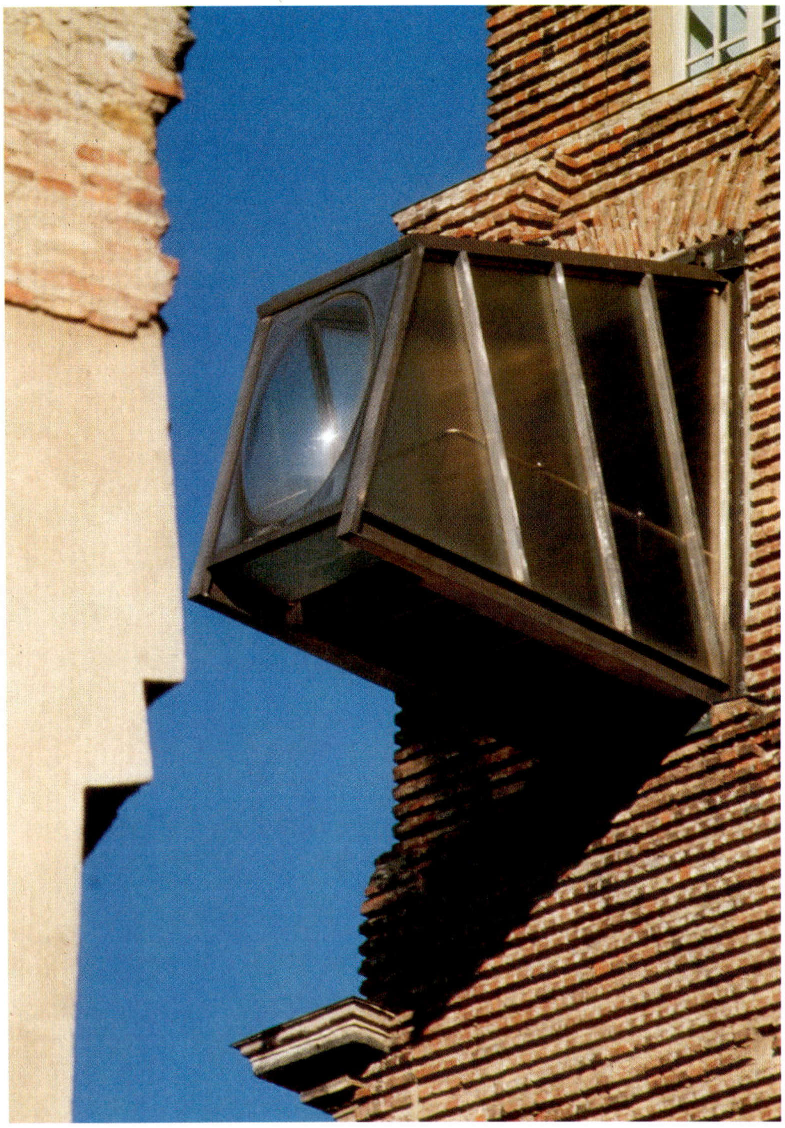

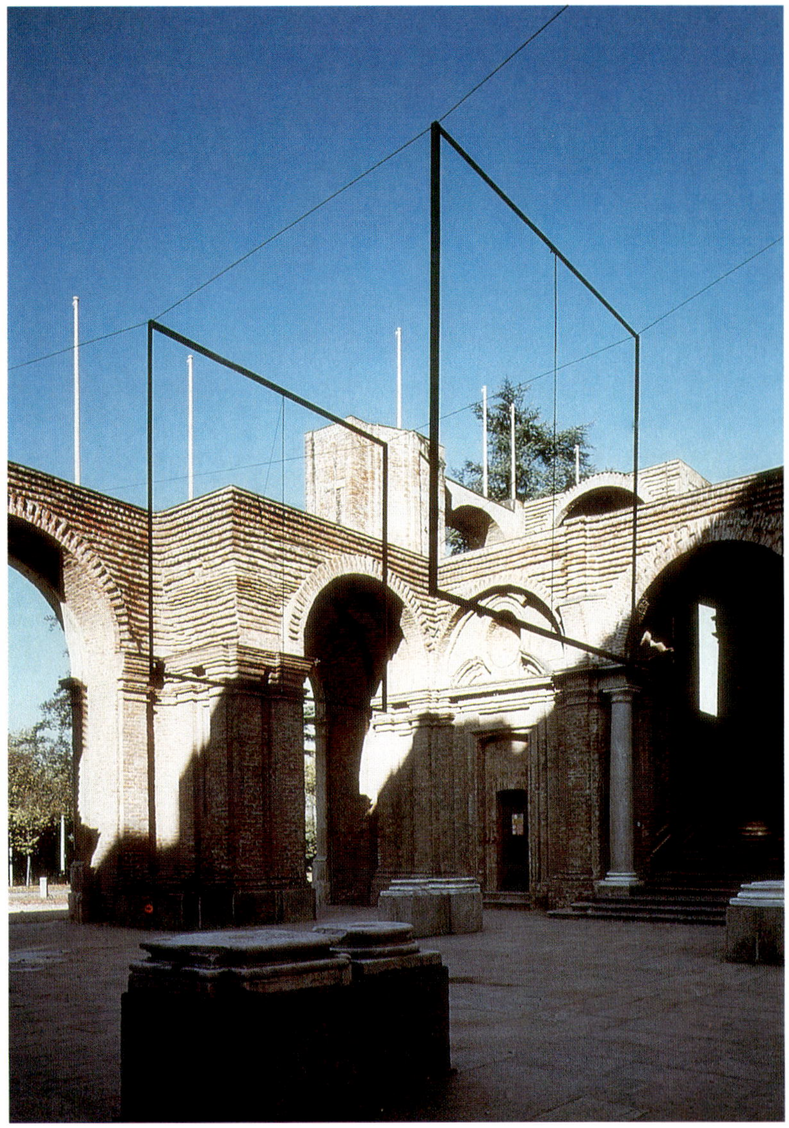

On the unfinished facade of the 17th-century palace, a glass observatory juts out from the wall. It is a virtual passageway from the past to the present, with a panoramic view over the luxurious atrium which Juvara had planned to build, the outline of which has been reproduced on the ground.

Reinforced beginnings of colonnades, arches and stairways around the empty space of the atrium.

Opposite page
Bruno's approach is not only to create a cohabitation of eras and works. Equally important here is anachronism, a dynamic revelation.

attenuating additions in order to recapture the exact moment at which Juvara had had to abandon his project. In so doing, today's building has found the force and vitality of a suddenly suspended gesture: stairways end in mid air, niches designed for statues remain empty and truncated pedestals accentuate the absence of colonnades. Unfinished structures have simply been covered and held in place by copper plates, whereas the large wall forming the discontinuous body of the edifice has been kept as it is, making use of the original building's incomplete arches and arcades.

One of the only interventions Bruno allowed himself consists of a small transparent observatory-like panoramic structure jutting out from the facade and overlooking a marble and stone outline of the ground plan of the atrium as Juvara had imagined it in his preparatory sketches. This could be viewed as an homage to this unfinished project and perhaps gives it a future, as everything is potentially reversible in Bruno's work. Necessary, but replaceable just

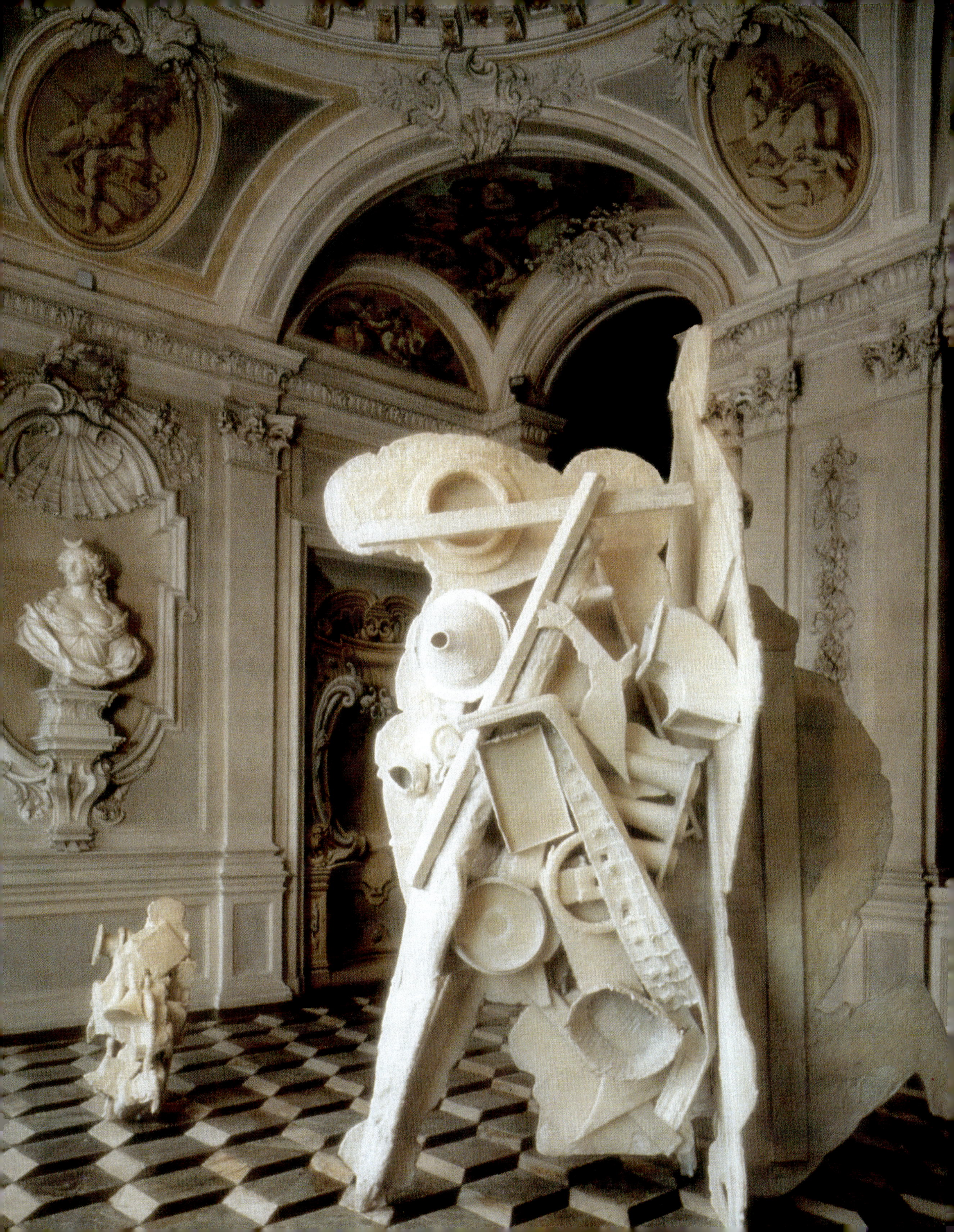

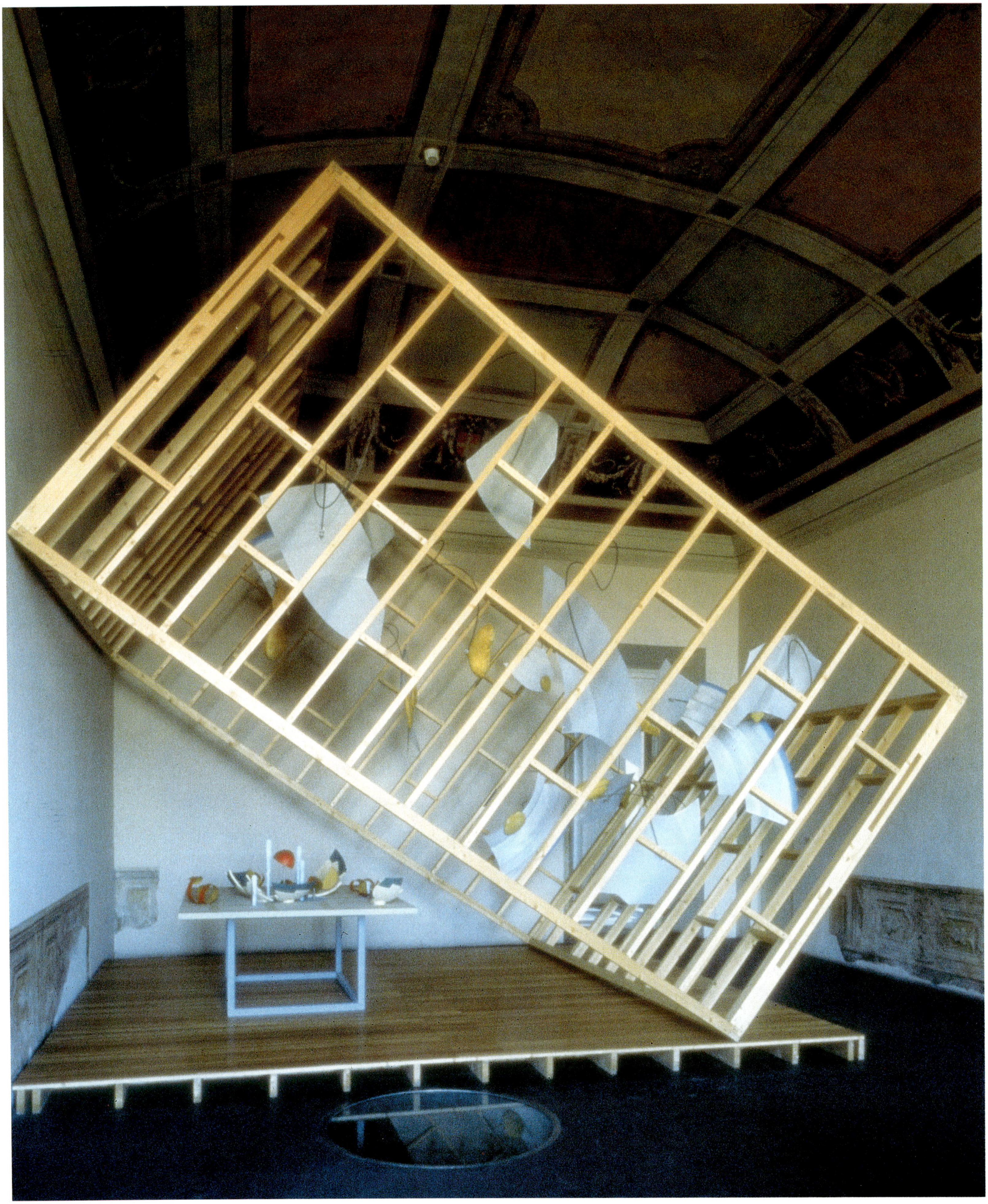

28 Castello di Rivoli, Turin, Italy

the same, is the great metal stairway suspended by steel cables which, along with a lift, occupies the location of the originally planned stairway. In anticipating future evolution while reviving the work of the past, the Rivoli Museum of Contemporary Art has been placed in a temporal dynamic, a true Modernism.

The 18th-century edifice thus restored, with the addition of a small theater on the basement level and considerably enlarged by the restoration of the previously inaccessible uppermost floor, now houses the permanent collections, laboratories and reception services.

Temporary exhibitions are held in the second monumental core of the Rivoli residence: the Manica Lunga, a long 17th-century building originally designed as a painting gallery which would have been destroyed if the Juvara project had been completed. This strange construction has reverted to its original purpose but with vastly improved conditions: lateral window lighting, which formerly obliged visitors to view the works against the light, has now been supplemented with natural light from the two lengthwise skylights of the new roof. A second "Manica Lunga," parallel to the first and with a suspended garden designed after the outlines in the 17th-century park, will complete this great museological complex, both futuristic and retrospective. In other words, decidedly contemporary. □

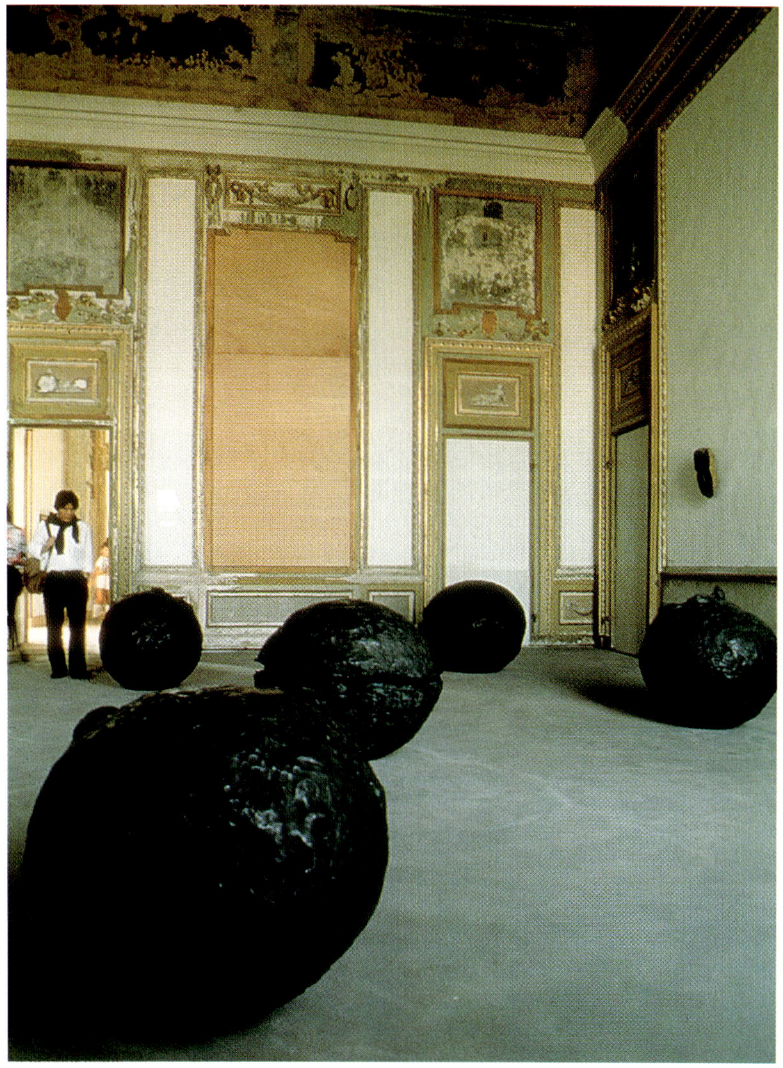

Certain rooms have been purposely left as they were revealed during the restoration process. Half-effaced frescoes and motifs take on a sort of poetic authenticity.

Cross section of the ensemble with Juvara's edifice on the left and the Manica Lunga wing extending to the right.

Opposite page
In a room of Juvara's building, the exhibition of a contemporary work gives new life to a decor of 17th-century ceiling frescoes.

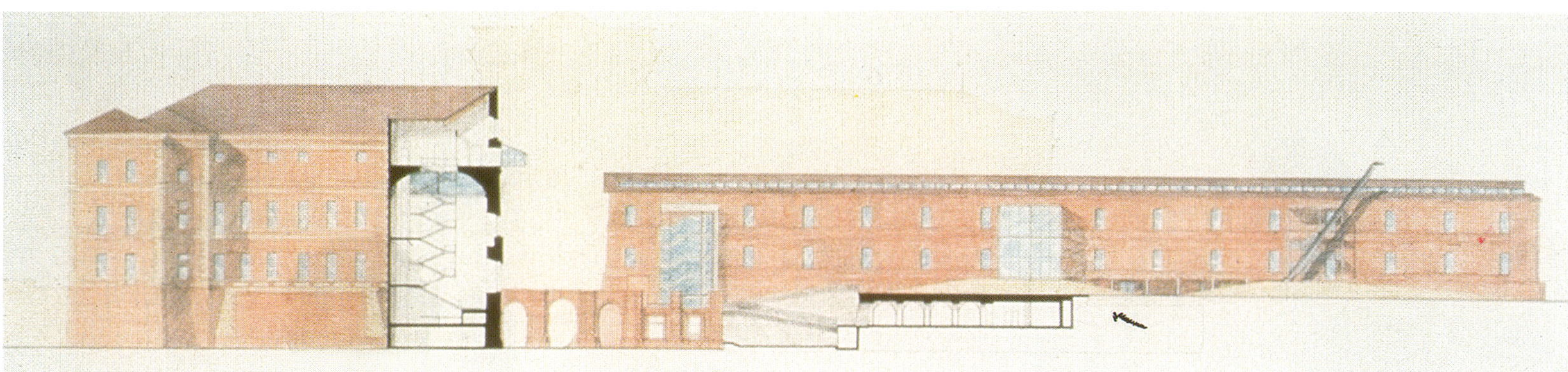

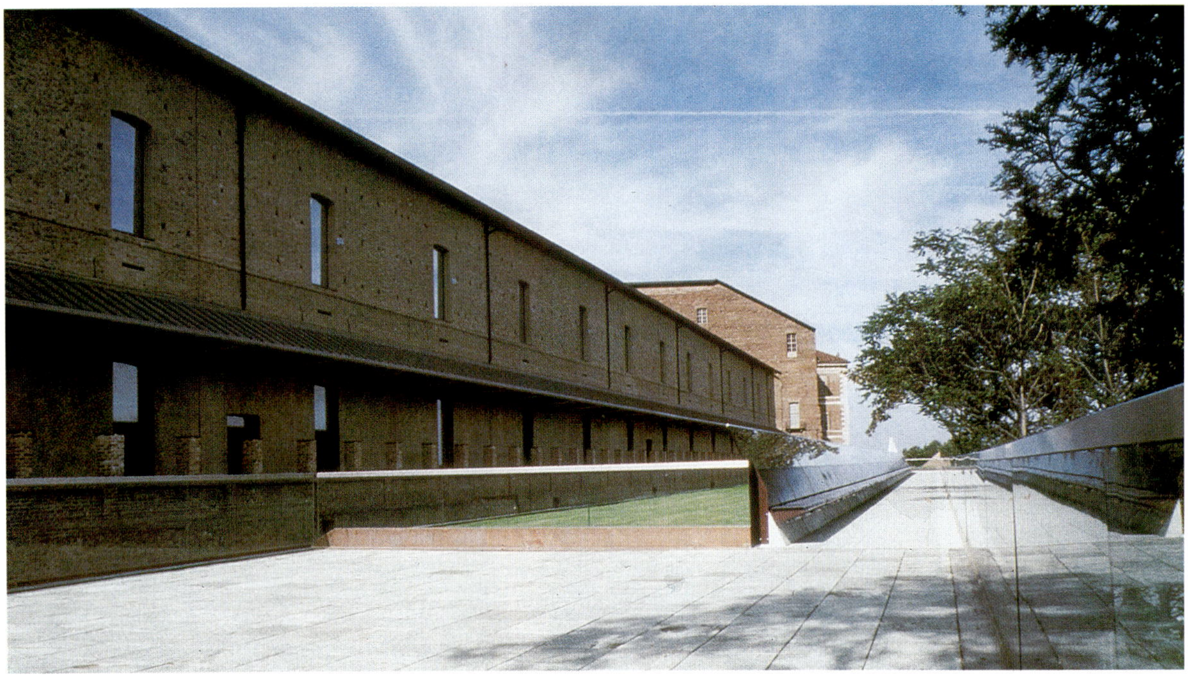

Outside perspective view of the Manica Lunga.

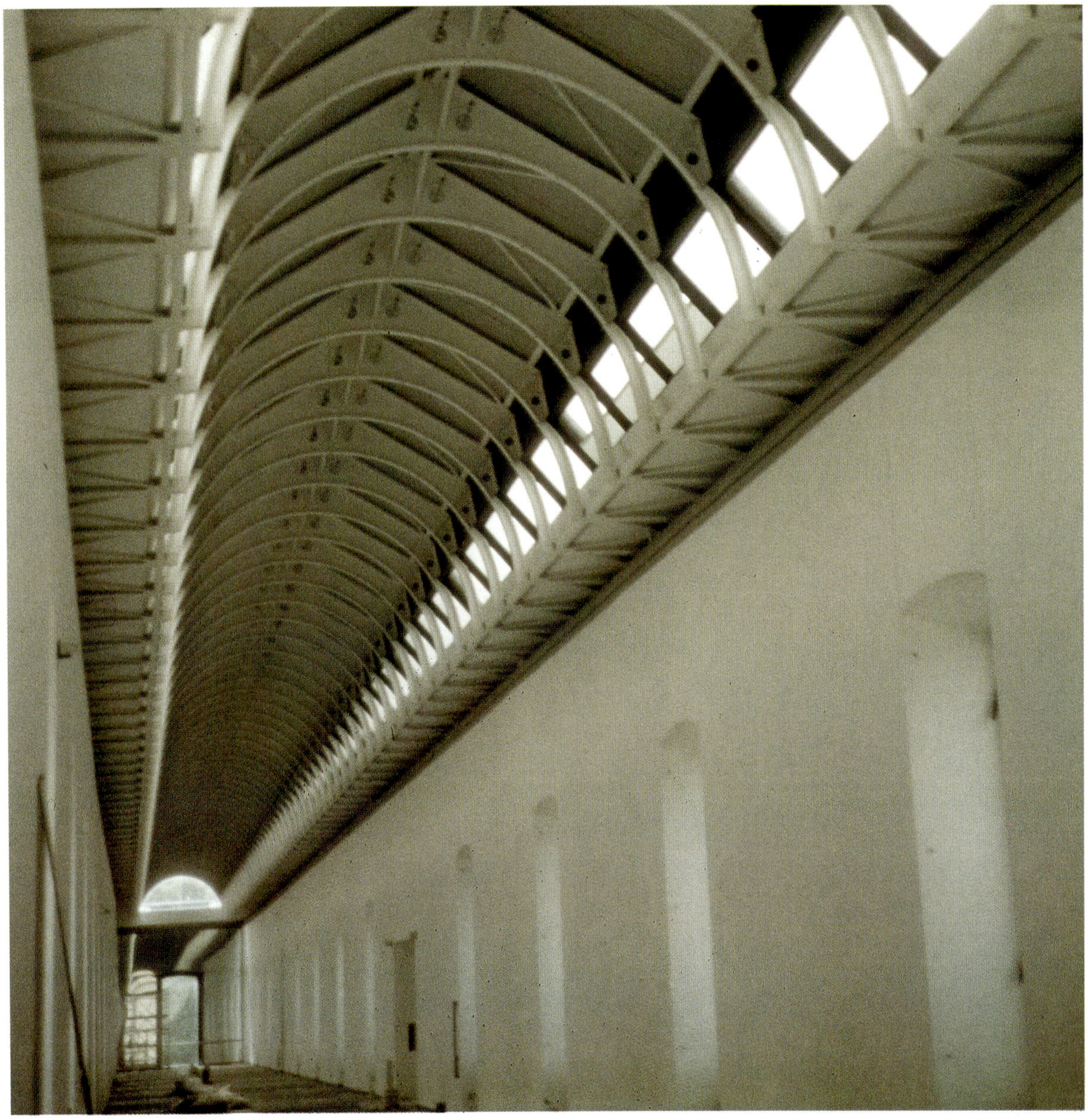

The new steel vault pierced by two parallel openings equipped with a sun-shade mechanism to control the natural light.

Opposite page

At the end of the Manica Lunga, neither the new stairway, the metallic roof, nor the glass walls erase the history of the edifice. Bruno preserved the very traces of the demolition work begun before the interruption of the construction in 1727.

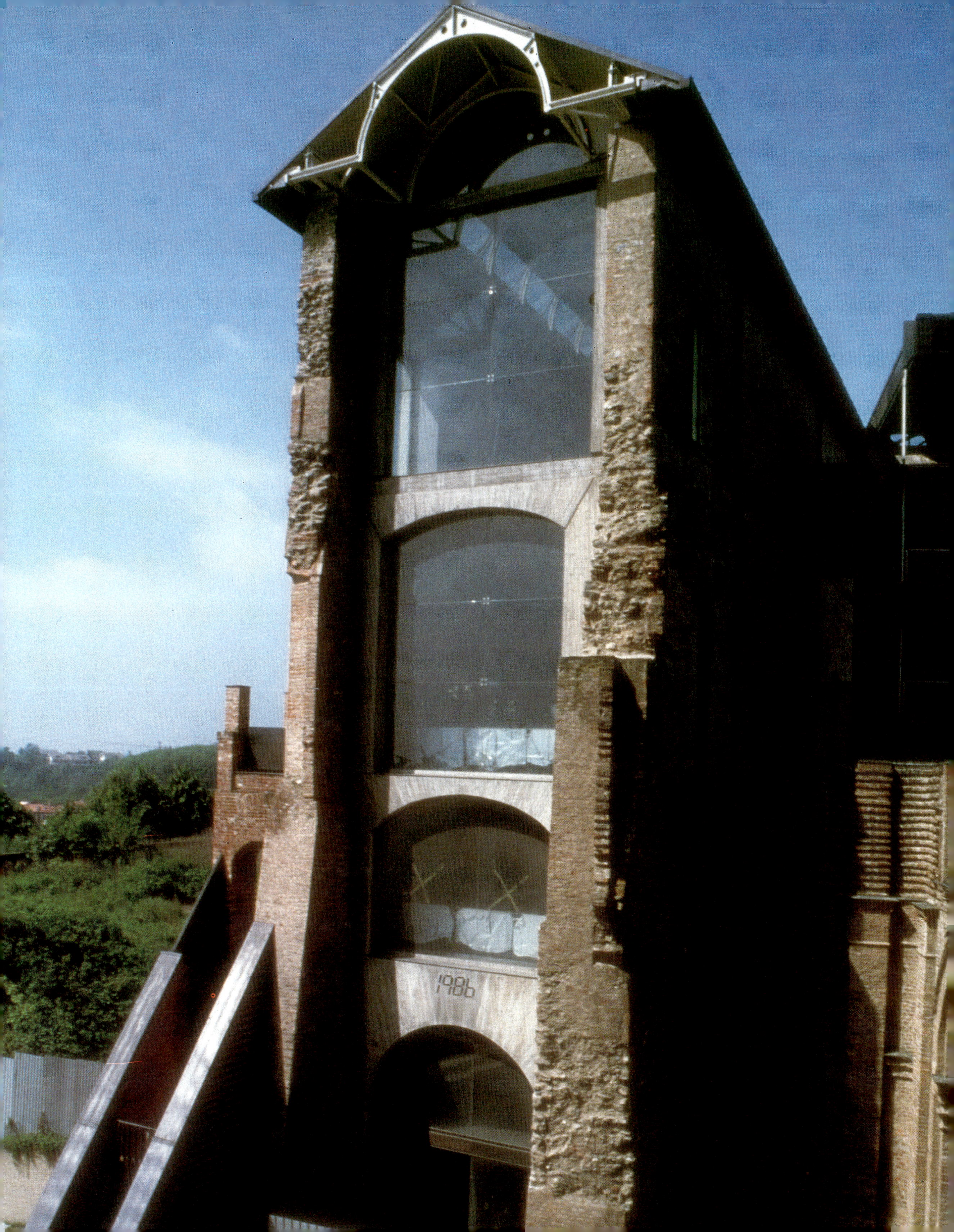
1986

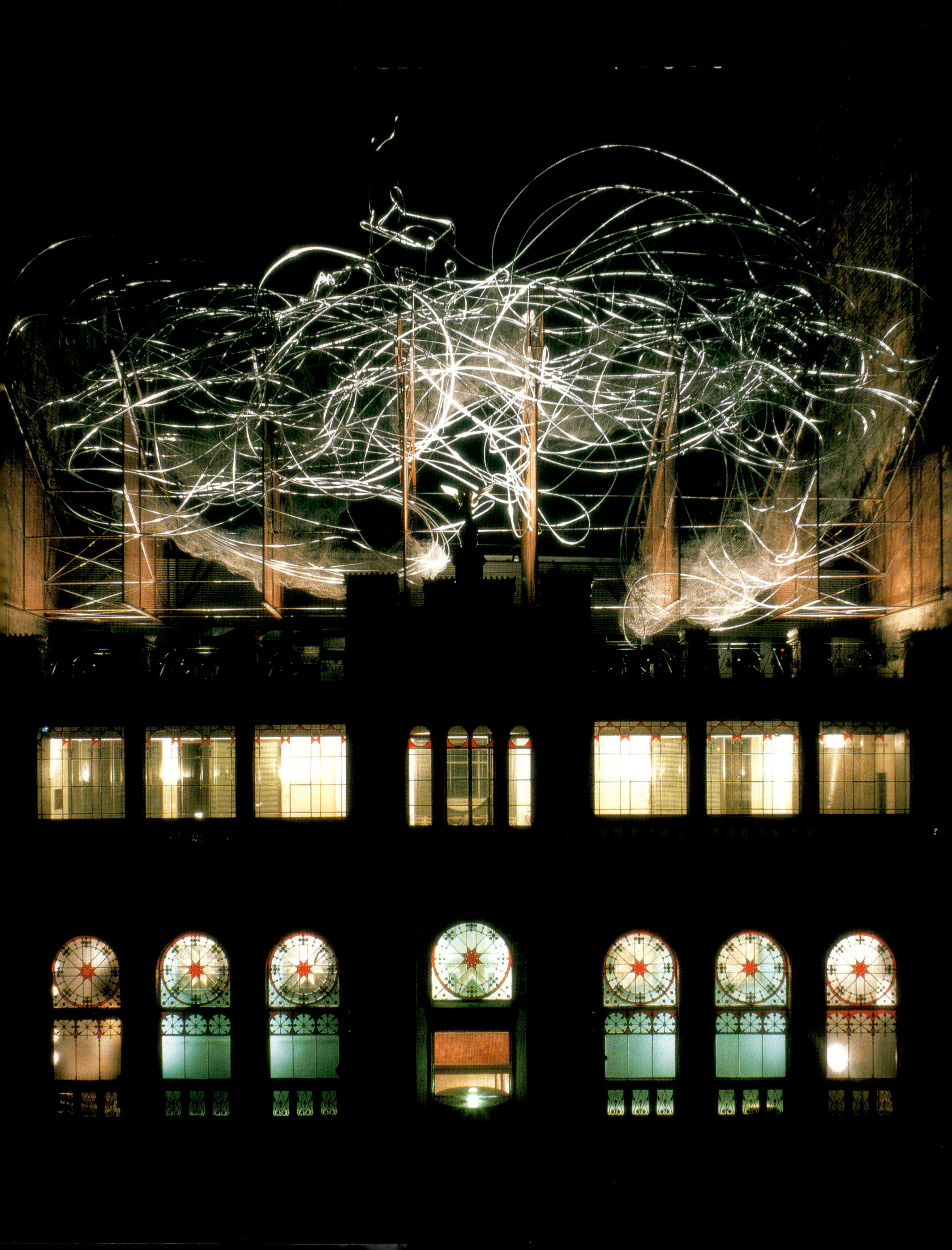

Amadó and Domènech

Fundació Antoni Tàpies

Barcelona, Spain

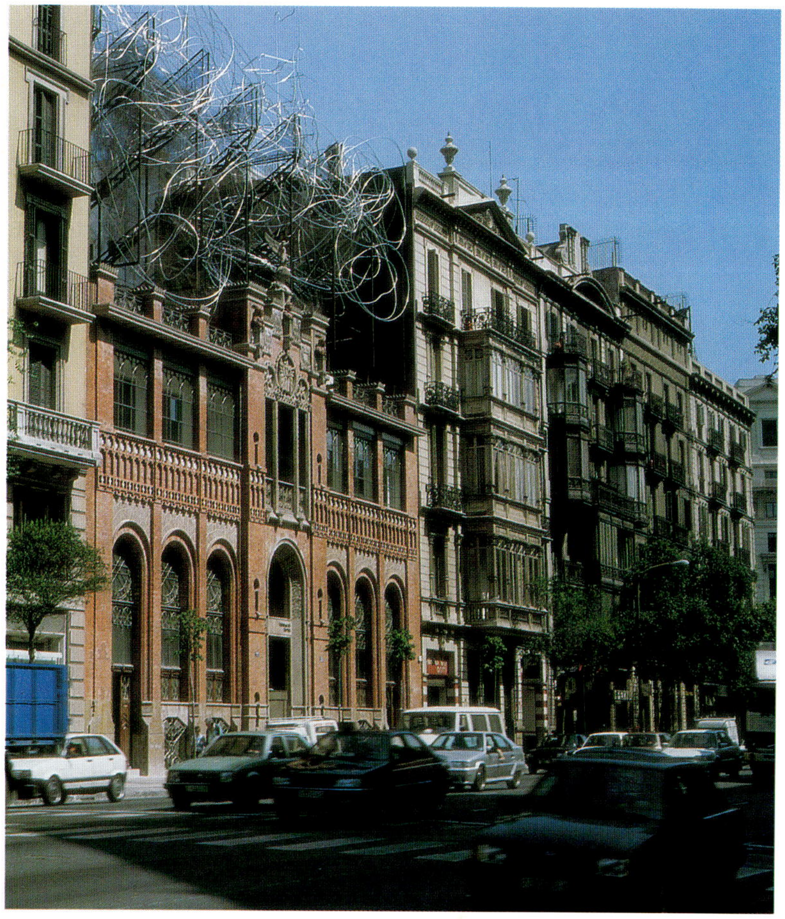

Affirming the new identity of this industrial building without detriment to the integrity of its 19th-century facade is one of the successful results of this new contemporary art center. With a clever strategy, the edifice was raised several feet by the addition of eight transparent panels of wire mesh. A minor intervention but one which enabled attaining the height of the lateral buildings. Also a playful intervention, as the panels serve as a support for a creation by Antoni Tàpies: a dynamic and festive invitation is made by the bubbling, interlaced cables providing nocturnal lighting and underlined by a row of leaded glass windows.

The increase in small museums with a specific function, often devoted to a single private or public collection and a particular theme or artist indicates that museums are showing a growing tendency toward specialization. This is certainly true for the Tapiès Foundation, a museum that inventories and exhibits a monographic collection. Its context is unique, however, in that the artist, Antonio Tapiès, has the rare honor of having a museum to his name within his lifetime, an homage that is usually the sole privilege of the posthumous.

This contemporary art center, which rotates the Foundation's permanent collection, took over an old publishing house, Montaner i Simón, a building designed by Modernist architect Lluis Domènech i Montaner and completed in 1879. The building, which introduced the industry into a residential neighborhood, combines cast-iron and brick, medievalism and technologism in what was one of the first examples of Catalonian *Modernismo*. Its restoration into a museum aimed, first and foremost, at

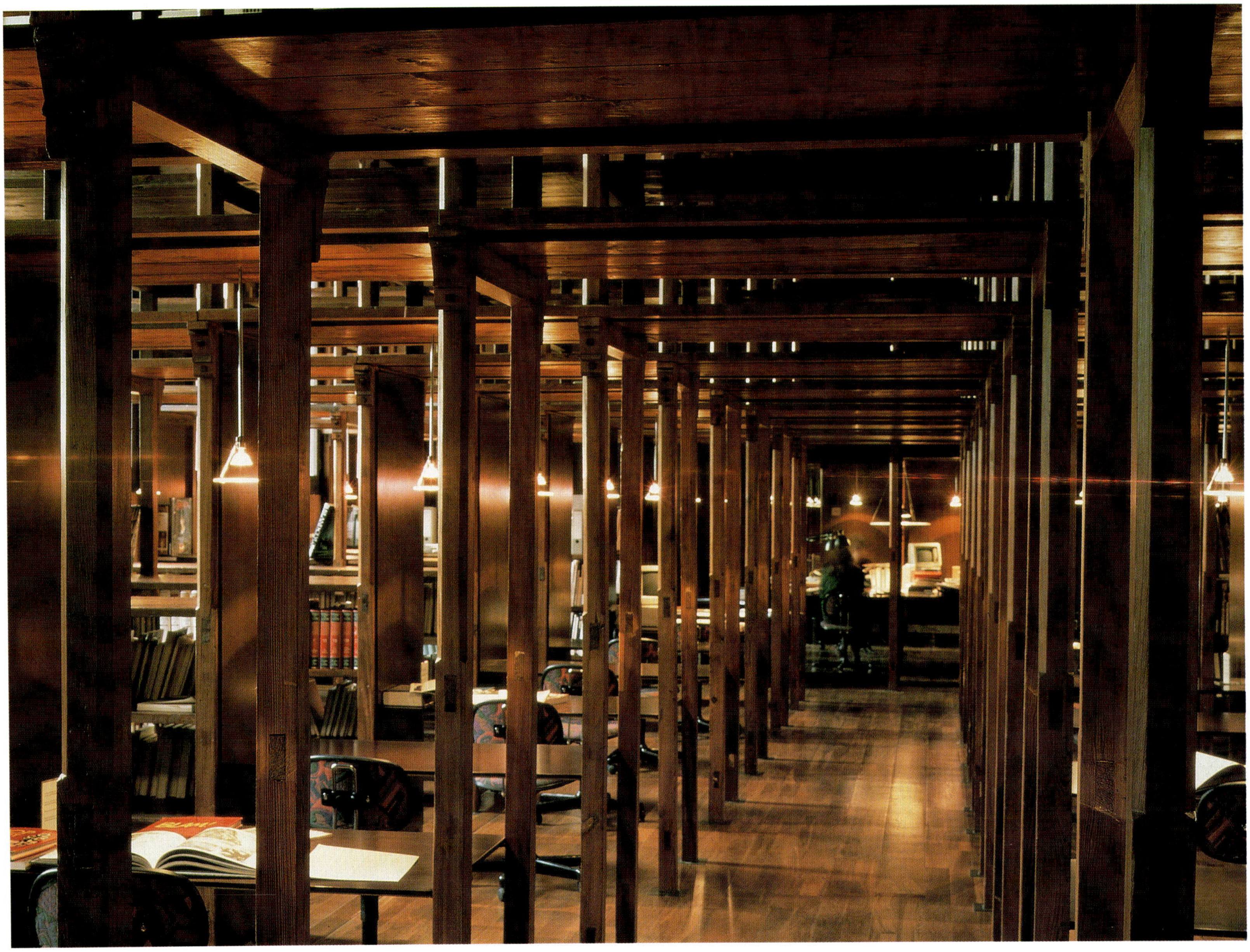

View of the library, where shelves of the building's former publishing house have been reused.

Opposite page
The mezzanine level seen from the library.

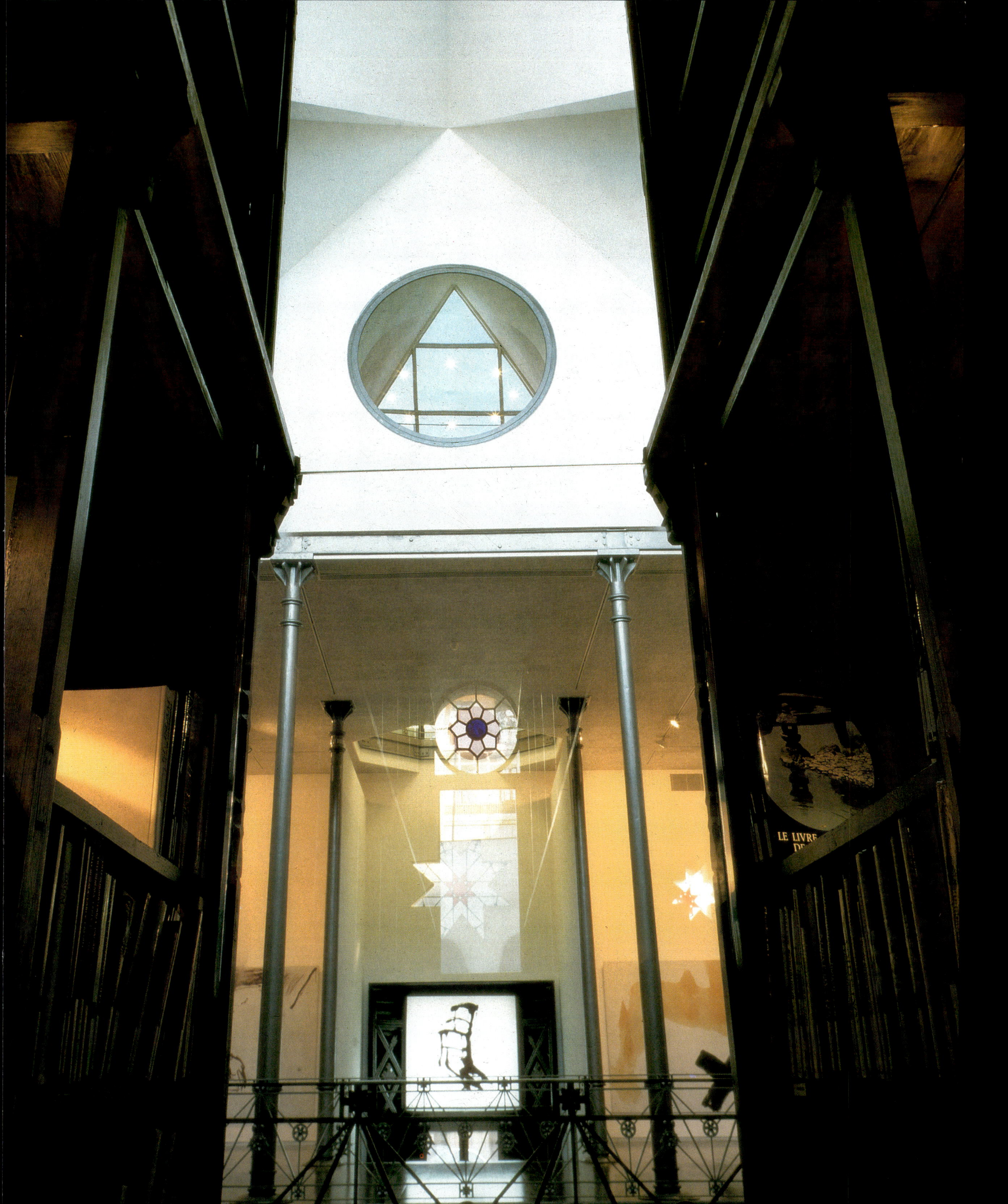
LE LIVRE

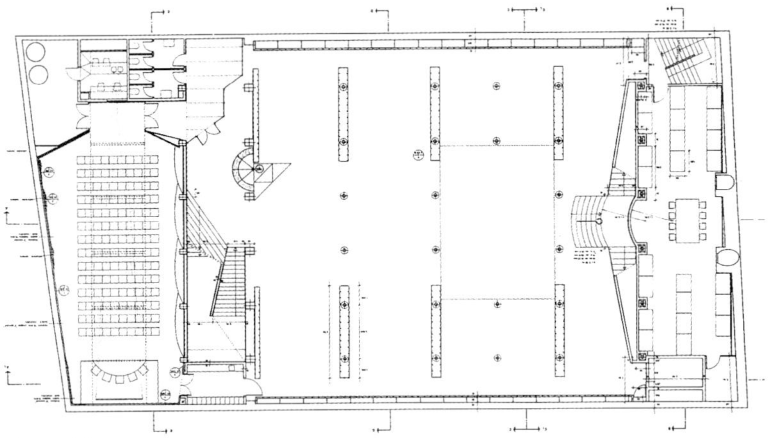

Ground floor

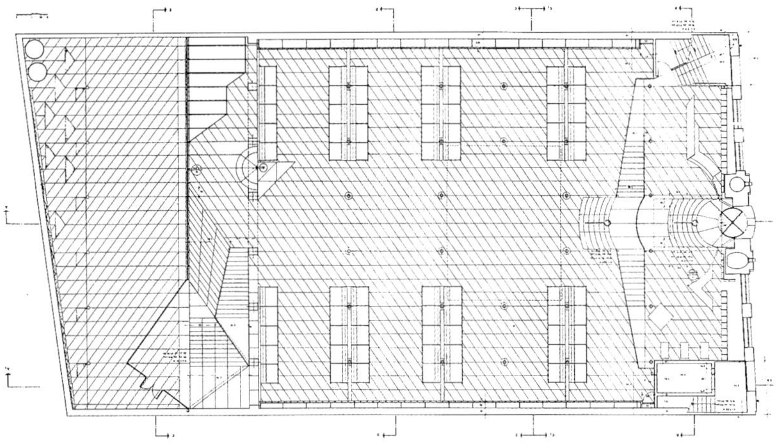

1st floor

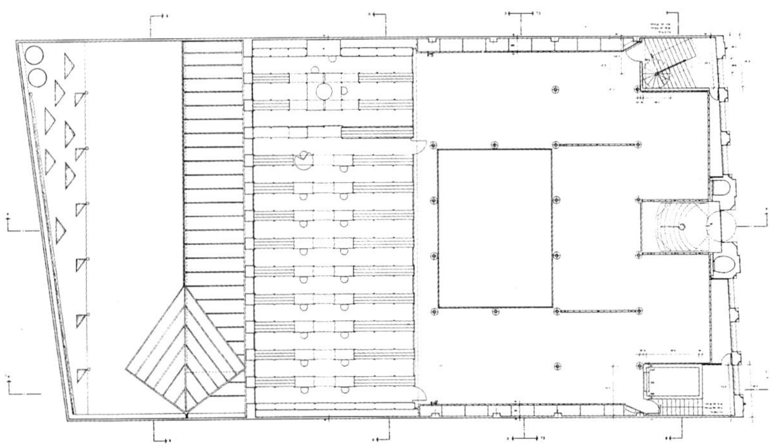

2nd floor

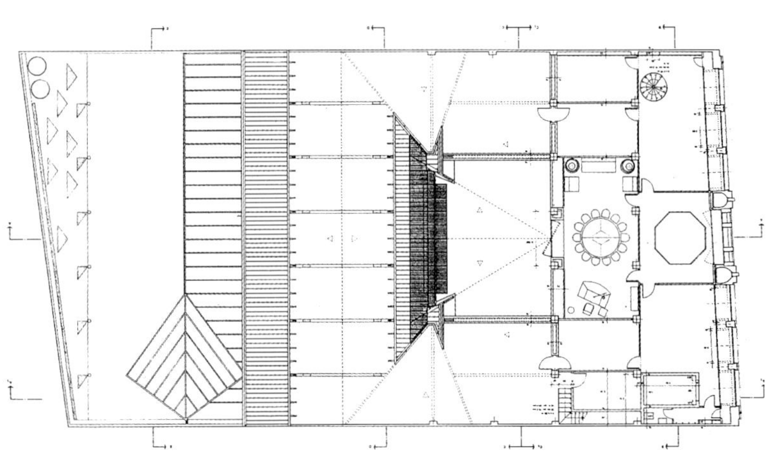

3rd floor

recovering the spatial and esthetic import of a building that had suffered from years of neglect. This involved taking down its interior partitions to retrieve the original layout of the space. Interspersed with tall, narrow cast-iron pillars and already benefiting from a source of natural, the interior had a system of skylights that merely required renovation. Once cleared out, this industrial space revealed three fine volumes: the largest on the street side, another in the middle comprised of large halls, and a section facing an interior patio. What remained was to design new staircases to link the central areas. All changes were done in an effort to keep the memory of the original place intact, re-using, for instance, the old shelves of the publishing house for the museum's library. A convivial summer terrace was added giving out onto the patio and accessible directly from the exhibition halls.

This elegant testimony of industrial architecture transformed into an art museum needed to announce its new identity from the street. The frames of the skylights were thus extended beyond the facade supporting eight beams from which hang long transparent panels held together within a wire mesh. This aerial addition, discrete and hardly noticeable from the front, was all that was needed to bring the Domènech building on par with its two neighboring buildings. It also plays the important role of announcing that this prior publishing house has acquired a public use. □

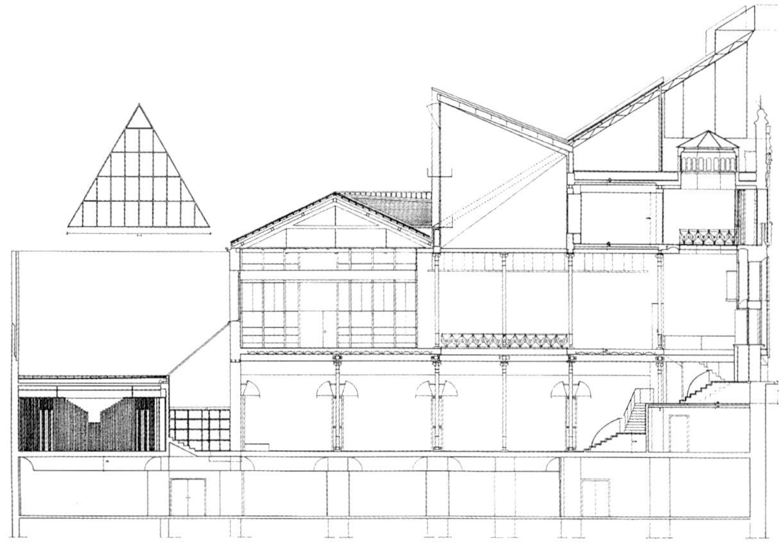

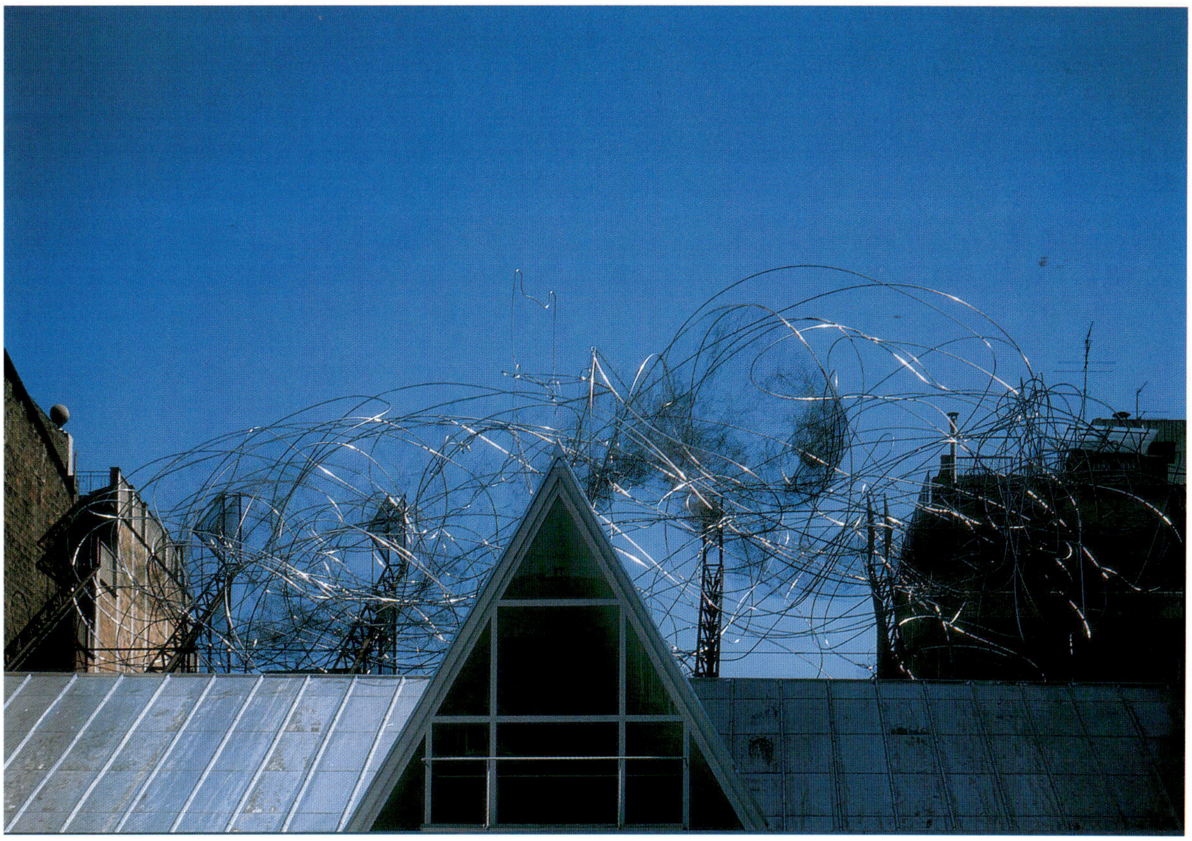

One of the qualities of the original edifice was the system of natural overhead lighting. Nonetheless, in order to improve the light in the exhibition rooms, the structure of the existing skylights was completely renovated.

Opposite page
Floor plans and transversal section of the building.

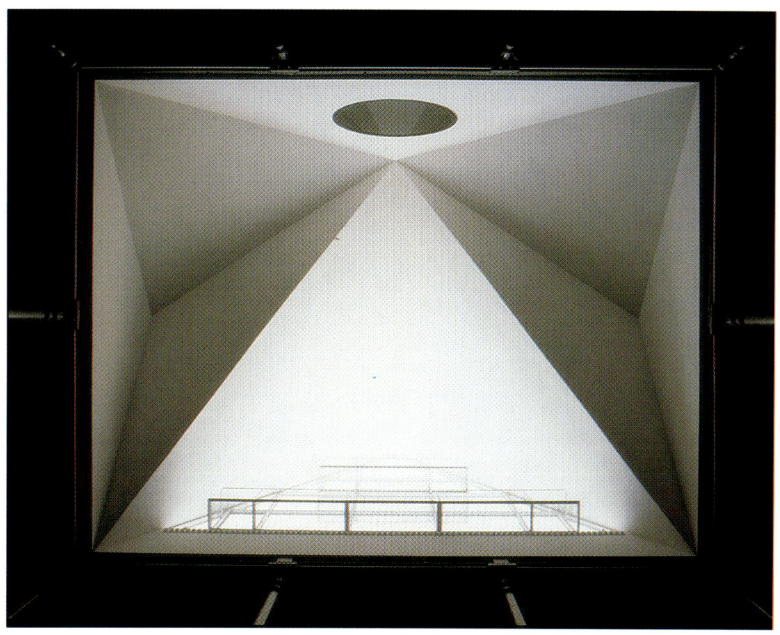

Following pages
The mezzanine. Taking advantage of the technological and aesthetic value of this beautiful industrial space by incorporating the building's slender columns and metal balustrades.

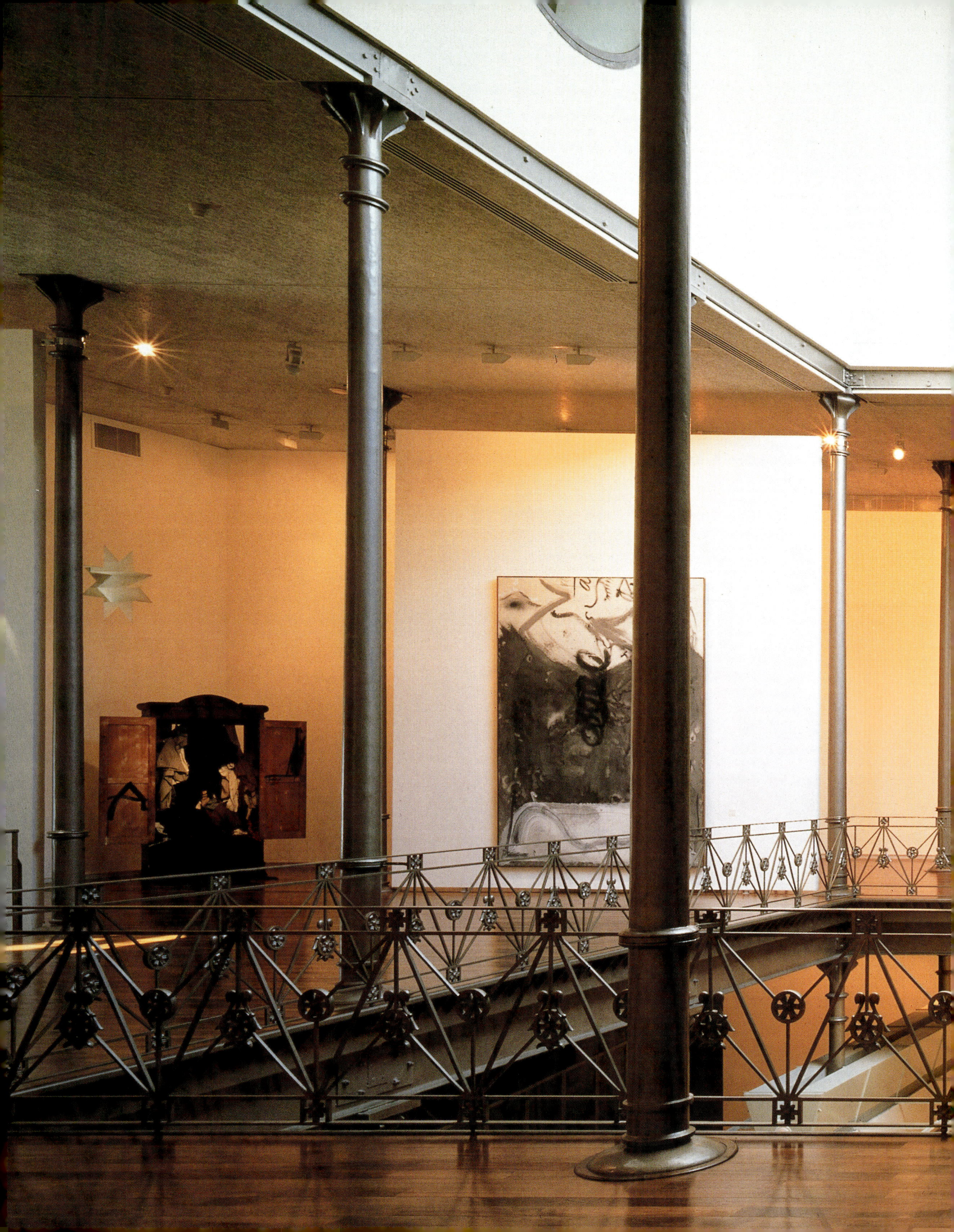

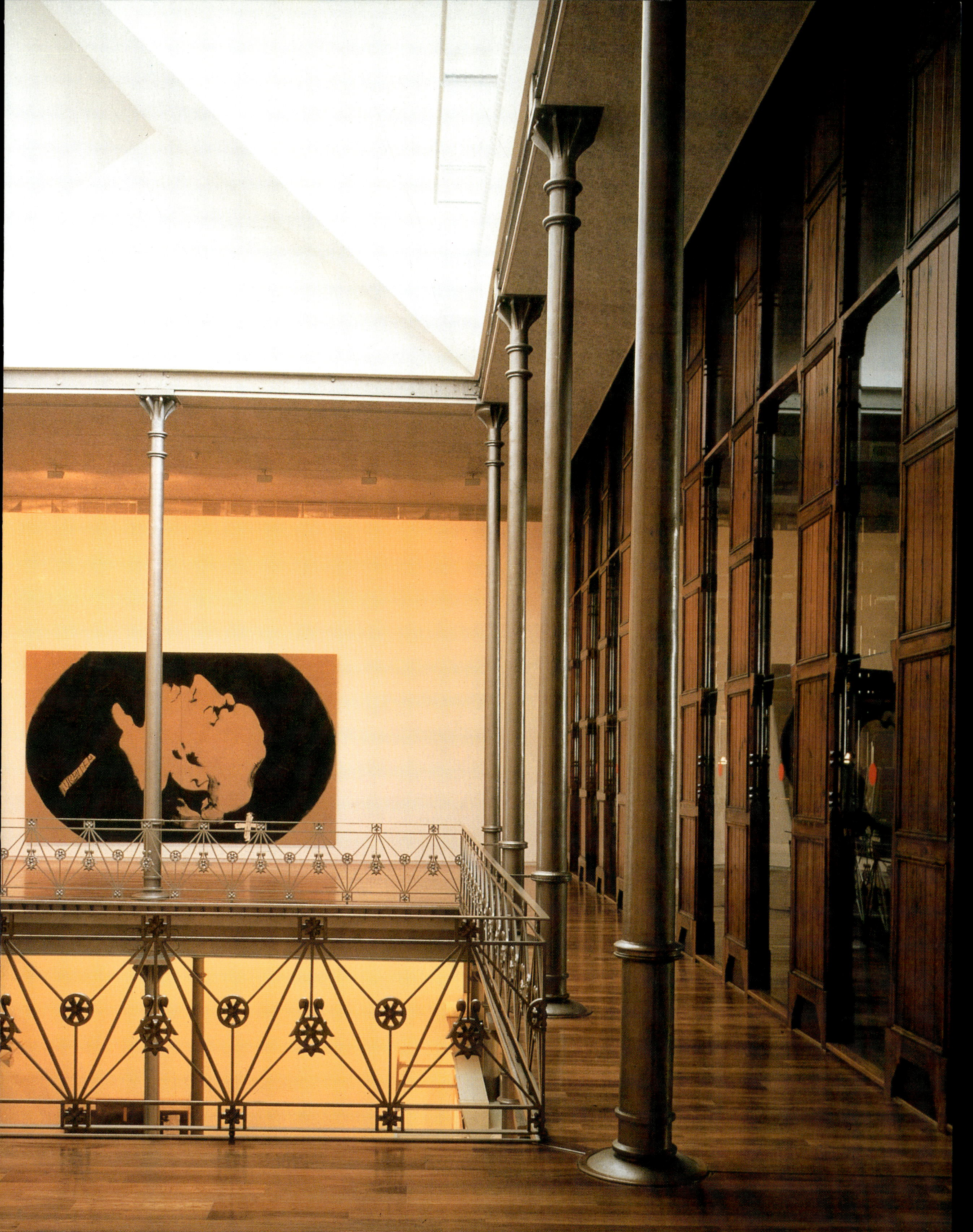

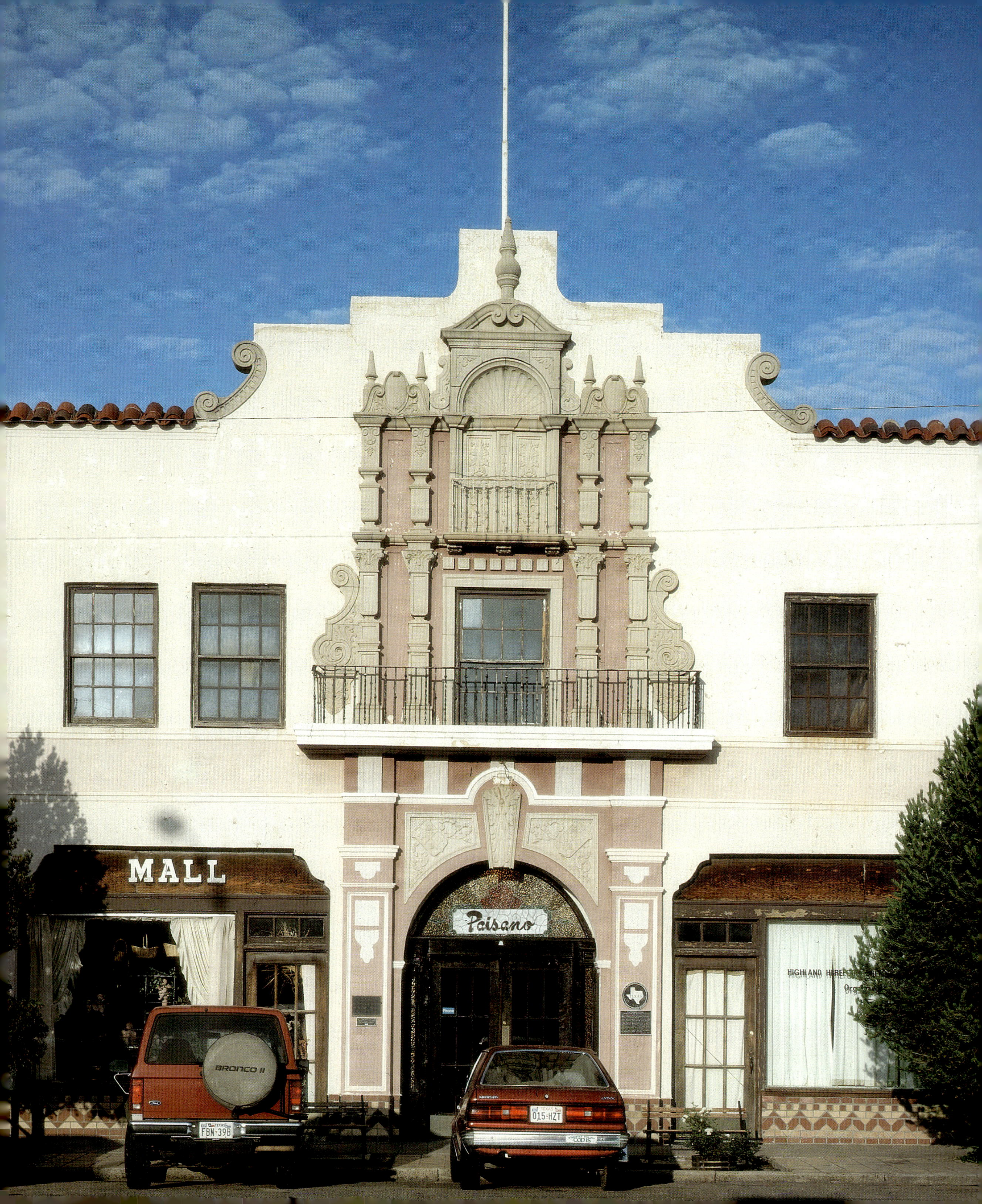
MALL
Paisano
BRONCO II

Donald Judd

Chinati Foundation

Marfa, Texas, United States

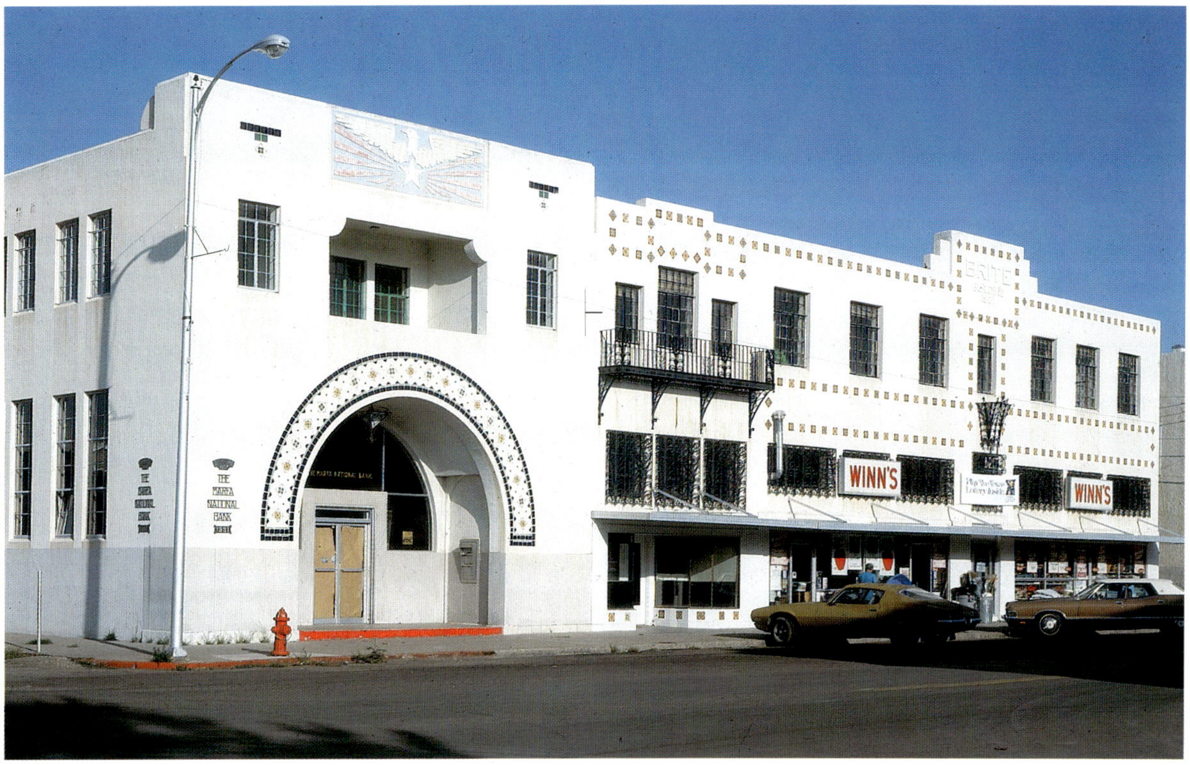

Marfa, a small town in south Texas, less than 200 miles from the Rio Grande and the Mexican border. Here on Main Street two Art Deco buildings with a touch of Hispanic flavor.

The idea of a permanent installation of works of art in Marfa Texas is diametrically opposed to the generally accepted idea of a museum, against which Donald Judd fought a constant battle. His arguments were and still are pertinent. It would even seem simple common sense if the generalization of the concept of culture had not interfered with art. Beyond the negligence to which artworks are constantly exposed, Judd denounced the incredible arrogance with which so-called experts assume the right to show art as they personally see fit. Judd was an angry artist: he denounced institutions, collectors and dealers (gránting the last extenuating circumstances) an entire power hierarchy of Fine Art in which artists are no more than an alibi.

Mobilizing his energy, the Chinati Foundation was a way for Judd to distance himself, first of all geographically. At the outset he looked for a site in Mexico but was dissuaded by the complexity of customs procedures. Marfa, a small, isolated, semi-deserted town in southwest Texas offered several advantages: huge empty hangars near an abandoned train station and a military site, once used by the U.S. cavalry, were perfect for the installation of large scale works of art. Begun in conjunction with the New York-based Dia

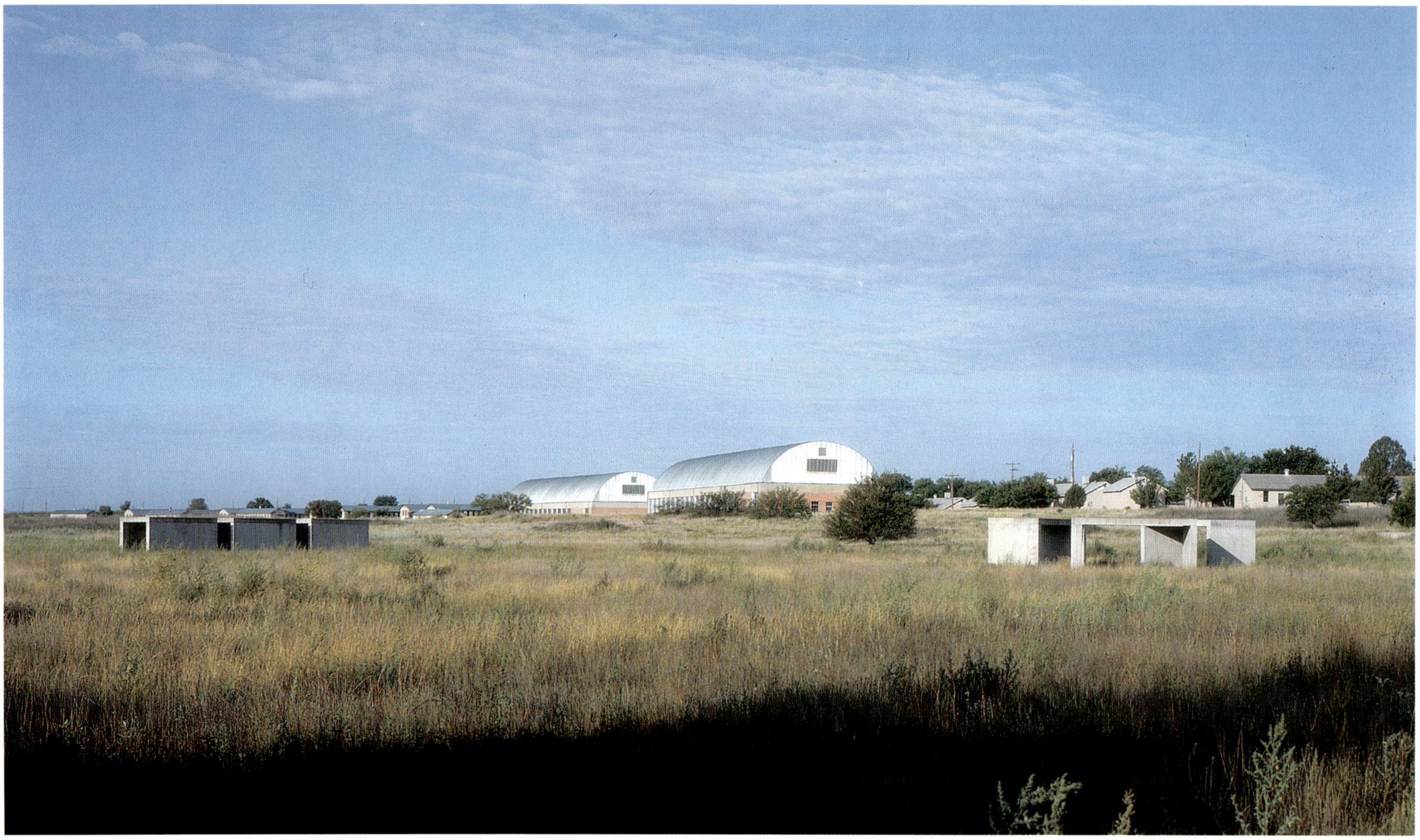

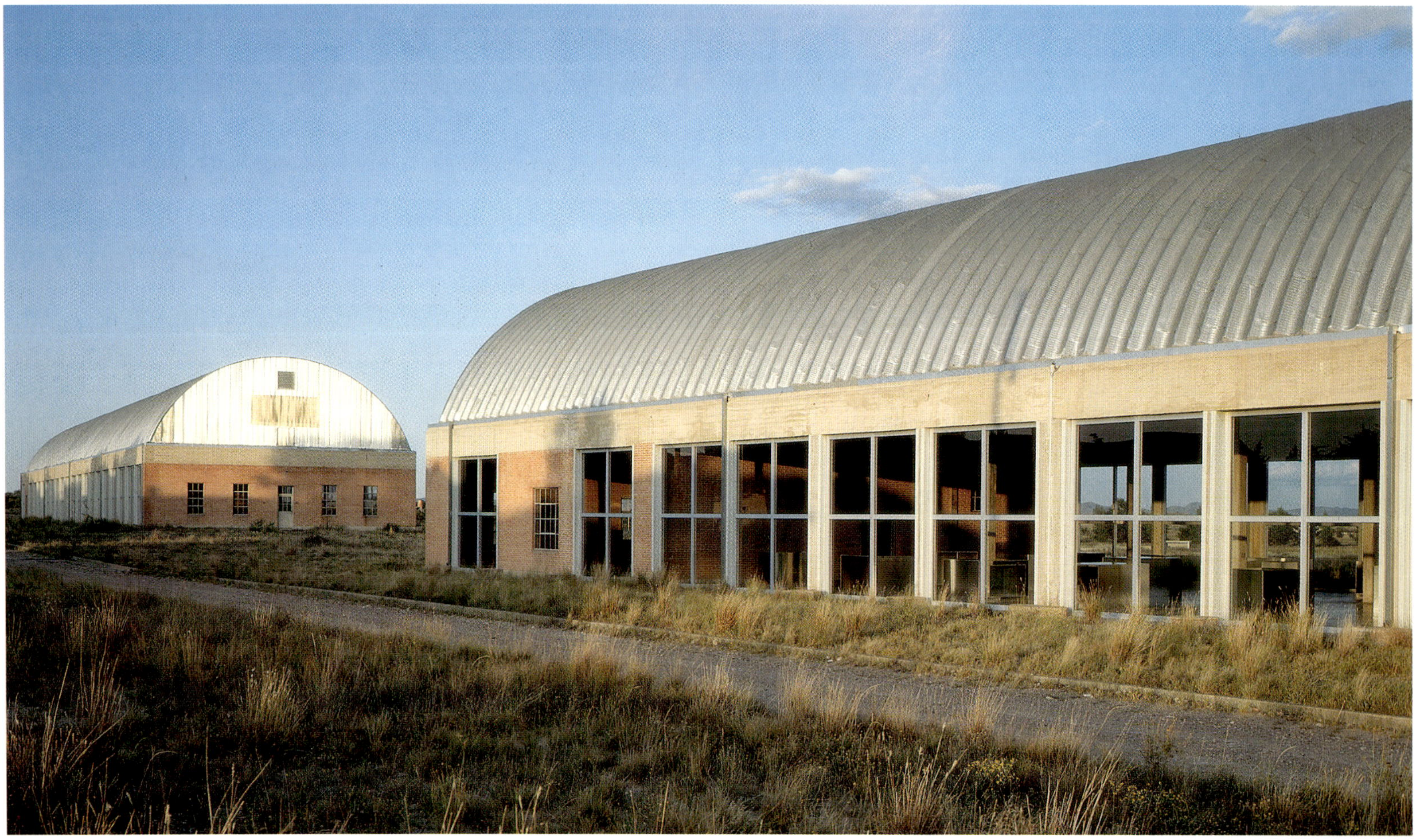

42 Chinati Foundation, Marfa, Texas, United States

The Fort Russell hangars which Judd transformed to install, with meticulous care, a series of specific stainless steel objects.

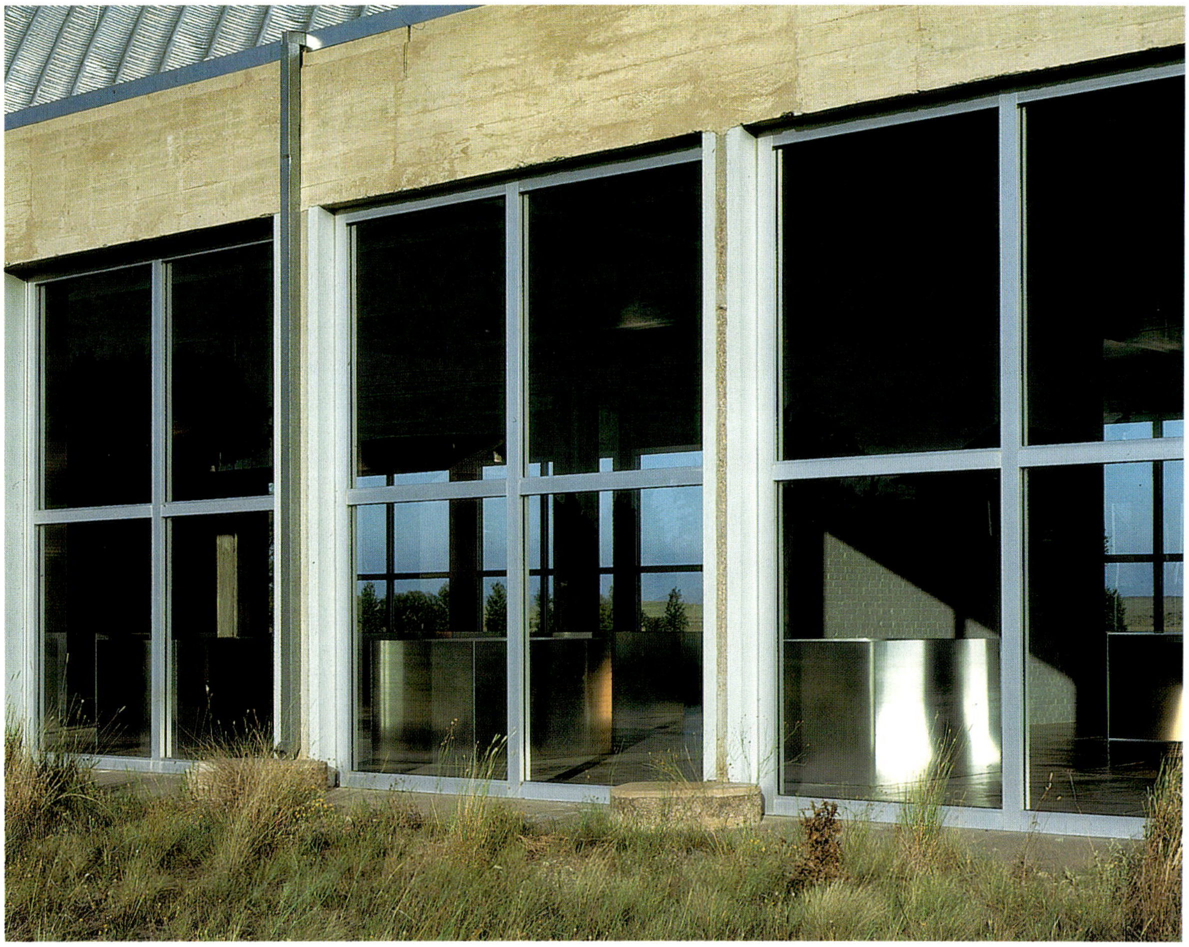

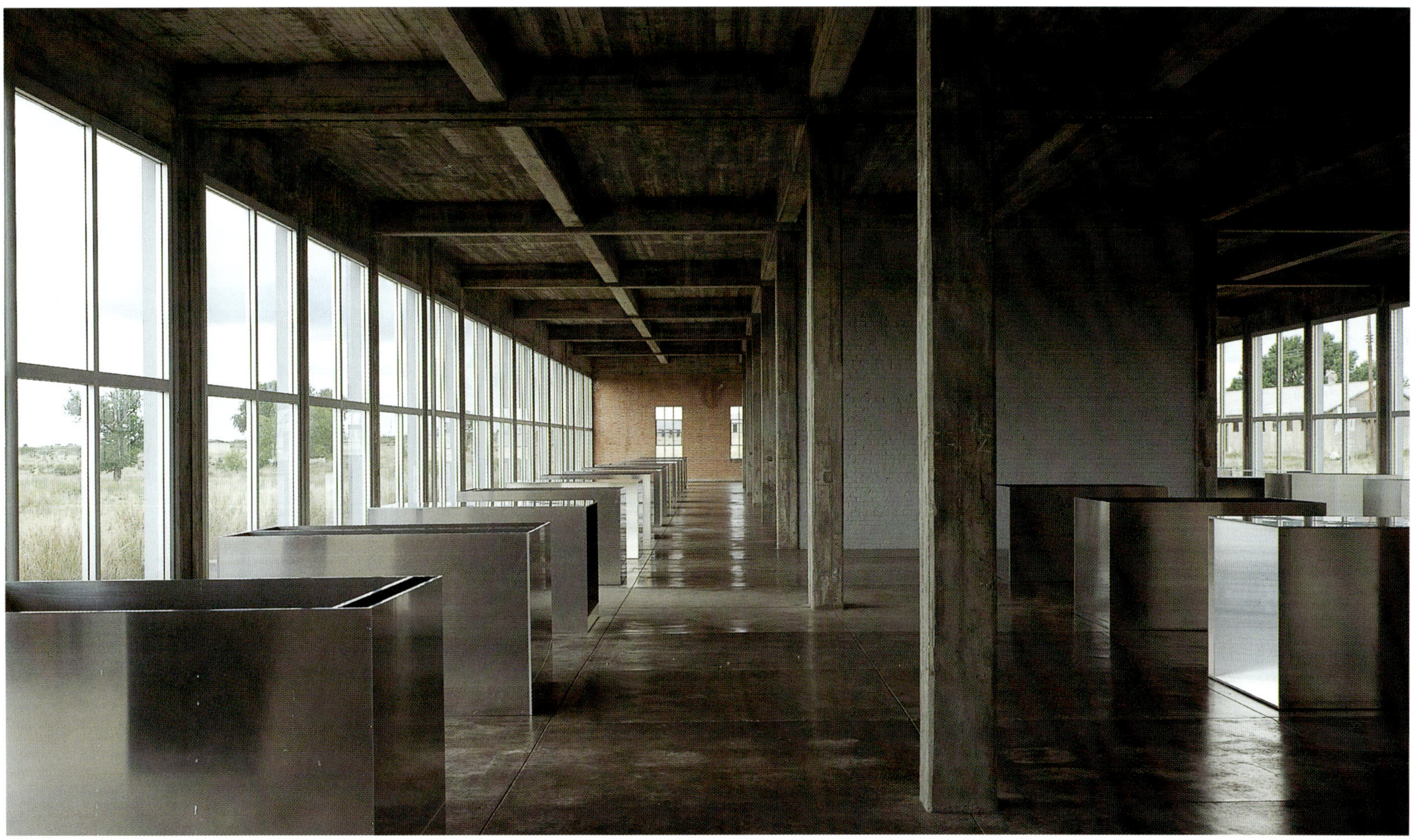

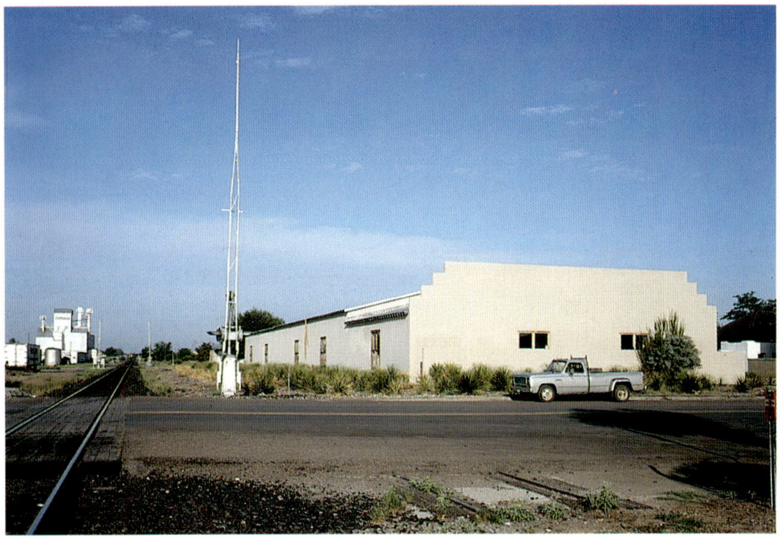

The large hangar of the abandoned train station near the grade crossing houses John Chamberlain's sculptures.

Opposite page and following pages
Restored to its original wooden structure with polished concrete floors, wood framed glass doors which pivot on their median axis: a Spartan vocabulary.

Foundation and continued by the Chinati Foundation alone, Judd's project came to life little by little: a hangar was transformed to accommodate sculpture by Chamberlain, the Fort Russell barracks are being prepared to house installations by Dan Flavin and drawings by Josef Albers and Barnett Newman. Still in the planning stages is the installation of a work in light by Larry Bell. Oldenberg, André, and Richard Long are other artists featured at the site. Judd's own works are installed in the complex, which for a time served as his residence in the Arena, and the two large Fort Russell hangars. A half mile long concrete work defines the limits of the military terrain. Judd thus realized the permanent installation of his works upon which he had so stubbornly insisted.

Donald Judd admitted to having hesitated for a long time before choosing art over architecture so as not to have to be subjected to the client. He practiced architecture for his personal use in his New York apartments, in the building he acquired in SoHo and later in Marfa. He refurbished a farm 45 miles away and a small hotel in Switzerland. He also designed furniture in the style of his artwork.

Judd had a dignified and not in the least puritan concept of architecture. He said the profession had died with Louis Kahn. He applied himself with the rigor he imposed on his artwork in a spirit of clean and complex geometry using mathematical variants and series. At Marfa, it was to renovate existing hangars and render them appropriate for the installation of a group of his sculptures. Judd's intervention on the Fort Russell buildings is exemplary of his tact and discretion: Judd cleaned the buildings to restore them as faithfully as possible to their original state; he then added polished concrete floors, wide carefully designed windows and a shingled, drum-shaped roof. The perfectly aligned stainless steel works play with the changing light. In this spartan atmosphere, the viewer finds the ideal conditions for contemplation and meditation.

For Judd, art was a dignified and serious affair. In the complex which served as his residence, the buildings were redone in adobe by local workers. Enclosed by its high walls, the "rancho" once again found an ageless physiognomy with its pergola and its unpolished wooden furniture. What is difficult, Judd once said, is to leave the earth in peace. □

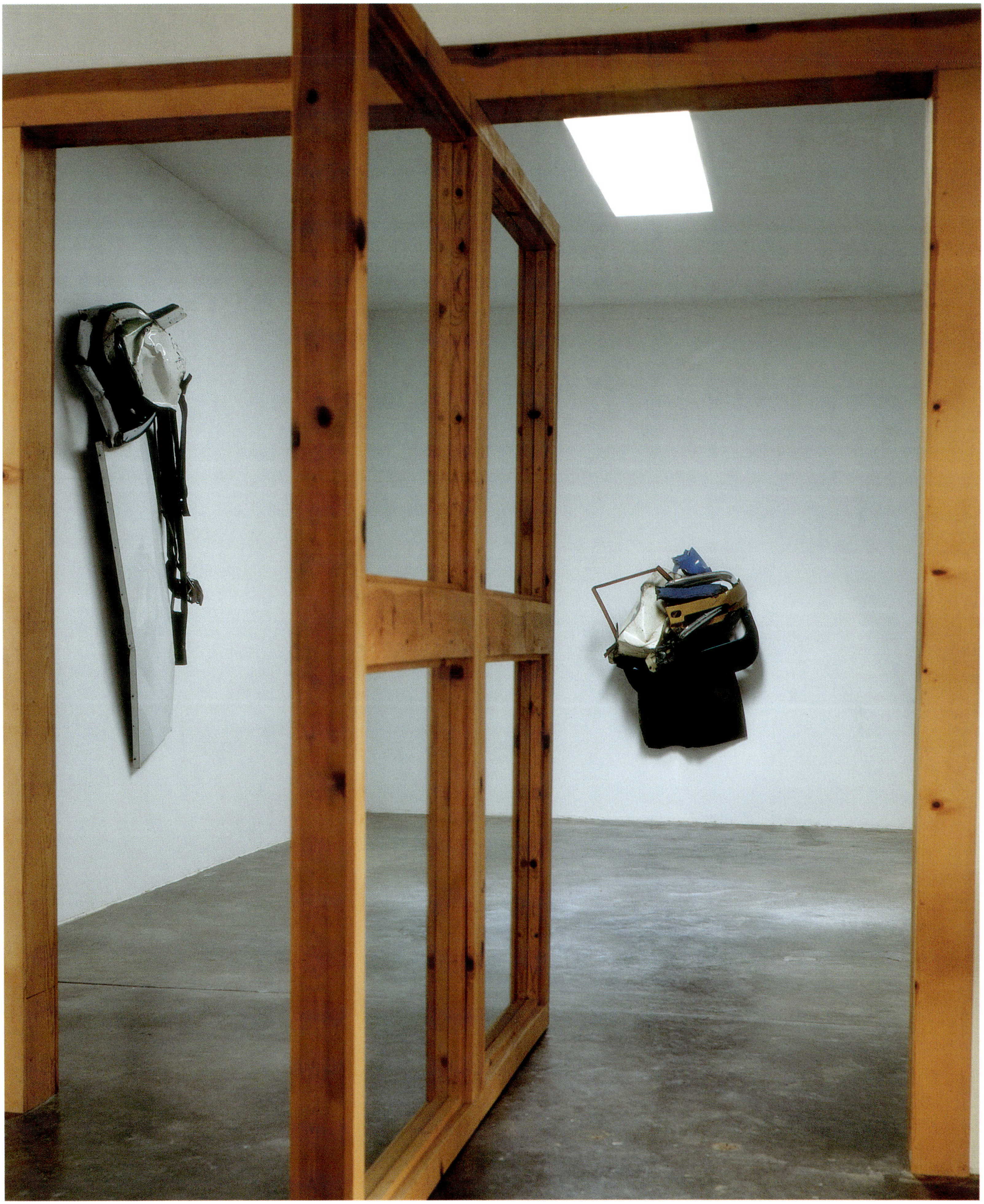

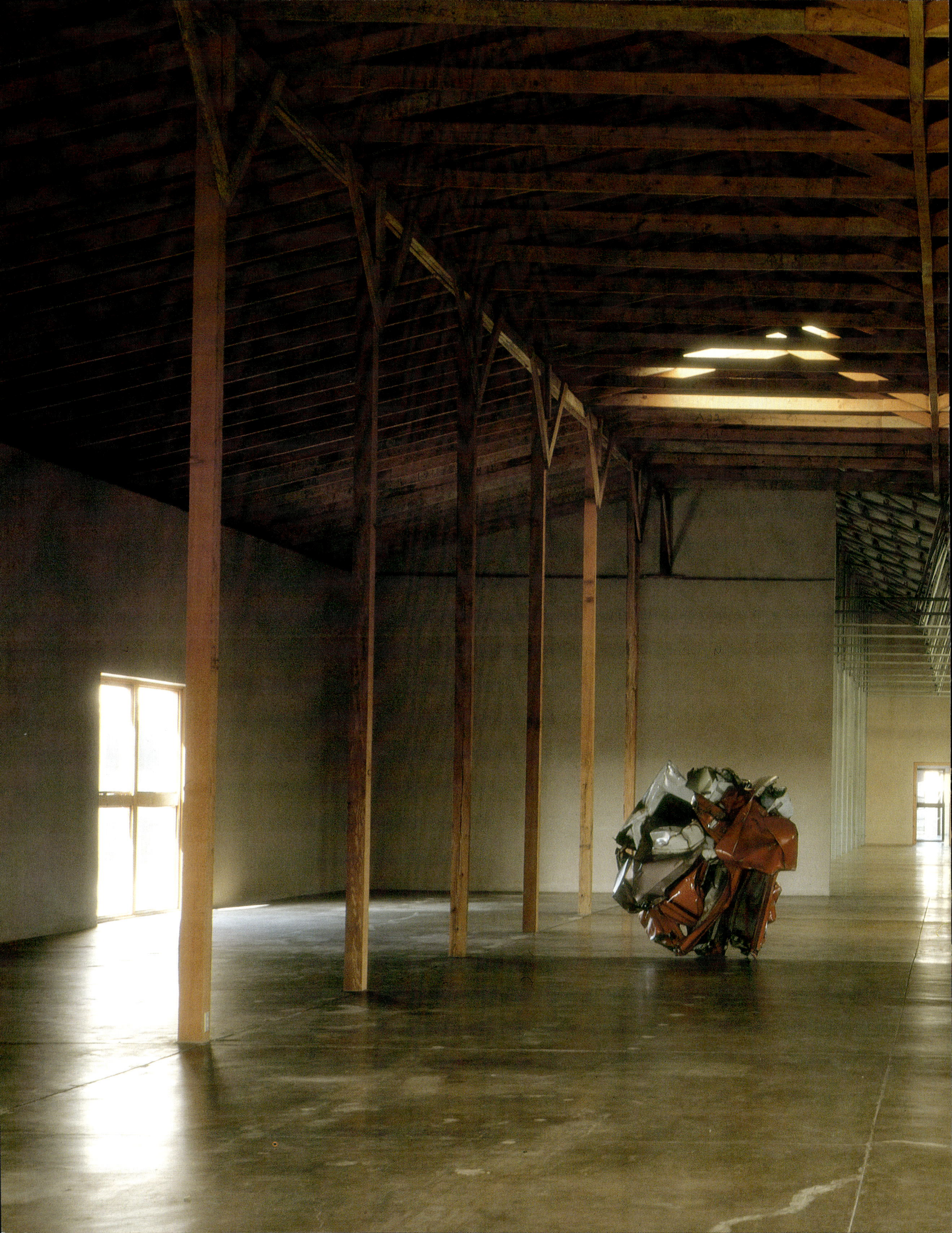

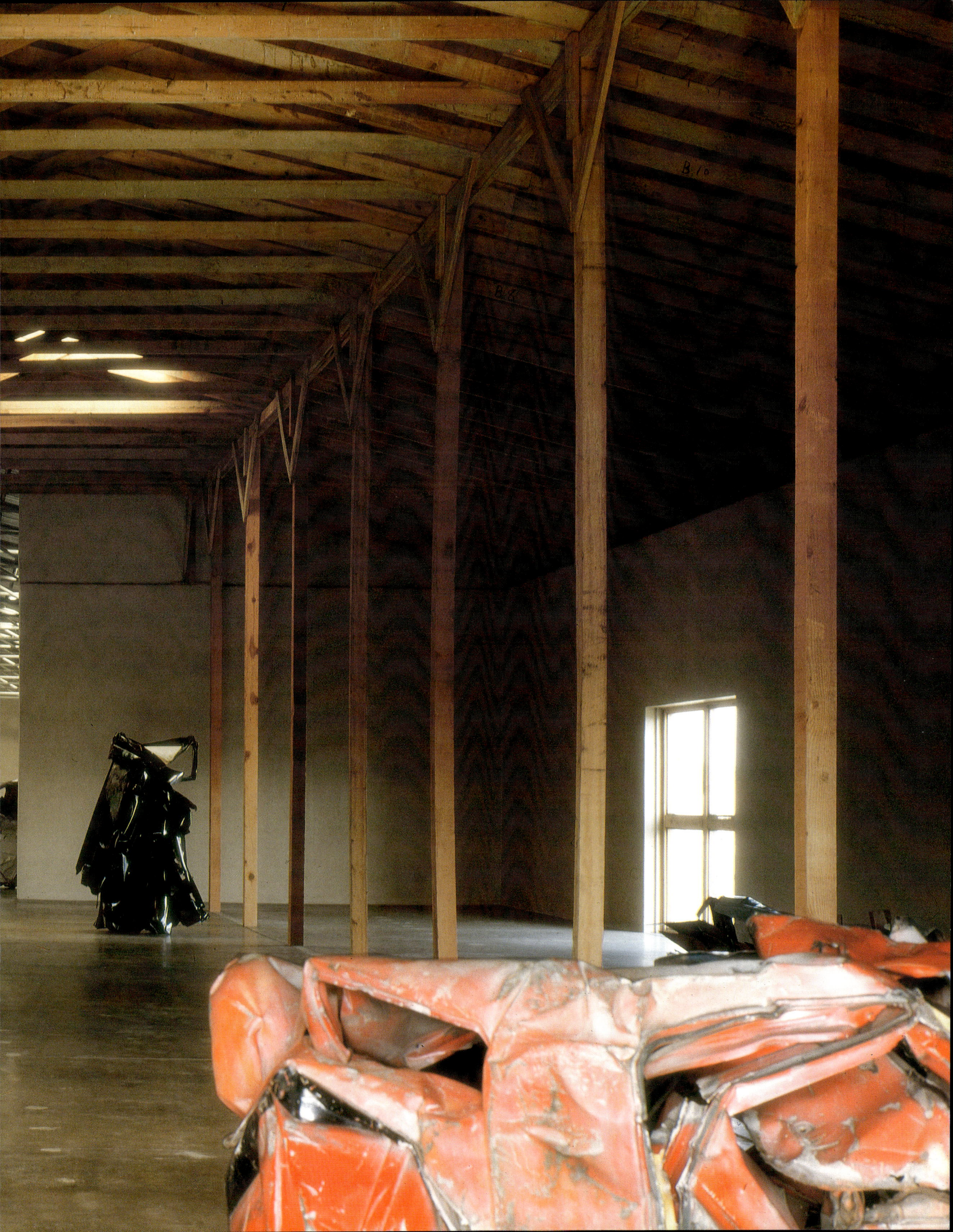

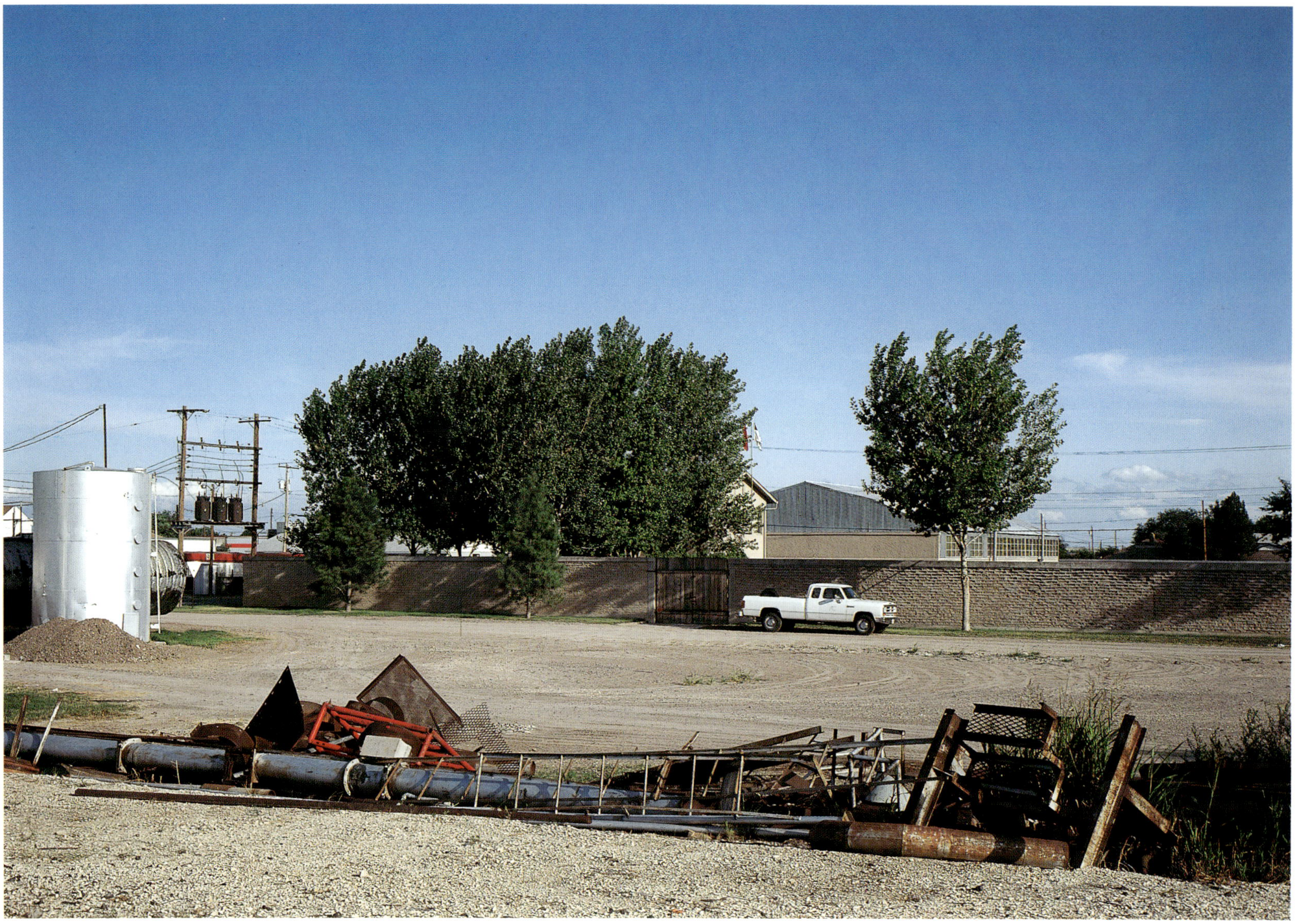

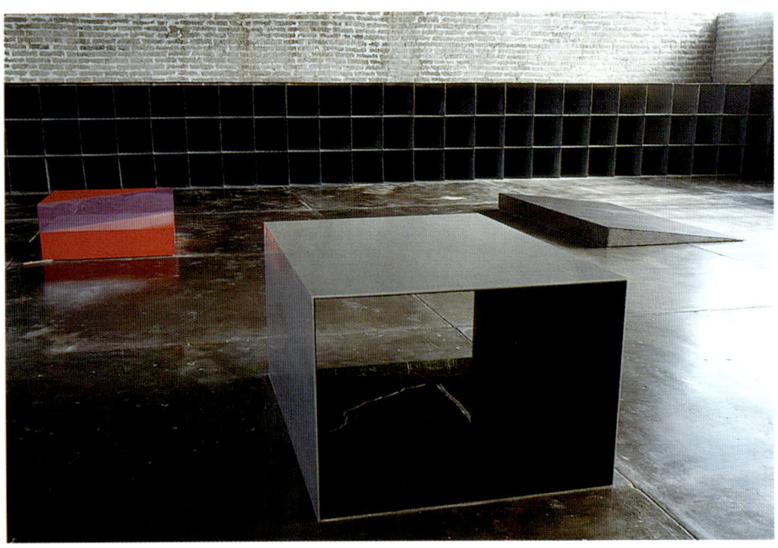

48 Chinati Foundation, Marfa, Texas, United States

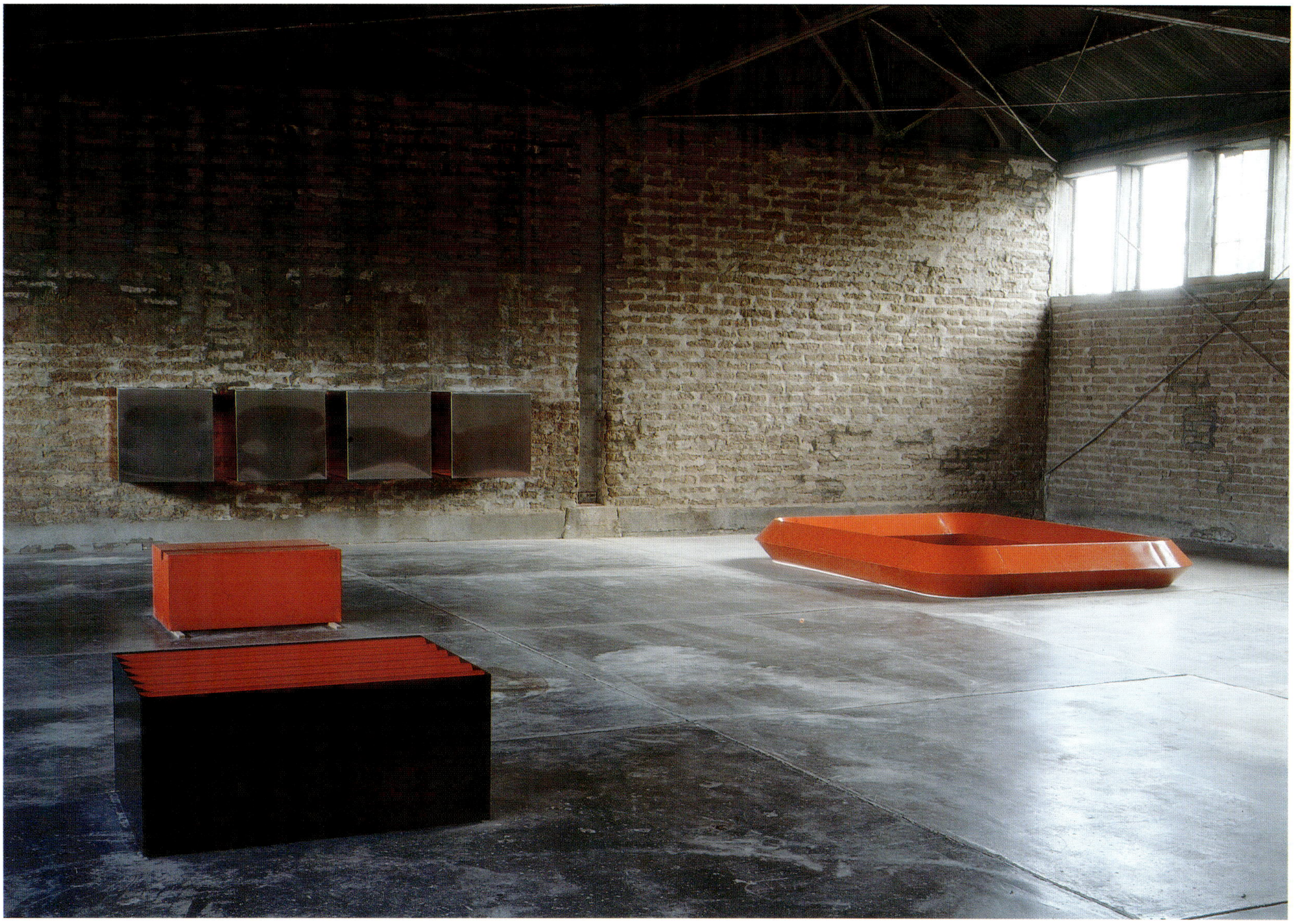

Judd's house is concealed by an adobe wall. Inside, older works by the artist have been installed.

Following pages
An alignment of variations on concrete tunnel forms in the Texan desert.

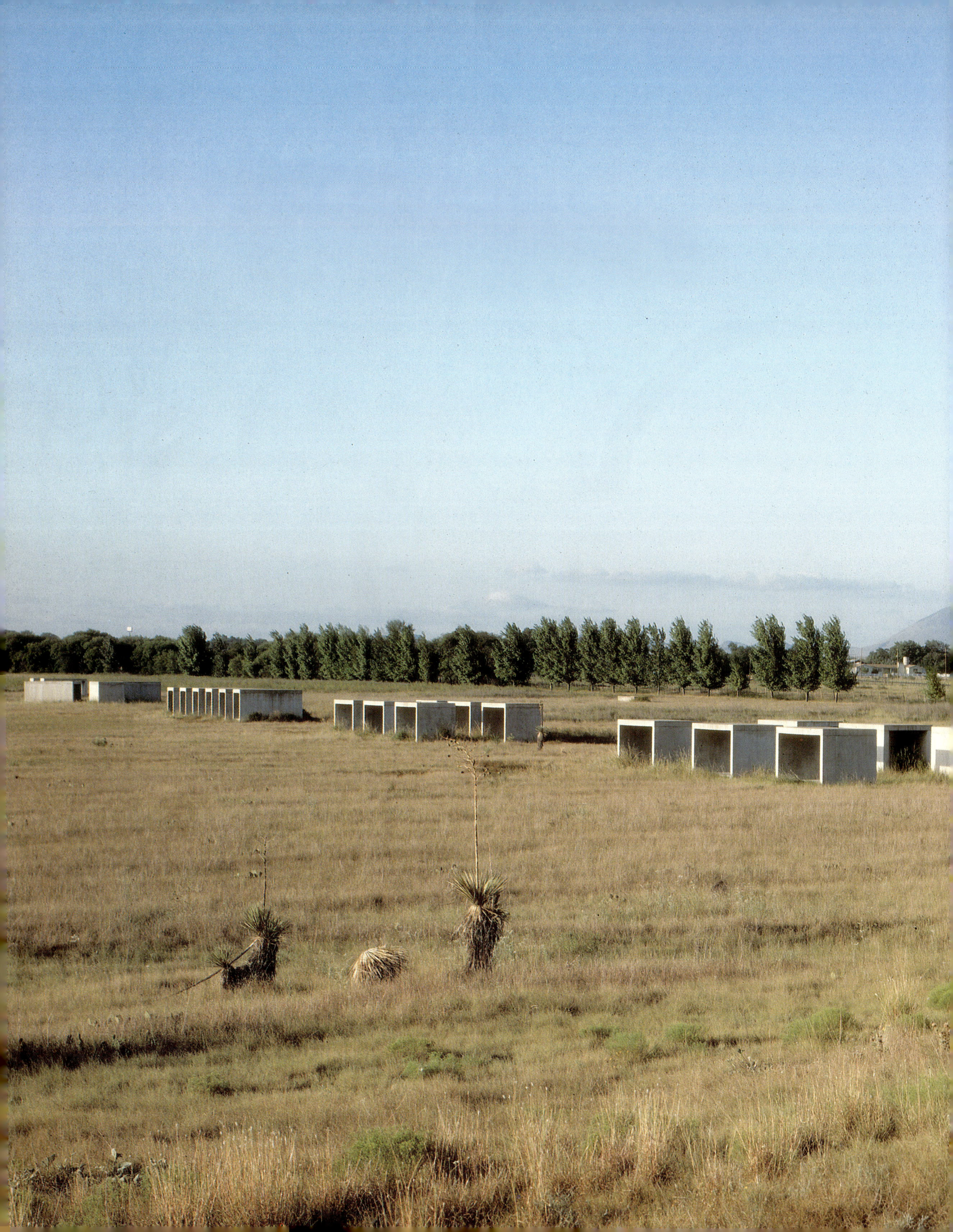

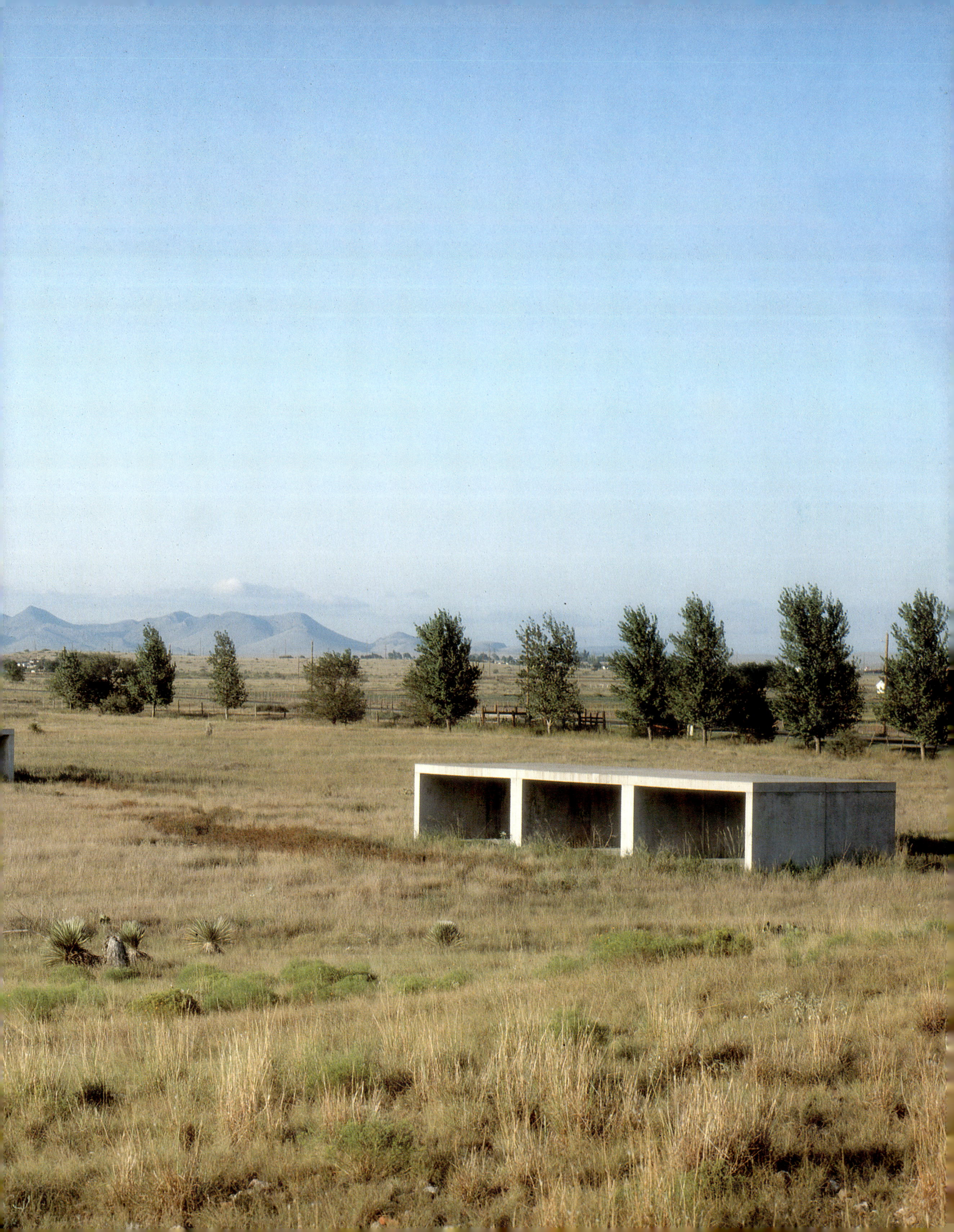

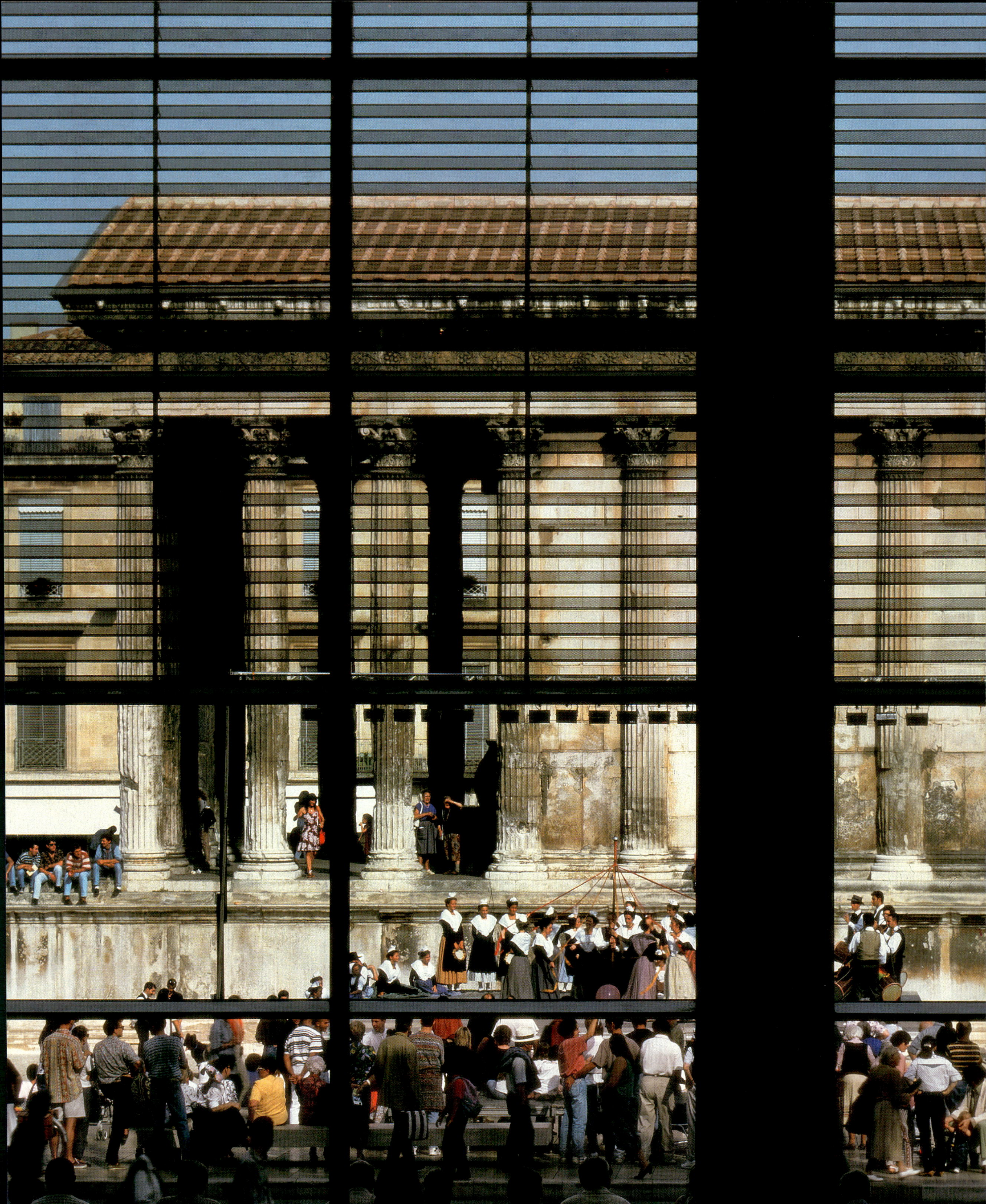

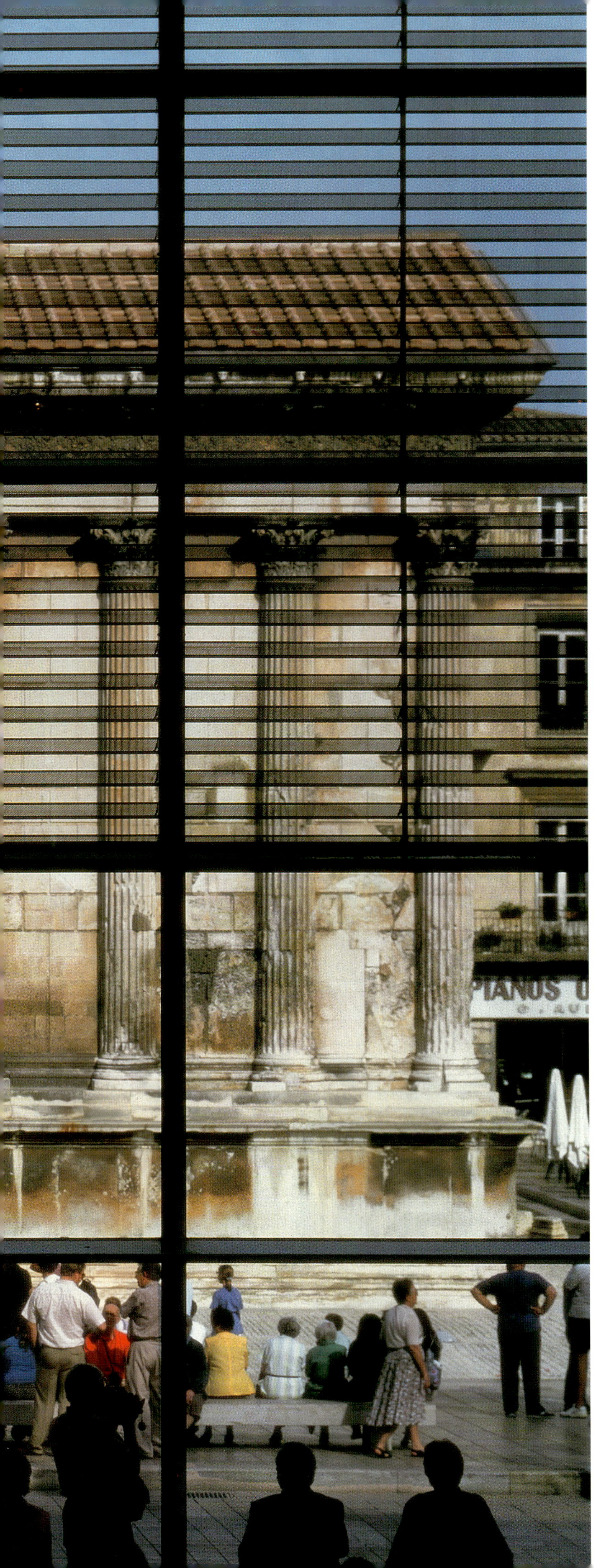

Norman Foster

Carré d'art

Nîmes, France

Far from a simple project, the Carré d'art in Nîmes, a media library and center for contemporary art, represented a true gamble. Local authorities were wary of its vocation to mirror the Pompidou Center in Paris and the proposed site was itself problematic. It was a bold decision indeed to have designated a site in the city center opposite Nîmes' most famous Roman monument, a small temple connected by shaded boulevards to the Roman arenas, on one side, and the Roman baths in the Fontaine gardens, on the other. This crossroads, although undeveloped, its bright esplanade serving as no more than a thoroughfare, was symbolically rooted in the urban fabric. It was thus not until 1984 after years of heated debate, petitions and campaign issues that the initial project could even be explored.

Adding fuel to the fire, where the media library now stands, stood the ruins of a theater that had burnt down in 1952 in particularly romantic circumstances; and although only its facade remained, its columns were considered to be in perfect harmony with the elegant peristyle of the Maison carrée, making it something of a monument. The decision whether to keep or destroy this neoclassical colonnade was among the alternatives confronting the twelve architects consulted about the project. When it was finally handed over to Norman Foster, he had to submit no less than ten propositions before a solution was finally reached.

Choosing to do away with the theater facade altogether, Foster built a glass cube in its place. The cube is shielded from the sun by immense screens protected, in turn, by a louvered canopy perched on the slender shafts of five columns in a reinterpretation of the portico of the Maison carrée. The need to enter into dialogue with its venerable neighbor was among one of the project's requirements. In response to another contextually related requirement, this

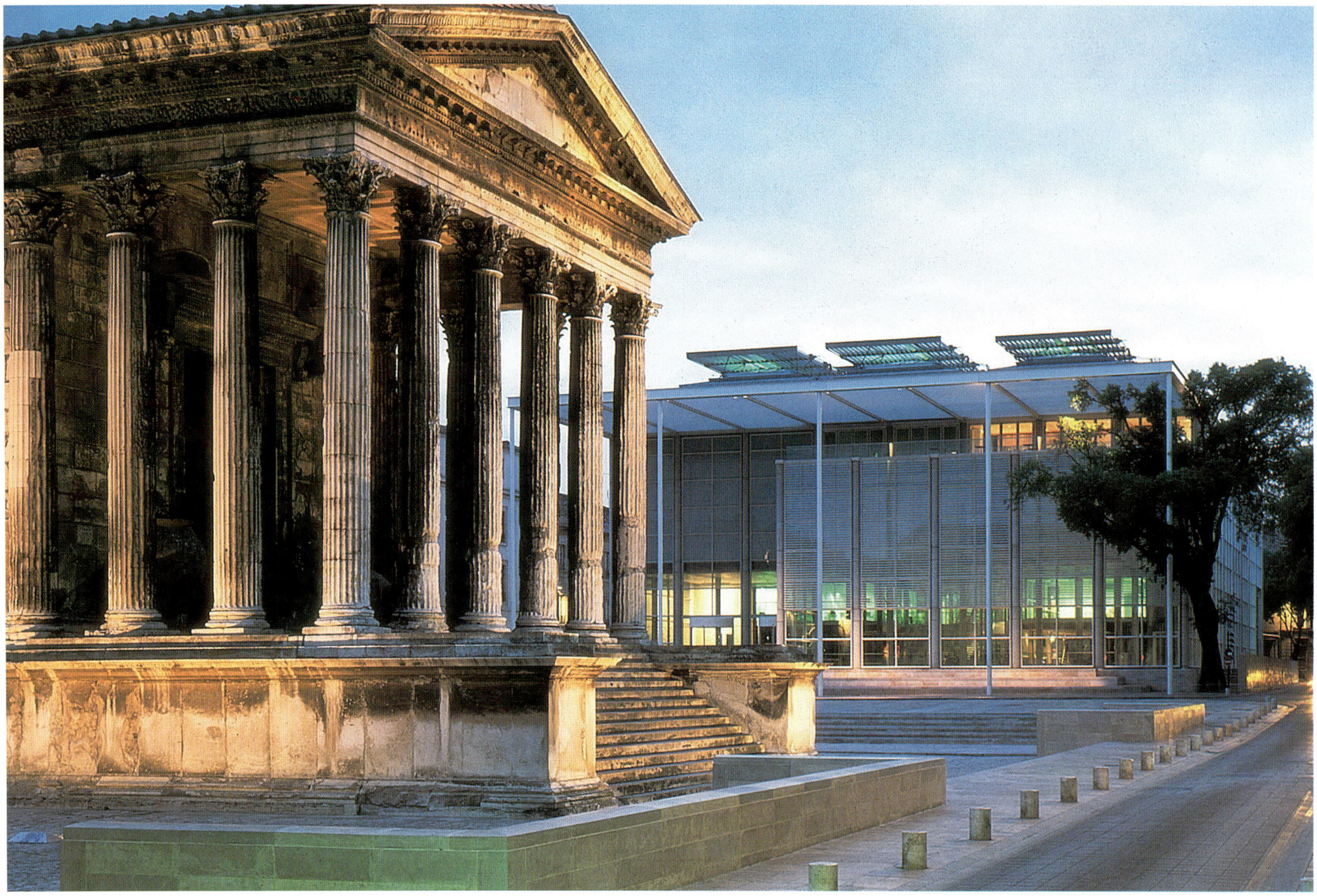

The Carré d'art can be considered as a contemporary declination of the classical style, devoid of all anecdotes by virtue of its extreme simplification. Foster repeated the proportions of the Maison carrée and reinterpreted the colonnade: thin concrete shafts articulate the facade of the new edifice. The portico marks the entrance way, shaded by an awning and a European hackberry tree.

Preceding pages
In the transparency of this glass structure, the Carré d'art maintains a constant dialogue with the city.

time not to exceed the height of the nearby structures, Foster partially buried the edifice. Most of this volume is used for storage, utility rooms and administrative offices, all of which can make do with artificial lighting. The other parts of the museum are organized around a central atrium that, in a play of open space and transparency, brings light to all five floors starting from the exhibition halls and media library upstairs to the library on the lower level.

Finally, the grounds separating the Carré d'art from the Maison carrée were repaved in granite and local limestone, forming a large central square to unify the ensemble. In good weather, this area becomes a place for meeting and conversation, restoring the traditional Roman forum which once took up this very site. This is a case in point for persuading the museum's detractors that juxtaposing two very different historical styles of architecture does not necessarily result in an antinomic relationship, but instead can lead to an authentic restoration of a place's original function. □

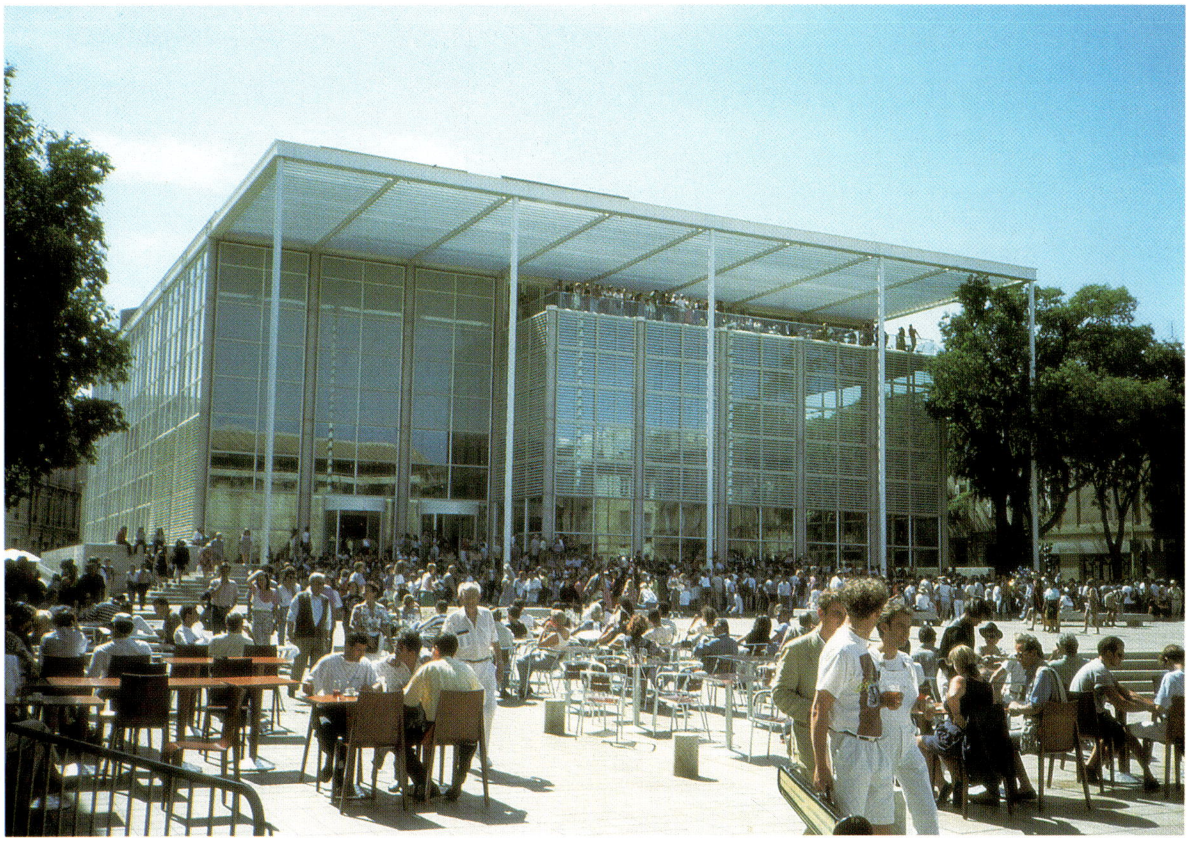

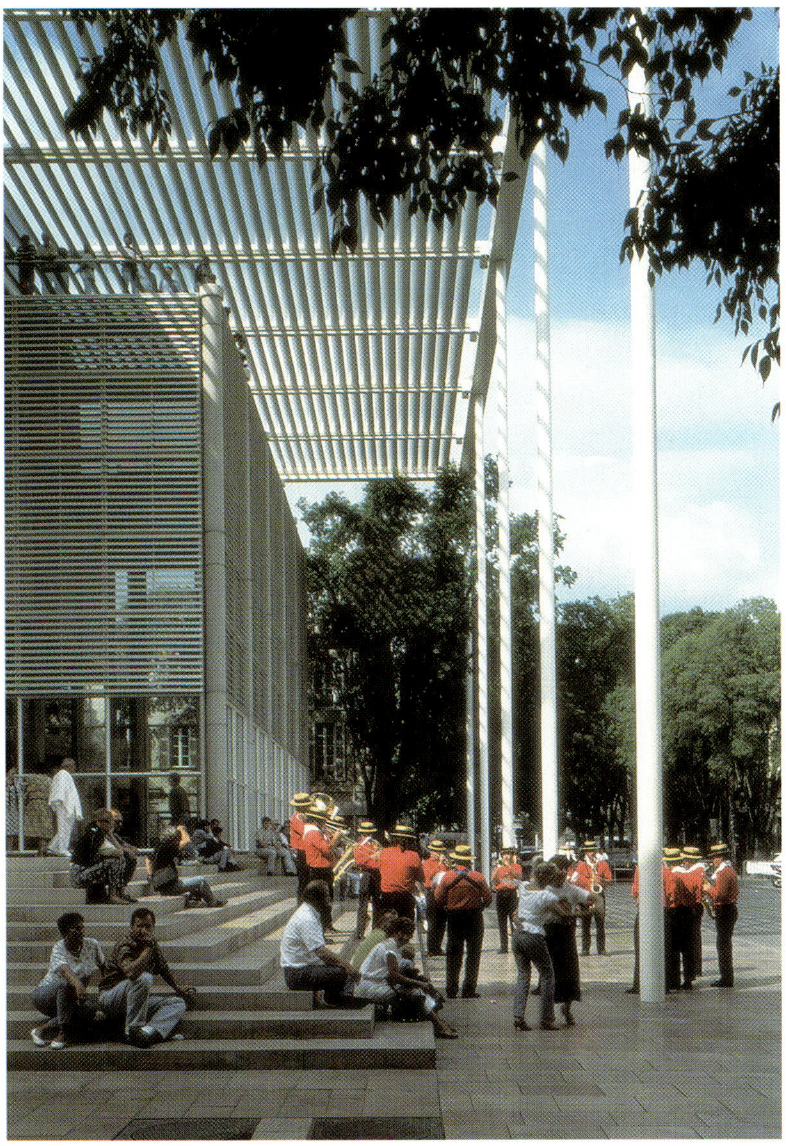

Front and side views of the principal facade giving out onto a large square. The space separating the museum building from the Maison carrée, which had for so long been nothing more than a passageway, has once again become a meeting place. The site rediscovers its original function of times past, the Roman forum.

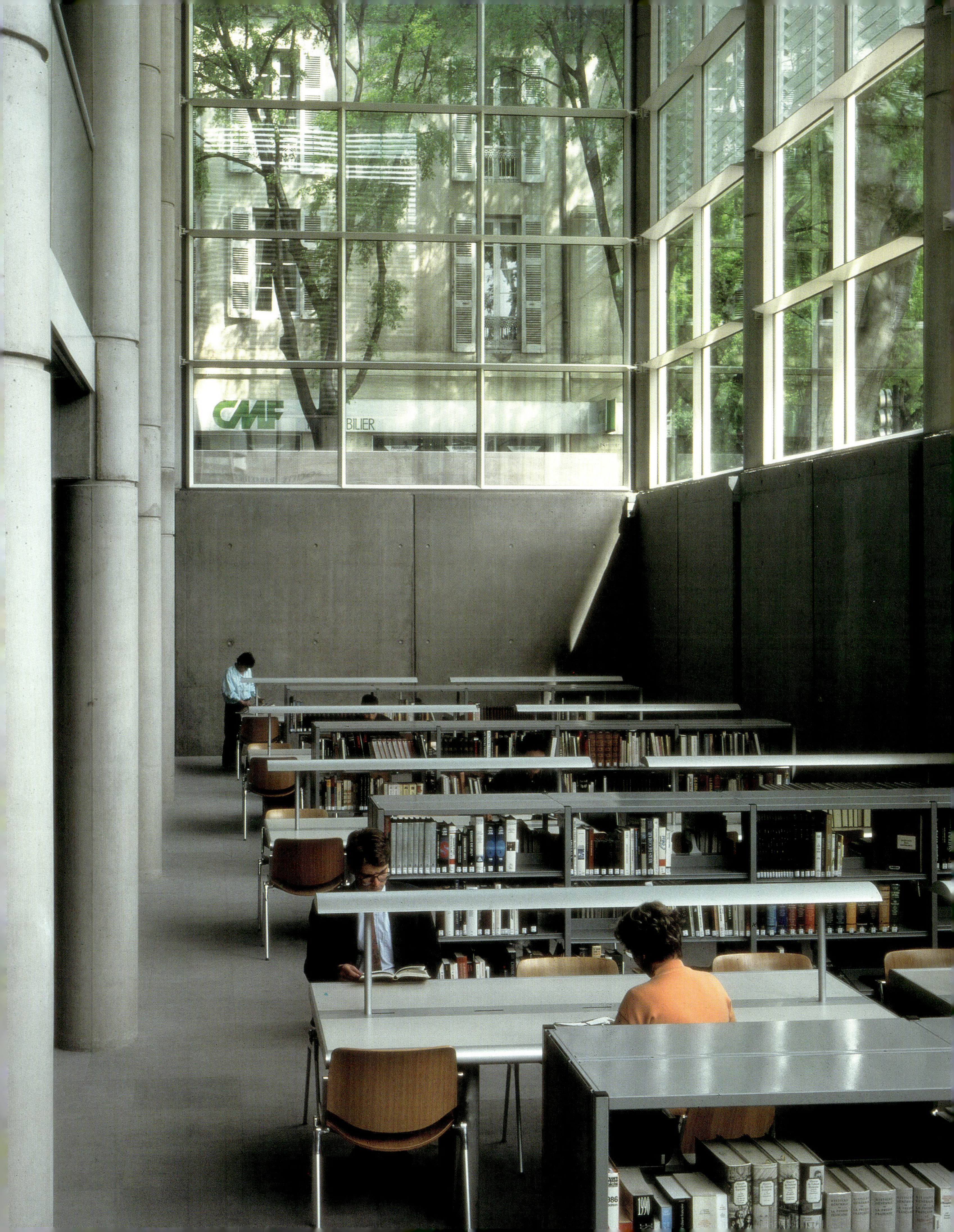
CMF
BILIER

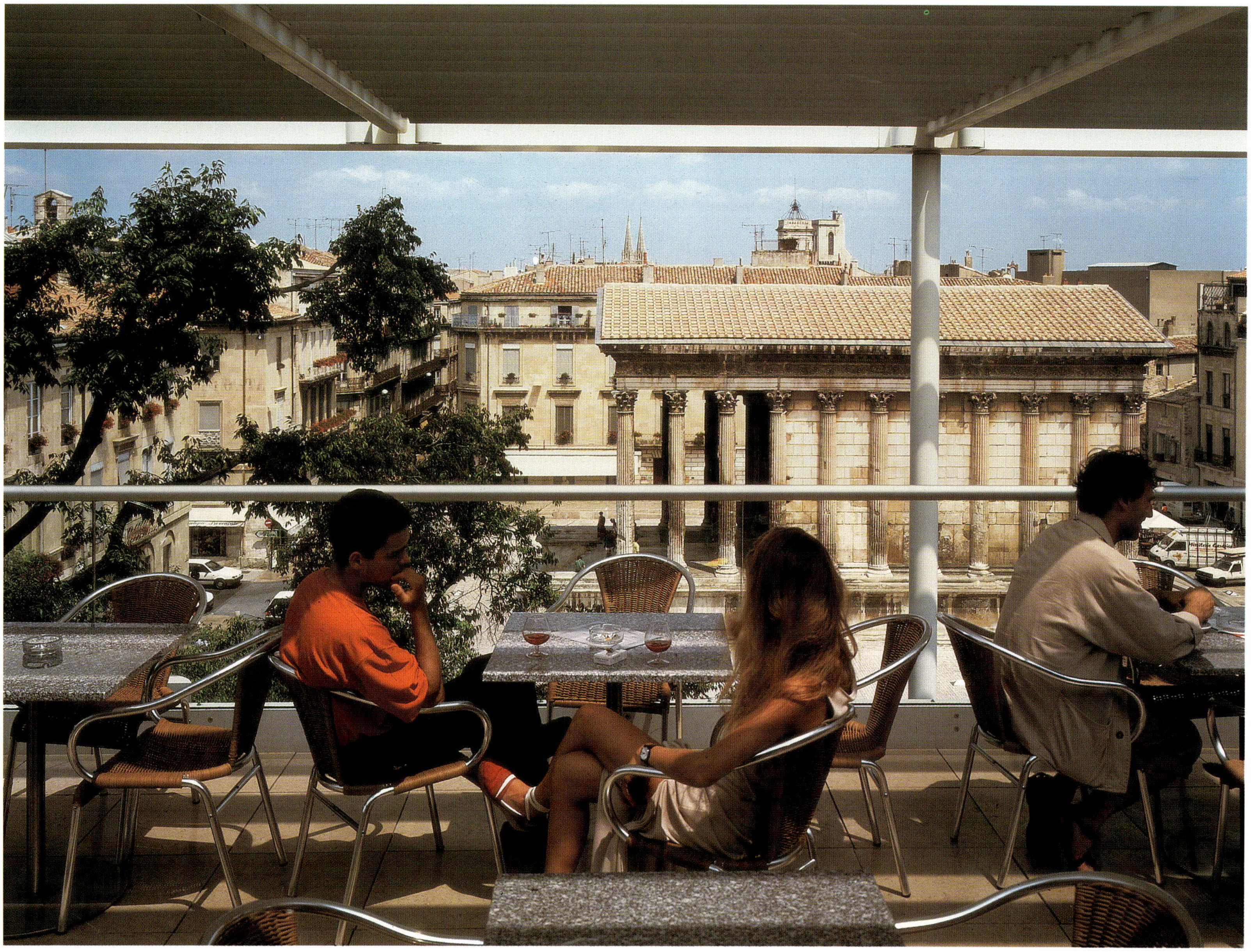

In the central atrium, the immense glass stepped stairway leads up to a terrace and the museum cafeteria. An occasion to discover the Maison carrée from this unusual angle, until now reserved for those few lucky Nîmes residents living on the uppermost floors of the surrounding buildings.

Opposite page

Detail of the library, where light from the atrium penetrates through to the lower spaces. More than three hundred sixty thousand volumes are gathered here, of which many are incunabula. Most of them come from the Séguier library collections, whose modernization and transfer were determining factors in the idea of the Carré d'art project.

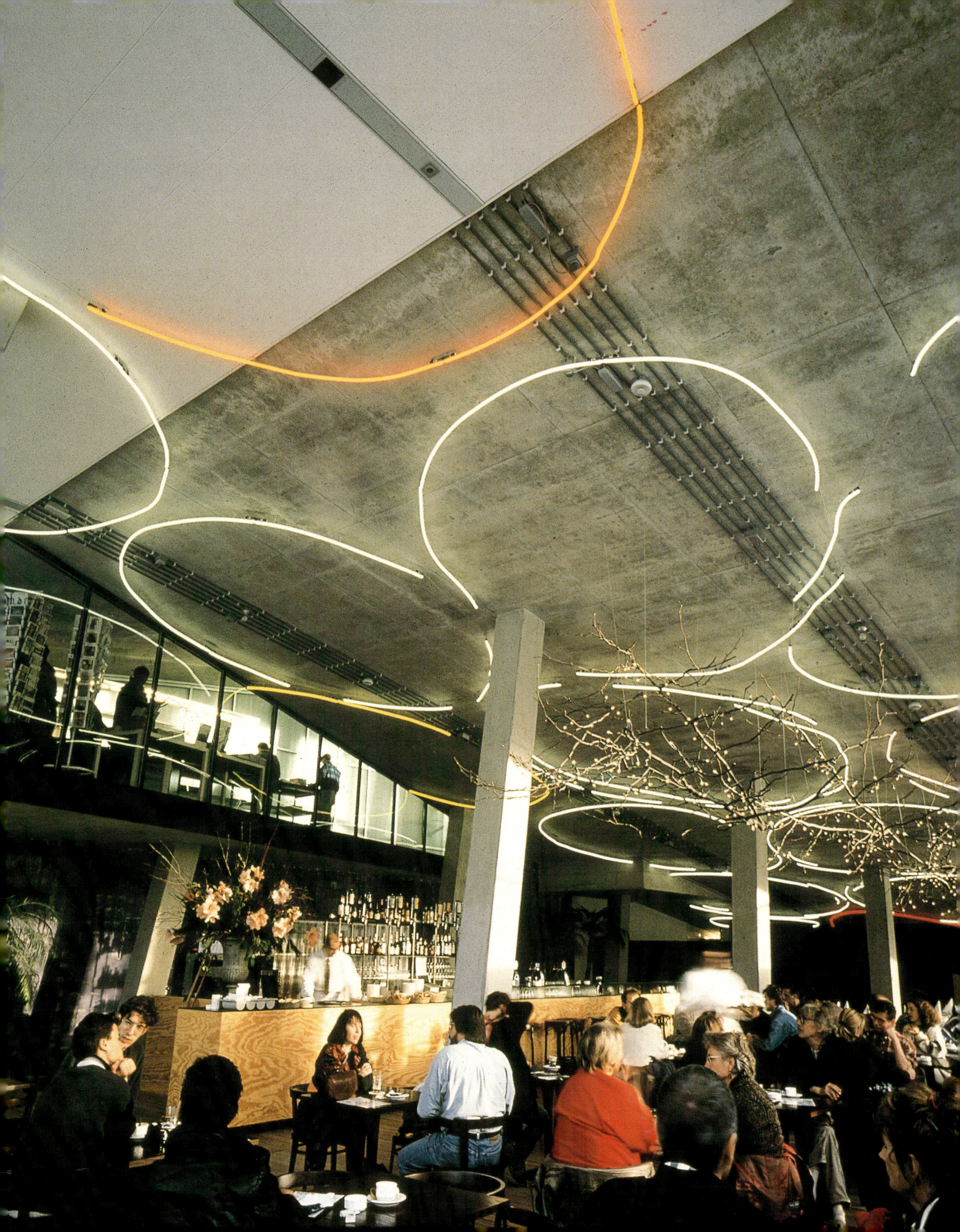

OMA - Rem Koolhaas

Kunsthal

Rotterdam, Holland

The edifice of the Kunsthal appears as a sort of synthesis of urban living and landscapes, adapting itself and playing upon this variety to bring together under one roof an array of complimentary experiences. The south facade, built along Maas straat, is directly confronted with the city and street traffic, whereas the pedestrian ramp which crisscrosses the building leads out, on the north side, to the peaceful space of a park.

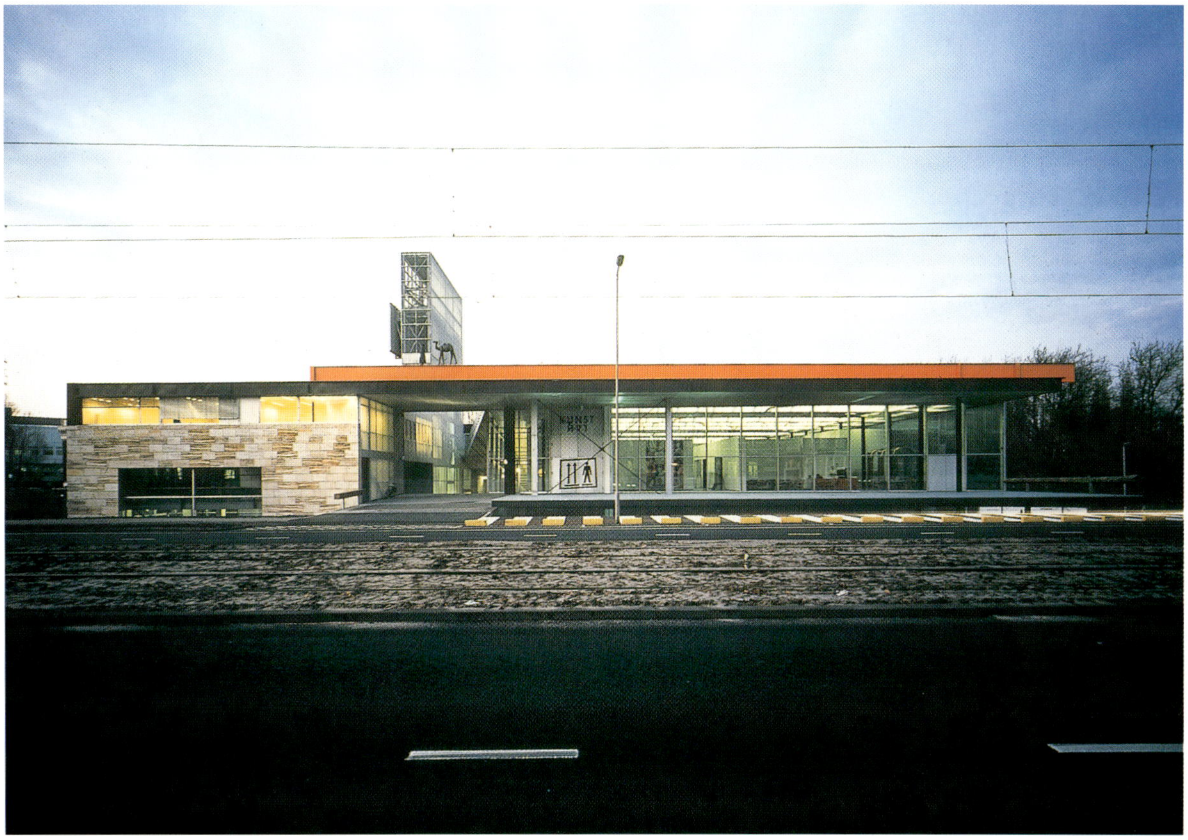

Opposite page
Detail of the interior design of the restaurant and its ceiling donned with circular neon lights. This convivial space opens out onto the park.

Having moved beyond the idea of a museum as a space for conservation and specialization, solutions for a new museum concept have converged to create urban buildings with multiple and varied cultural uses. The Kunsthal in Rotterdam illustrates this new wide-reaching vocation. There is nothing of the traditional museum here: the Kunsthal has no permanent collection and it hosts myriad exhibitions, often with no preconceived thematic or chronological design. In other words, it is an event space that puts emphasis on art exhibitions.

Koolhaas has formulated this arena of flexibility and cultural tolerance as an open circuit connected directly to the city, complete with its urban contrasts and contradictions. The site itself juxtaposes diverse elements with, to the north, a peaceful border of park and, to the south, a raised embankment road with heavy non-stop traffic. Free of any artifice, in the shape of a simple box, the Kunsthal stands between these two extremes like a door between city and nature. Crossing over the edifice, a pedestrian ramp stretches from one end to the other, connecting the road to the park. This public passage, separated from the indoor

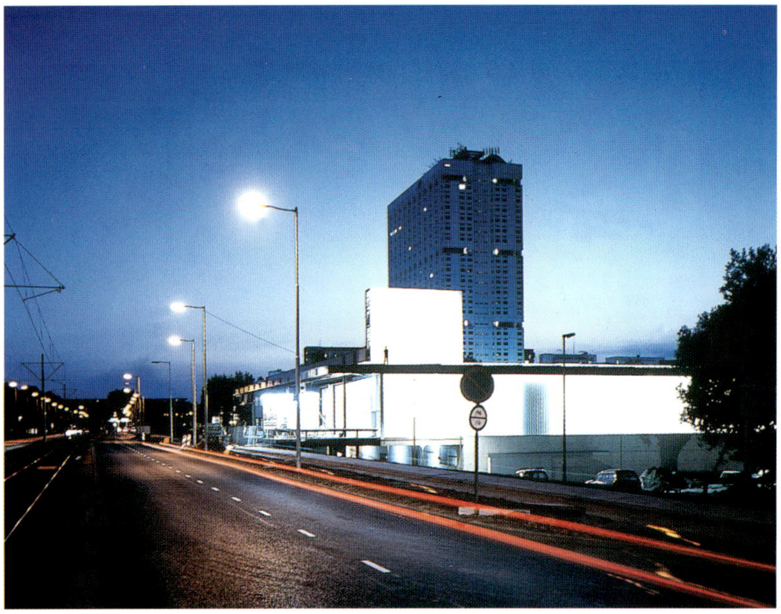

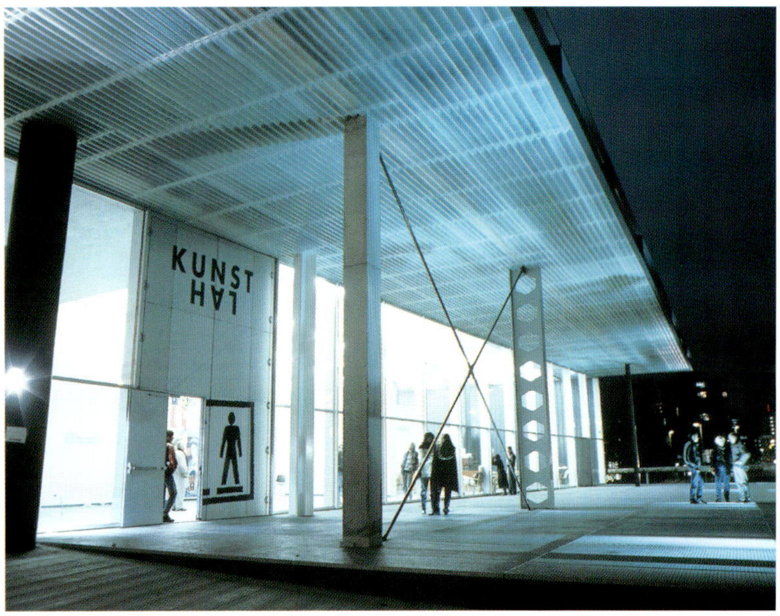

Side views of the south facade.

area by a glass partition, is in fact an integral part of the Kunsthal's circuit. Through the passageway's glass panels, it offers a view of the parallel itinerary of the gallery; and by what appears to be a mirror crossing, it leads directly to the exhibition halls. On the western portion of the building, this ramp meets up with a second one going in the other direction. This meeting point is also what forms the main entrance.

From here begin the passages to the main exhibition areas, which follow one another in sequence. Going down the ramp, one reaches Hall I on the park level, while going up and crossing the central ramp one reaches Hall II on the street level. A third ramp crosses over the first ramp at an angle, leading to Hall II and rising all the way up to the roof. Here a terrace with a garden of fruit trees, like a suspended orchard, overlooks the road and its trucks – another of these well thought-out and enjoyable contrasts that are emphasized wherever possible. Another interplay of opposites, this time in the structure of each hall, sets up a binary relationship between opacity and transparency. In Hall II, for instance, only the street side is transparent, while all the other blind walls, under their glass ceiling, are white. Conversely, in Hall I the nature side takes precedence and transparency favors the park, its plants extending all the way indoors, echoed by the tree trunk pillars supporting the black ceiling.

Clearly, there is an attempt here to multiply the visitor's experience by juxtaposition, but one in which free association comes into play. After all, the Kunsthal has the sole vocation of being an instrument of freedom. Astride between city and garden, calm and noise, indoors and outdoors, it avoids being pinned down by any one system. □

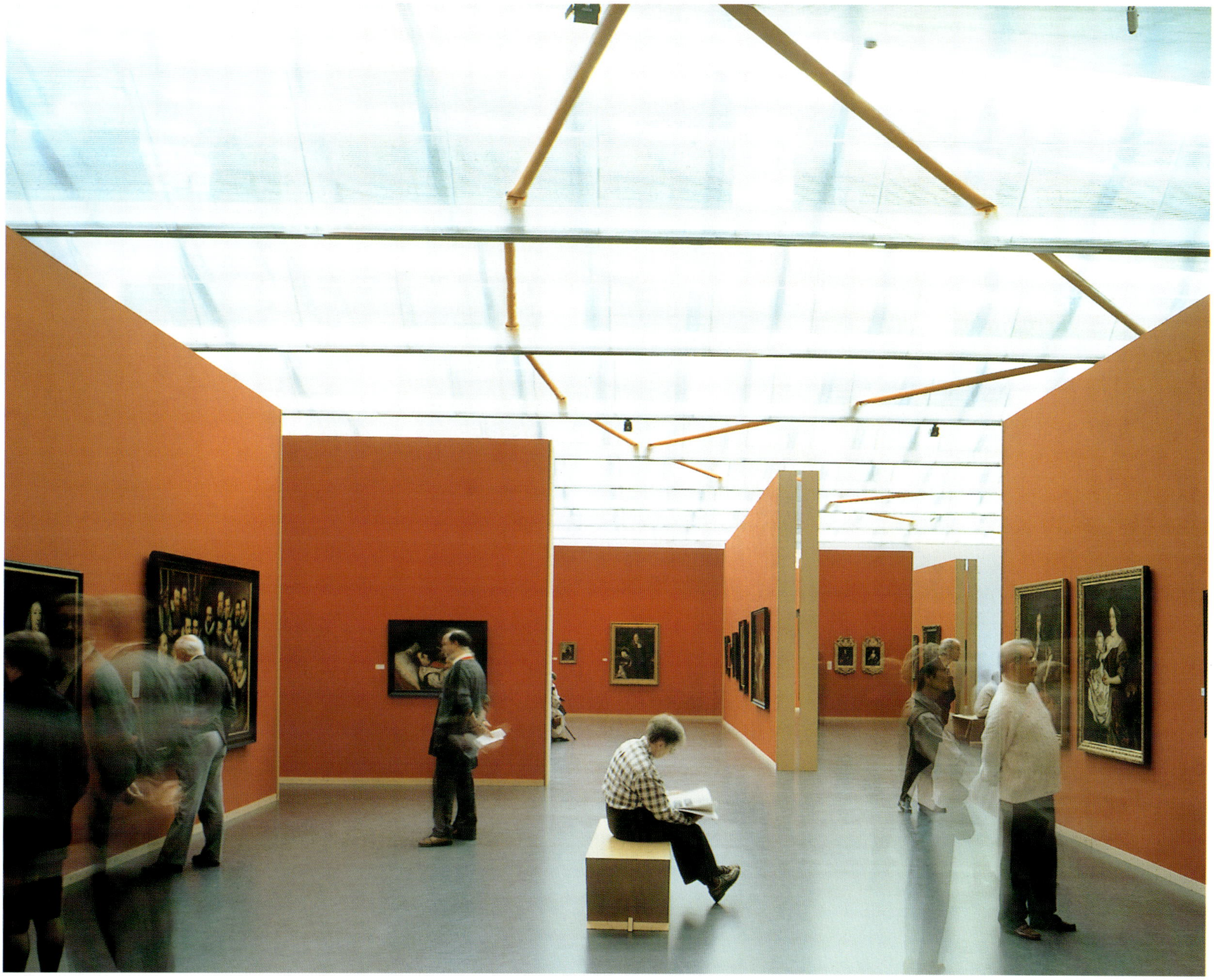

Hall II exhibition space: the luminescent ceiling suggests, in transparency, the technology involved in the structures of the decor, rhythmically repeating the red ocher of the walls.

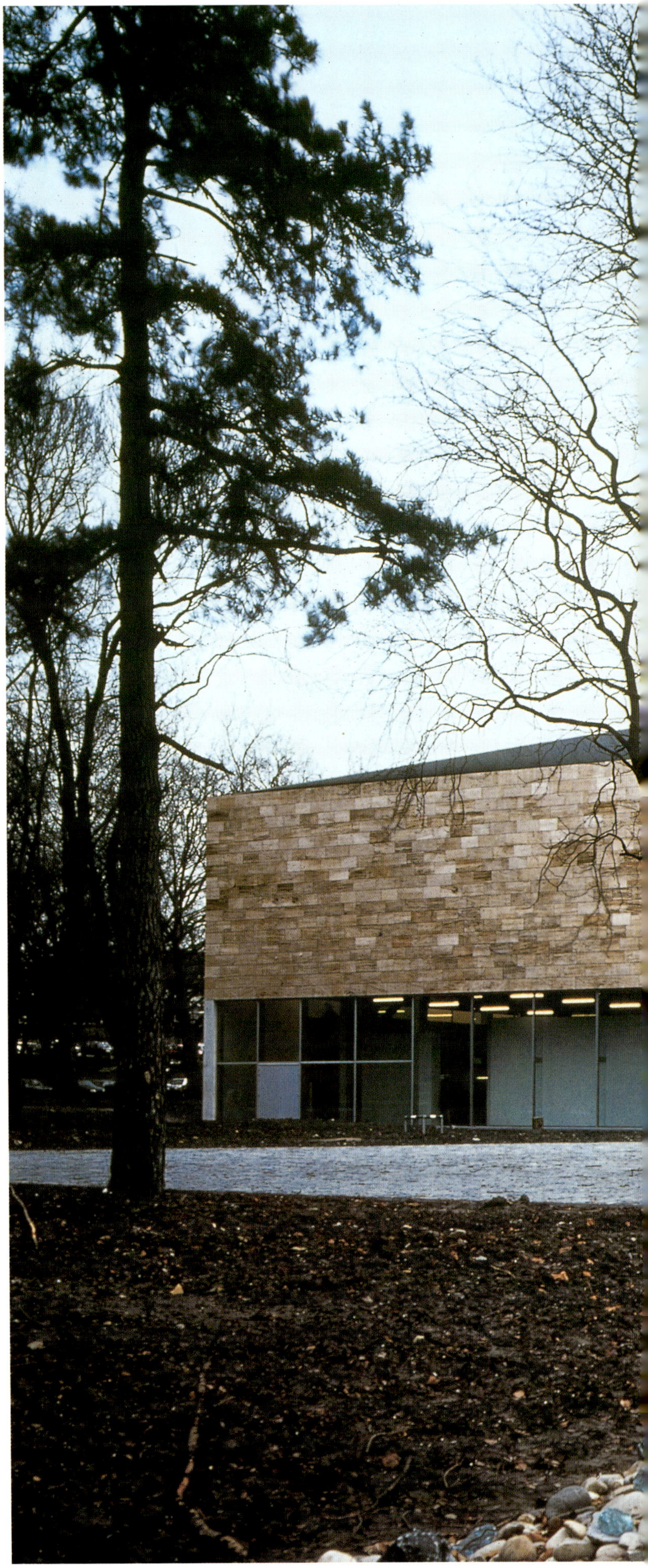

From the park, the silhouette of the trees is superimposed upon the facade whose glass walls reveal, from certain points on the access ramp, the horizontal rows of neon lights in Hall I and the swirling fluorescences of the adjacent café.

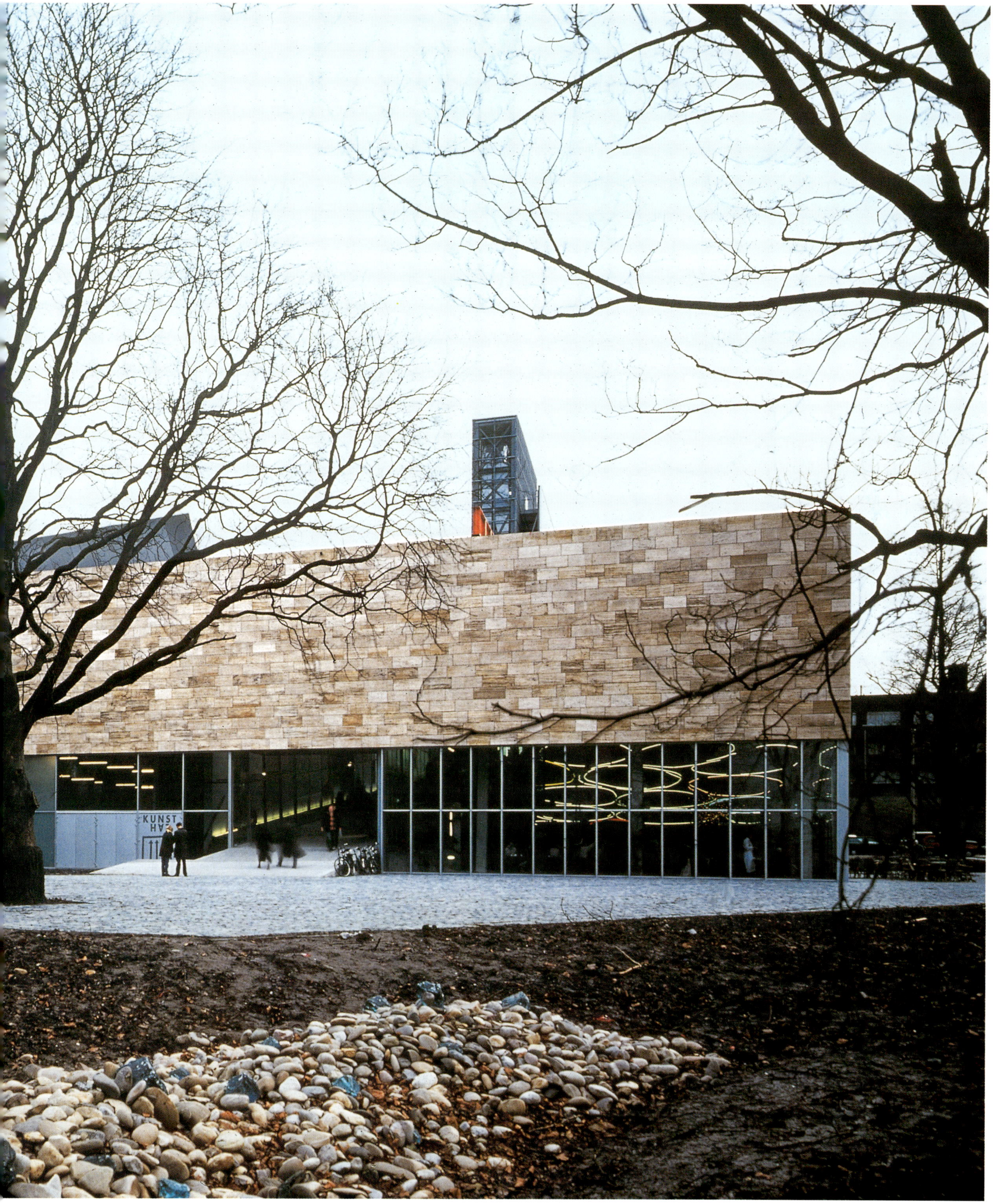
KUNST

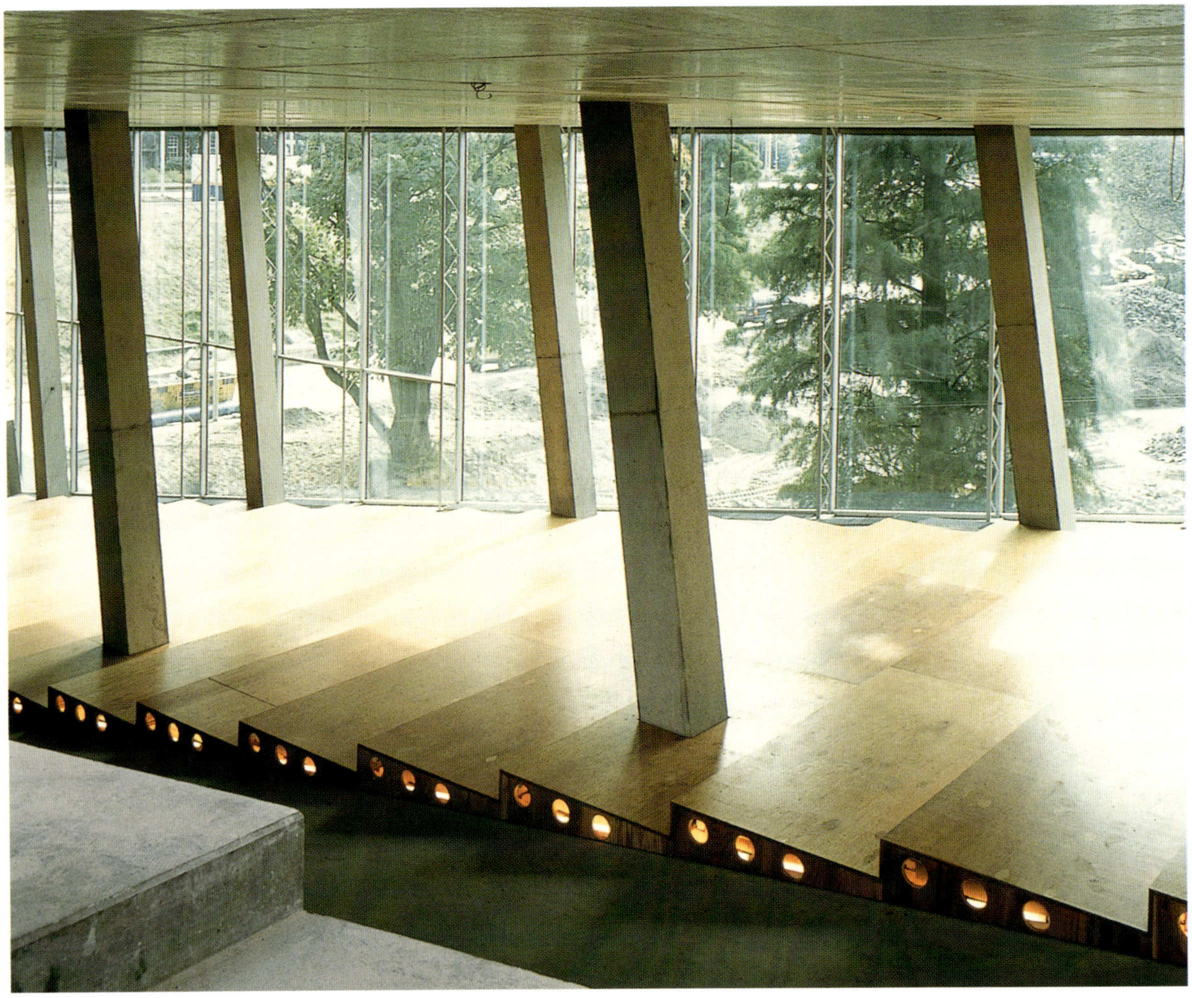

View of the auditorium whose floor and tilted pillars create an ambiguity of potential instability.

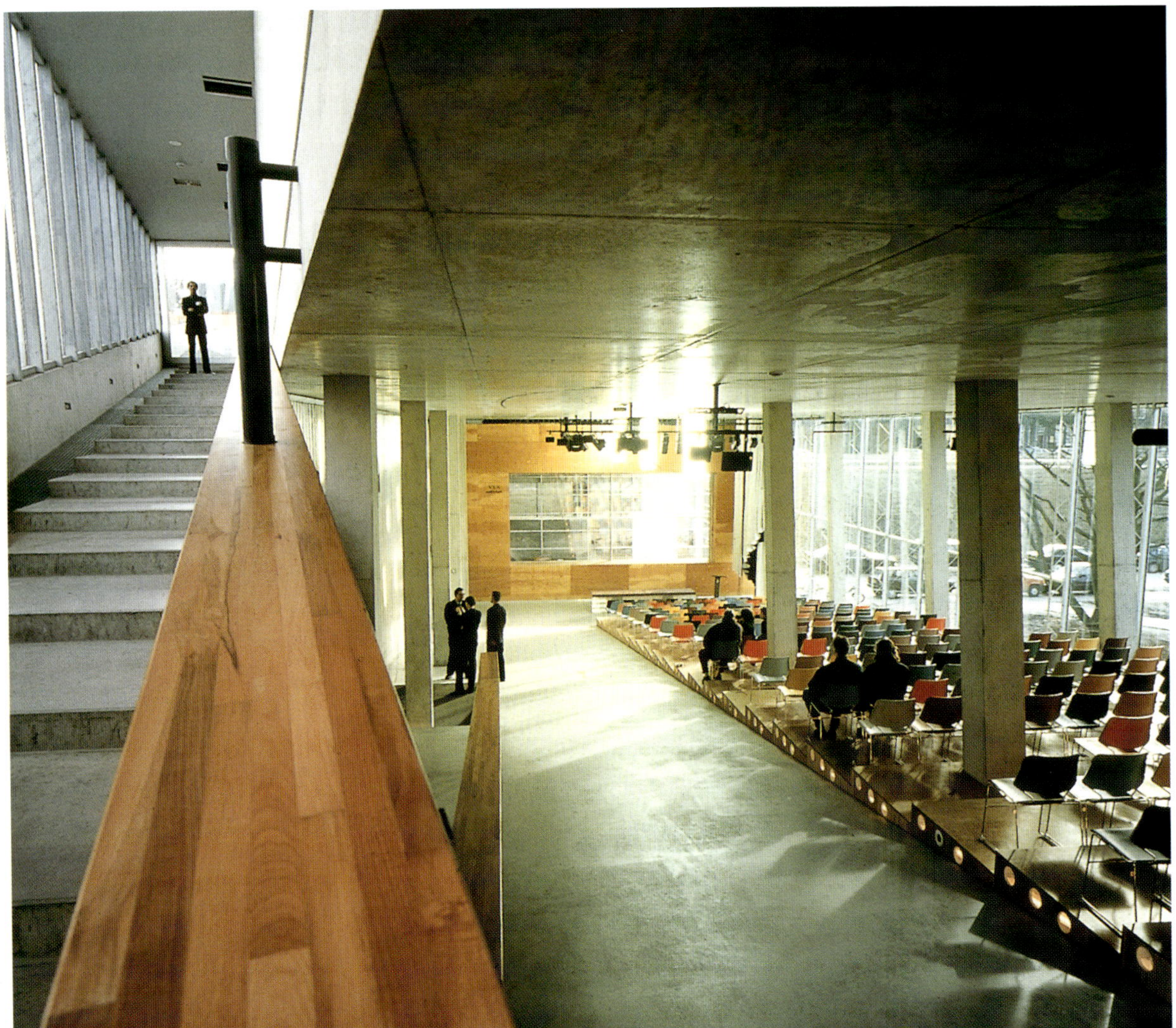

Ramp leading from the auditorium to the exhibition spaces.

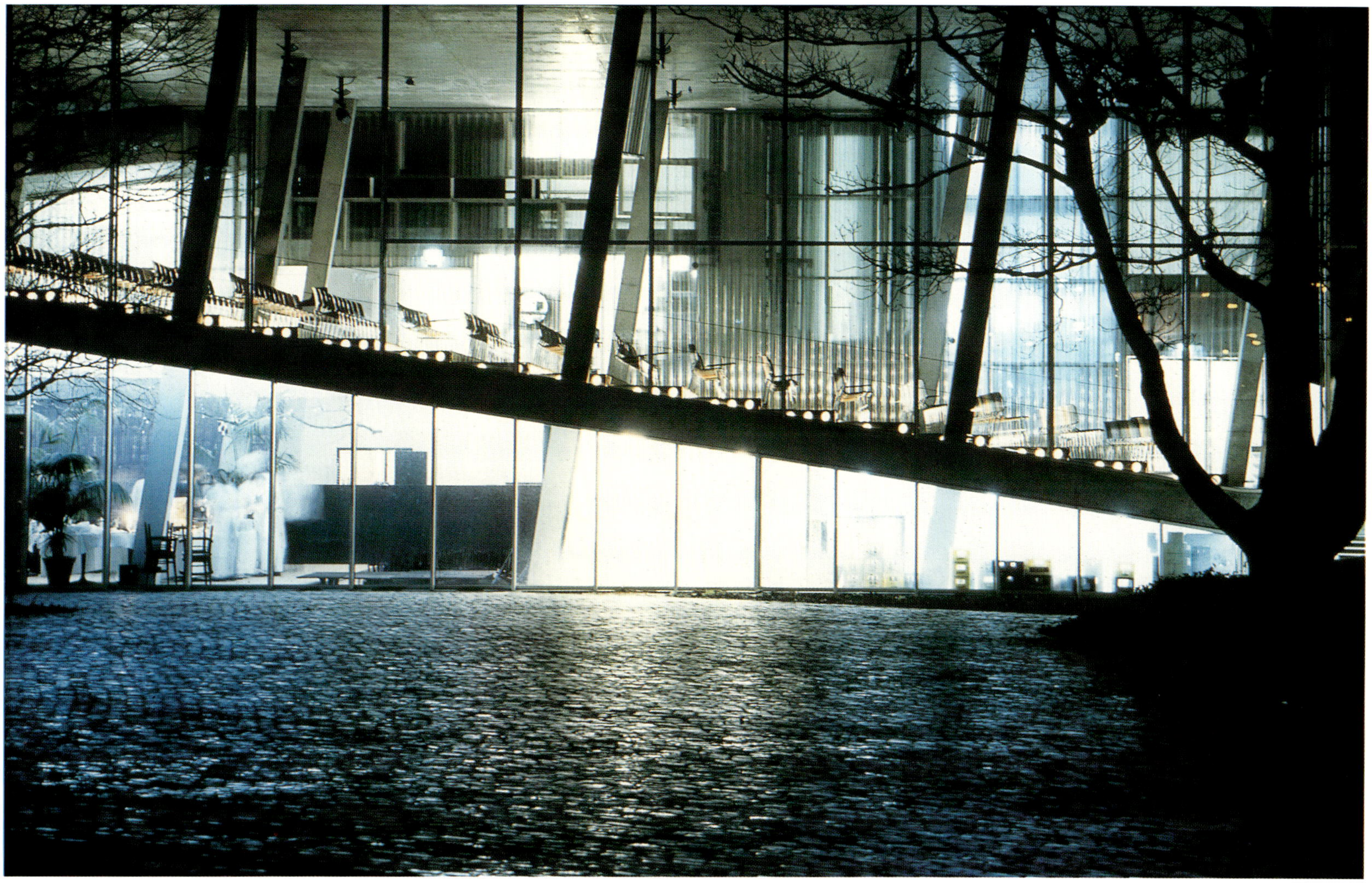

Detail of the west facade
crossed by the oblique
line of the auditorium.

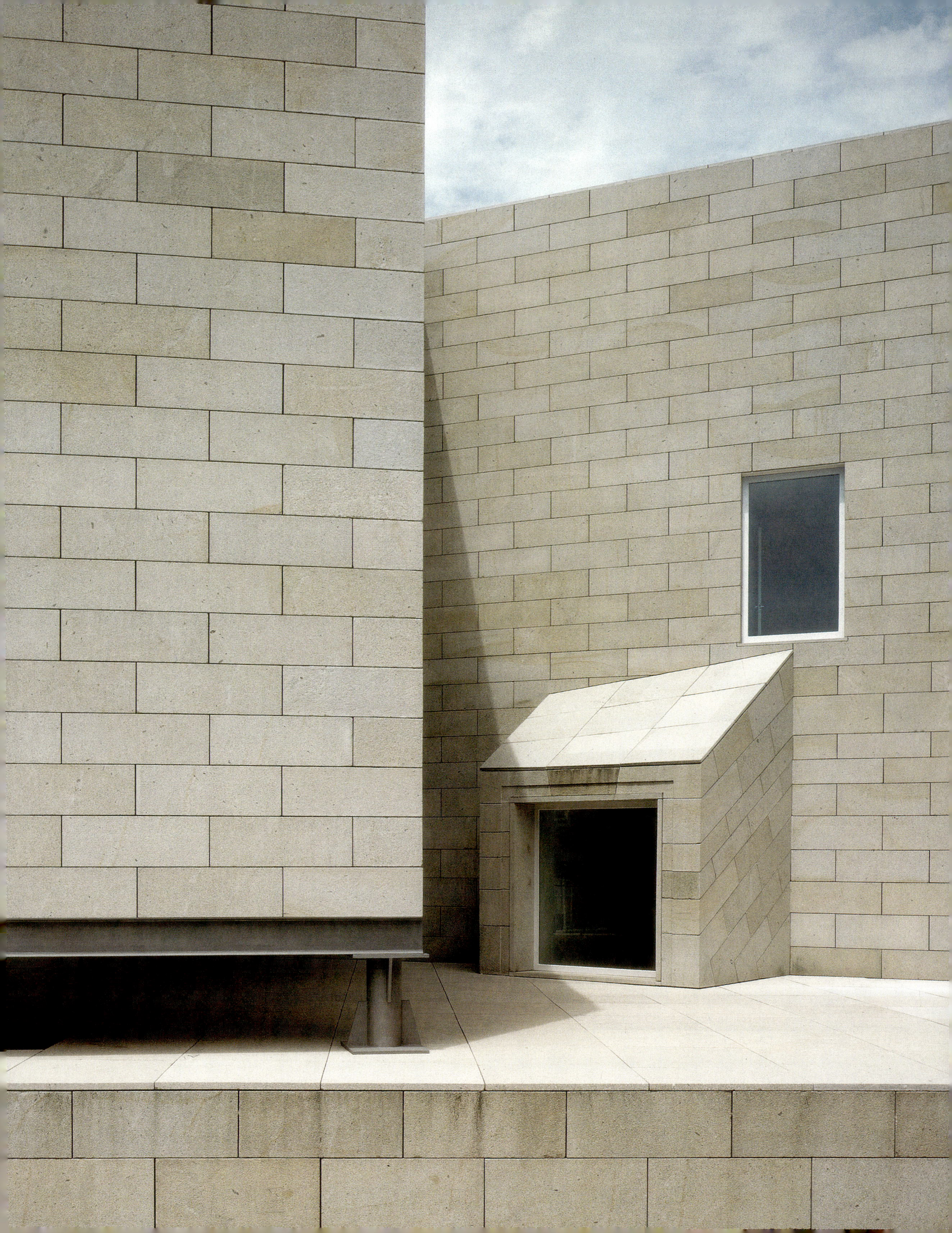

Alvaro Siza Vieira

Centro gallego de arte contemporáneo

Santiago de Compostella, Spain

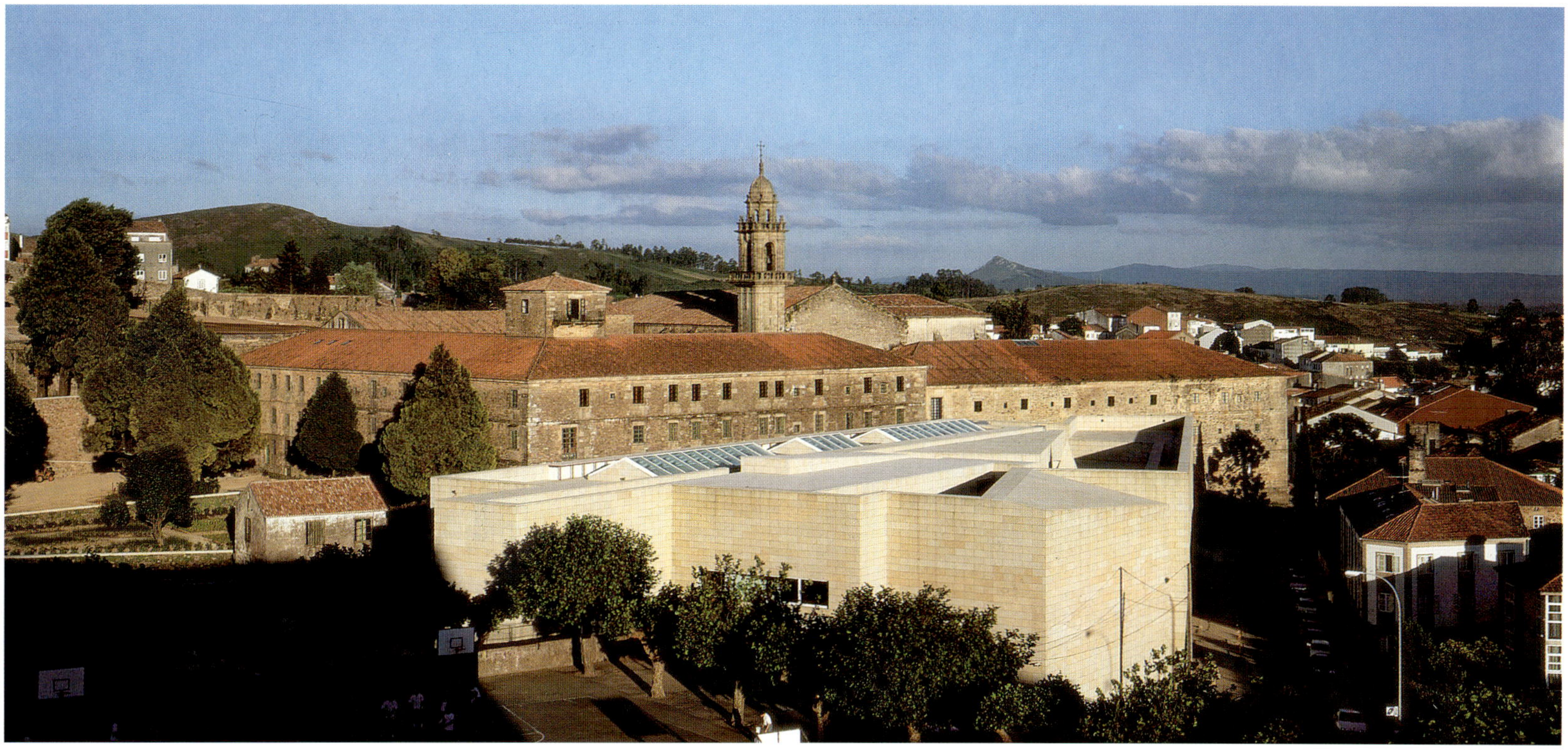

The sombre, compact structure of this granite edifice illustrates the great adaptability of Siza, careful to use only local materials and concerned about capturing and interpreting the spirit of local architecture. Resembling popular Galician housing, the Center of Contemporary Art hides within its stone shell and sets its grey mass against the ardors of the climate.

Located in the historic centre of Santiago de Compostella and sharing a site with the Santo Domingo de Bonaval convent, the construction project of the Galician Center of Contemporary Art had more than its share of difficulties: it involved juxtaposing a modern museum and an old convent on a site with an irregular and disjointed topography.

The project was thus as much one of urban renewal as architectural. Considering the likelihood of there being varied and unexpected developments, Alvaro Siza seemed well-suited to the task. His career began in the effervescence of the Carnation Revolution in Portugal. Accustomed to working as a team, Siza and one of his collaborators set themselves up directly on the site in order to tackle the problems as they arose. This hands-on approach was also in perfect keeping with Siza's methodology and abided by his rigorous economic principles: "Attention to quality, the need to optimize cost and limit delays demand an active involvement in the actual construction of the project."

This approach resulted in what appears to be a compact edifice comprised of two volumes, one parallel to the street, the other parallel to the facade of the convent. The configuration of these two geometric shapes forms a triangular atrium taking up the full height of the building.

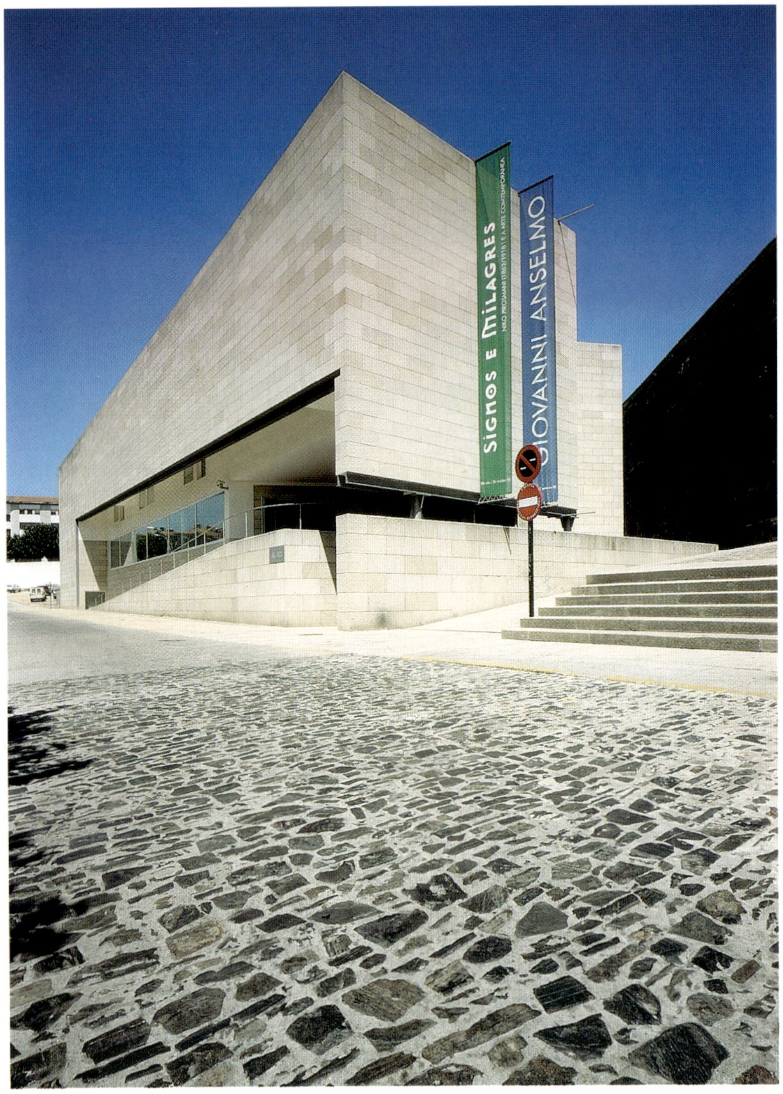

Here, a large reception hall articulates the circulation to and from the exhibition halls. As for the difficult topography of the site, Siza managed to turn it to his advantage. He created a zig-zag tour whereby a network of ramps and staircases leading to the galleries offers the visitor varied perspectives and overviews of the exhibits, a tour that culminates in a roof terrace overlooking the convent and the city below.

This fluidity of movement is coupled with the use of relatively rare building materials such as the dense gray granite slabs on the outside. The architect's choice of granite, however, demonstrates his good old common sense as it is the most commonly used and least expensive stone in the region. A similar practical consideration underlies his choice of white marble, also a local material, which he has generously used to line the atrium. Other materials include the stucco on the ceilings and partition walls and the light-colored oak floors in the exhibition halls. Floating in a diaphanous whiteness, these materials have been treated and combined to create illusions of transparency; Siza's true tour de force, after all, is his talent as an illusionist. A visual interplay of light and shadow, the sculpting of perspectives and outlining of volumes create an overall sense of weightlessness.

The natural brightness afforded by the openings in the atrium and the skylights of the upper galleries is controlled and softened by large hanging screens and compensated, where needed, by indirect lighting, the whole captured in the dark skeleton of the granite facades. □

Openings in the building cut the block of the facade like loopholes.

Opposite page
The Center of Contemporary Art surrounded by the redefined esplanades and terraces.

The roof terrace of the building overlooking the city and the Santo Domingo de Bonaval convent.

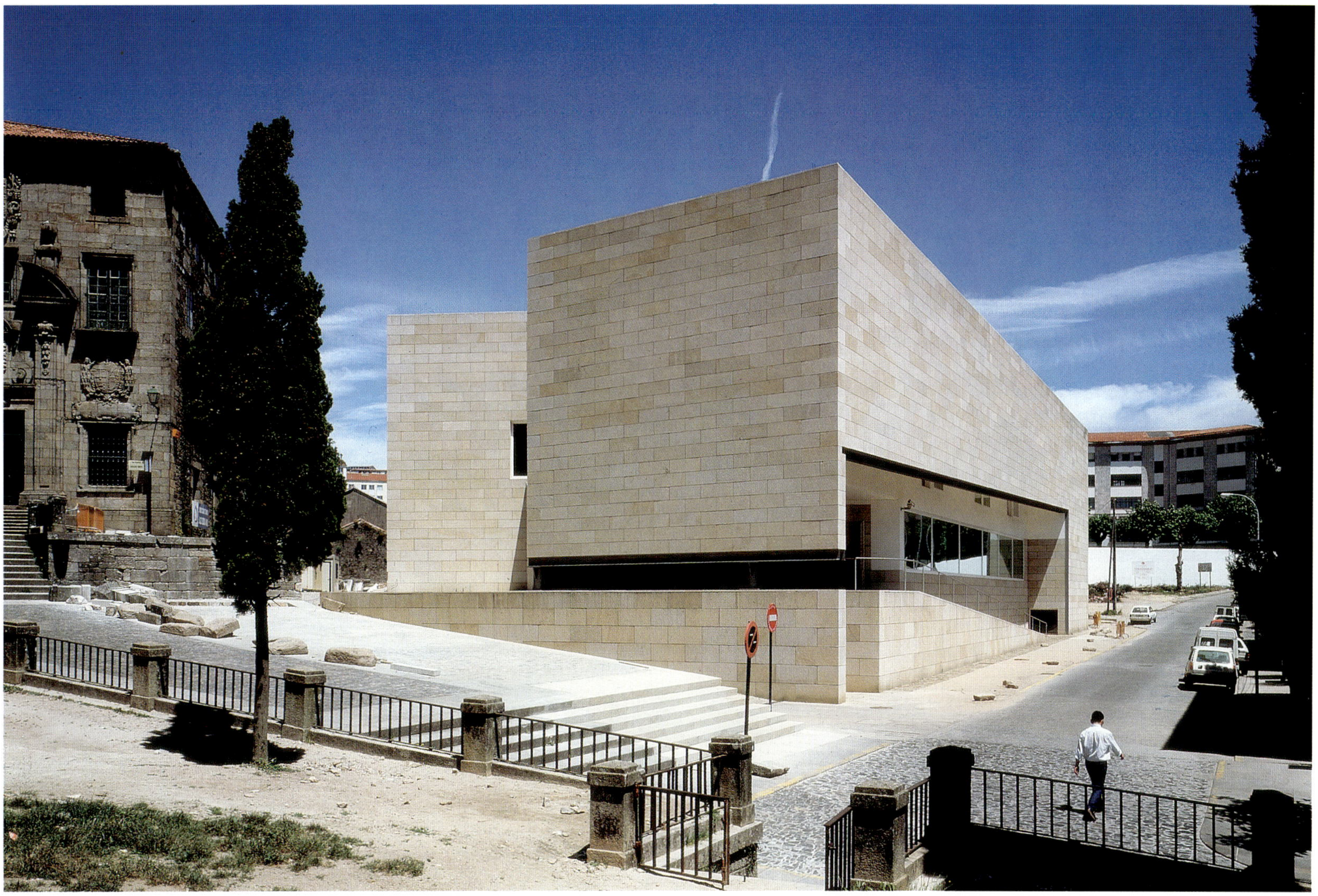

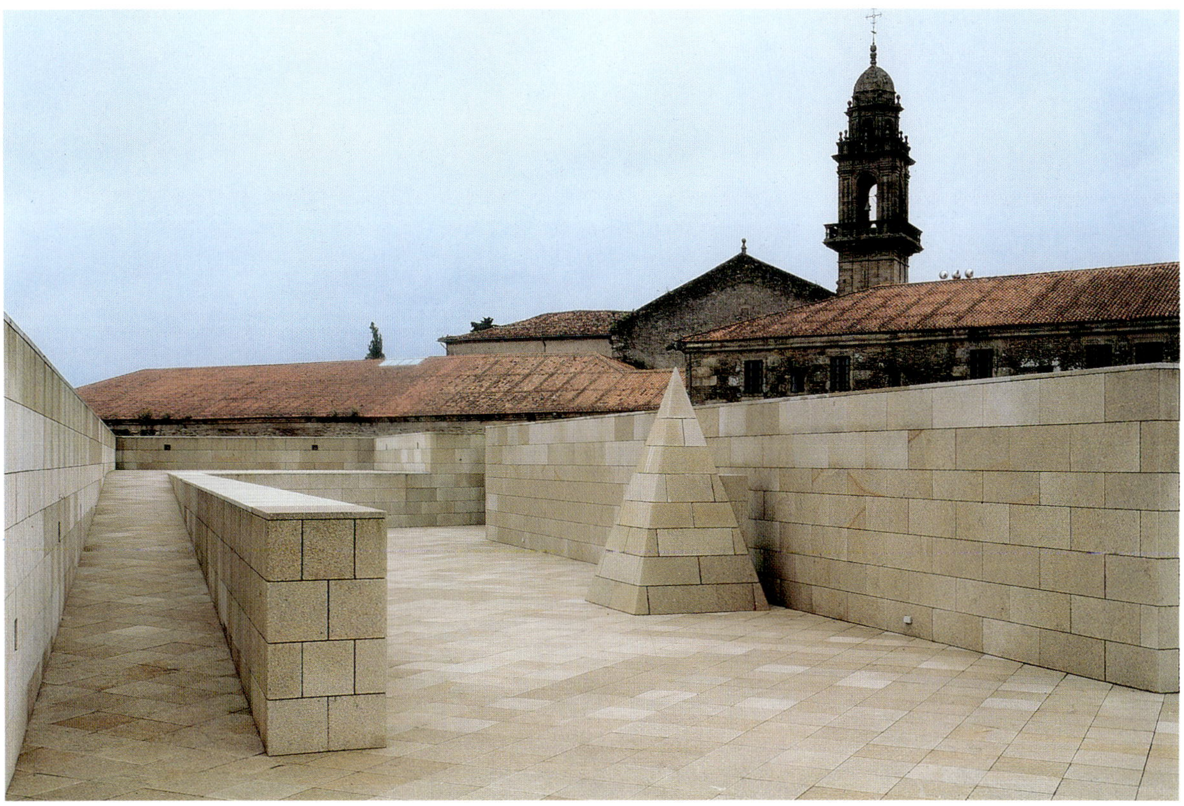

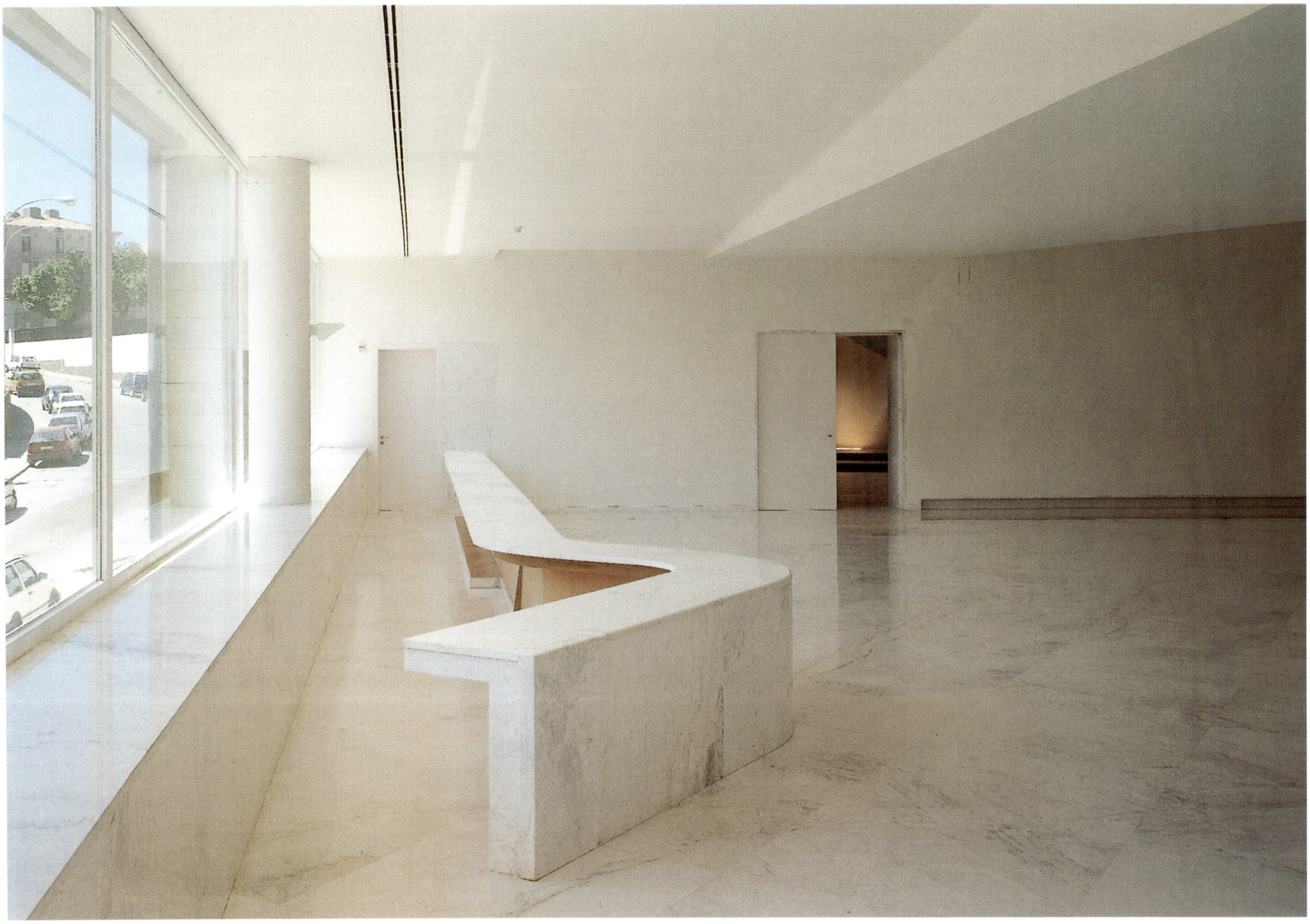

Details of a ground floor room: in contrast to the sombre grey of the facades, the interior spaces capture the light, greatly enhanced by the diaphanous white of the walls and the marble.

Opposite page
Neither anecdotal allusion nor superfluous decor: it is the superb and surprising play of light and perspective which dramatizes the ensemble.

Following pages
Views of the conference room on the ground floor.

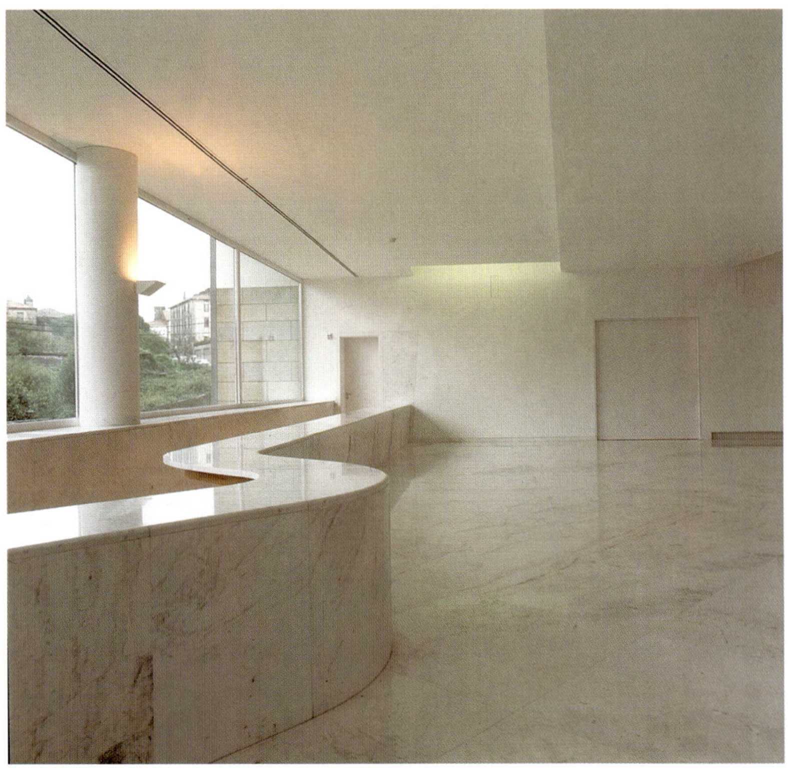

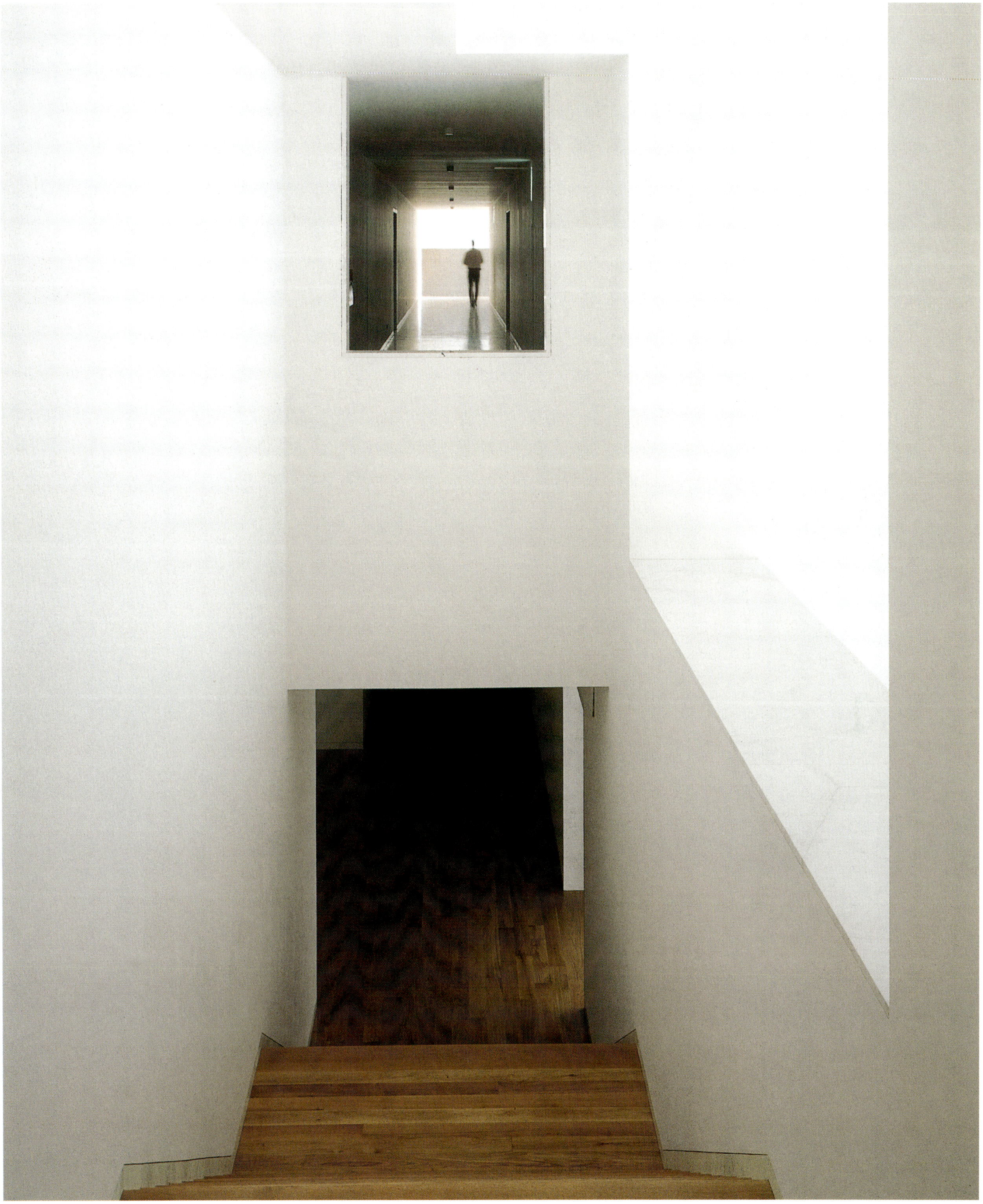

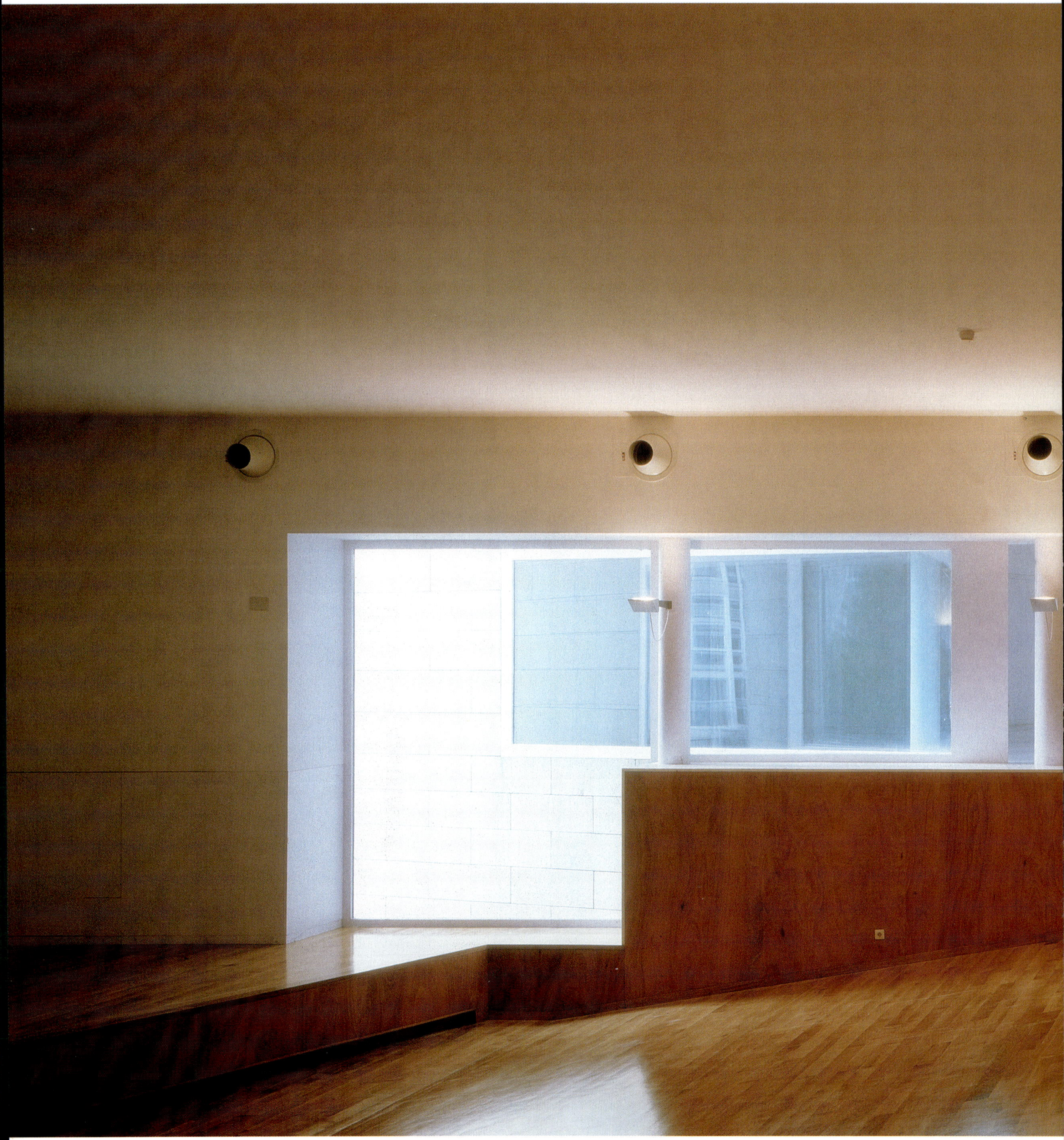

72 Centro gallego de arte contemporáneo, Santiago de Compostella, Spain

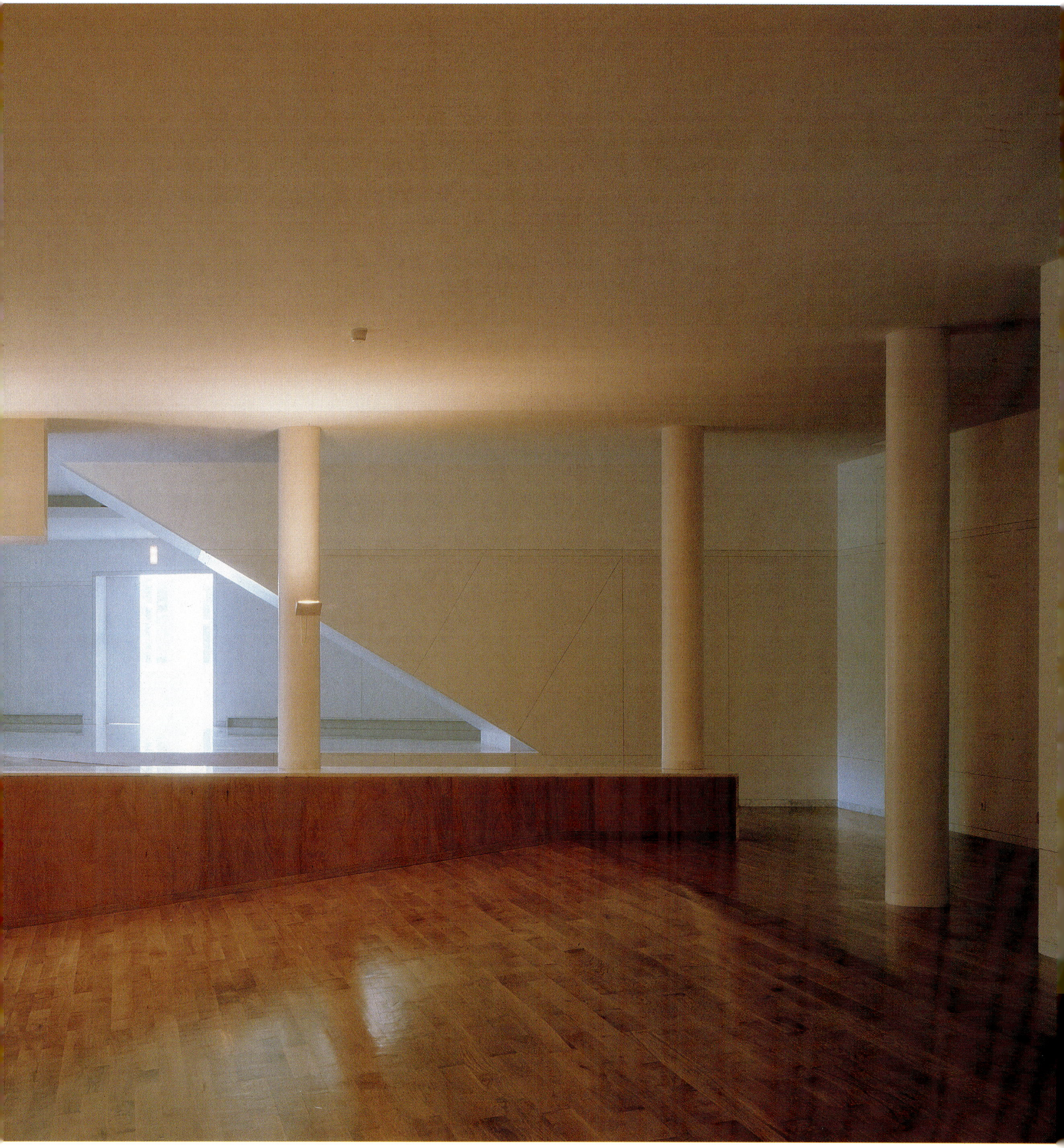

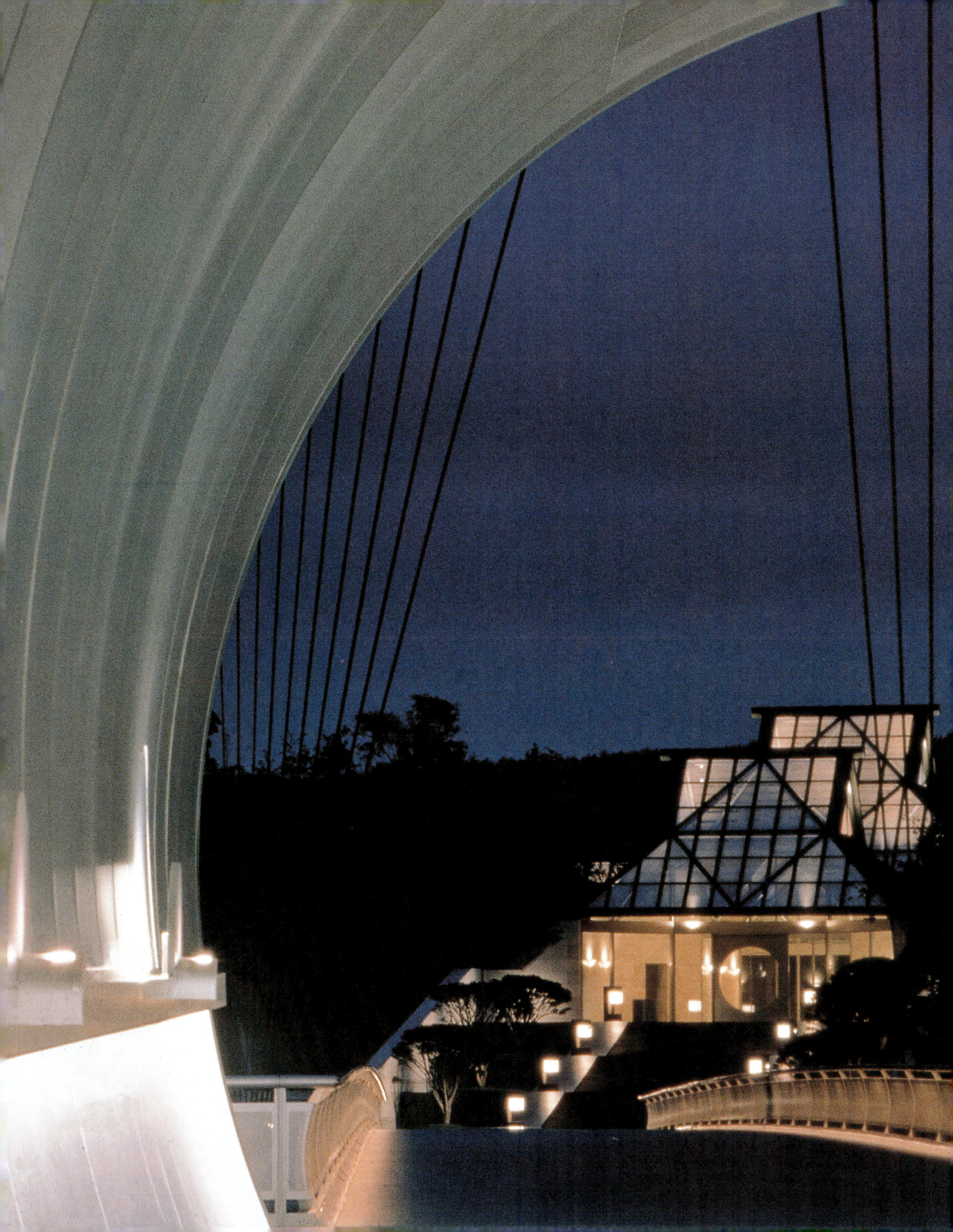

I. M. Pei

Miho Museum

Shiga, Japan

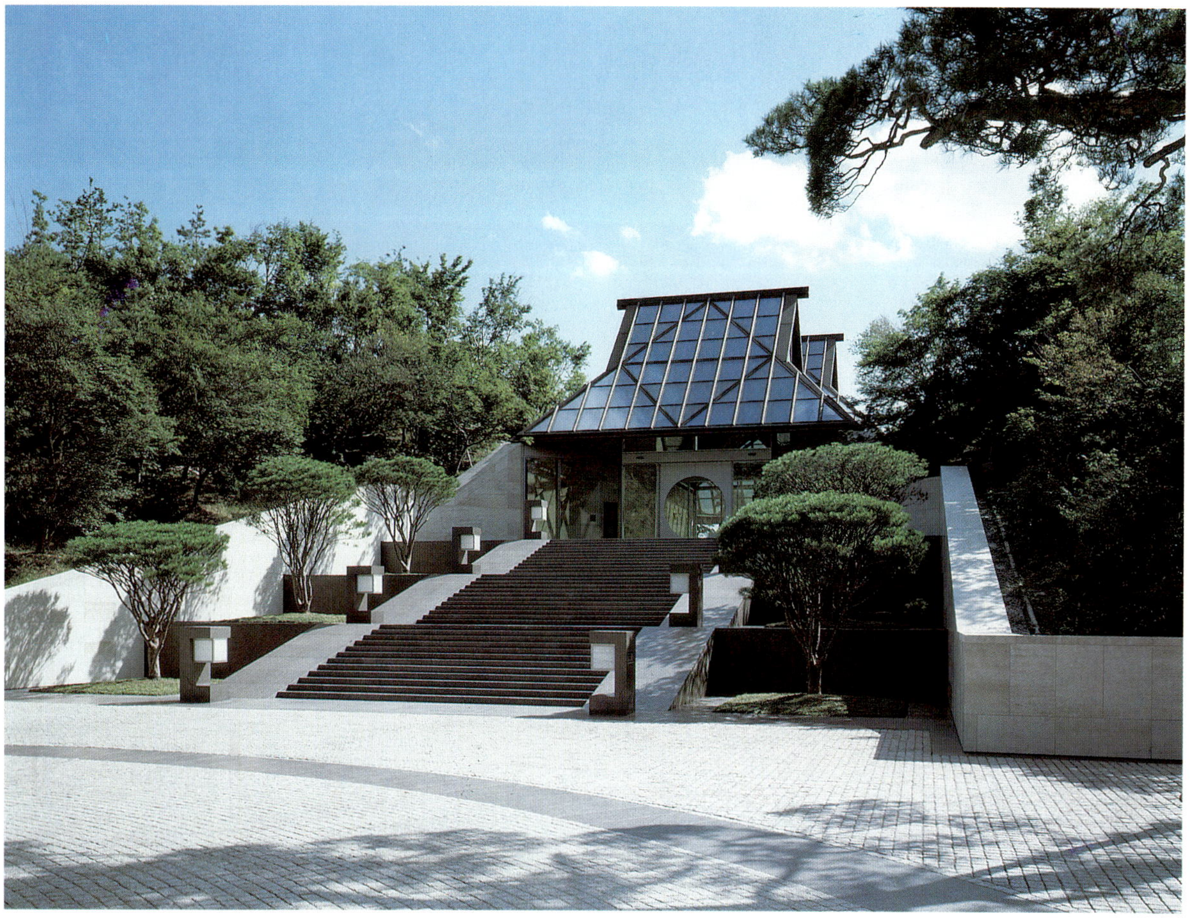

In the fall of 1997 Ieoh Ming Pei reached 80 years, his birthday, coinciding with the opening of his latest and probably most curious creation, the Miho Museum. This surprising project, by definition a public establishment, was built on a remote, almost inaccessible mountain site. Also atypical, the commissioner is none other than a sect advocating the conjunct contemplation of art and nature for the health of humanity. A highly spiritual enterprise but nonetheless well backed by worldly possessions. The Shinji Shumekai sect invested more than 165 million dollars in the creation of this museum intended to house and exhibit the fabulous collection of art objects donated by its founder, Mihoko Koyarna.

Today could very well be the era of museums, just as there was once an era of cathedrals. These new temples devoted to culture take on an almost spiritual quest in bringing about a transition from the profane to the sacred. In the case of the Miho Museum, designed by Pei, Cobb, Freed & Partners, the concept could not be more on the mark. The museum is the synthesis of its commissioner's philosophy, its commissioner being the Shinji Shumeikai sect, a religious community devoted to the ceaseless pursuit of beauty and all forms of expression, whether natural or artistic.

Chosen by the sect's spiritual leader, Kaishusama, the site – superb indeed – takes up a natural reserve of forest between twin ridges, just an hour's drive from Kyoto and a mere half mile from the sect's sacred grounds. Spreading out over 17,400 square meters (186,000 square feet) in this stunning landscape, the museum houses the sect's art collection of ancient Japanese and European relics – one of the finest such collections in the world. A primary concern

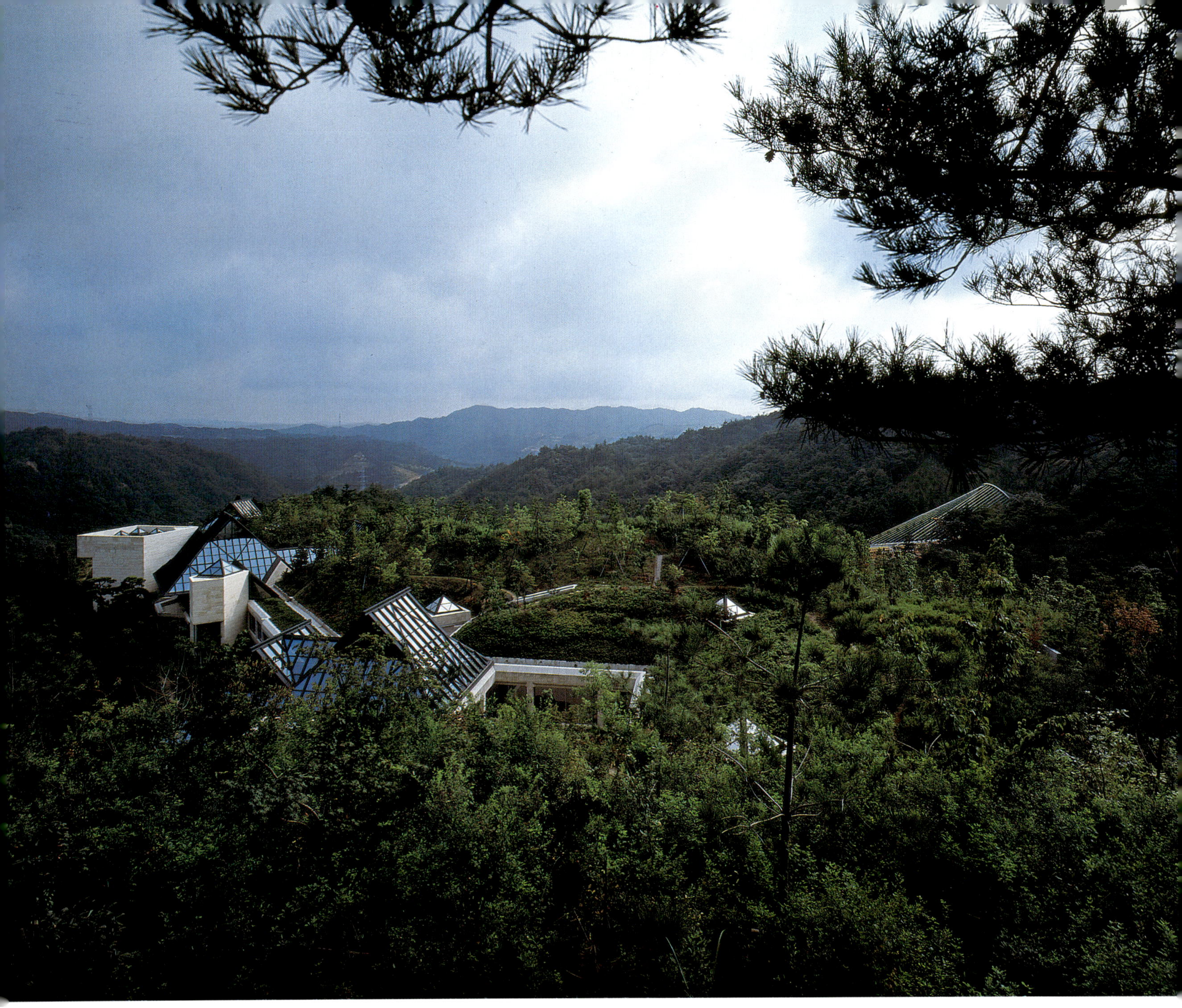

In order to accomplish its work of salvation, the sect acquired a vast terrain located in a forest reserve classified as a protected zone. First, a temple with a 6,000 person capacity was built, designed by Minoru Yamasaki , the architect of the Twin Towers in New York. Added to the temple was a bell tower designed by Pei, who was also chosen to build the museum ensemble a half mile away. Due to pressure from the environmentalist lobby, all the buildings had to be three-quarters underground. Discreetly nestled into the hills, only the immense skylights show through, facing the heavens.

was to fully integrate the museum into the scenery without altering its natural beauty. The bulk of the building was subsequently partially recessed into the ground and all its access routes are underground.

Beyond the project's spiritual concerns are other – this time more prosaic – concerns. Unlike a private sanctuary, the museum is intended as a public foundation with an estimated 70,000 visitors per year, which called for a Japanese-style planning with its particular sense of organization, leaving little room for improvisation... Visitors coming from Kyoto by car or bus assemble in a triangular reception pavilion with a cafeteria and a ticket office. From here they are taken by small electric cars through one of the

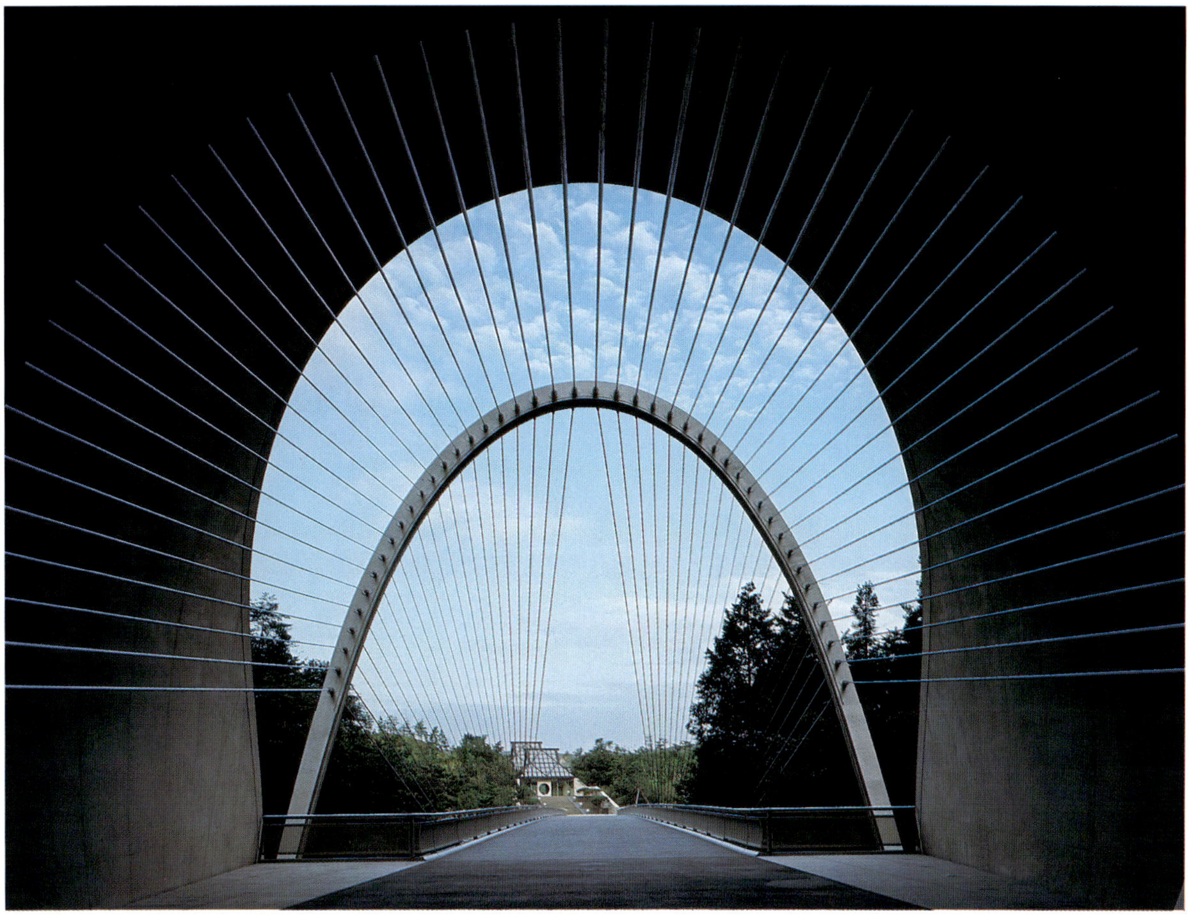

The cathartic itinerary of the tunnel opens onto a bridge suspended over a ravine. Beyond, and turned slightly from this axis to avoid a frontal view, is the museum entrance: reminiscent of a Shinto temple reached by the traditional initiatory climb up of a great stairway.

Museum Directory

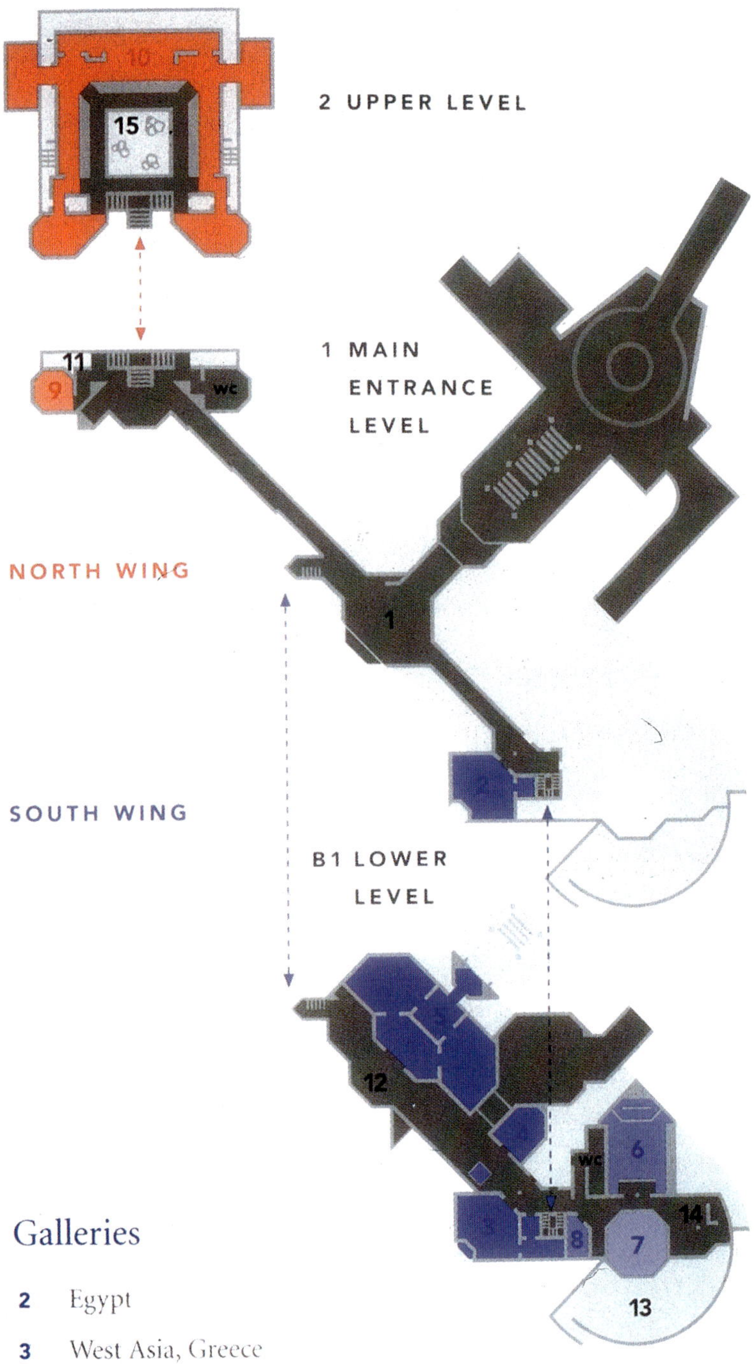

Galleries

2 Egypt

3 West Asia, Greece and Rome

4 South Asia

5 China

10 Japan

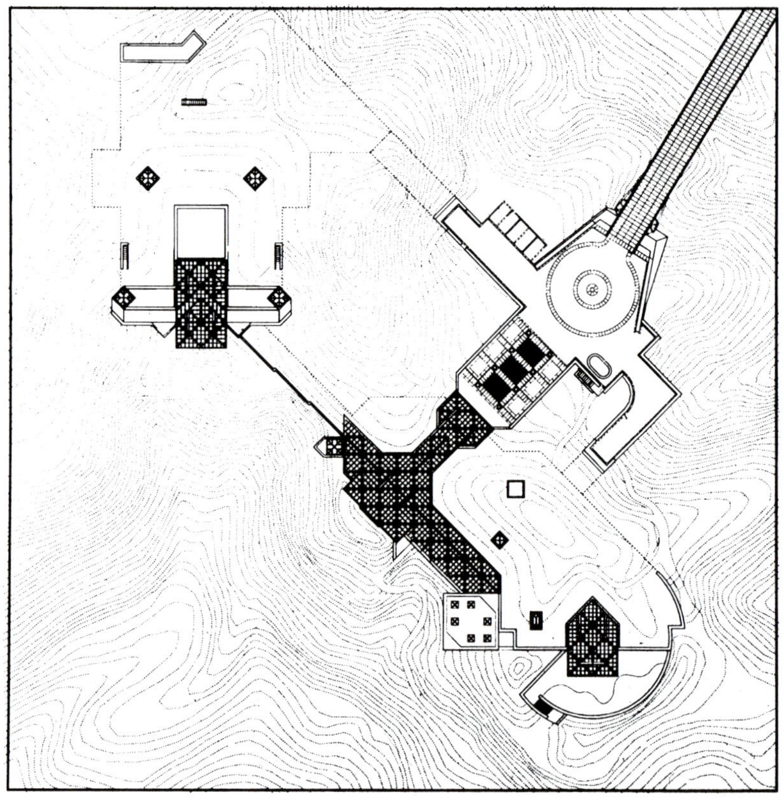

Plans of the edifice: the north wing holds Japanese art galleries and to the south, the Western collections.

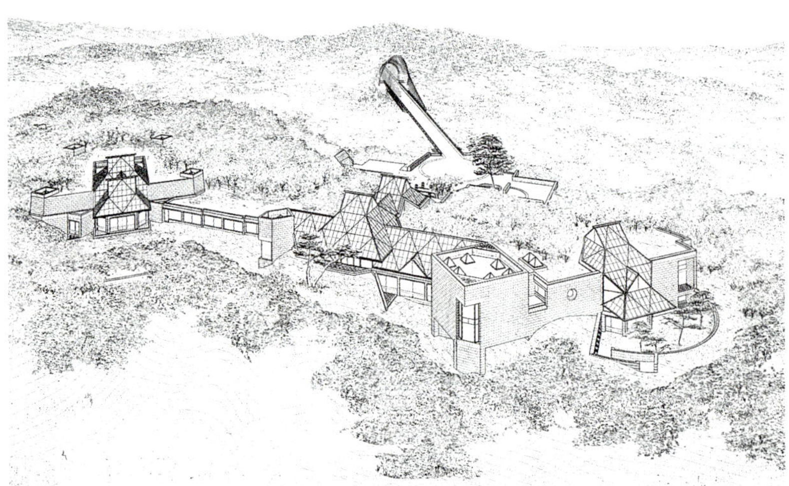

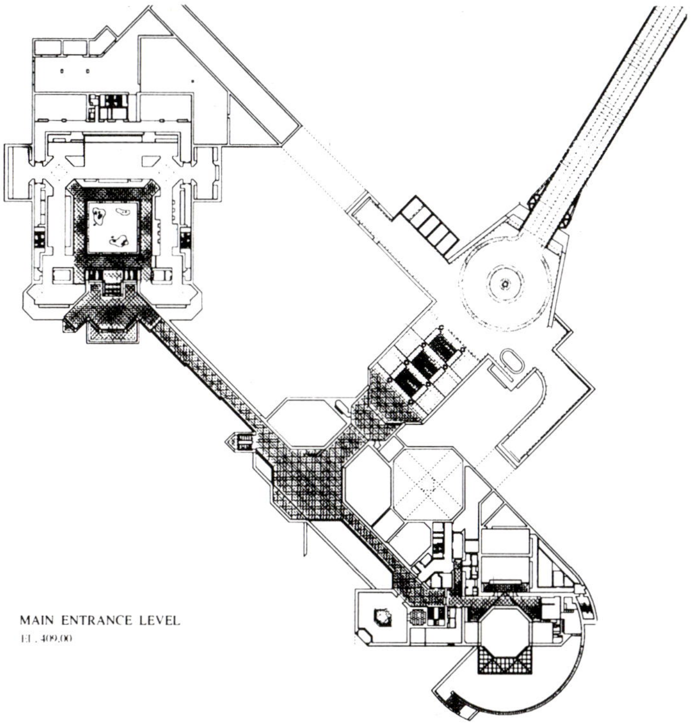

MAIN ENTRANCE LEVEL
EL. 409.00

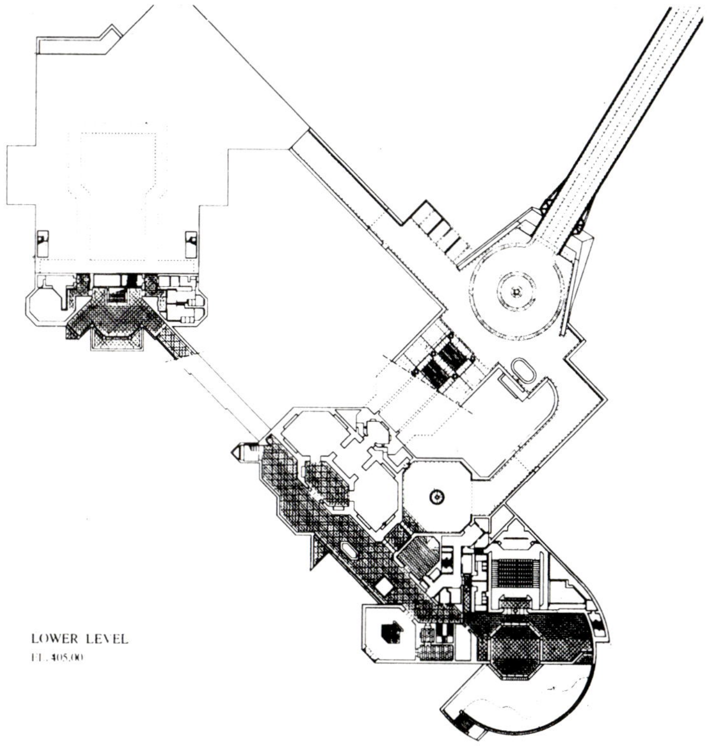

LOWER LEVEL
EL. 405.00

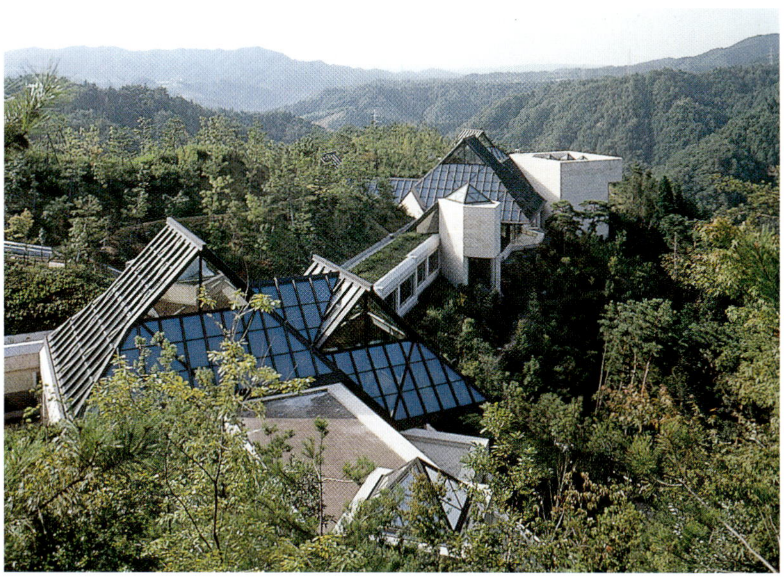

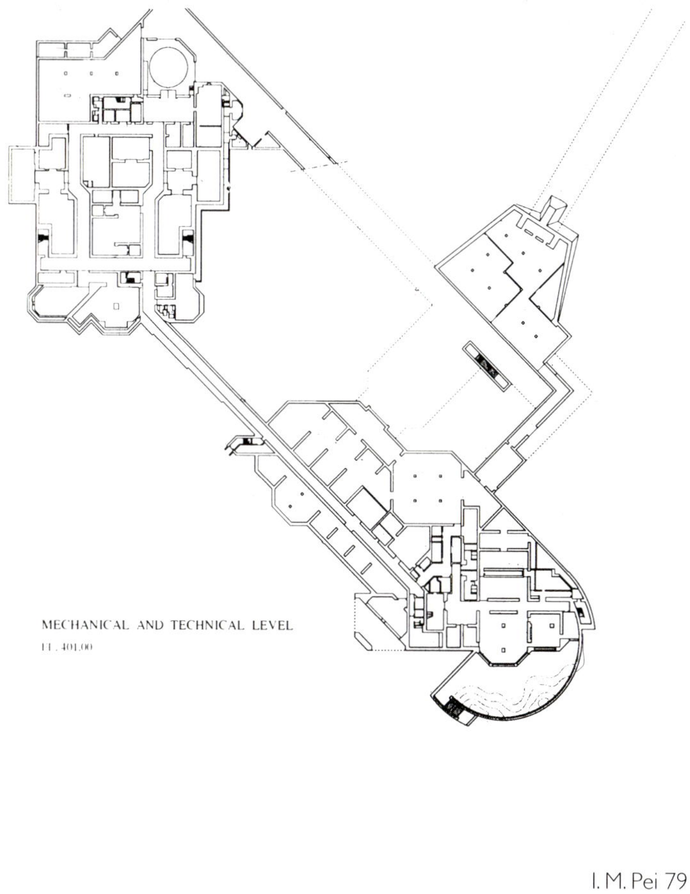

MECHANICAL AND TECHNICAL LEVEL
EL. 401.00

two tunnels leading to the museum – the second tunnel being reserved for transporting artworks and as an emergency exit. This underground journey in the strange brightness of indirect lighting is the first in a series of ritualized and progressive steps to visiting the museum. Beginning at the mouth of the tunnel, a suspension bridge crosses over a ravine to a square leading up to the museum. From here, one has only a partial view of the edifice set against its paradisiacal backdrop of mountains, giving no sense of its actual size. Geometric window panes like giant skylights reach all the way to the ground and the vertical elevation on the opposite facade follows the site's folded contours, never exceeding 13 meters (43 feet) in height

Visitors ascend a series of leveled terraces – reminiscent of the local temples – to the reception hall lined in glass and fitted with aluminum sunscreens. From here, the view embraces the entire valley to the west. The reception hall gives access to the north and south wings, both of which have identical surfaces and differ only in their layout, each one according to the dictates of the site. The north wing, around a central Japanese open-air garden, holds the Japanese art galleries, in addition to laboratories and storage space. The south wing, by contrast, is three-stories high and holds the Western art collection, the curatorial offices, an auditorium and a tea room.

All surfaces have been combed to bring forth the grain, the texture and warmth of the wood, thus achieving the ideal of universal harmony at the origin of the project, a harmony as present in the fusion of the edifice with its surrounding forests, as in the joining of tradition and modern technology, or the synthesis of East and West. □

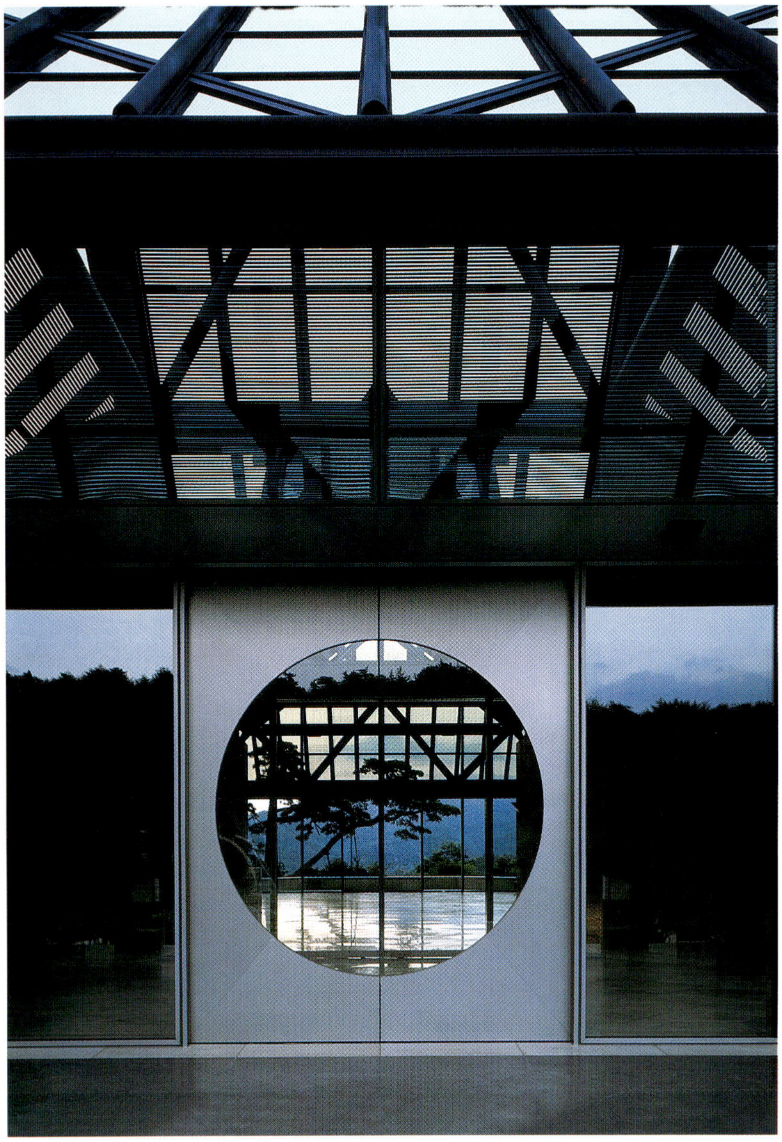

Museum entrance in which the geometry of the circle symbolizes the access to harmony and perfection of the spirit.

Opposite page
Another predominant geometric form, the isosceles triangle. The nocturnal view of the museum transforms the edifice into a series of small pyramids of light, like look-out posts lost in the immensity of the landscape.

Following pages
The steel and glass ceiling of the great central hall, where blinds sculpt the shadows and diffuse the light.

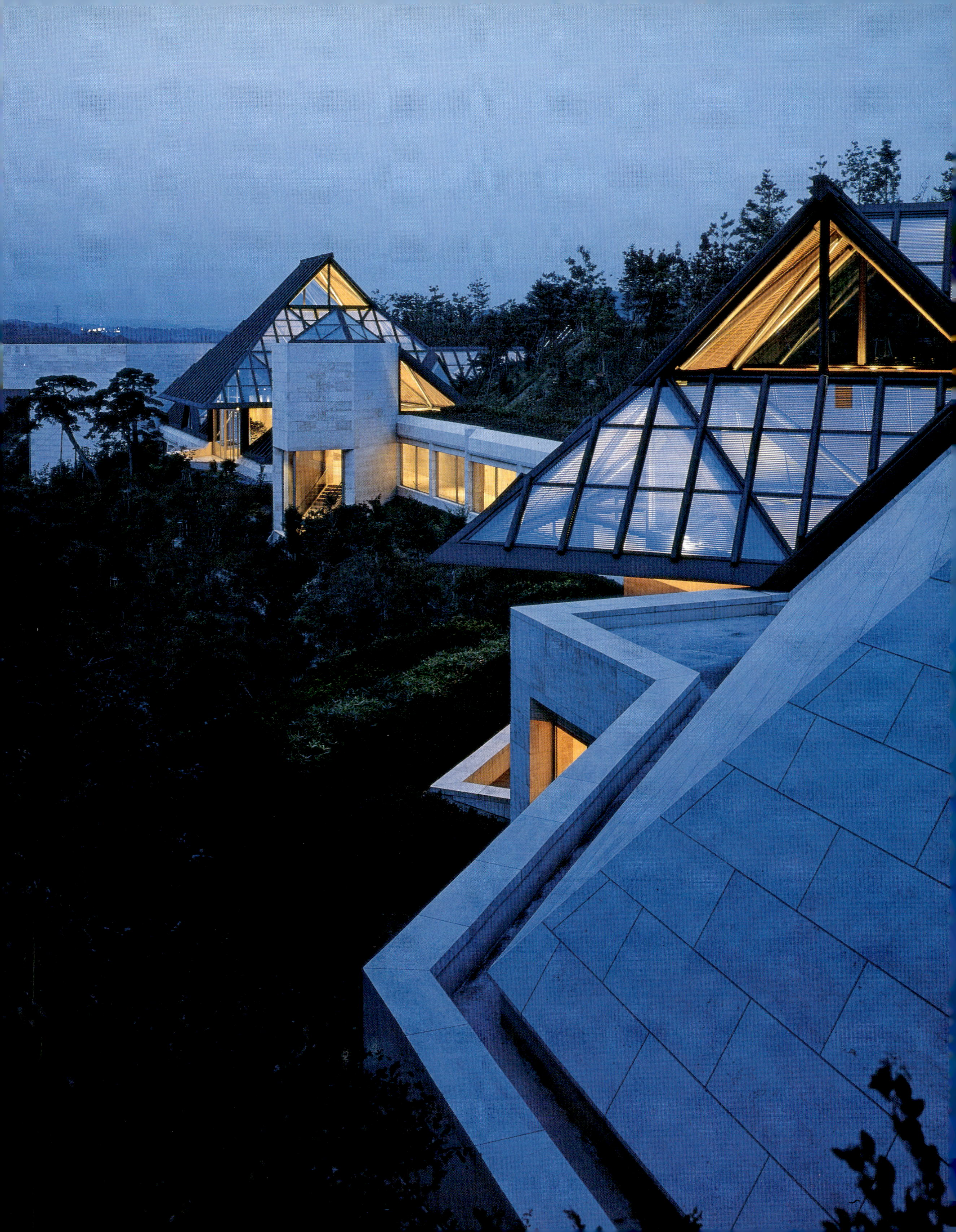

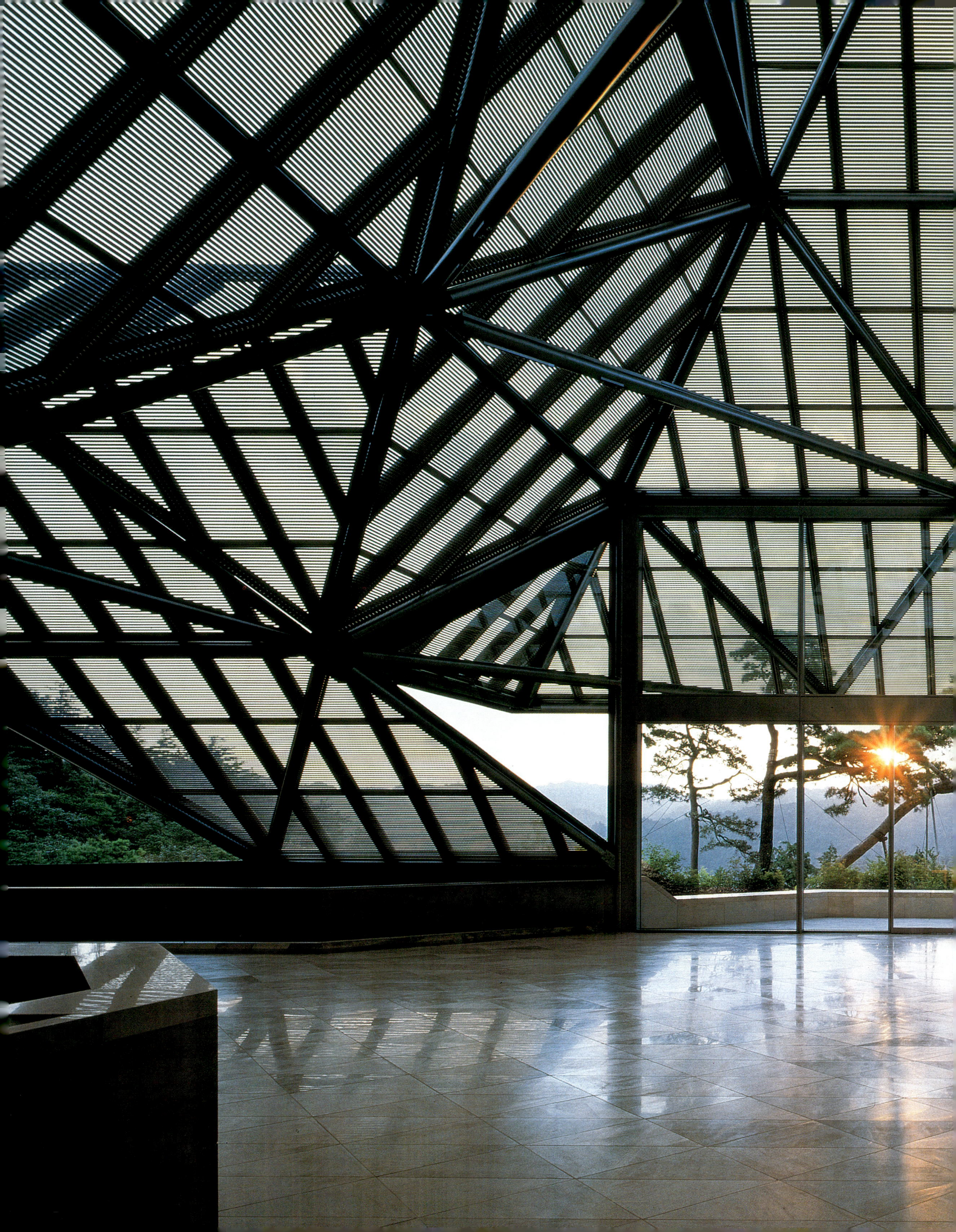

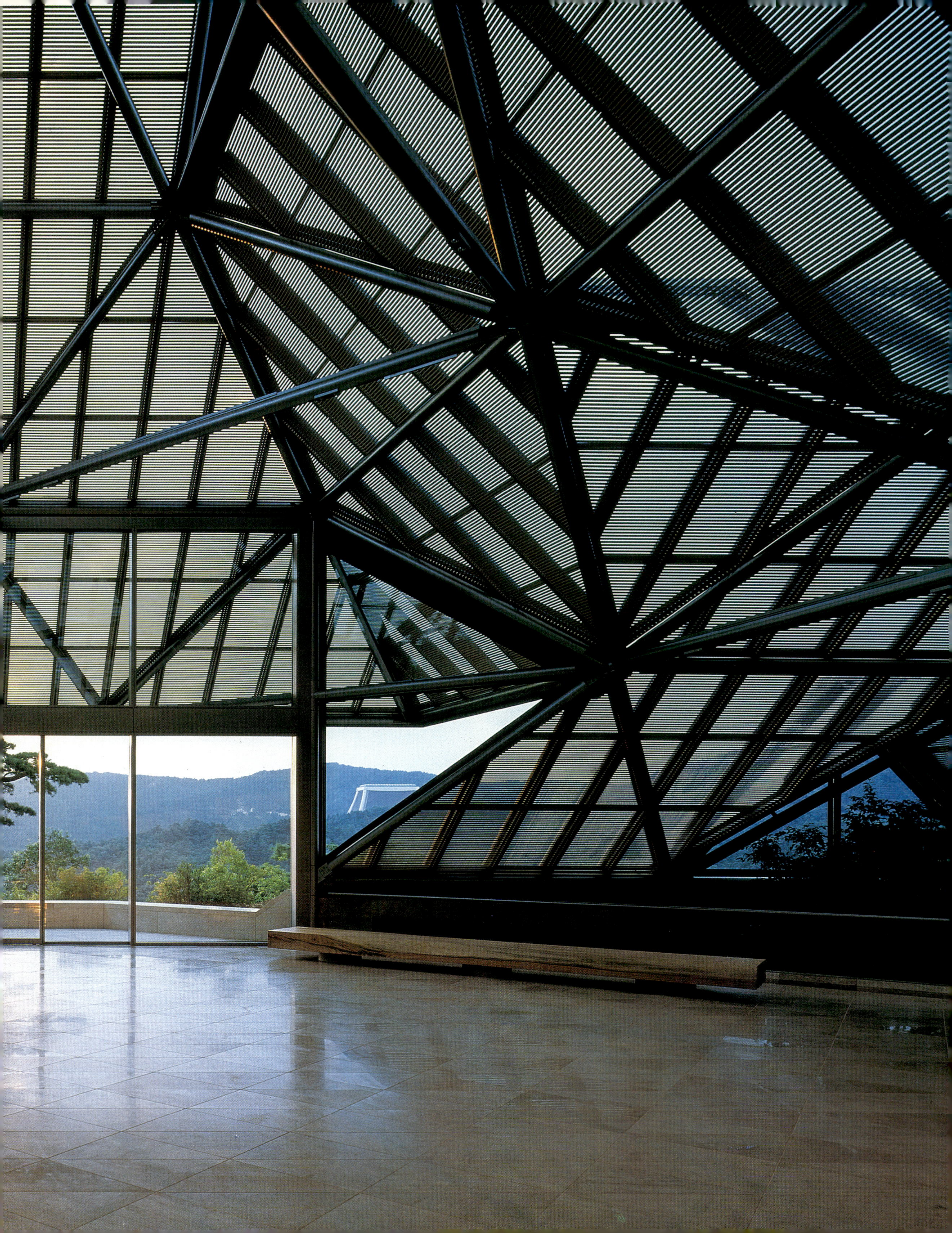

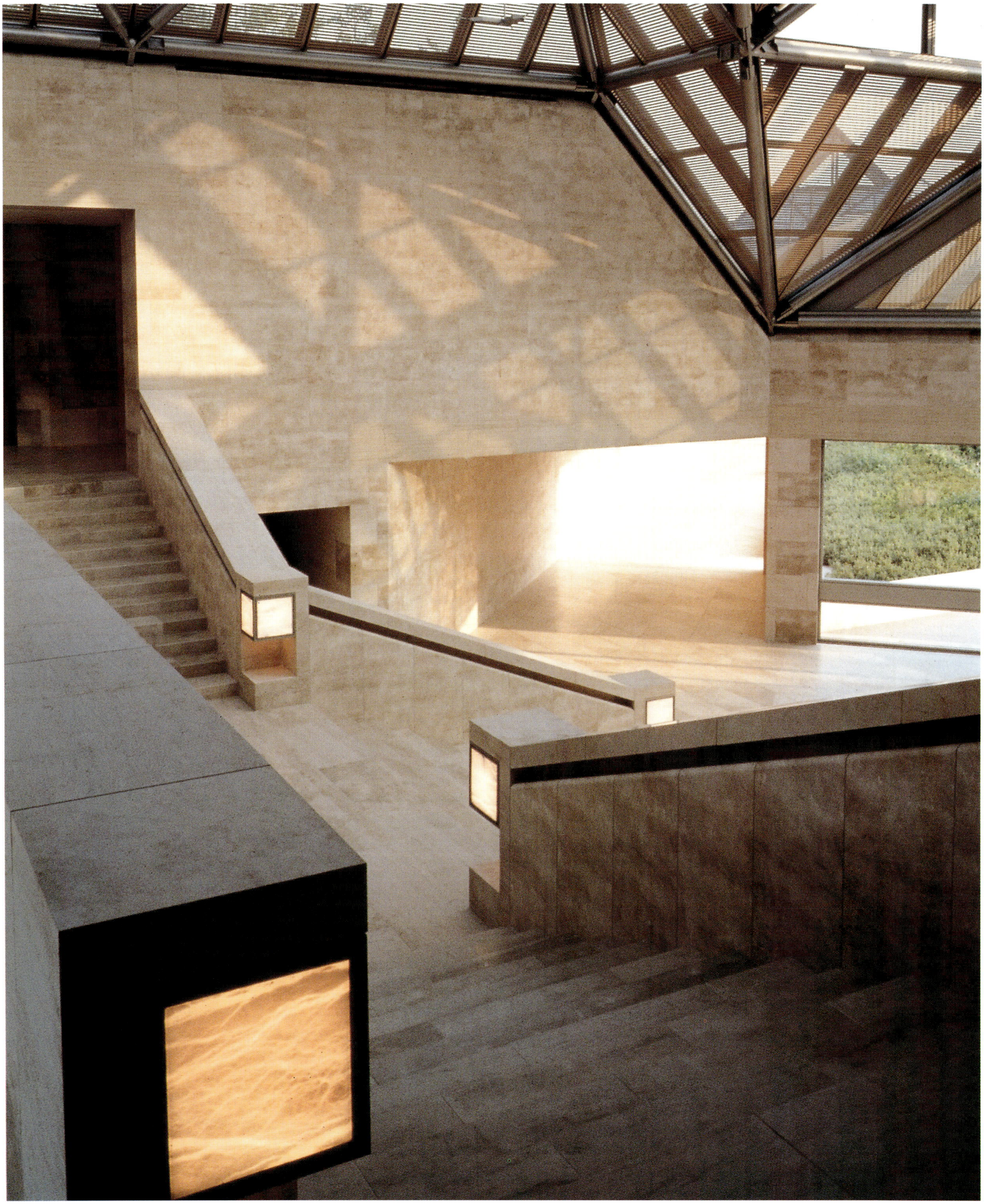

84 Miho Museum, Shiga, Japan

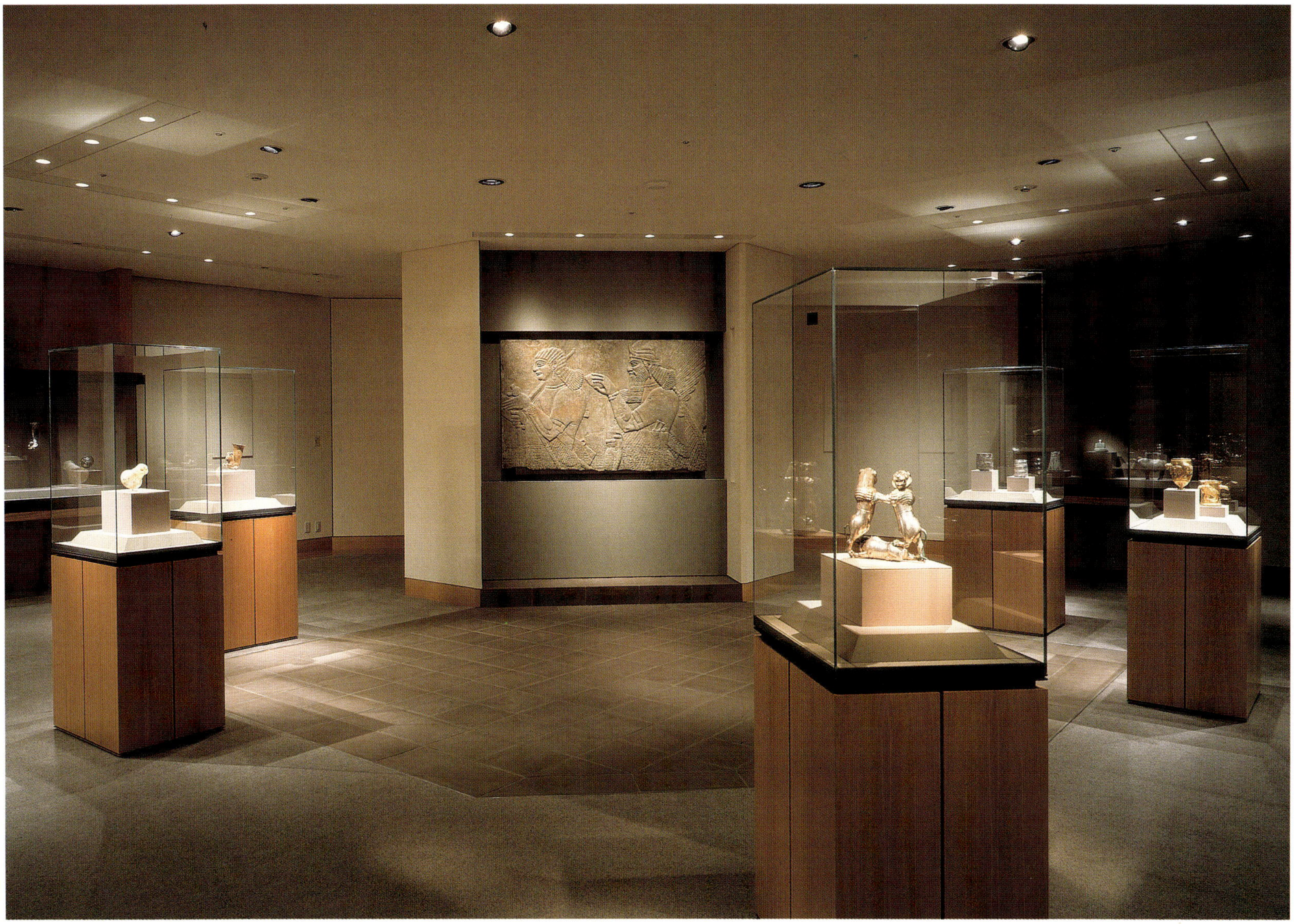

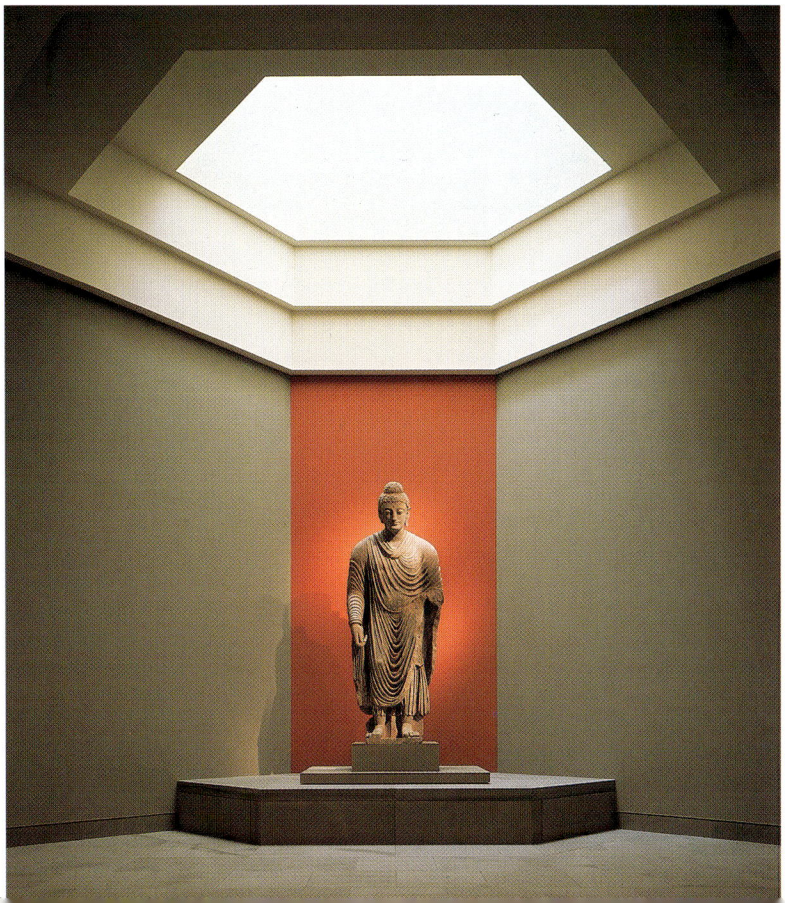

The exhibition rooms in which invisible light sources magically illuminate each object, are each centered around a chosen object, an Indo-European stele or a statue of a Gandhara Buddha.

Opposite page
From the central hall, the corridors leading to the galleries: filtered through the large glass roofs, sunlight enhances the pale tones of the Magny stone, especially imported from France.

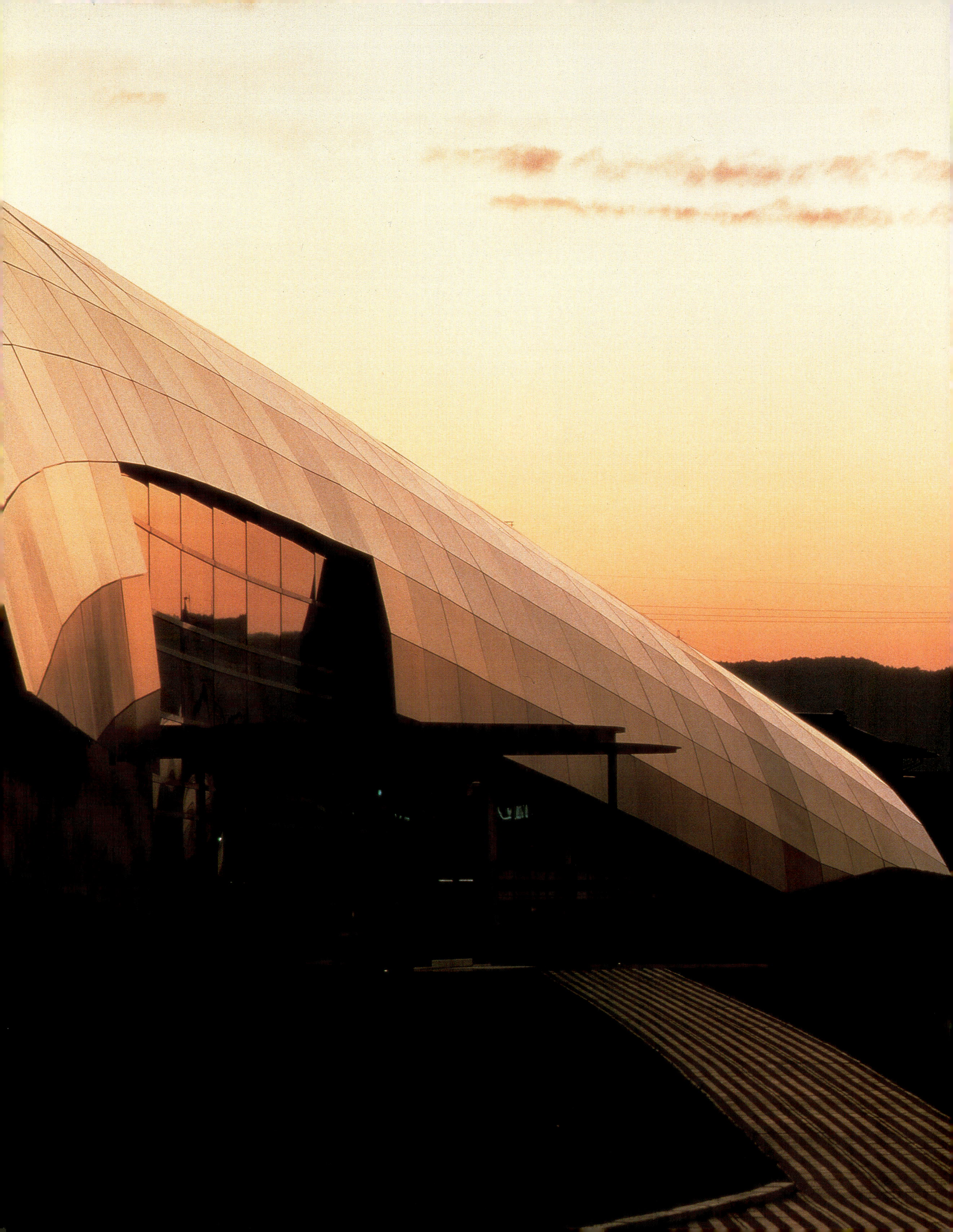

Toyo Ito

Shimosuwa Museum

Nagano, Japan

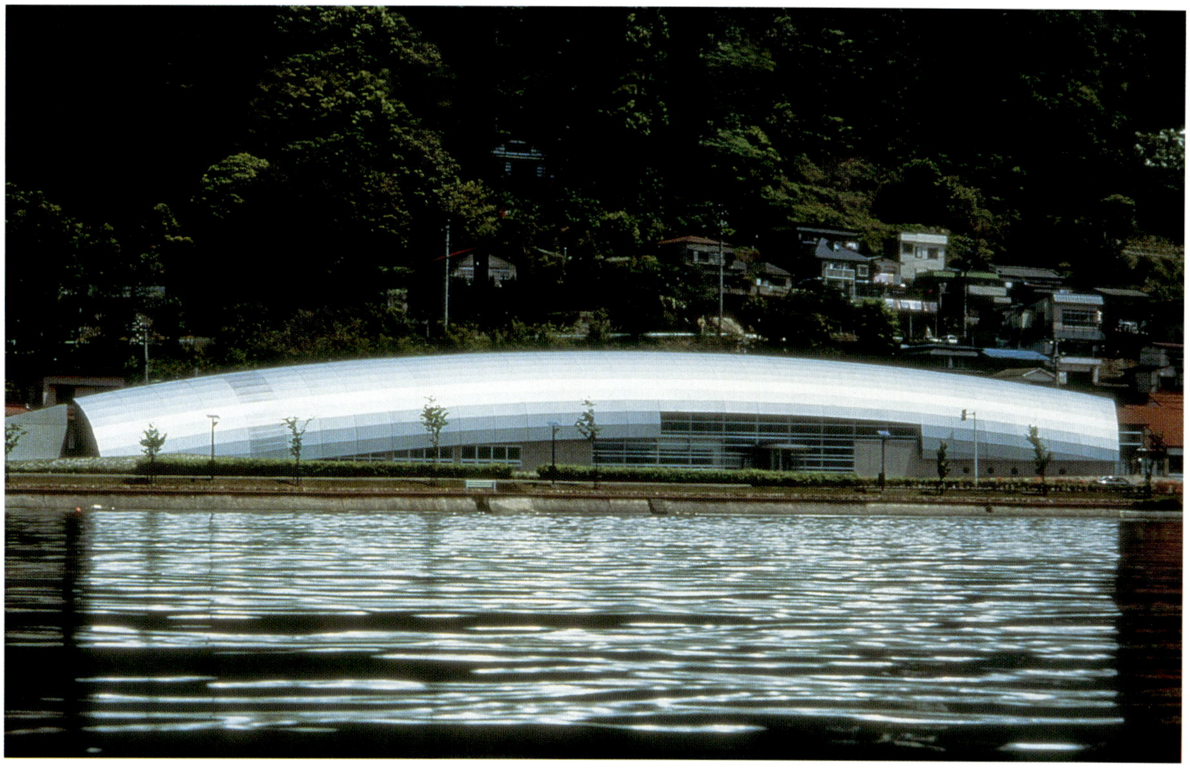

Seen from the lake, the Shimosuwa Museum, whose main entrance faces the water, takes on its full force and meaning. Truly imitative of the landscape, it blends with the liquid surface from which it seems to emerge, ship's hull or silver cetacean. Like a wave, swelling and curving back, it hugs the mountainous shore onto which it is built. Between lake and mountain, architect Toyo Ito's strange building proclaims the identity of this superb and heavily touristed area whose folklore and traditions are preserved in the Shimosuwa Museum.

Not long ago, the Shimosuwa Municipal Museum would have been called a "small town" museum. This is not to suggest, however, that it shares the characteristics usually associated with such an institution. The museum, with its large metallic "hull" anchored on the shores of Lake Suwa, was part of a construction project celebrating the identity of the town, a town with one of the highest elevations in Japan, surrounded by a striking mountain range.

This new museum was designed by the winner of the 1990 competition, Toyo Ito, and houses two permanent collections. The first treats the history and natural surroundings of Lake Suwa; the second, the archives of the local poet Akahiko Shimaki (1876-1926). Toyo Ito's design is in close dialogue with its immediate environment. The museum's reserves are contained within a large cube on the rocky facade, while, on the lake side, the various exhibition halls share the long arched "hull." The roundness of this silver arch, lined with thin aluminum sheets reflecting the sky and the lake's waters, is the distinctive feature of the ensemble.

Beyond its spectacular esthetic and lyrical appearance, the building's design responds to more prosaic concerns such as the region's harsh climate. Here, the aluminum shell acts as a primary thermal shield superimposed on a steel framework

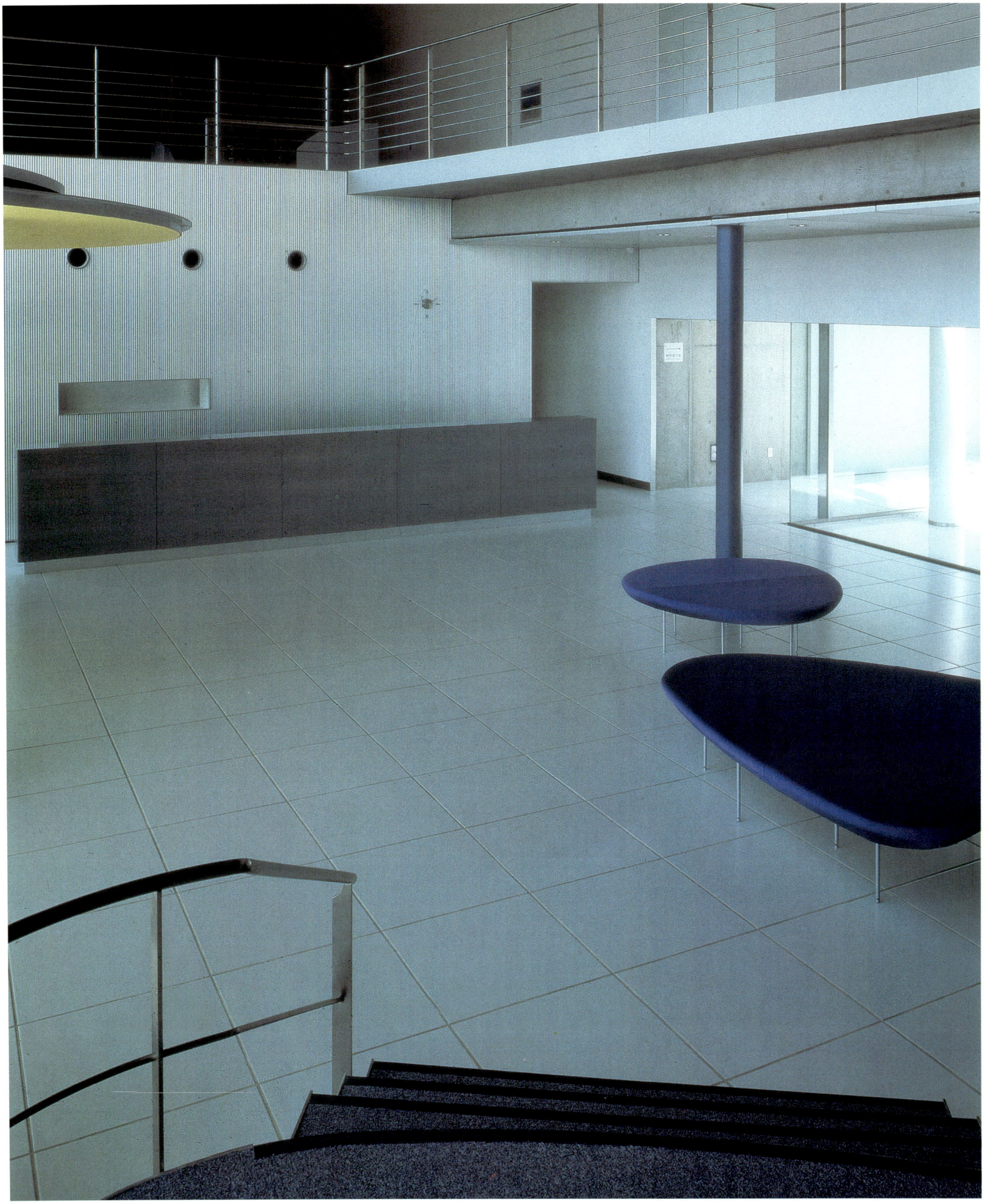

 Shimosuwa Museum, Nagano, Japan

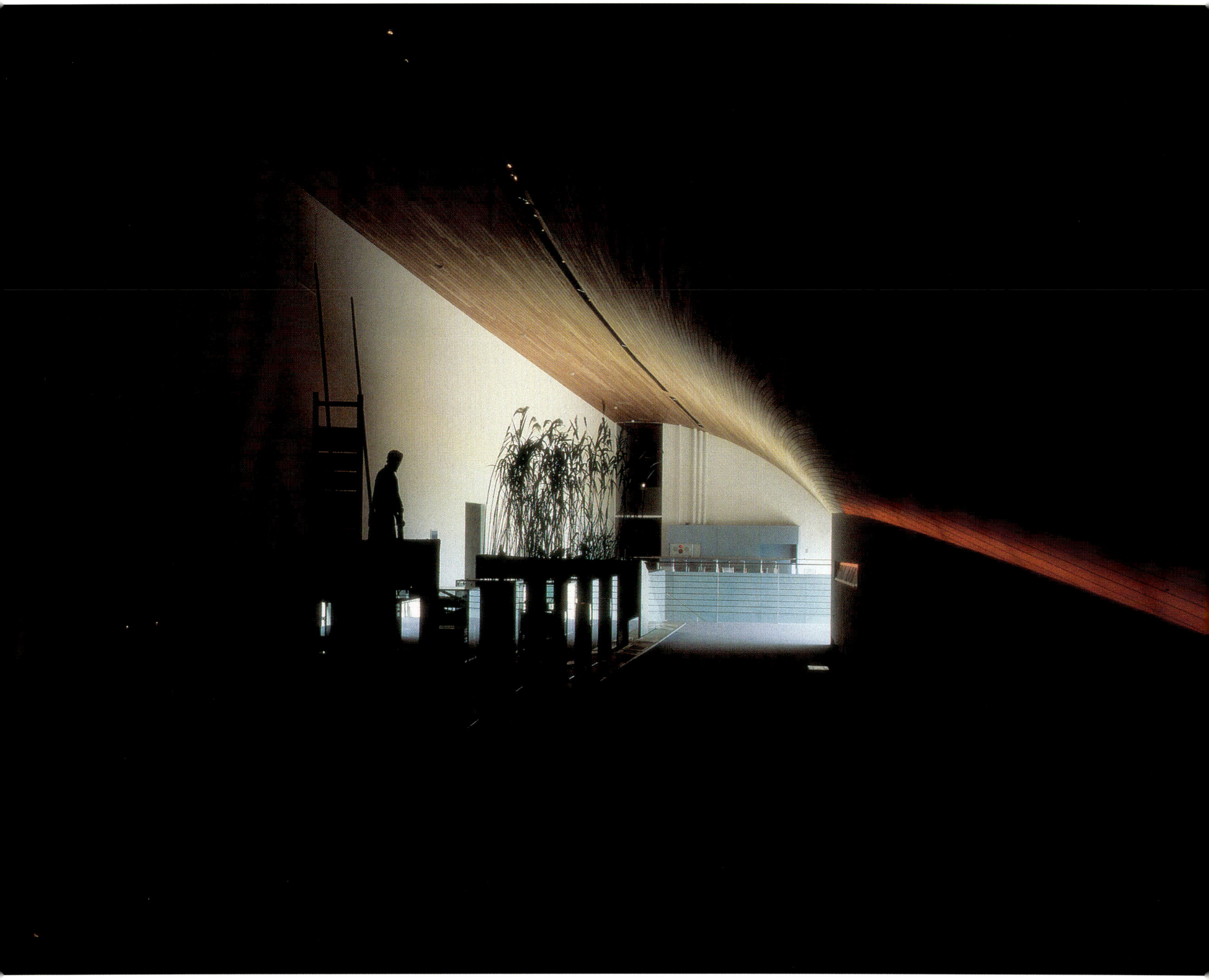

The aquatic allegory of the exterior facades continues on the interior of the building. The wooden membrane of narrow laths forming the ceiling of the exhibition rooms of the mezzanine overlooking the main hall flows, slides and curves like a stream of running water.

Opposite page
Detail of the main hall, where everything reflects the proximity of water: whiteness of foam, porthole openings on the wall or railings of the mezzanine.

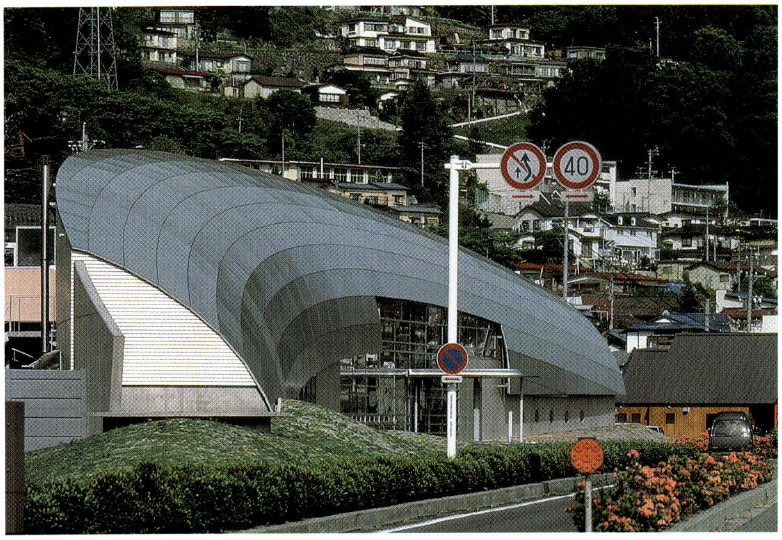

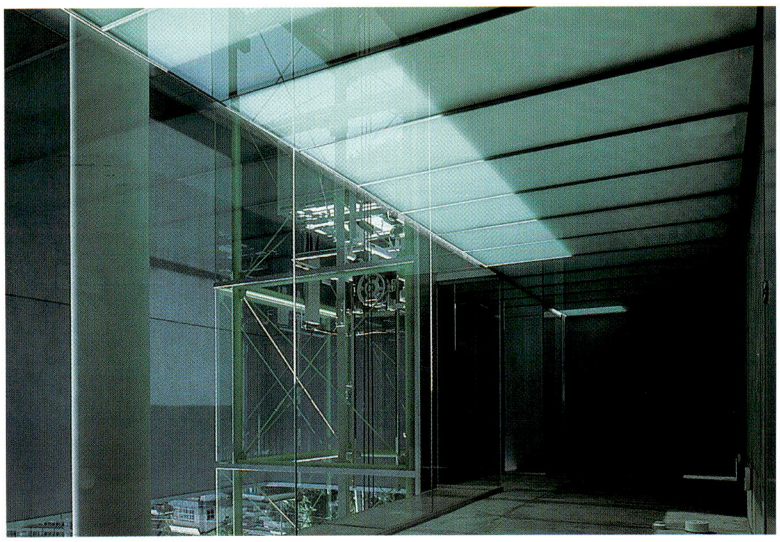

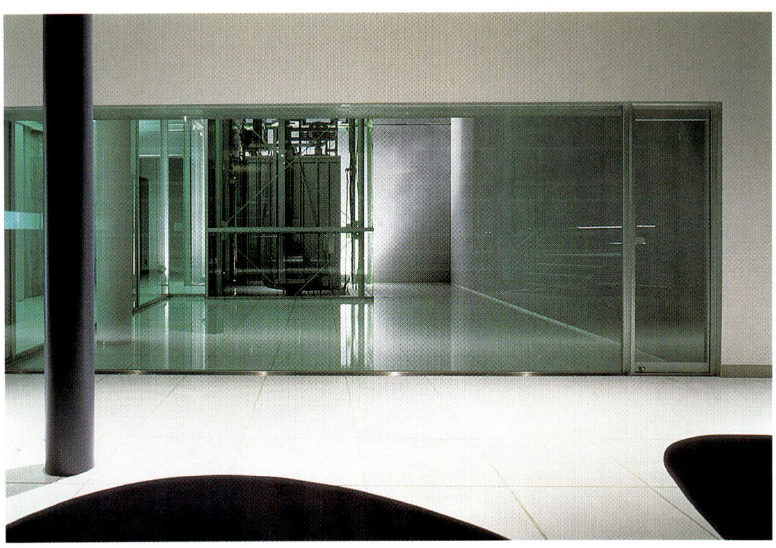

lined with a wooden "membrane." To insulate the building from the cold, the ceilings are paneled and an underground natural heat source next to the lake ensures a constant temperature.

Every aspect of this museum is under the sign of water: the frosted glass in the galleries is reminiscent of the frozen waters of the lake celebrated in local customs; the layout of the room dedicated to the photographs and manuscripts of Akahiko Shimaki evokes the deep bright blue of the lake in summer. The interplay of transparencies and the subtle distortion of the curved, and sometimes off-center volumes accentuate the sense of fluidity and floating in another, often repeated, aquatic illusion. The spectacle of the lake is reinvented and projected onto a glass screen that lies only a few inches from the top of the waves. There is a shimmering reflection from a fine sheet of water on the white pavement of the entrance hall. Even the outside gardens swept by the wind have small waves of green leaves.

Like a liquid fusion, the dialogue between the shimmering lake and the silver "hull" joins in homage to the town of Shimosuwa, its history and its surroundings. □

Lateral view of the principal facade from the lakeside shore.

Perspective views of the glass elevator shaft, transparent and bluish like an ice cube: one of the numerous allusions to the frozen waters of the lake which in winter becomes the stage for various traditional activities, both crafts and recreation.

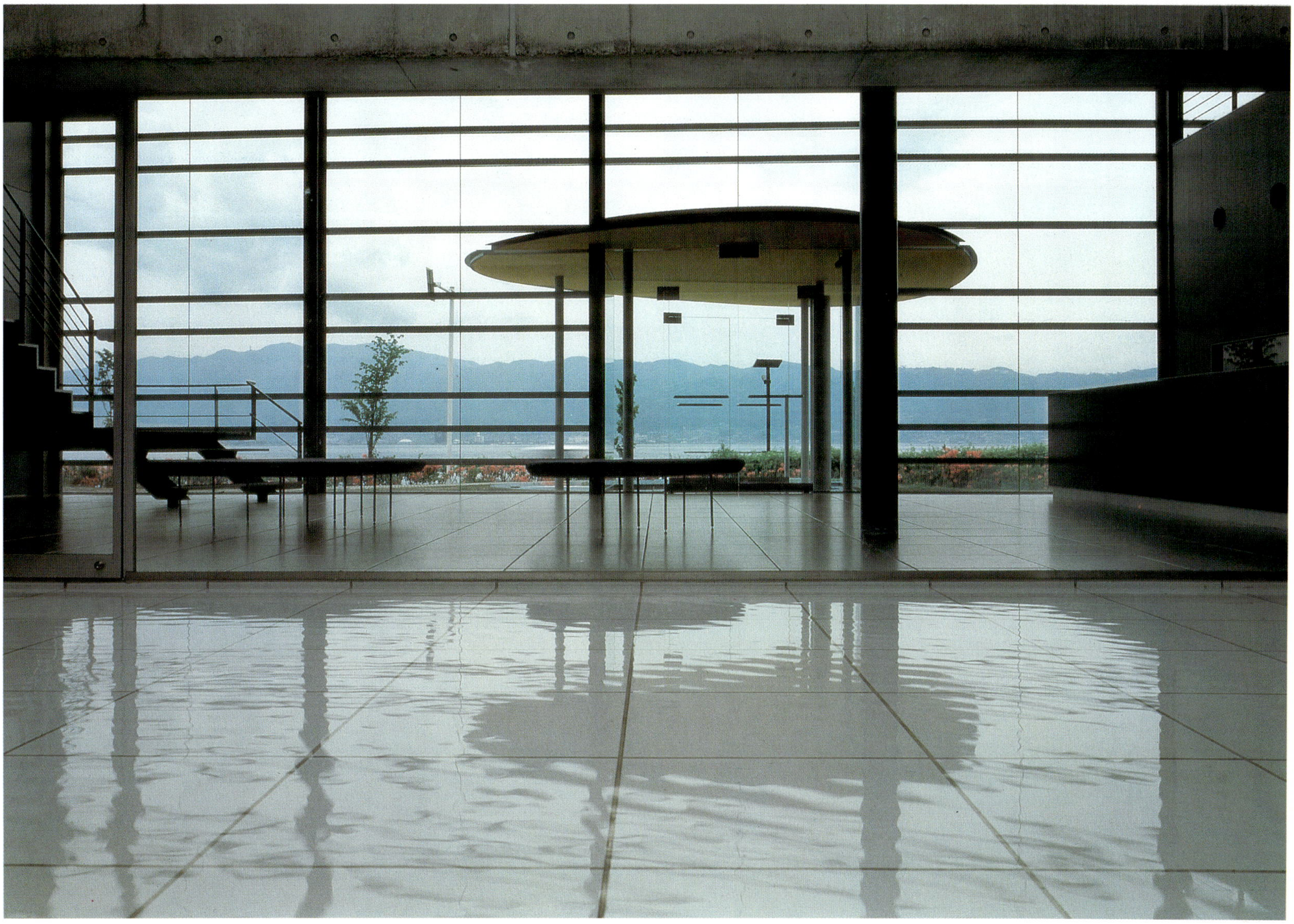

View of the main hall from the patio, which, covered in a fine sheet of water, fuses the interior and exterior spaces: liquid reflections of glass walls and sky, repeated farther away in the lake's horizon and the scalloped outline of the mountains.

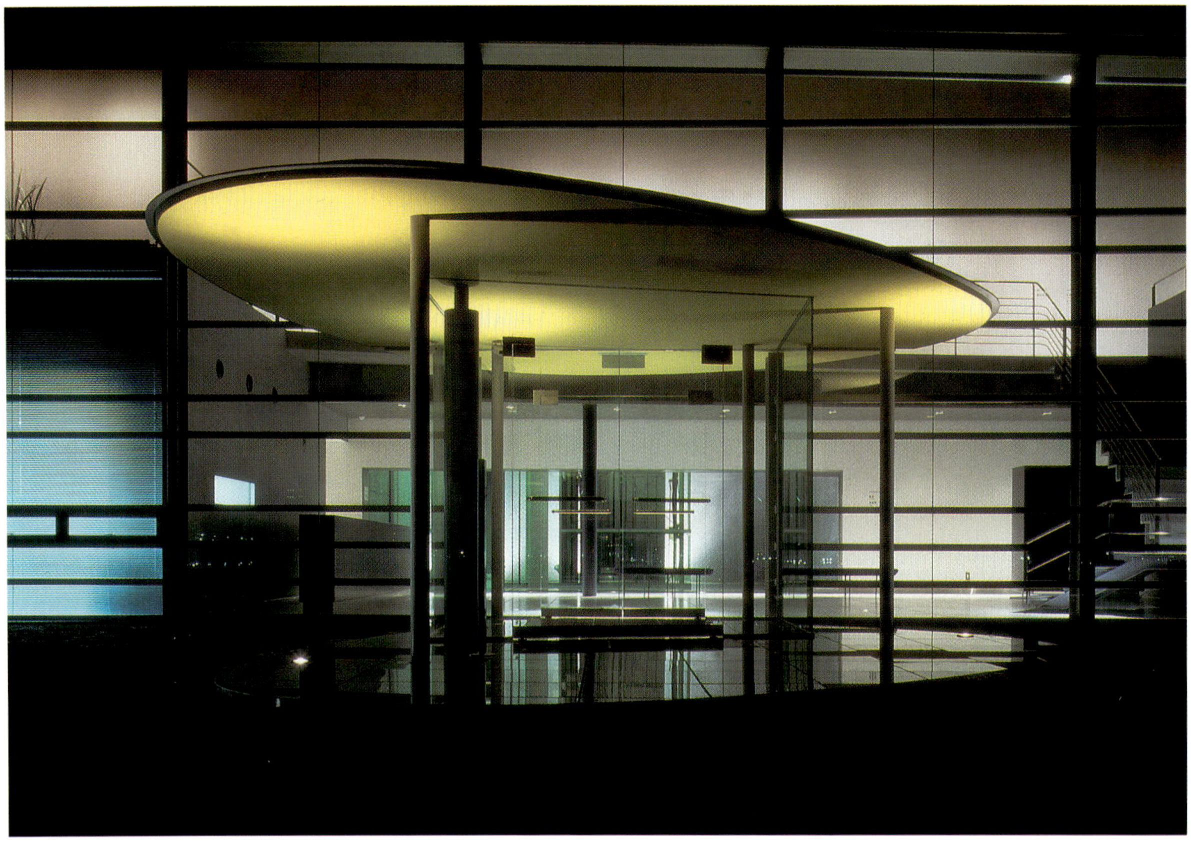

Nocturnal view of the main hall and entrance way sheltered by the oval wave of its awning.

Opposite page
Detail of the mezzanine and the small cafeteria located to one side from which one embraces the panorama of the lake.

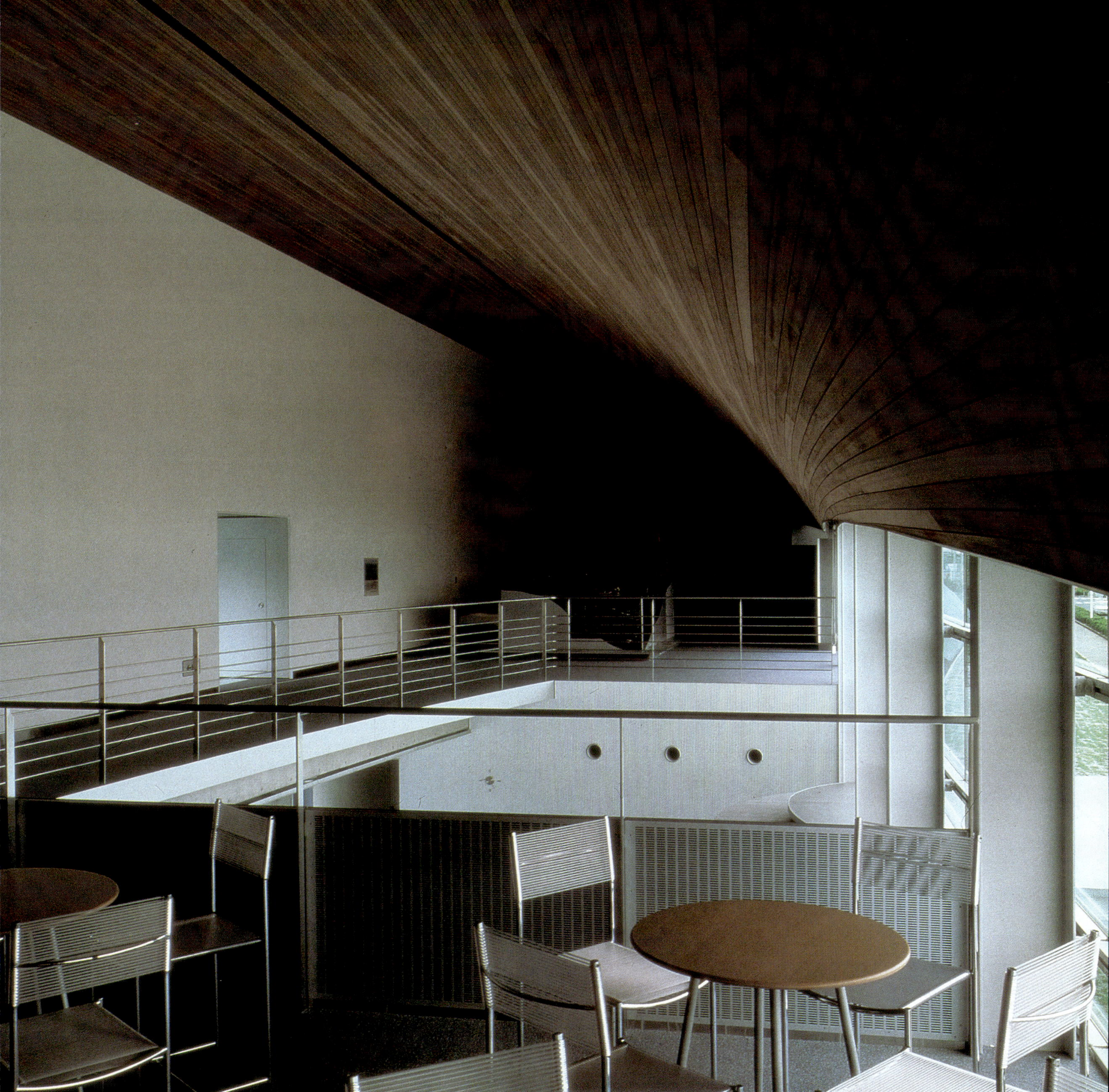

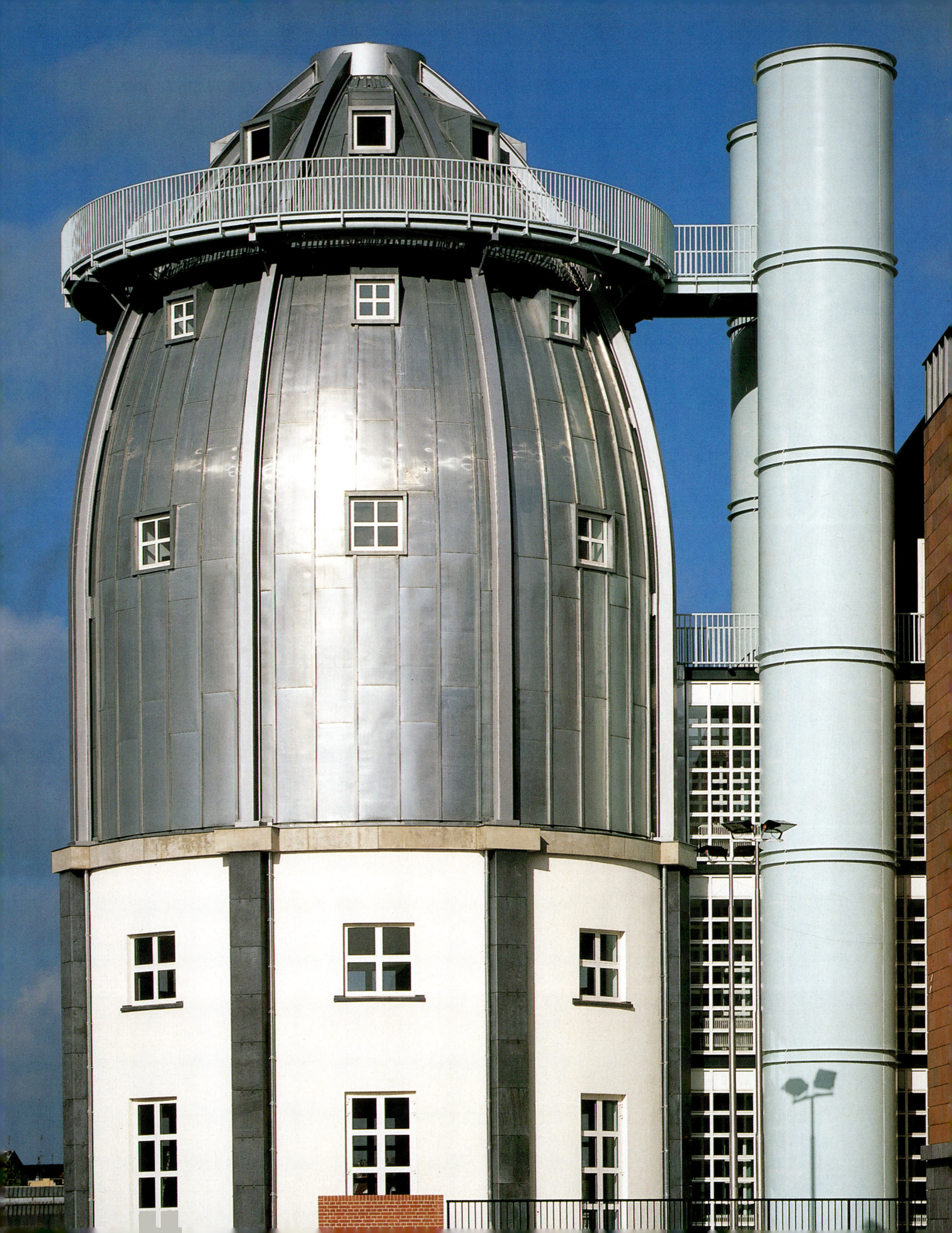

Aldo Rossi

Bonnefanten Museum

Maastricht, Holland

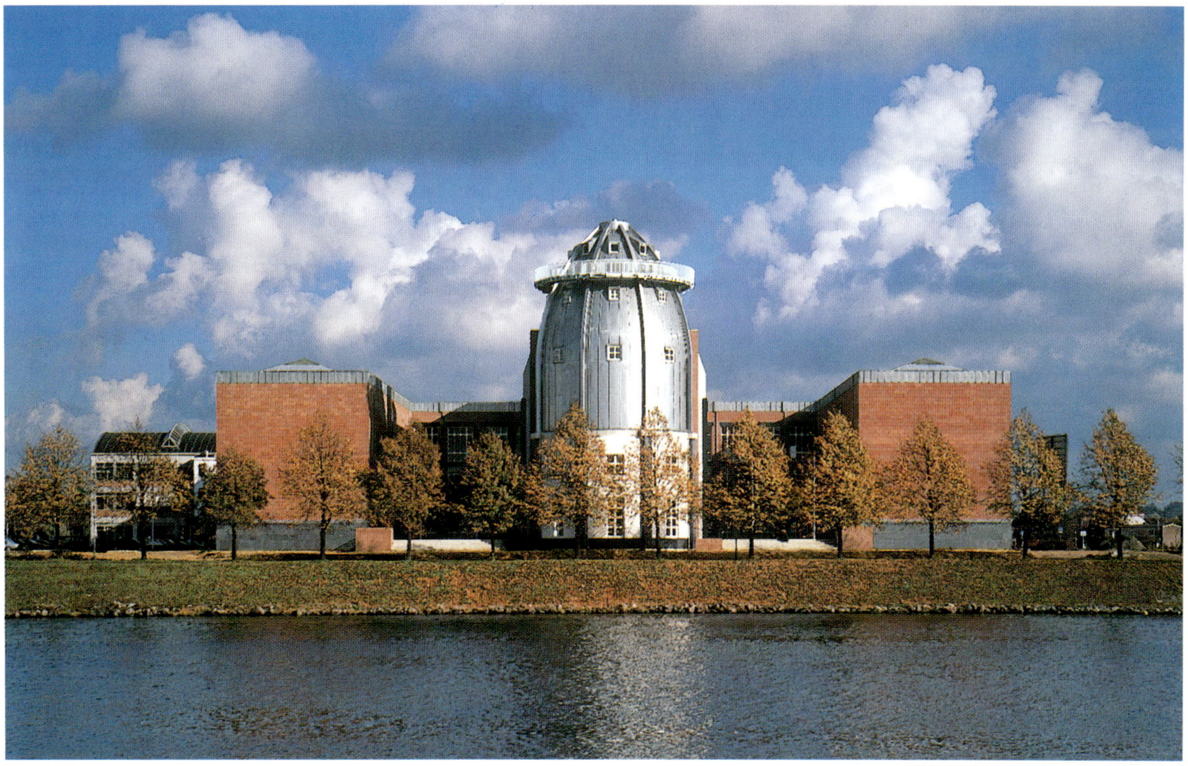

One of his last works, this edifice once again illustrates Rossi's approach to architecture, midway, as he said, between "inventory and memory". Memory of the old industrial complex formerly occupying the site, of which one of the buildings was kept and restored, inspiring both the spirit and style of the new structure. Inventory as well, constantly renewed and reinvented in all the possible declinations of the tower: here an immense metal bombshell measuring 28 meters (90 feet) distinguishing and overlooking the ensemble.

The Bonnefanten Museum in Maastricht is the last offering of the late Aldo Rossi, victim of a car accident in 1997, and illustrates, in all its simplicity and clarity, some of the ideas most dear to him. Rossi believed in the preeminent use of eternal archetypes and that the discipline could remain independent, for this was the expression of a man who refused to align himself either with Modernism or post-Modernism.

Only masters in architecture, its seems, have the privilege of responding to the particularities of a given context while maintaining their signature style. Holland is a country that has been and remains the fiefdom of a modern architecture characterized by simple orthogonal shapes and pared down volumes devoid of superfluous decoration. Rossi's design in Maastricht is in perfect keeping with the preexisting structure while asserting its individuality: a tall outline of a tower in the form of a metal-clad bullet. Towers were Rossi's obsession, present as much in his numerous drawings as in his buildings. Frank Gehry once commented: "Aldo and I have a lot in common. The only difference is that I play at being a fish while he plays at being a coffee pot." For Rossi, towers spoke of an urban loftiness. He was not swayed by the moralism of the Moderns who claimed every

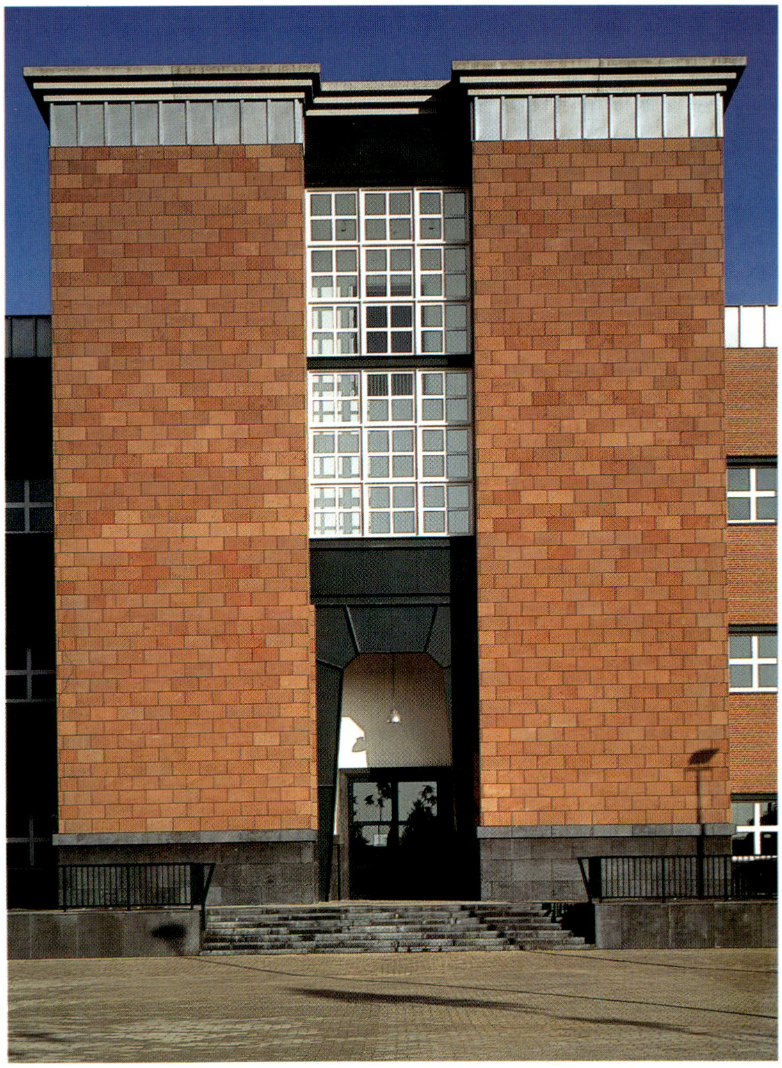

Main entrance of the museum.

Opposite page
The main staircase set between red brick walls reminiscent of the surface of the exterior facades

architectural element should have a purpose and proudly built his towers without a purpose to stand as mere signs in their urban or rural landscapes. He confessed to his fascination for Sardinia's nuraghi, dry-stone towers that remain unexplained as to their exact use whether as grain silos or watch towers, freely entrusting his own structures with sacred mystery. Bonnefanten too holds something of a mystery: a 28 meters (90 feet) high tower enclosing a luminous virtually empty space and devoid of any affectation, except perhaps for its "Grand Café" on the first floor and the Cupola Room, redecorated by a different artist every four months.

Only the Wiebengahal, a restored industrial building from 1912, remains of the old Sphinx Ceramics factory that used to stand where the museum is now. Located opposite the museum's main entrance, it holds the collection's large sculptures. The new red brick and stone edifice—its lateral wings framing the tower and opening out onto the river Meuse—houses the collection from the Bonnefanten Museum (Museum of Good Children) which it received in 1995, as well as the magnificent medieval Neutelings Collection. The archeological and medieval collection is on the second floor, while contemporary art is exhibited on the third. This art center with its numerous areas accessible to the public belongs to a neighborhood still under construction that includes, most notably, a building entitled "Government" where the Maastricht Treaty was signed in 1992. □

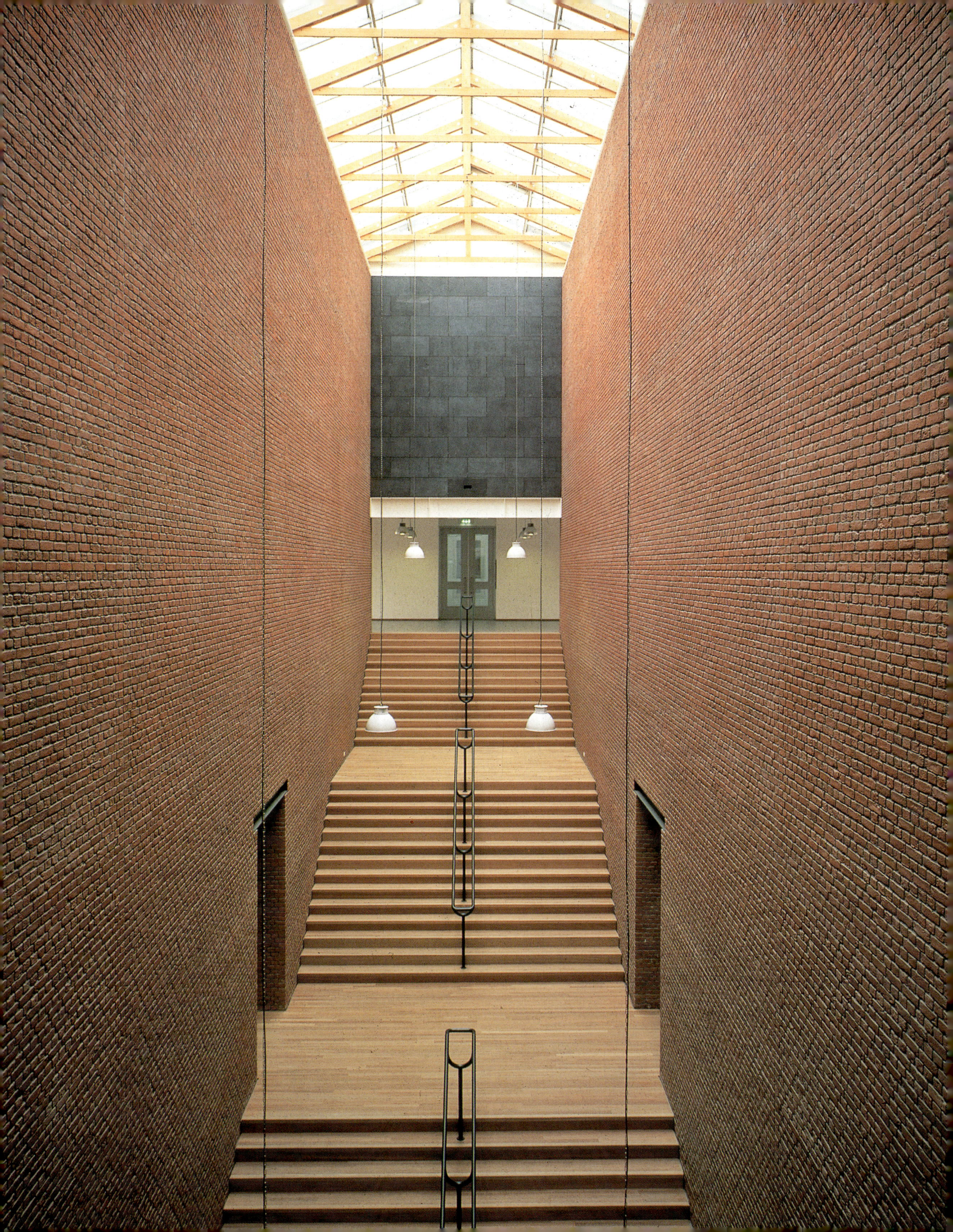

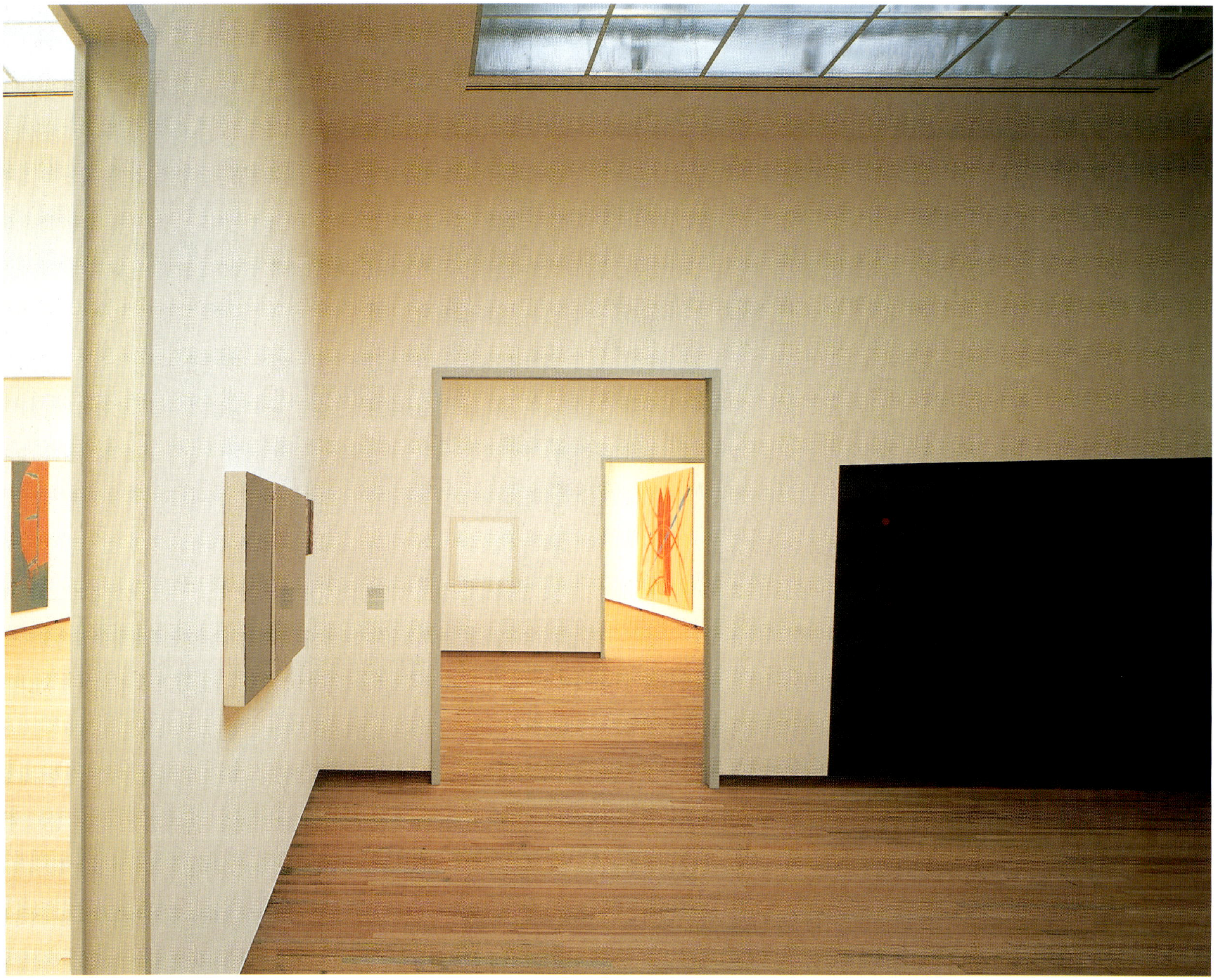

Neutrality of exhibition spaces illuminated by the ceiling's skylights.

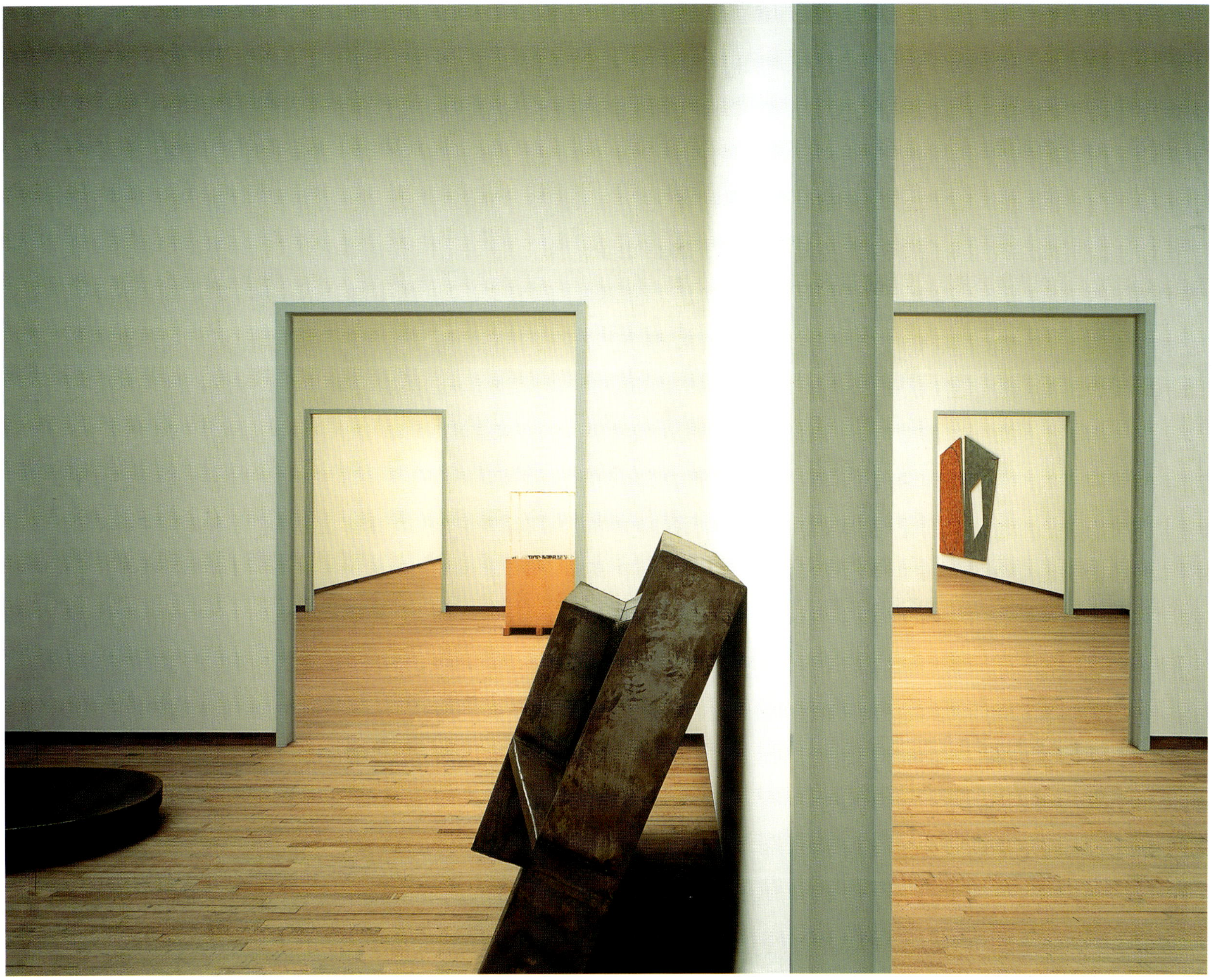

The relative regularity of the more or less square spaces, is animated by views into the adjoining rooms.

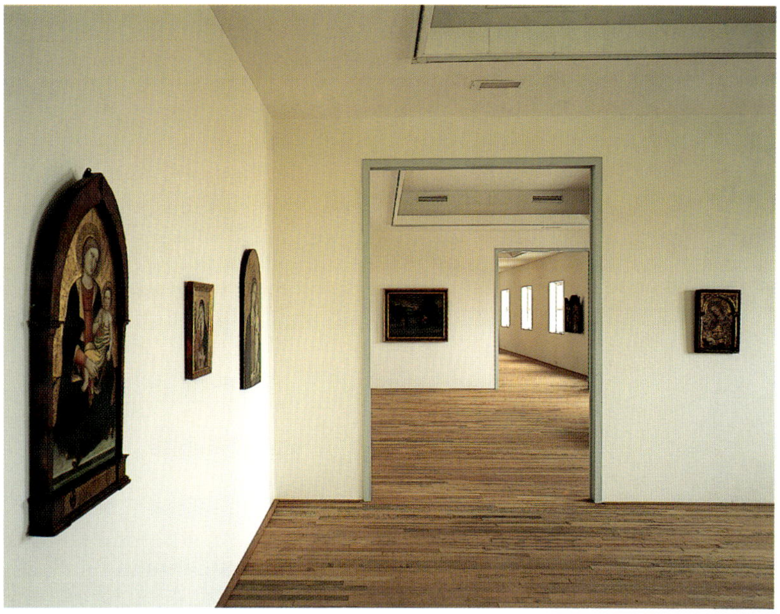

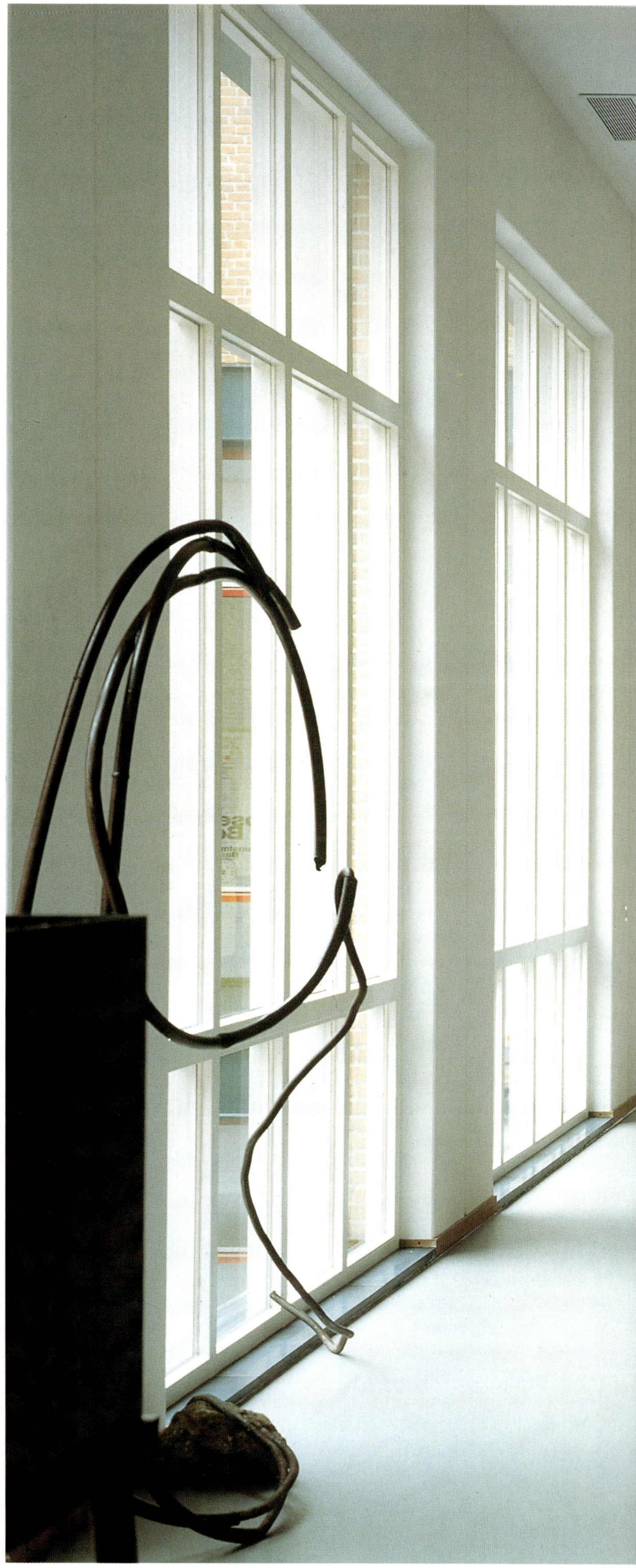

Detail of the exhibition rooms on the second floor, consecrated to archeological and medieval art.

Two views of the contemporary art rooms.

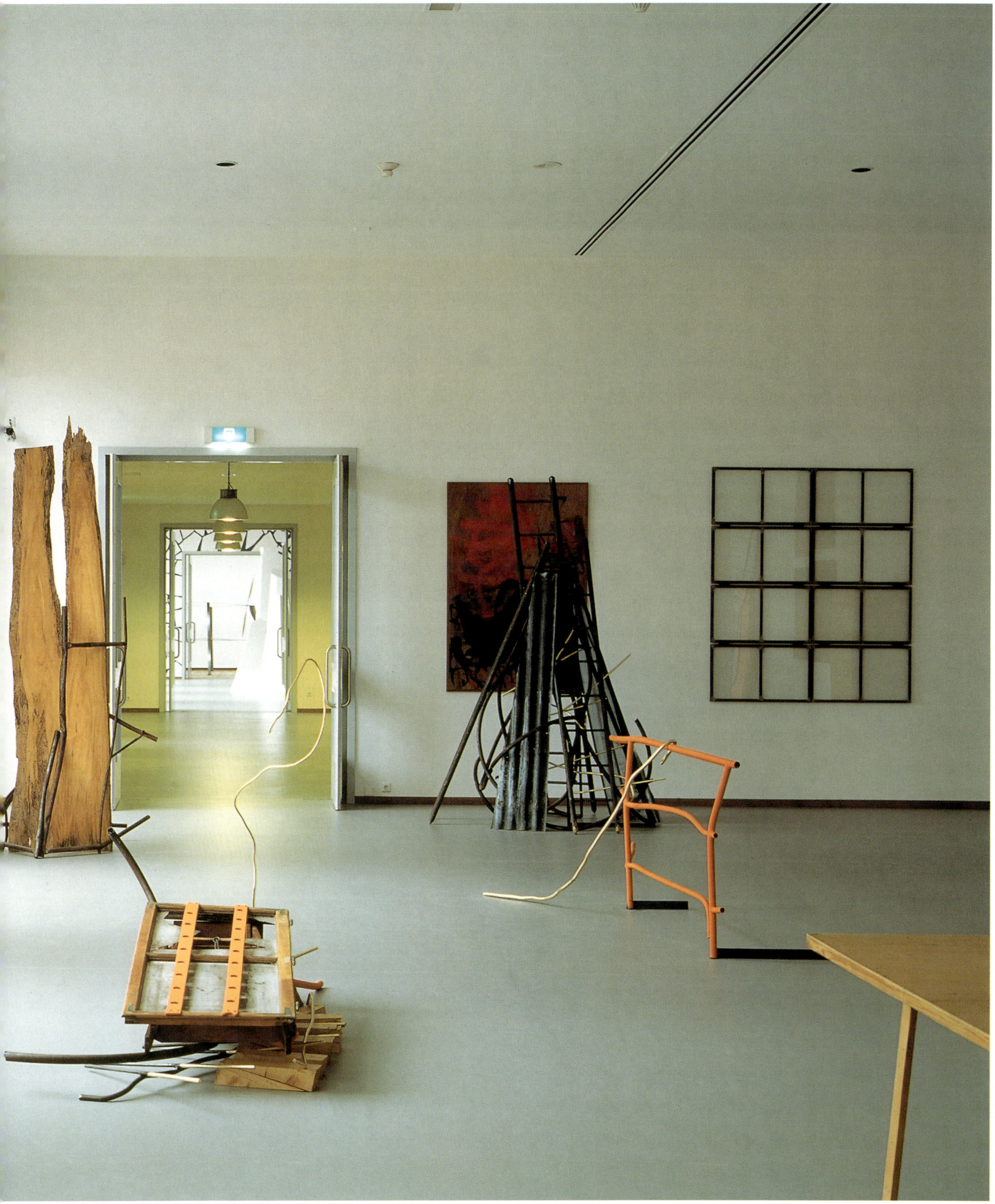

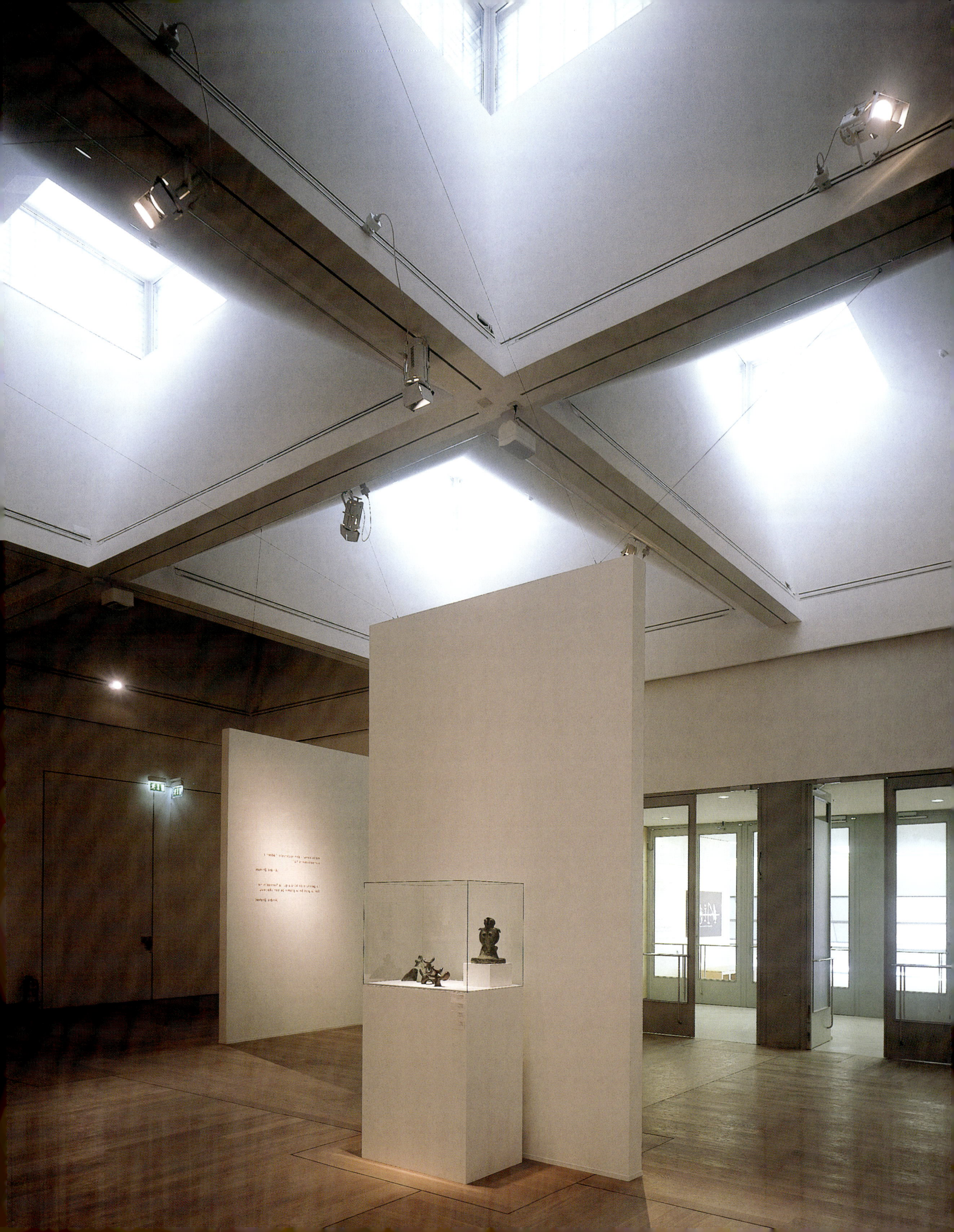

José Rafael Moneo Valles

Moderna Museet

Stockholm, Sweden

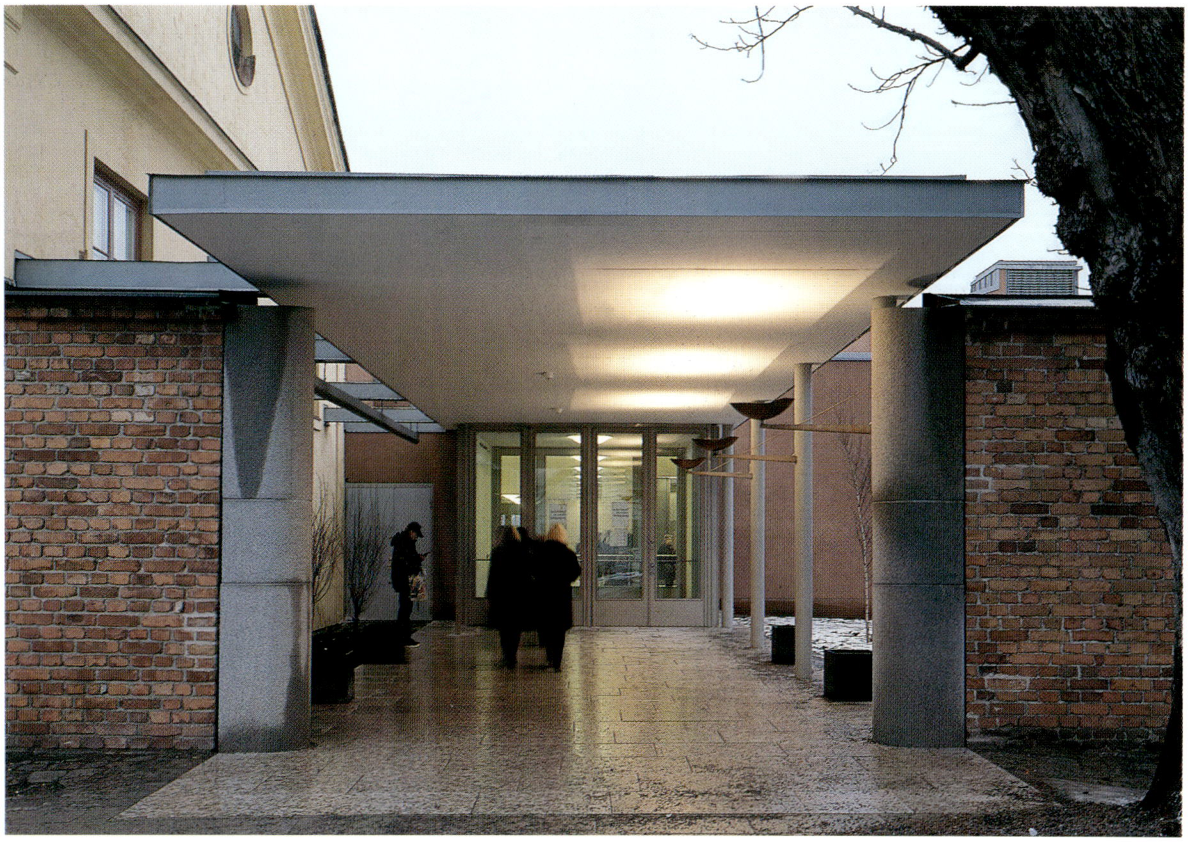

Two crucial factors in the design of the new museum of modern art: the installation of a system of pyramidal roofs permitting natural lighting of the rooms (opposite page), and the integration into the edifice of a high school building existing on the site (above, museum entrance).

The small Moderna Museet was built at the end of the 1950's on the island extending beyond the National Museum under the aegis of a young curator who would consequently make his mark, Pontus Hulten.

By the 1960's the museum was famous: Hulten had organized spectacular exhibitions of young Americans such as Rauschenberg and Johns, of Jean Tinguely, Martial Raysse and he had even convinced Marcel Duchamp to make a "certified copy" of the *Large Glass* for a thematic exhibition or movement.

As a national museum, the Moderna Museet has since acquired an important collection of contemporary art. At the beginning of the 1980's it had become clear that the museum required a considerably larger space. Having now become a noble art, it was decided to add an architecture museum. A competition was launched in 1991; the winner was Rafael Moneo.

The island extends lengthwise on a northwest/southeast axis and has a slightly rounded relief with occasional outcroppings of granite. The buildings line the quays on one side and border the road which divides the island along the

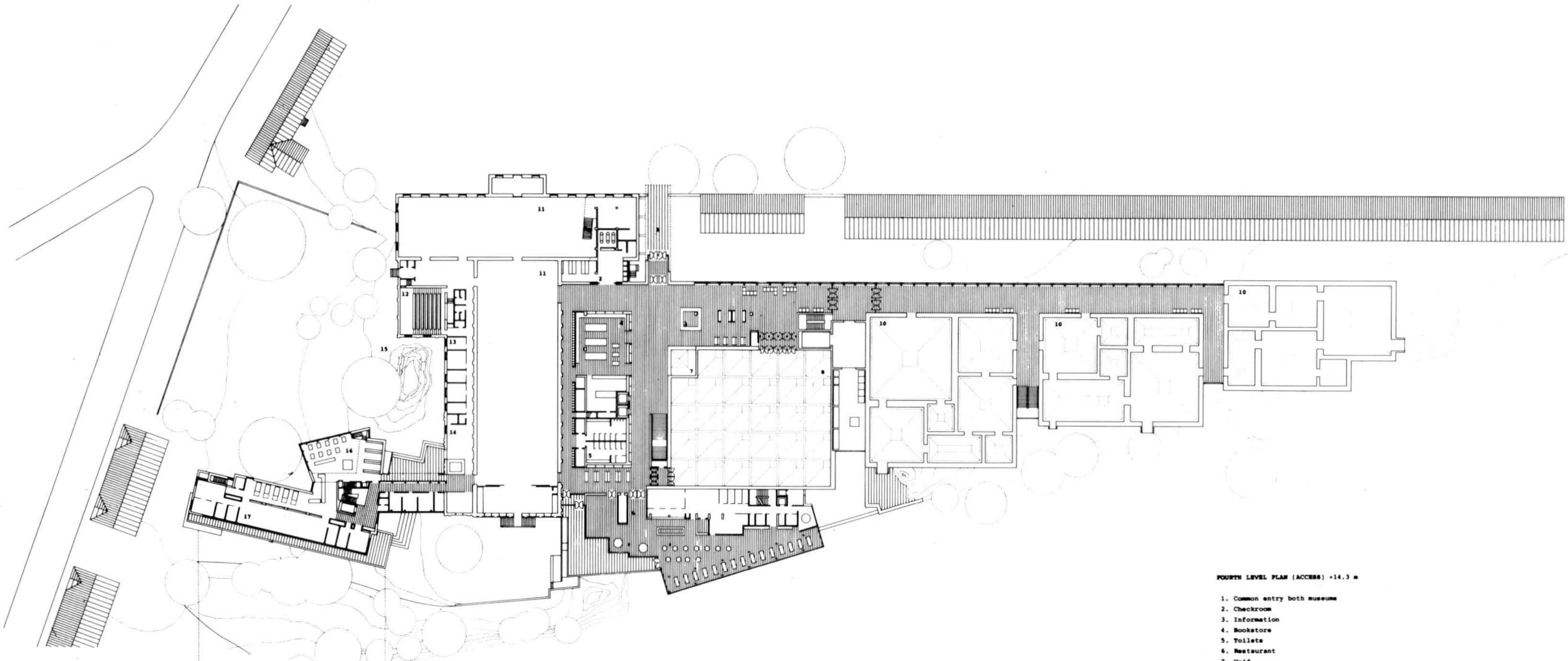

FOURTH LEVEL PLAN (ACCESS) +14.3 m

1. Common entry both museums
2. Checkroom
3. Information
4. Bookstore
5. Toilets
6. Restaurant
7. Void
8. Temporary exhibits
9. Storage and setup temporary exhibits
10. Permanent exhibits Modern Art Museum
11. Permanent exhibits Architecture Museum
12. Conference room
13. Offices
14. Cafeteria
15. Architecture Museum court
16. Library
17. Research laboratories

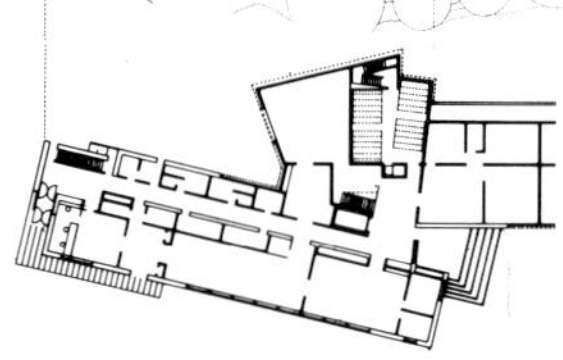

THIRD LEVEL PLAN +10.6 m

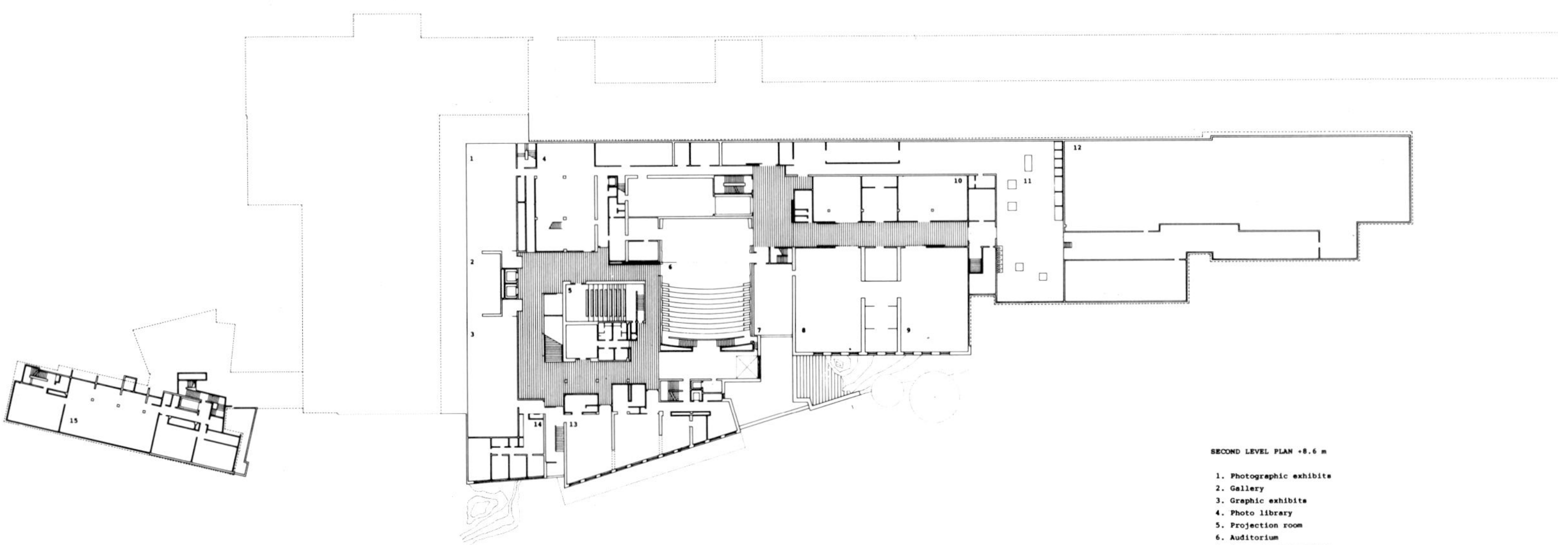

SECOND LEVEL PLAN +8.6 m

1. Photographic exhibits
2. Gallery
3. Graphic exhibits
4. Photo library
5. Projection room
6. Auditorium
7. Document restauration
8. Painting restauration
9. Sculpture restauration
10. Archives
11. Technical room
12. Storage
13. Workshops
14. Offices
15. Architectural drawing archive

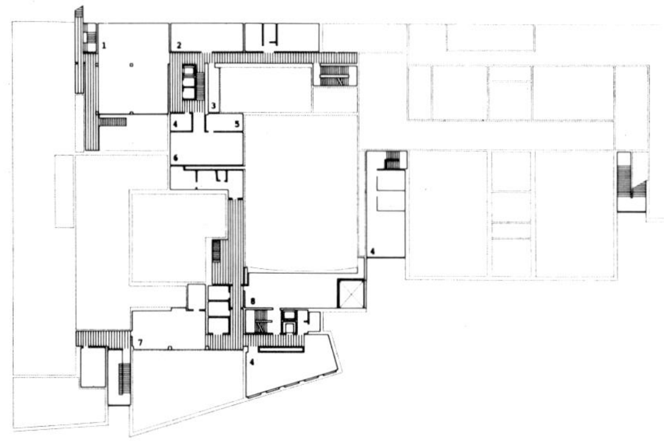

THIRD LEVEL PLAN +11.4 m.

1. Photo library
2. Photo storage
3. Balcony above photograph studio
4. Office
5. Laboratory
6. Photograph conservation
7. Personnel room
8. Projection room

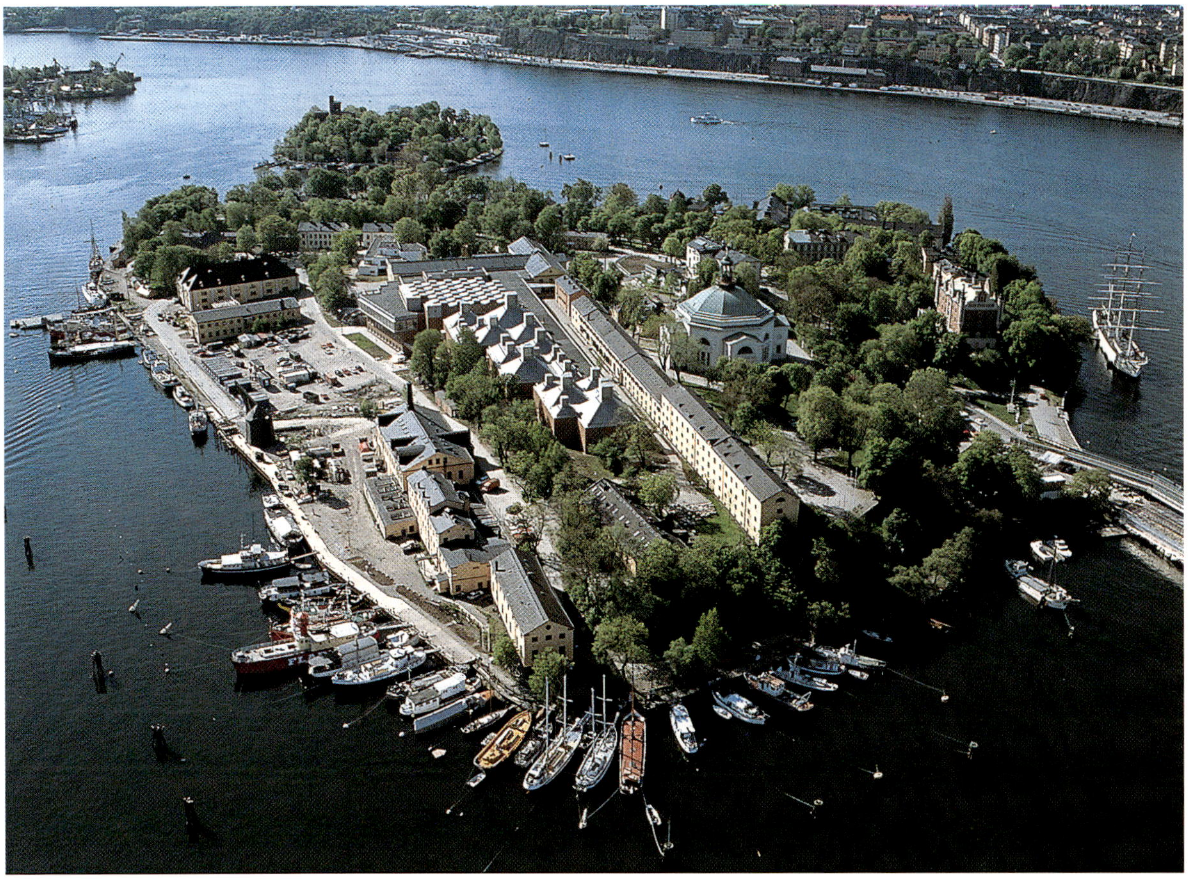

Aerial view of the island: the building is recognizable with its pyramidal roofs.

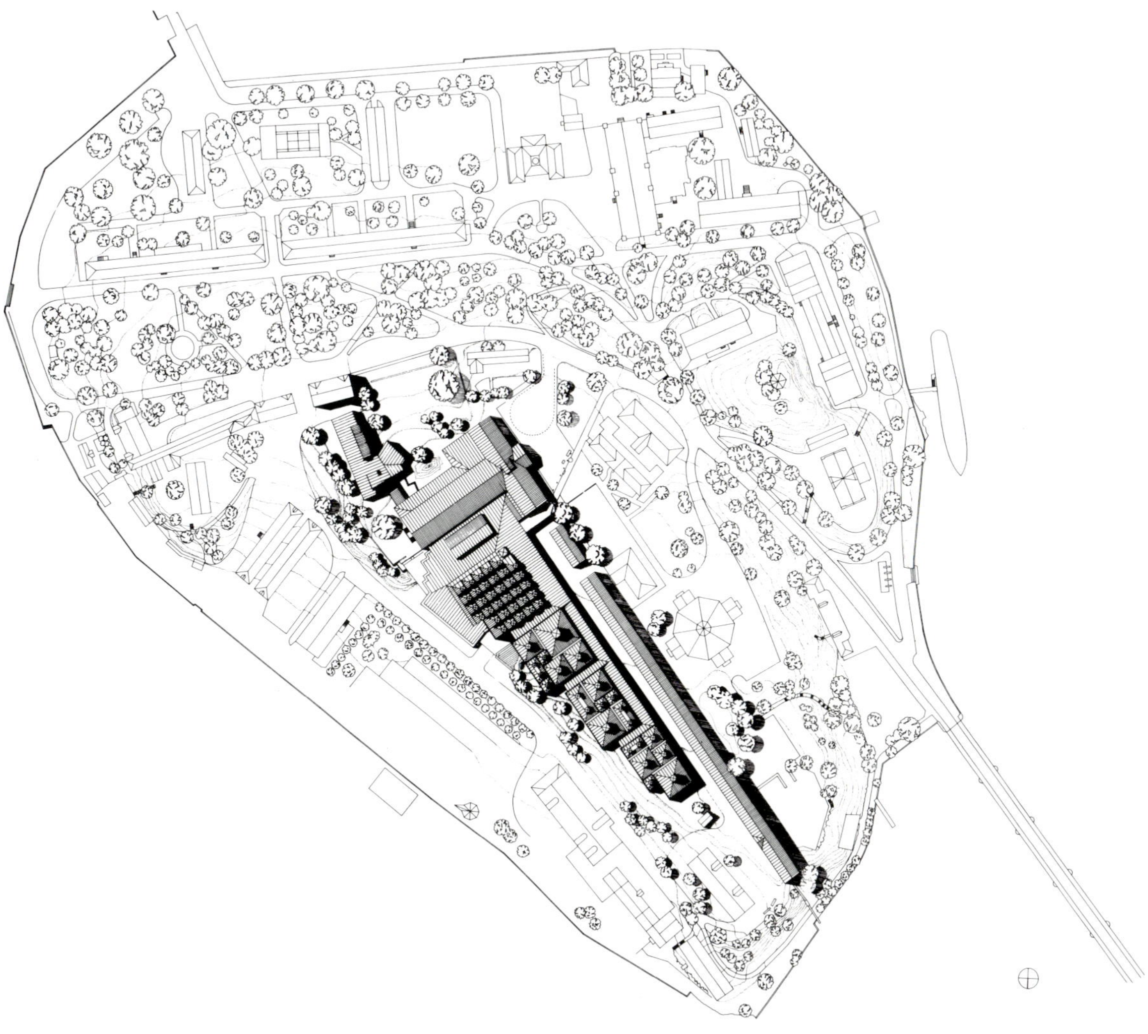

Site plan

Opposite page
The linear disposition of the plan is dictated by the island's watershed and the distribution of the spaces conforms to the slope.

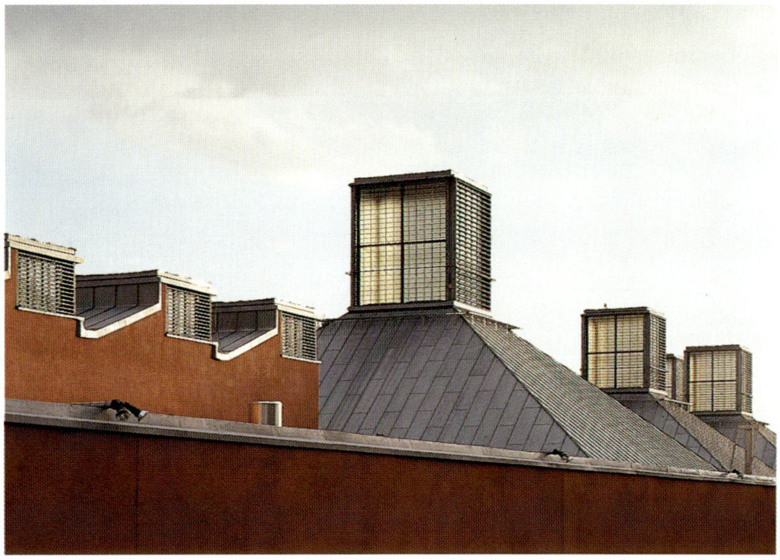

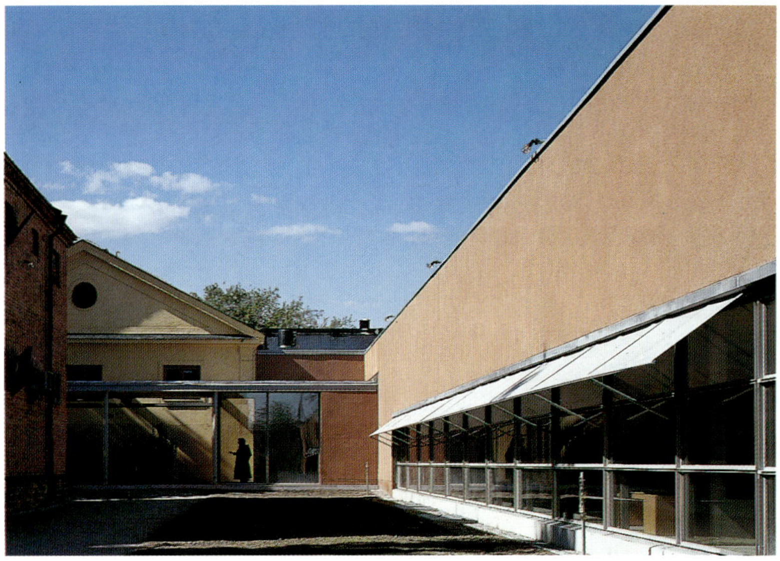

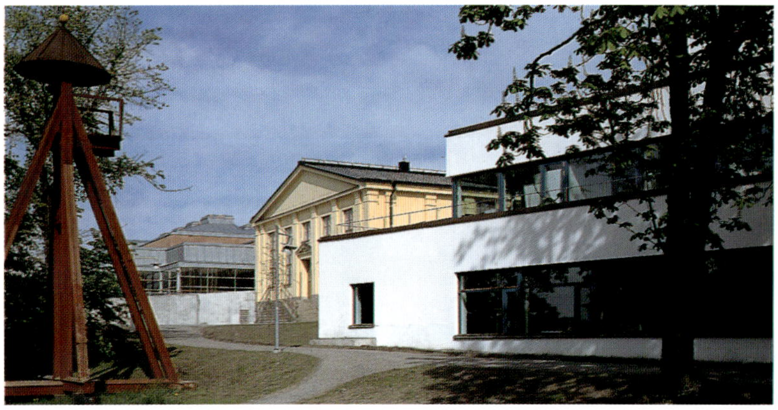

Above: the copper roofs topped with glass cubes.
Middle and below: the new buildings integrate the old neo-classical high school.

watershed on the other. Their style blends discrete neo-classicism and Swedish turn-of-the-century Romanticism. A small pinnacled temple is all that can be seen from a distance. The quays now serve as nothing more than a yachting harbor without as such having lost their dignity. Moneo's course of action undoubtedly enabled the preservation of the fragile balance of the site.

The architect recovered a high school building in the form of a "T" and integrated it into the program by ridding the site of the existing museum building: the museum of contemporary art wing was developed towards the northwest in a series of basic geometric exhibition halls, square or rectangular, with pyramidal roofs and skylights. This enabled a discrete insertion on the scale of the surrounding buildings. The remainder of the museum project, graphic arts and photography galleries, were integrated onto the hillside descending toward the bay with service, maintenance and loading facilities accessible from the quay.

From the common entrance, the architecture museum juts out at an angle toward the southeast. The two buildings are easily distinguishable: the art museum is covered in a red ocher coating, the architecture museum in white. Moneo used all his virtuosity in an ensemble that blends into the local architecture – an unheroic gesture, against the current of the theatrical requirements of today's museography.

Inside the two buildings there is an atmosphere of calm and comfort: simple materials, polished stone and parquet floors, plaster walls and wood furniture provide the art works with a setting of great simplicity, benevolent neutrality.

In a recent interview, Rafael Moneo emphasized that the buildings hadn't a single curve. What could he have meant by that? □

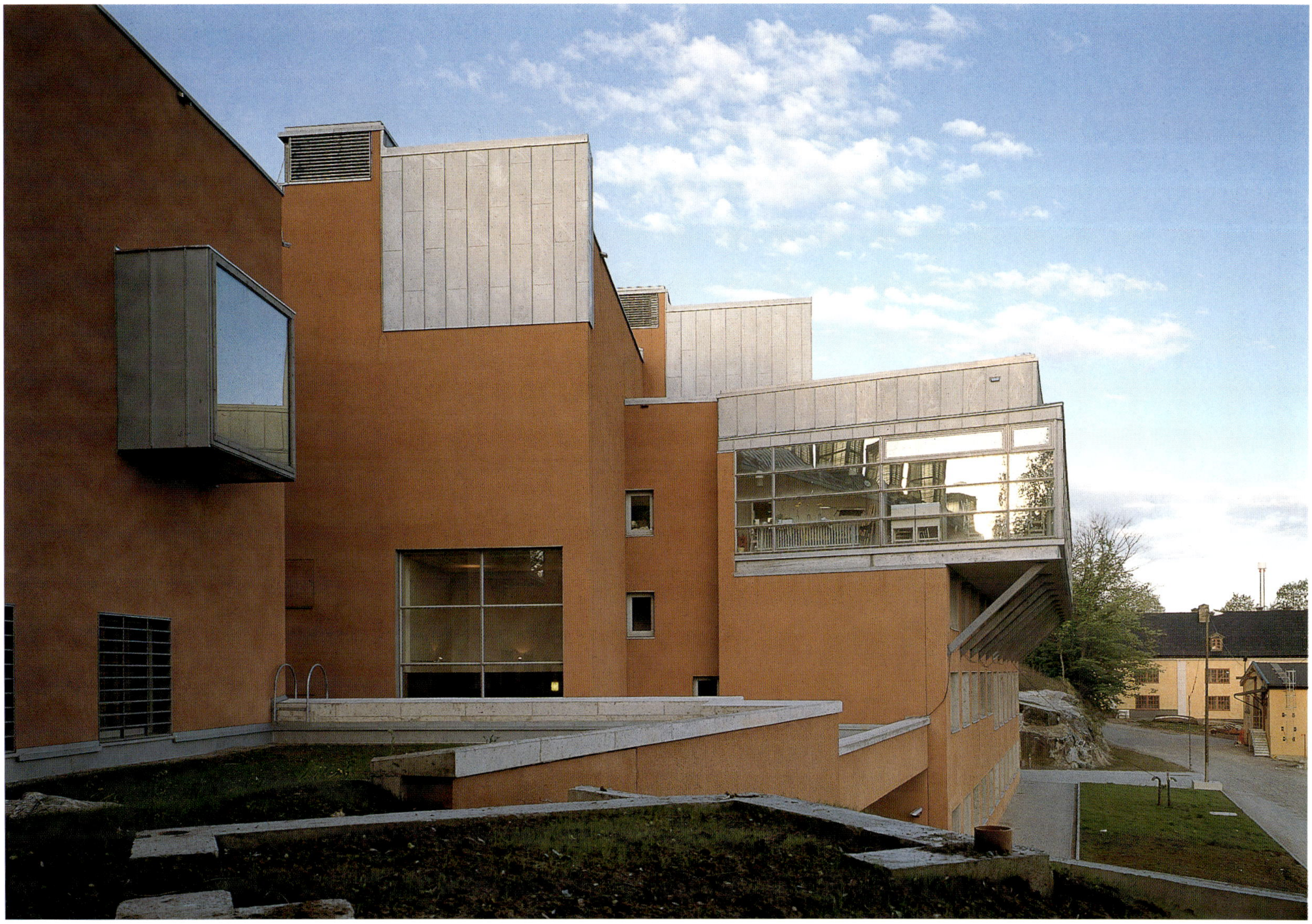

A series of recesses break up the volumes and temper the new museum's impact on the site.

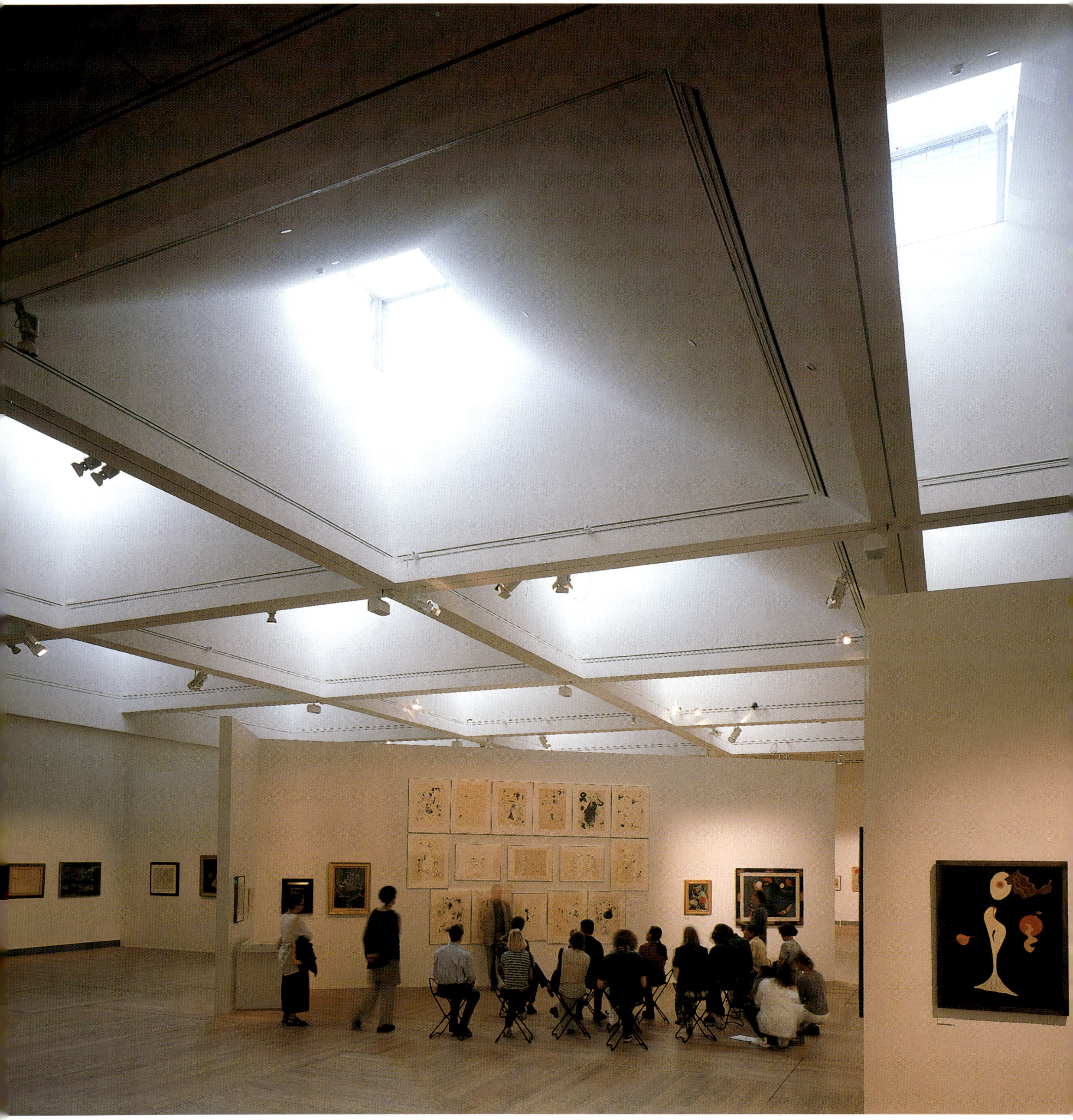

108 Moderna Museet, Stockholm, Sweden

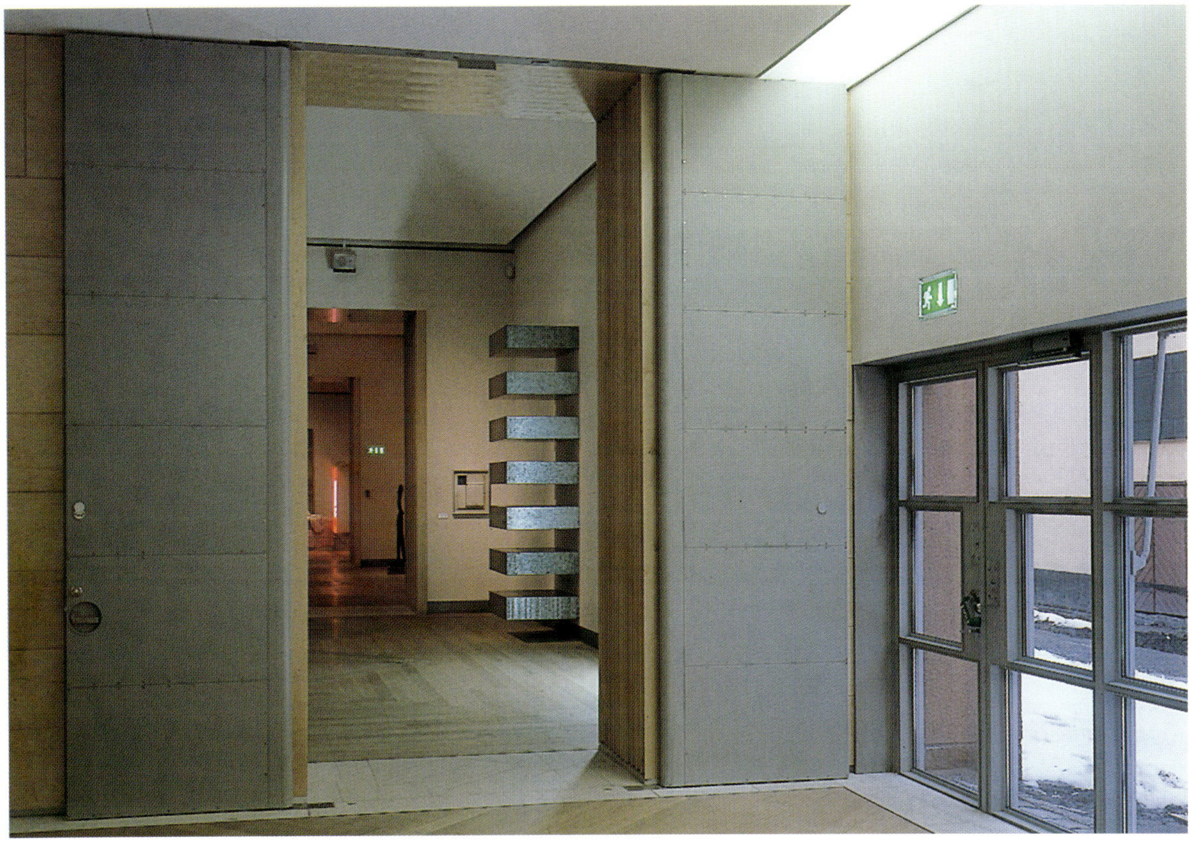

Rigorous design and discreet materials provide a neutral setting for the works.

Opposite page
High ceilings and controlled natural light allow visual comfort and a great flexibility in exhibition methods.

Following pages
The beautiful Surrealist and Dada room: to the right, a replica of the *"Large Glass"* made for the museum by Marcel Duchamp.

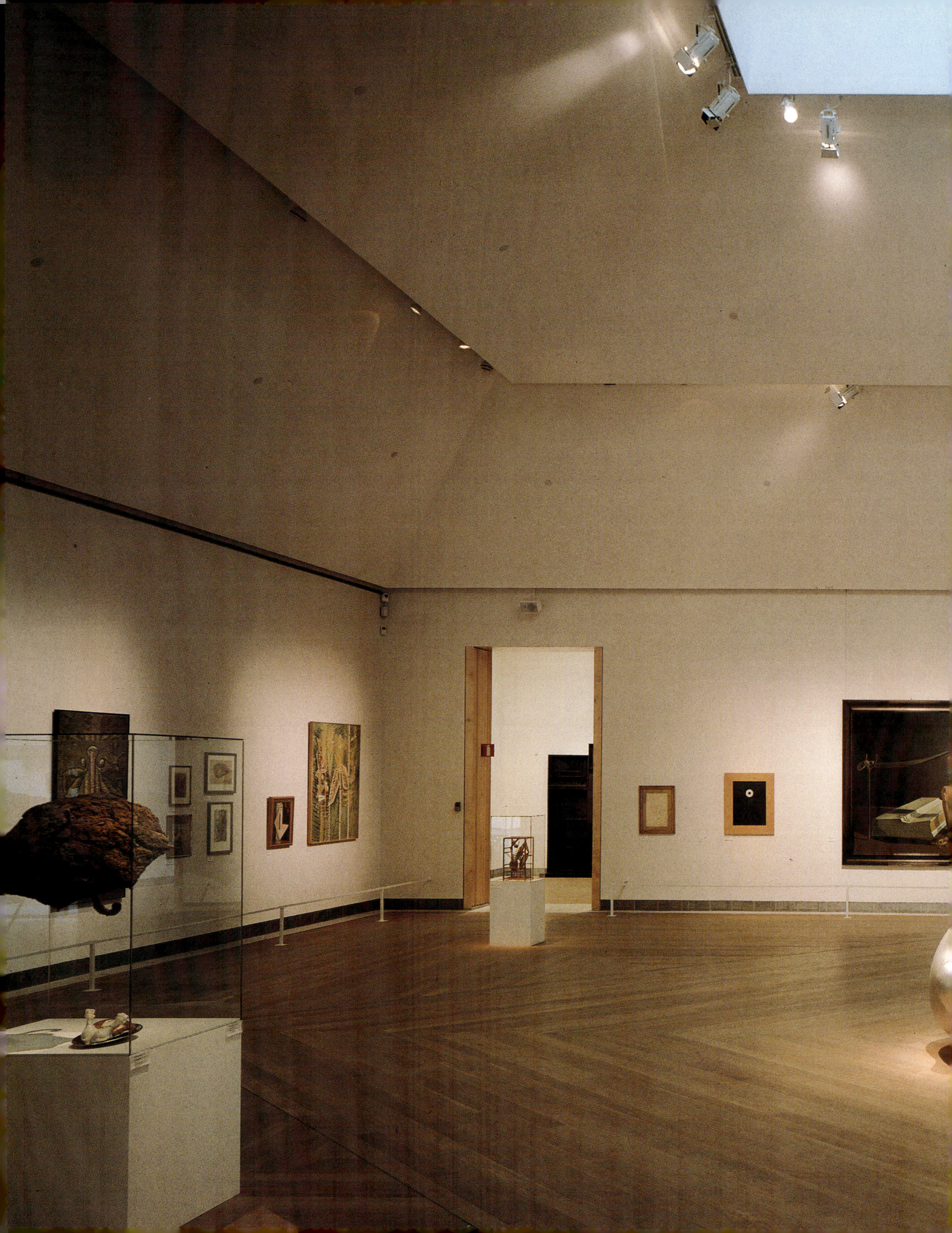

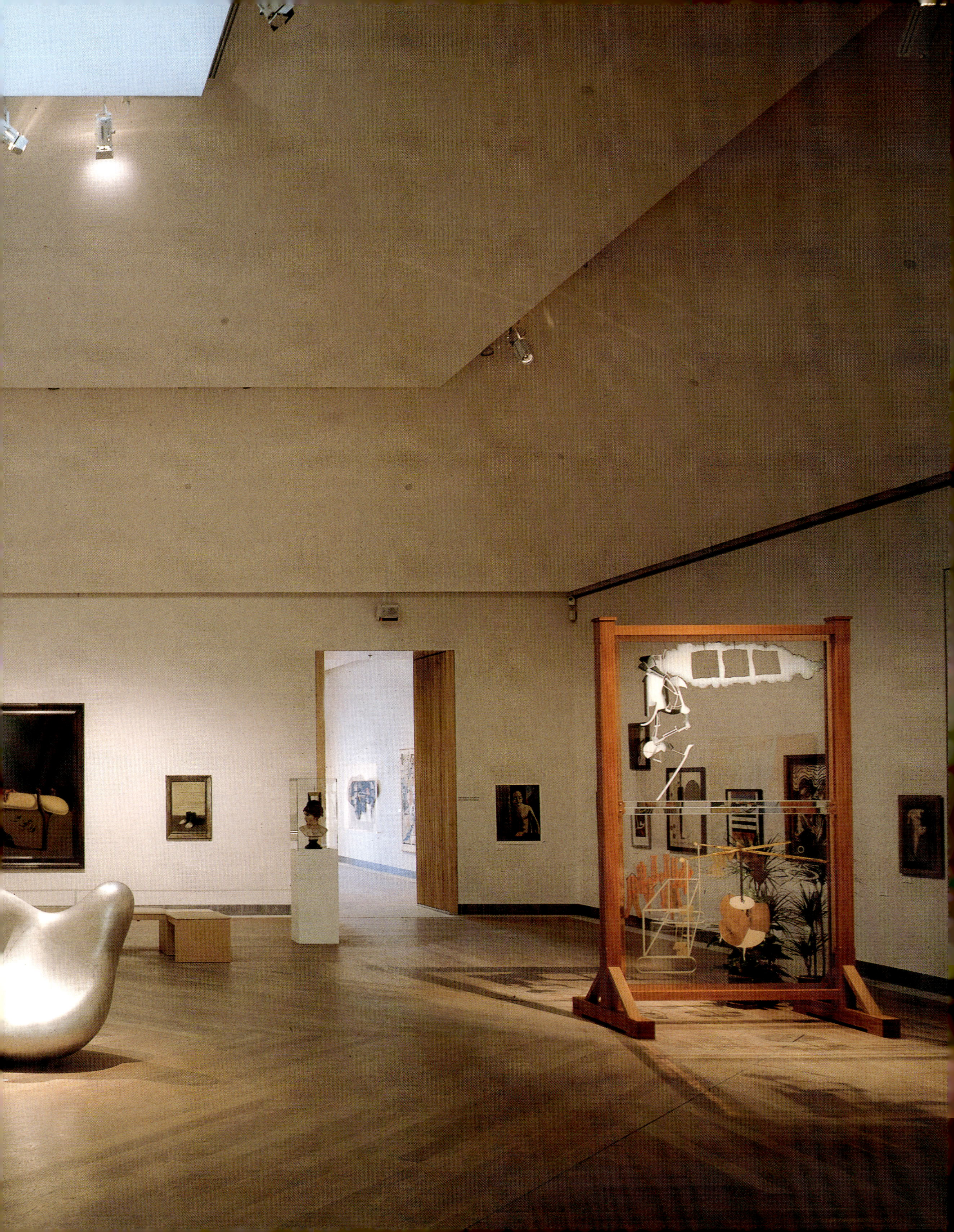

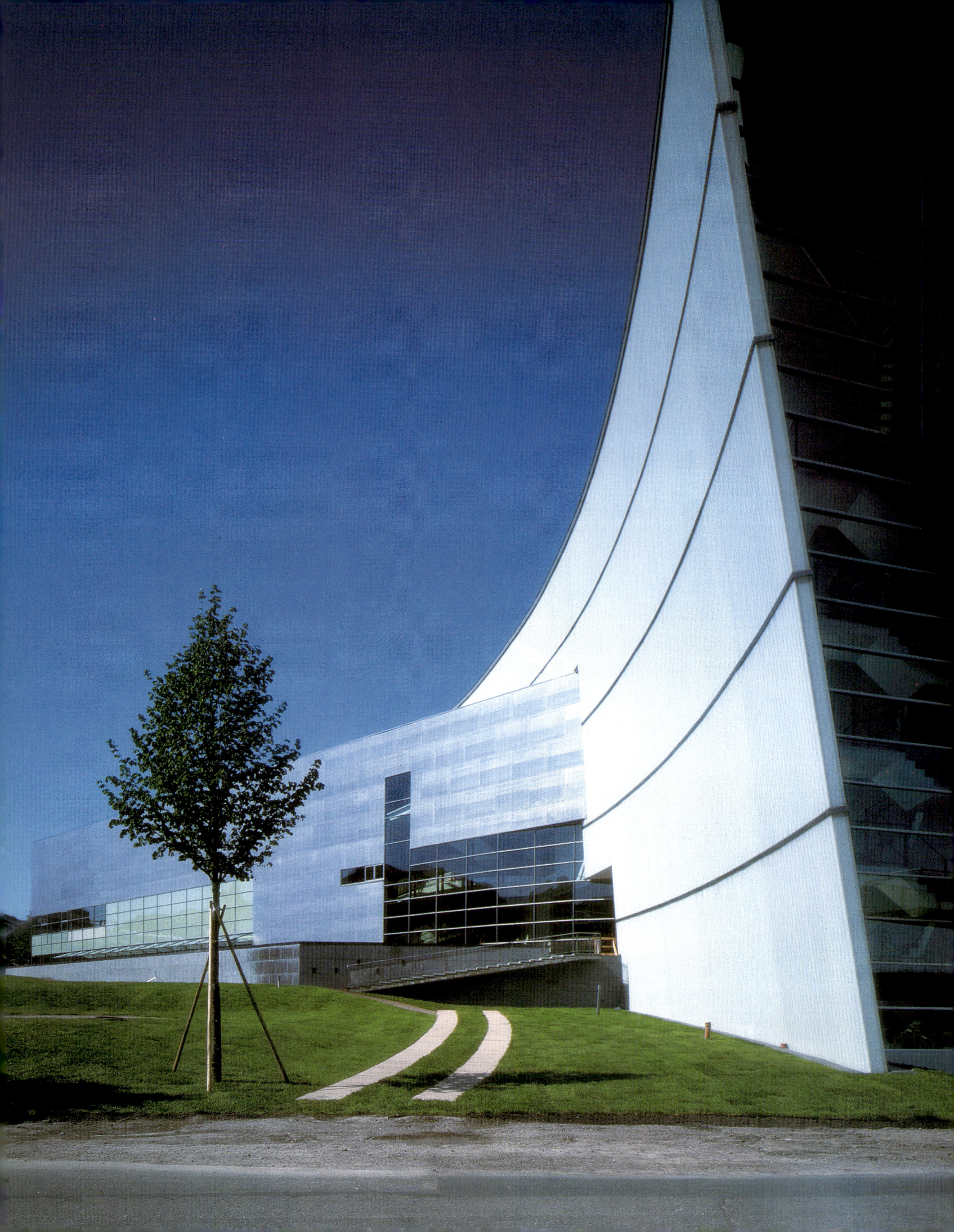

Steven Holl

Kiasma

Helsinki, Finland

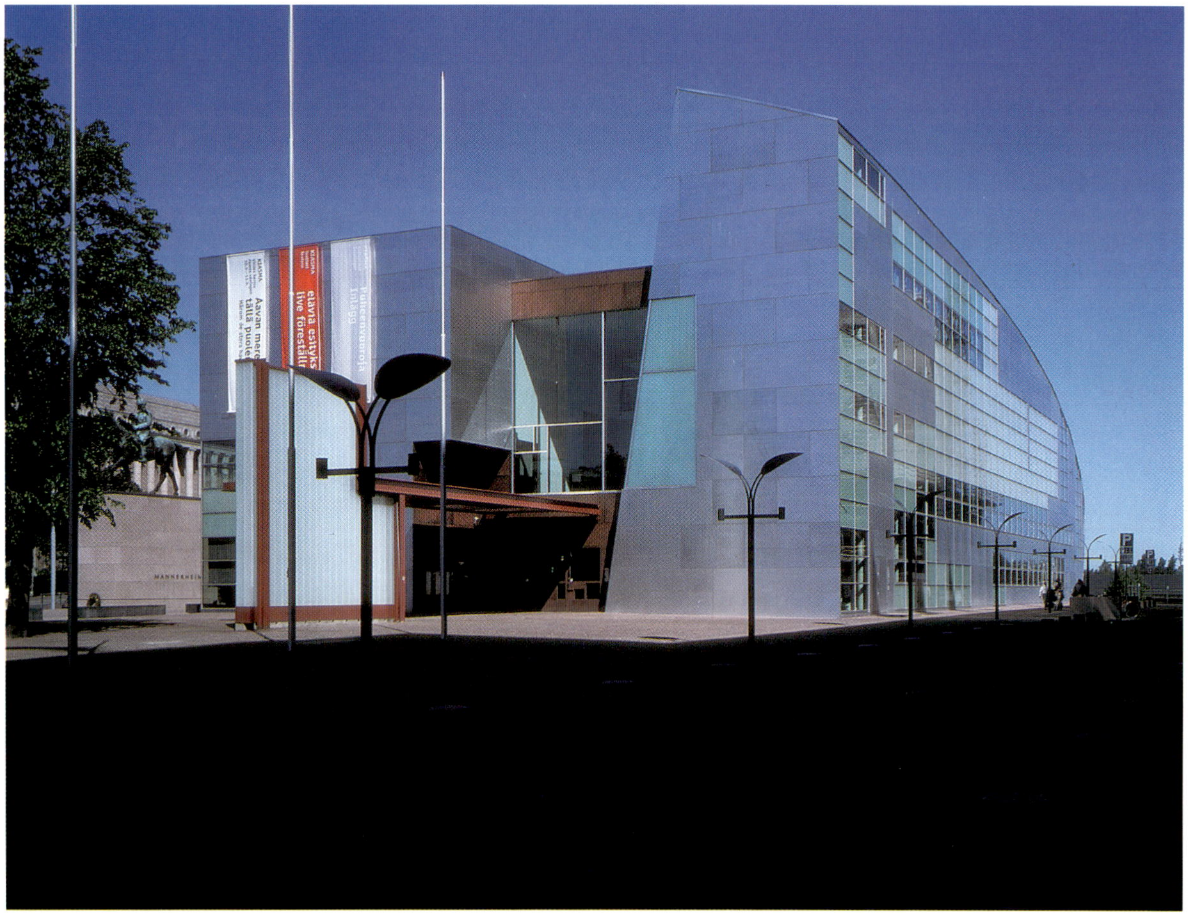

Tightly linked to the cultural and spatial landscape of Helsinki, Steven Holl's edifice works its way in by combining rectangles and curves.

Code name: "Kiasma." It was with this title that American architect Steven Holl won the competition launched by the Finnish government for creating a Museum of Contemporary Art in Helsinki. The rhetorical principle of "chiasma" – a spatial and conceptual intersection – deliberately set the new building in an area of convergence. The sculptural construction fits into a triangle, its furthest point plunging into the urban traffic to the east, not far from the station built in the 19th century by Eliel Saarinen. To the north, the edifice widens out and curves around two axes: a cultural axis joining the cultural center by Alvar Aalto and a natural axis connecting the "Kiasma" to the Töölo Bay.

The intersection of these views and diverse influences is given a certain harmony by bringing the water from the bay through the center of the museum itself. Water crosses the length of the museum before emerging in the open air where it reaches a large rectangular pool built on the west facade. The babbling sound of this rivulet follows the visitor all along his or her visit, interrupted only in winter when the

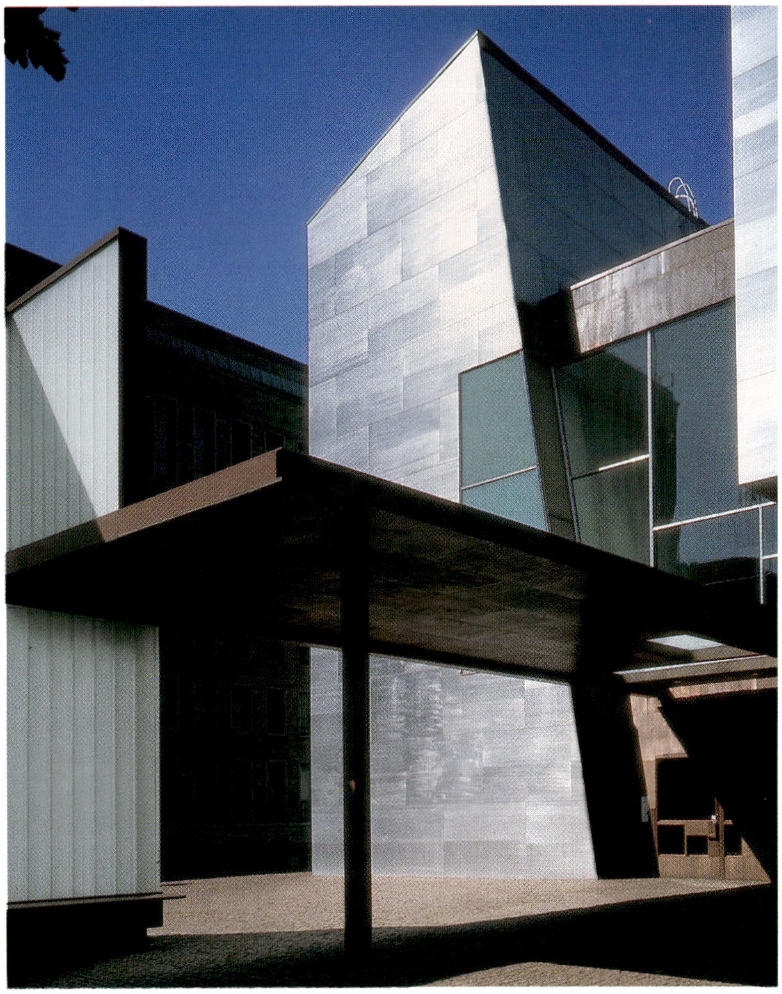

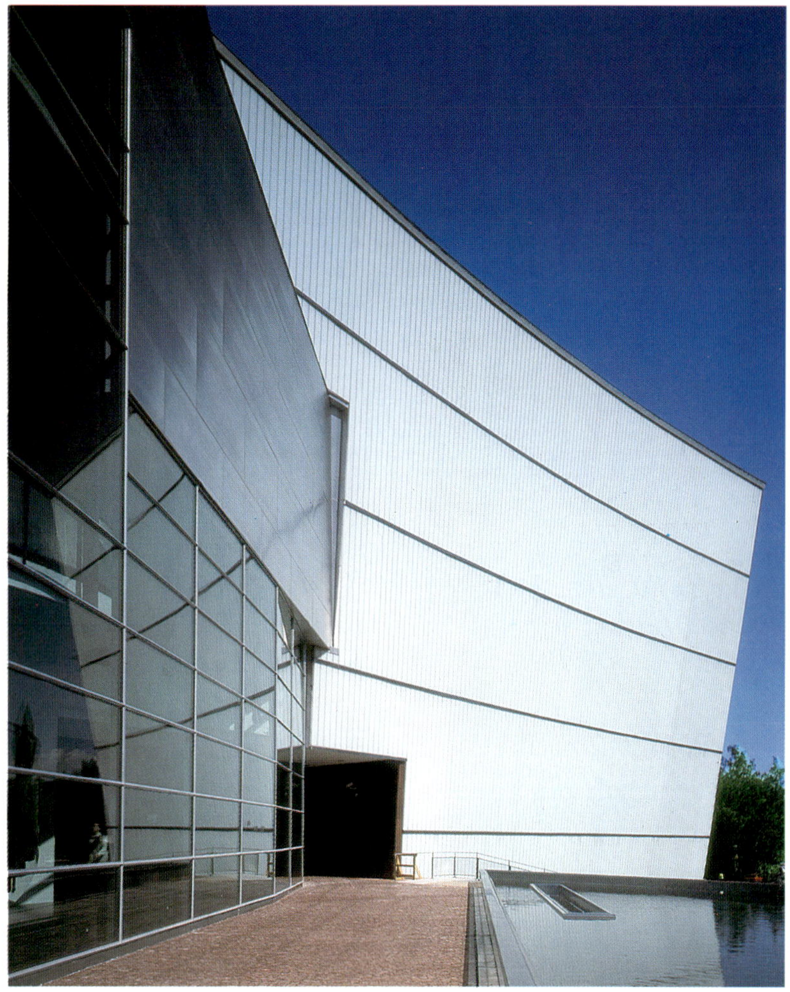

Detail of the principal facade and the canopy leading to the main entrance.
Two views of the west elevation and contiguous long, rectangular basin (right).

Opposite page
North-west facade of the "conch" which opens out here toward the Finlandia Hall and simultaneously follows a natural axis connecting the building to the Töölo Bay.

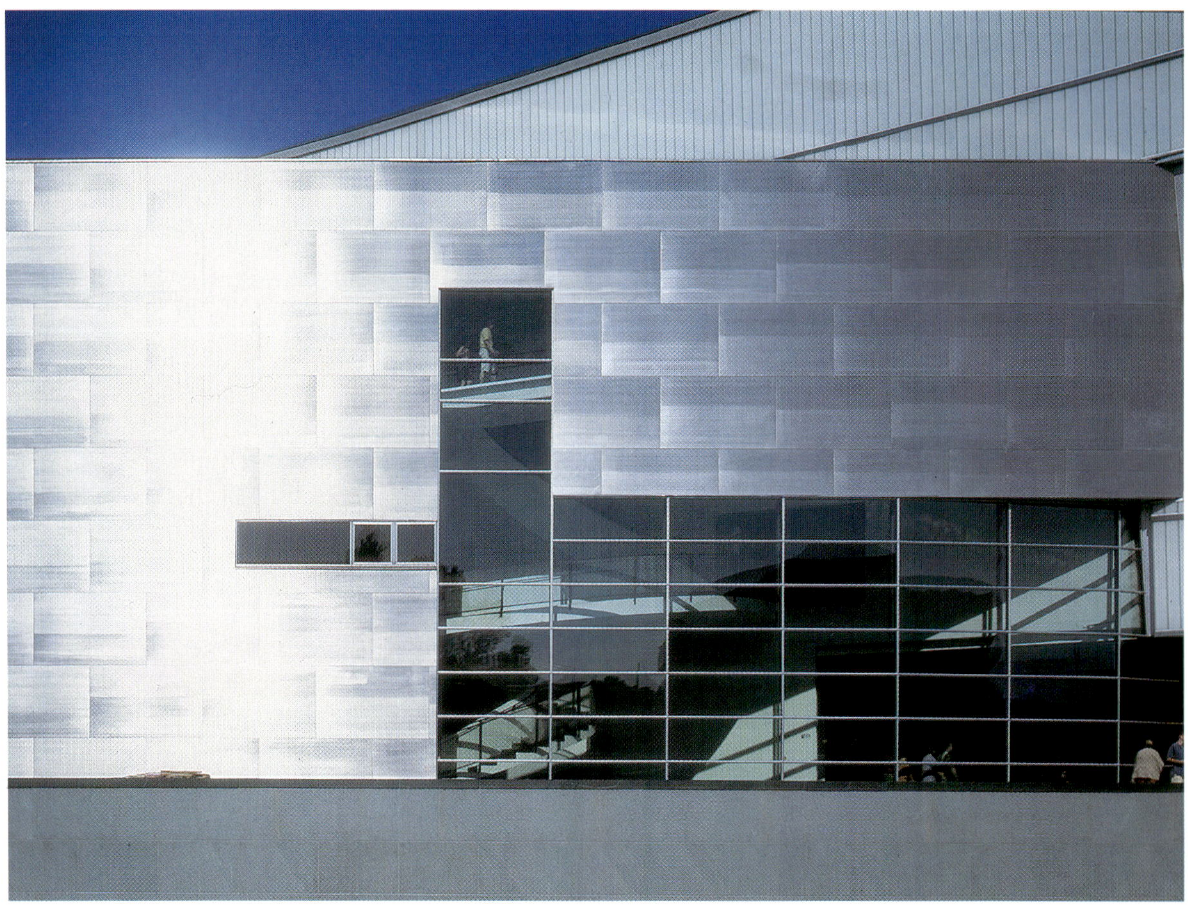

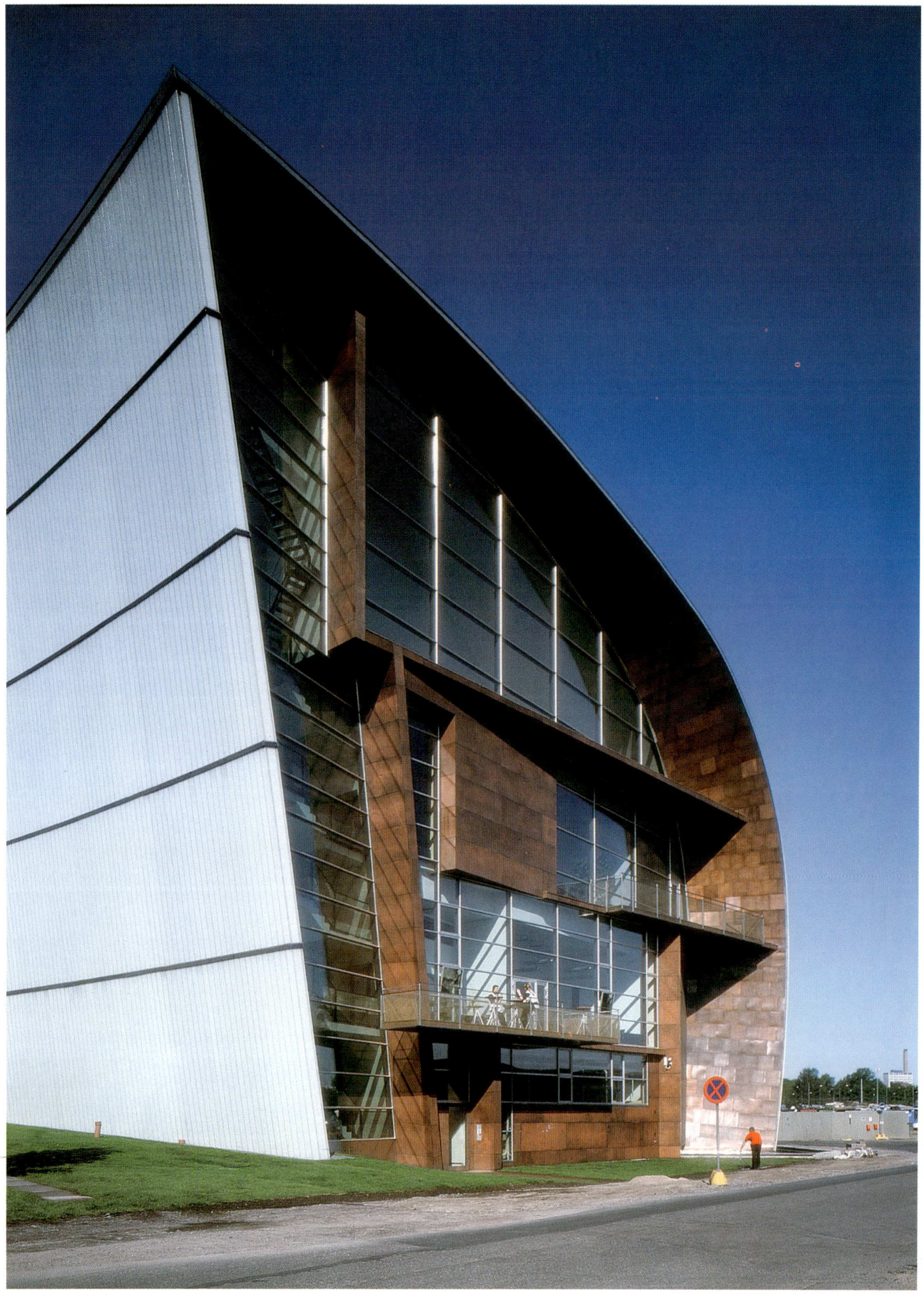

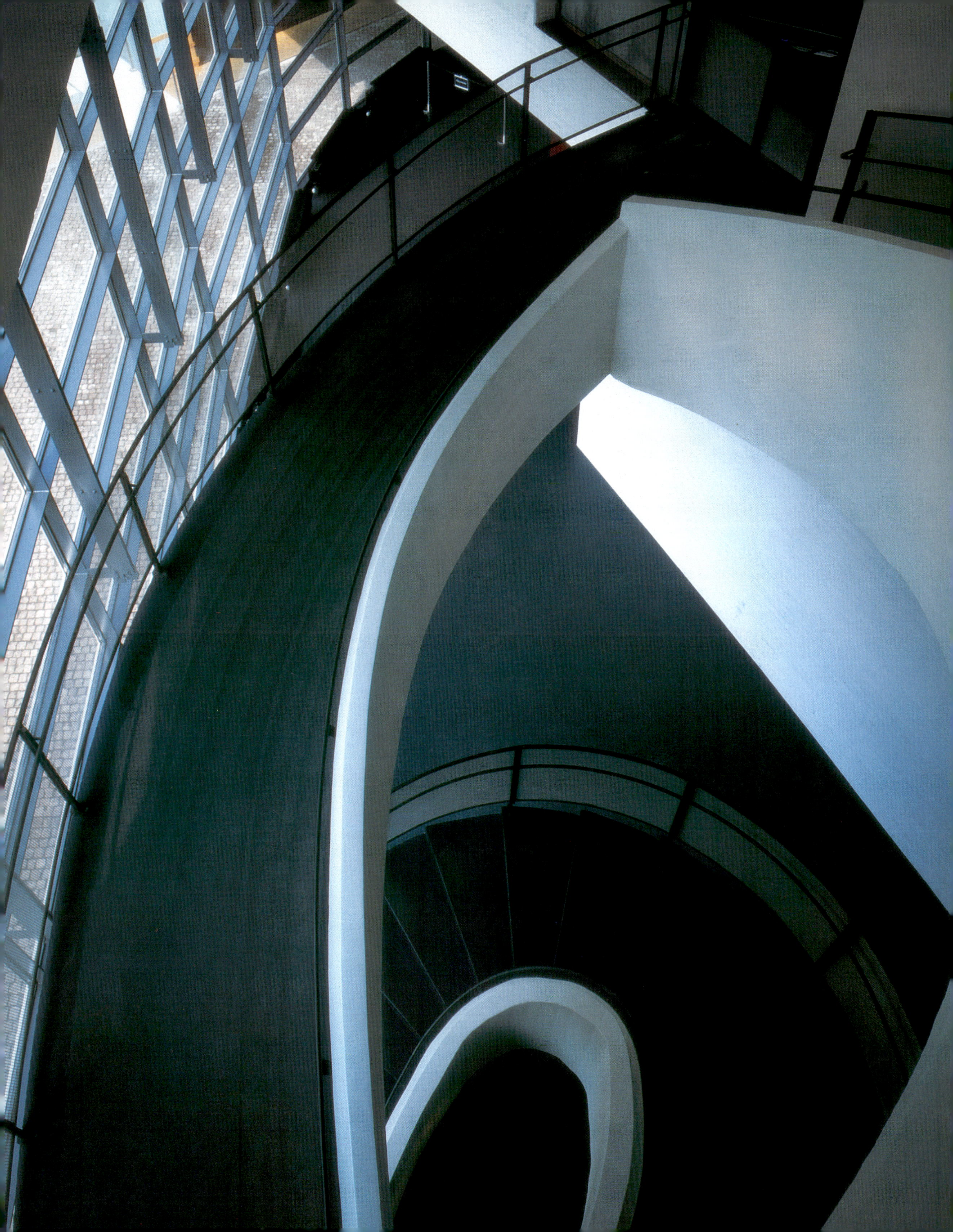

water freezes and the pool, like a mirror of ice, reflects the building lit up at night.

The architecture itself has a remarkable flexibility, attentive to the different currents it integrates and literary gives shape to. The structure is forked, made up of four sides that encompass an overhanging shell open toward the bay. These two components, joined by hallways, enter into a spatial dialogue and, most notably, a play of light. The curved contours of the shell function like a giant solar panel, capturing light by intercepting the horizontal rays of the Nordic sun and distributing them as they rebound off its surface toward the rectangular building. The interior is thus inundated by natural light, diffused by the carefully-angled skylights.

Furthermore, the spatial interplay in the roundness of the shell's walls anticipates the diversity of the artworks. In a deliberately neutral and silent atmosphere, this sequence of curves offers the visitor a continuous unfolding of changes in perspective with a succession of mysterious detours, thus connecting the indoor experience with the overall concept of the "Kiasma."

The same principle governs the functioning of the museum as a whole. Conceived of as an Art Forum, it can adapt to all forms of cultural events from exhibitions, dance performances, concerts to seminars. Even the cafeteria can be transformed into a meeting place for round table discussions or readings. Facing both the entrance hall and the garden, it is equally a place for enjoying the peaceful atmosphere of the nearby bay which, when the visibility is good and in the words of Alvar Aalto, "extends as far as Lapland." In other words, this network of openings and convergence forms a perfect chiasma. □

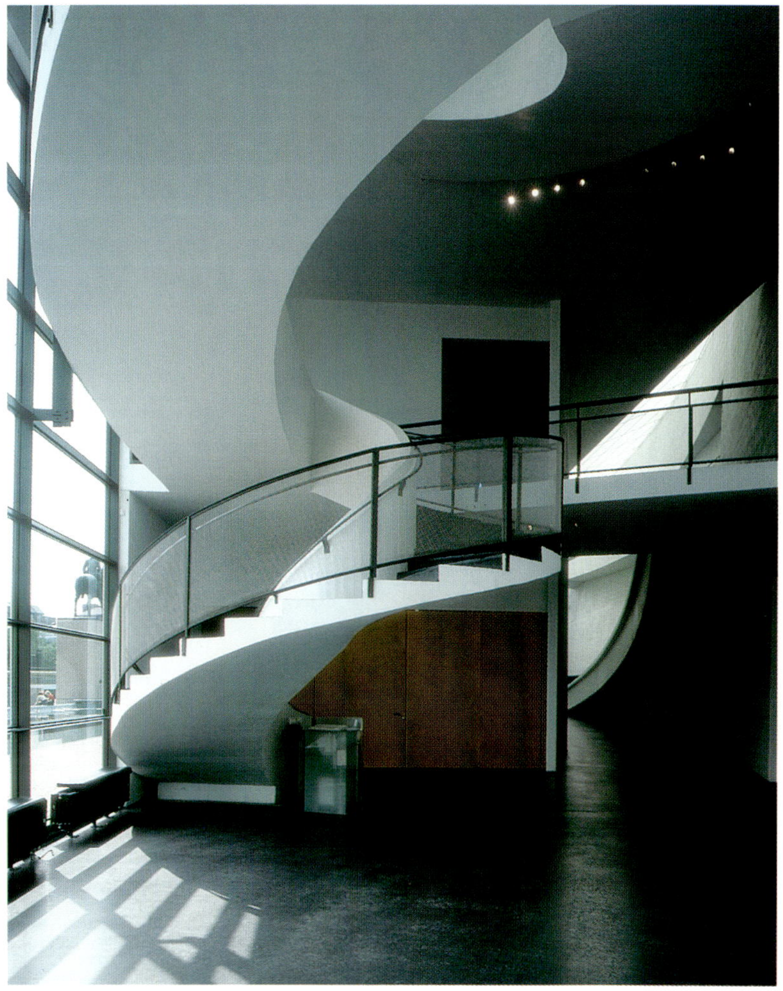

The concept of the curve or rather torsion, as applied to the interior spaces, and in particular, to the twisting and flowing stairways and access ramps.

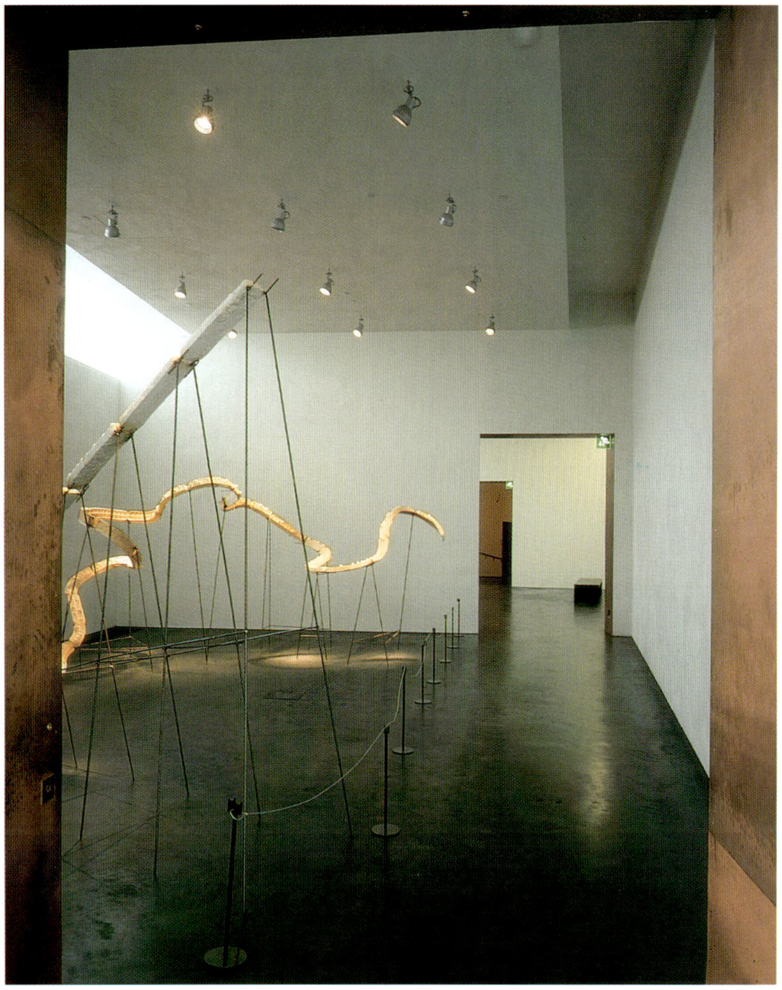

The general nature of the rooms – rectangular with a single curved wall – forms a silent but dramatic exhibition space. From one gallery to the next, slight variations in size and form due to the building's curve, introduce dynamism and surprise.

Following pages
The refractive surface of the "conch" integrates a system of skylights which distribute the light and liven up the neutral mass of the walls.

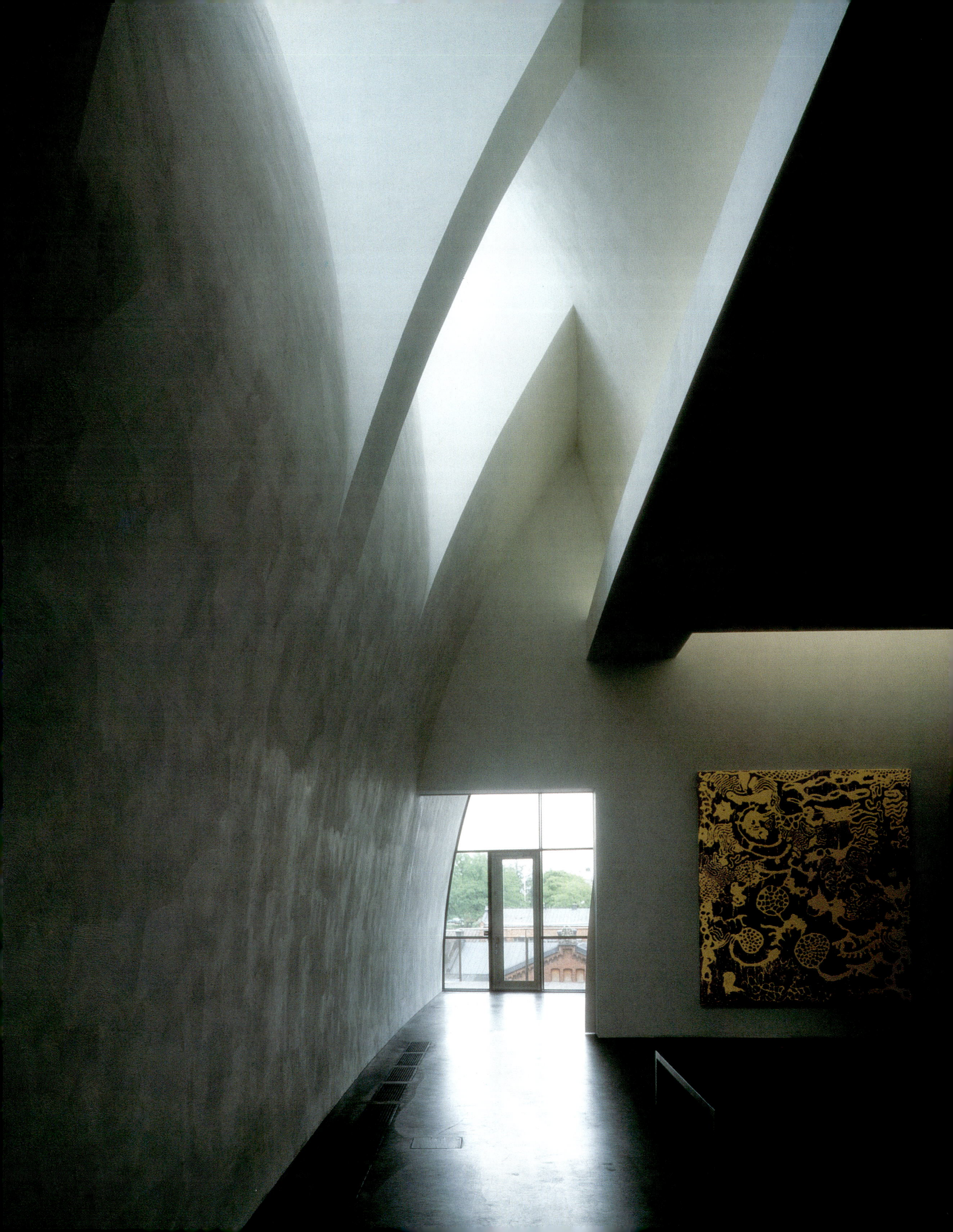

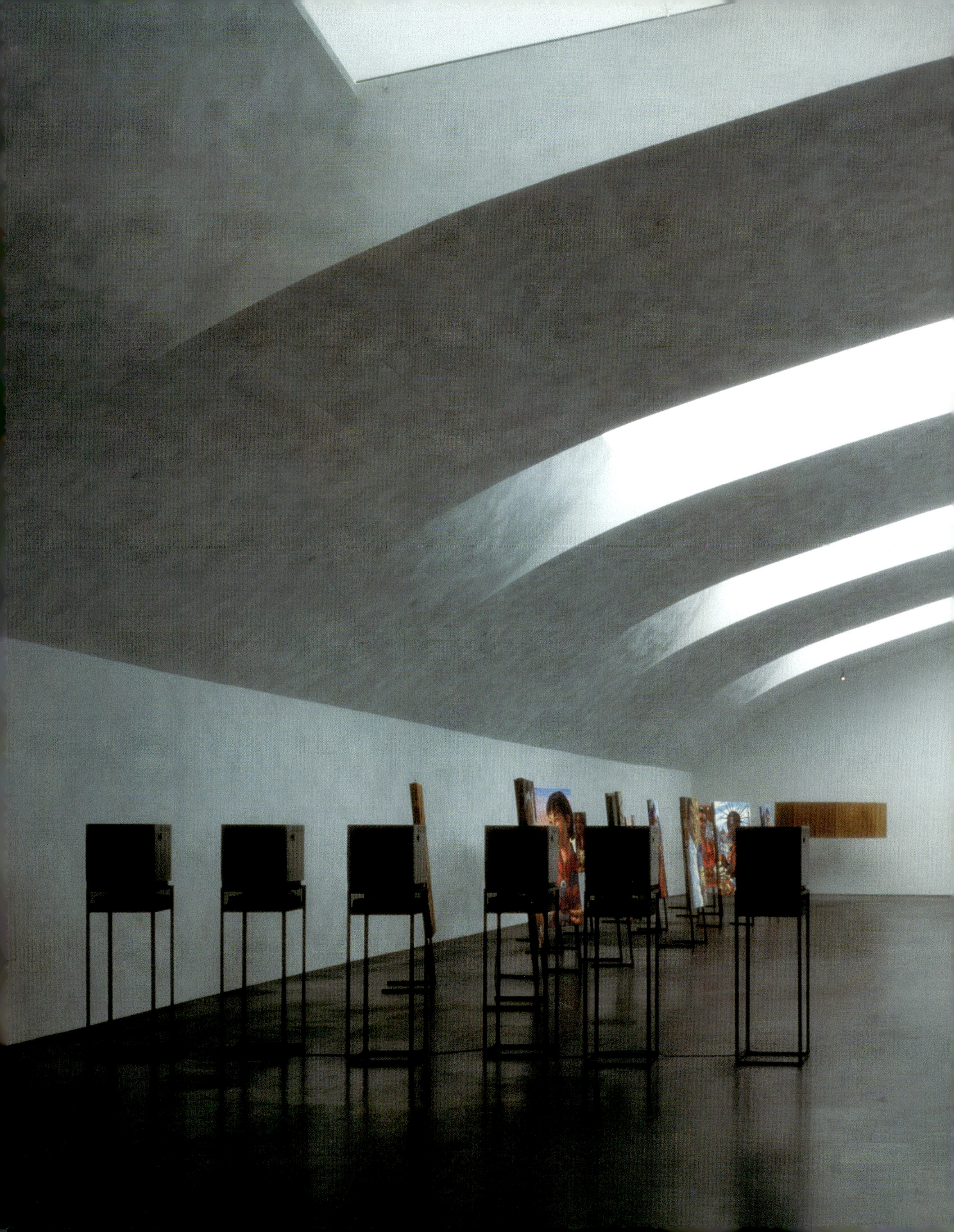

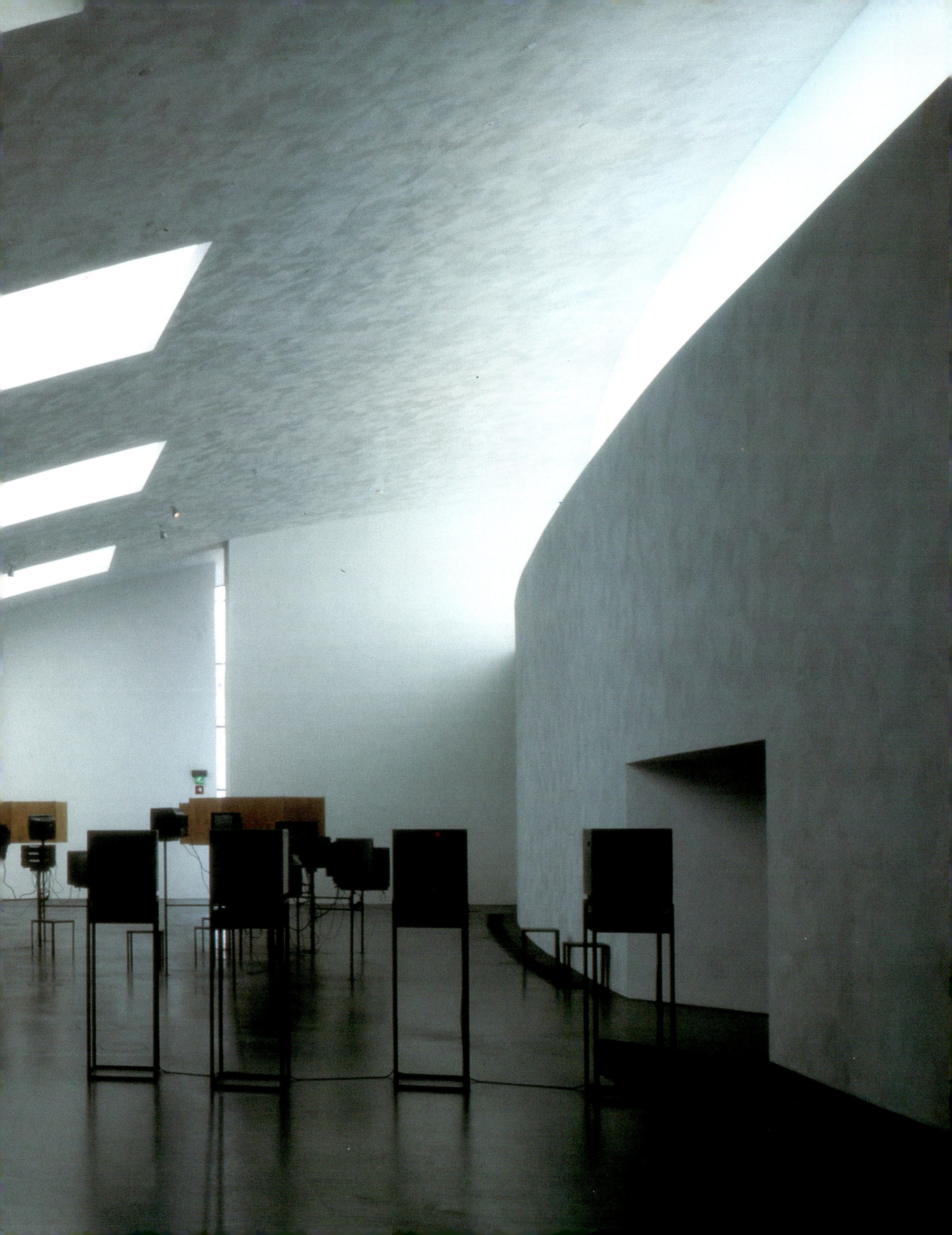

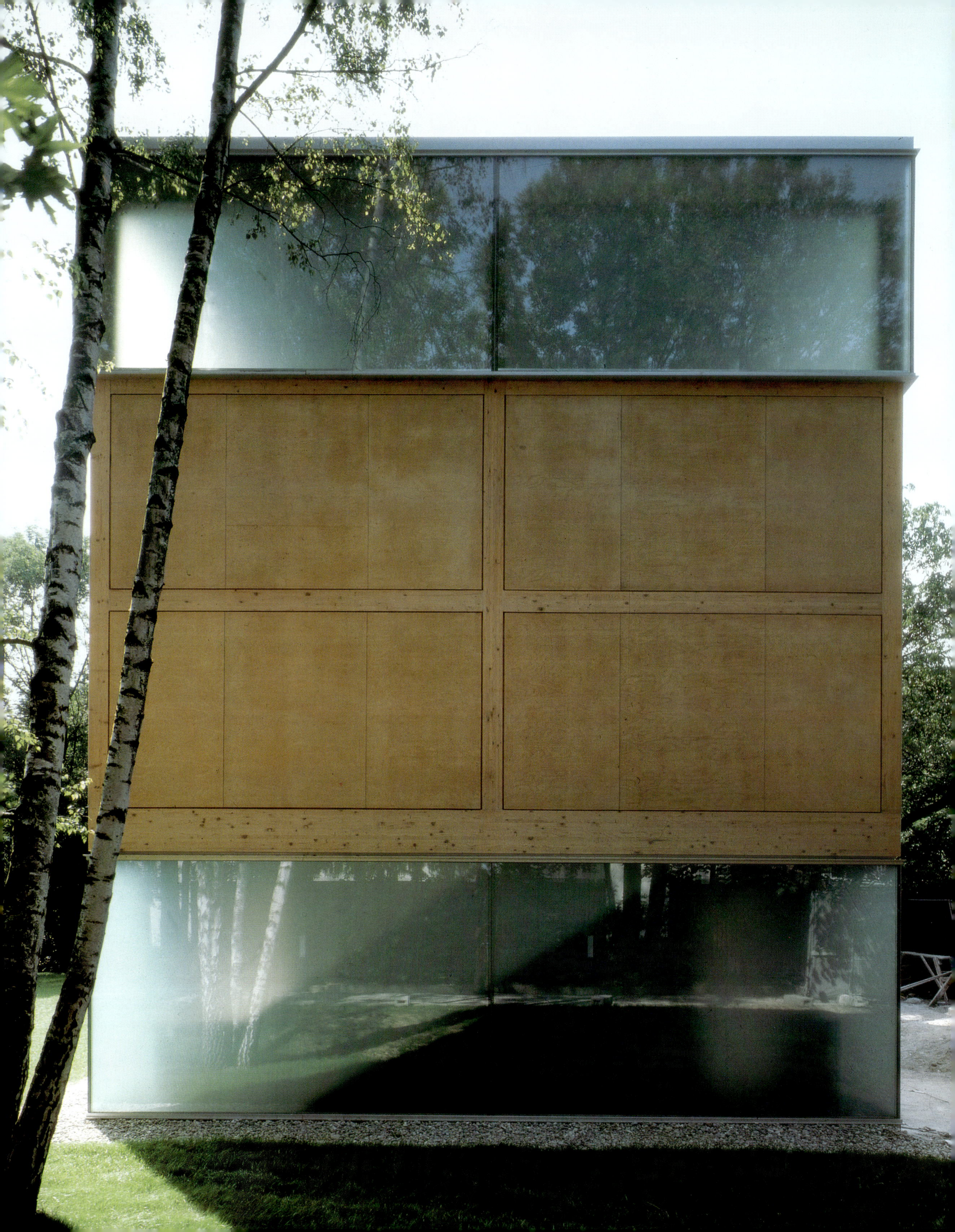

Herzog & de Meuron

Sammlung Goetz

Munich, Germany

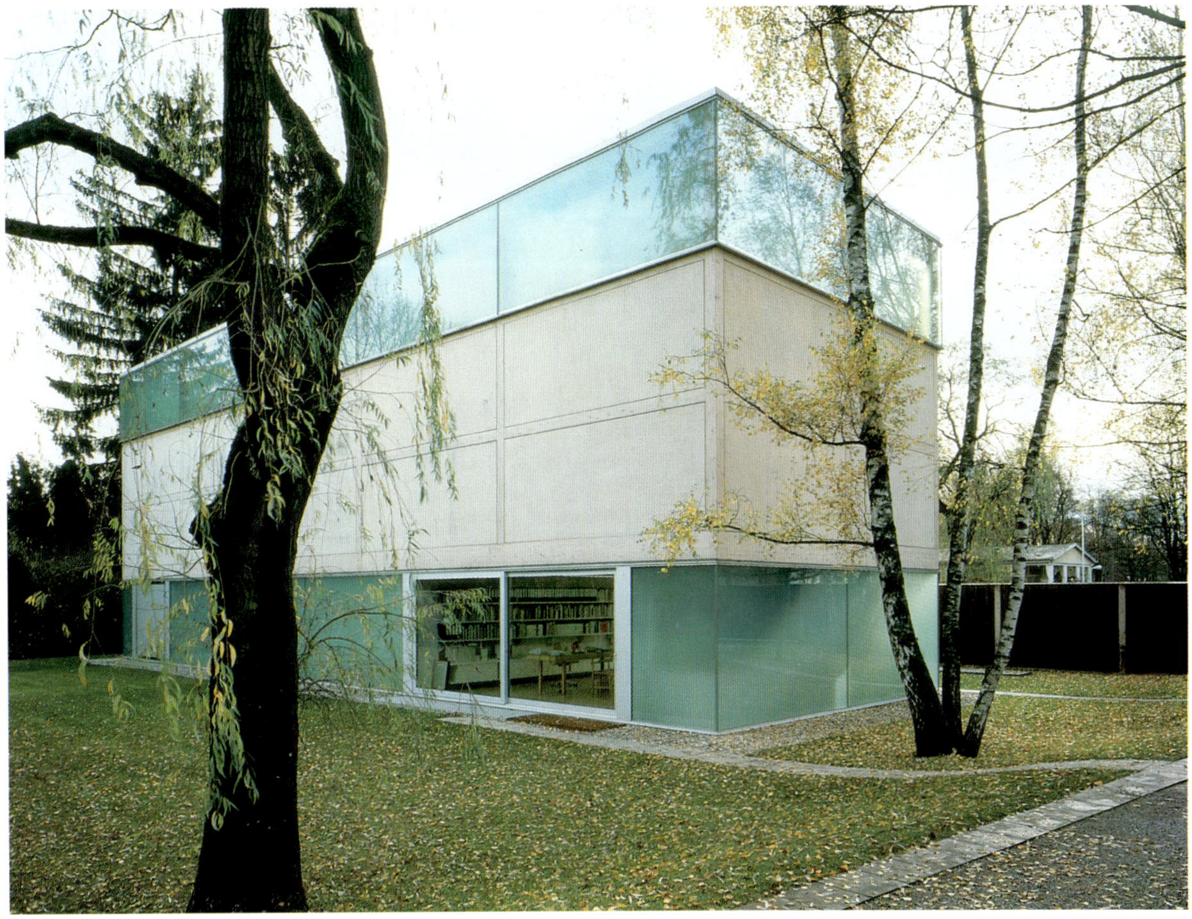

A "shoe box" set in a park: an impression quickly proven wrong by the subtlety of a specific, perfectly geometric object.

Jacques Herzog and Pierre de Meuron have never tried to hide their penchant for art: both could have become artists (or biologists as they like to say) but opted instead for architecture, taking advantage of our times as especially propitious to exchange; besides, architecture is a form of art. Their frequent advisor and collaborator the artist Rémy Zaugg once stated that he is drawn to "strategies and forms capable of making changes in cities and the public domain," a statement that sums up well the vocation of architecture.

This was Herzog and de Meuron's first museological project; they would later win the competition for designing the new Tate Gallery building in London. Their client, a collector in Munich, commissioned this gallery to be built on her private property, dotted with silver birches and pines. The gallery evokes as much an expression of folly as a place for reflection, its architectural aim being to link itself to the artworks, pieces dating from 1960 to today by such demanding artists as Cy Twombly, Robert Ryman, Bruce Nauman or Iannis Kounellis... This intention undoubtedly

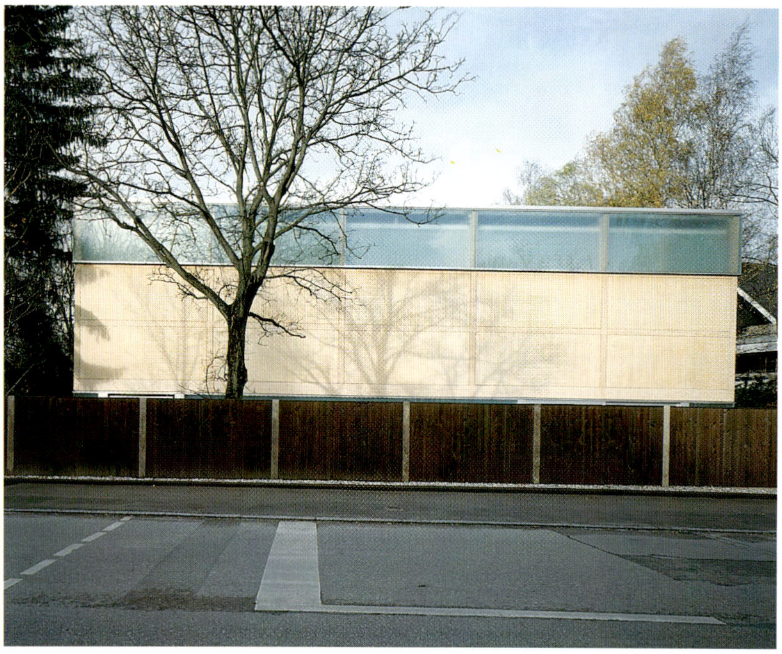

underlies the building's rather austere dignity: a rectangular parallelepiped without the slightest relief. When modernity was going through its crisis with the critics, the construction came to be known as the "shoe box." It is, in fact, made up of two boxes, one on top of the other, the first box half recessed into the ground and the second perched above it. Its spartan design is tempered by a subtle interplay of materials and light: sanded glass framed in aluminum on the garden level and a window encircling the upper part of the building with wide plywood panels at mid level.

This approach of placing a pared down geometric object in an entirely natural setting is in perfect keeping with the architects' open refusal to mark the boundaries between natural and artificial processes. Instead, they view the two as a continuum and not as dialectically opposed. They also see a link between the visible and the invisible world.

Viewed in this light, the Goetz gallery acquires a certain ambiguity and its status as a specific object or simple container glimmering uncertainly among the full-grown trees becomes unclear: the mystery, it seems, is greater than its tangible, physical incarnation. An old trick of (modern) art is to know how deep to bury a mystery if you intend it to be uncovered. □

View from the street: a mute, intriguing object.

Opposite page
The glow softened by bands of sanded glass and the fugitive vision of the library hint at the building's function.

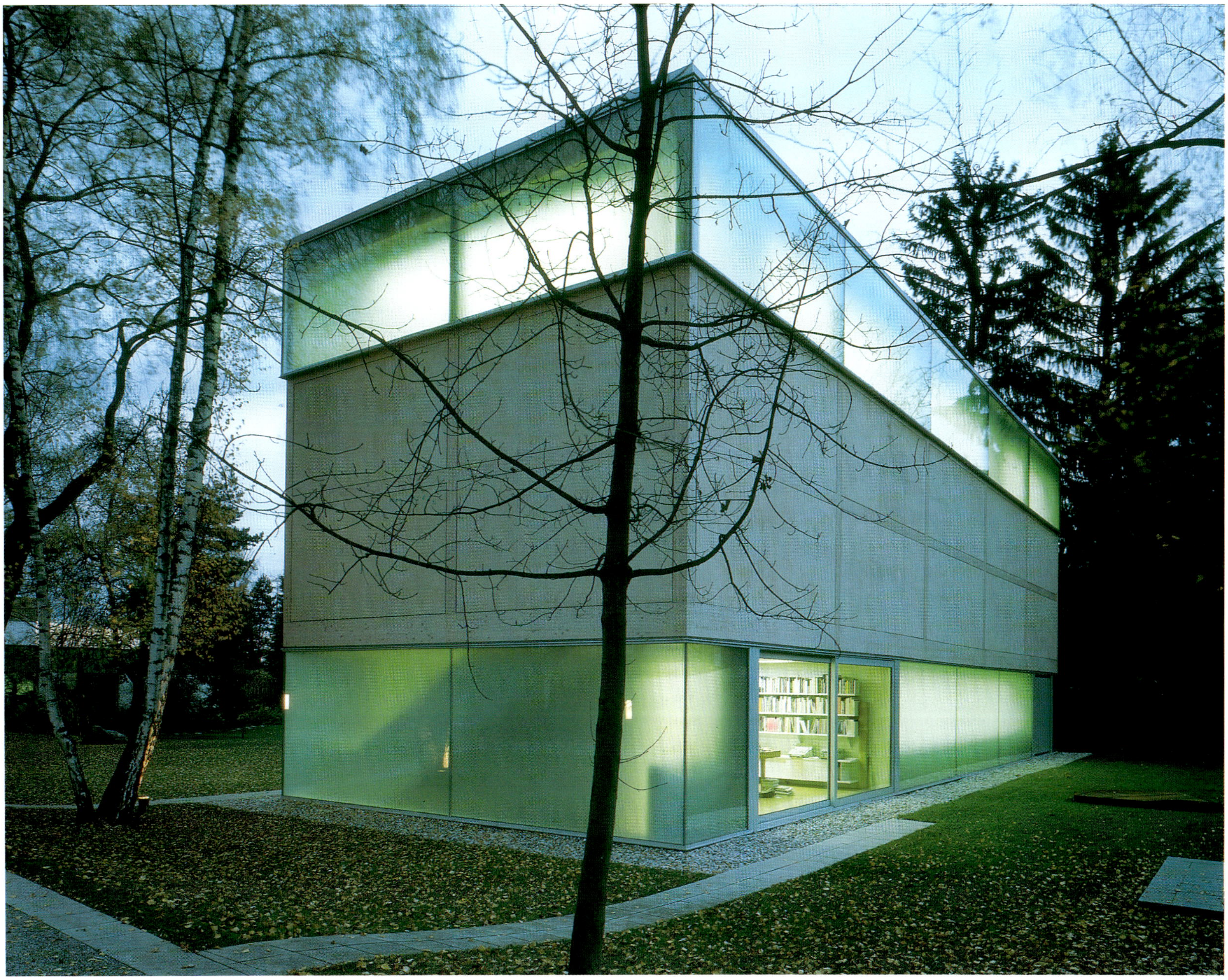

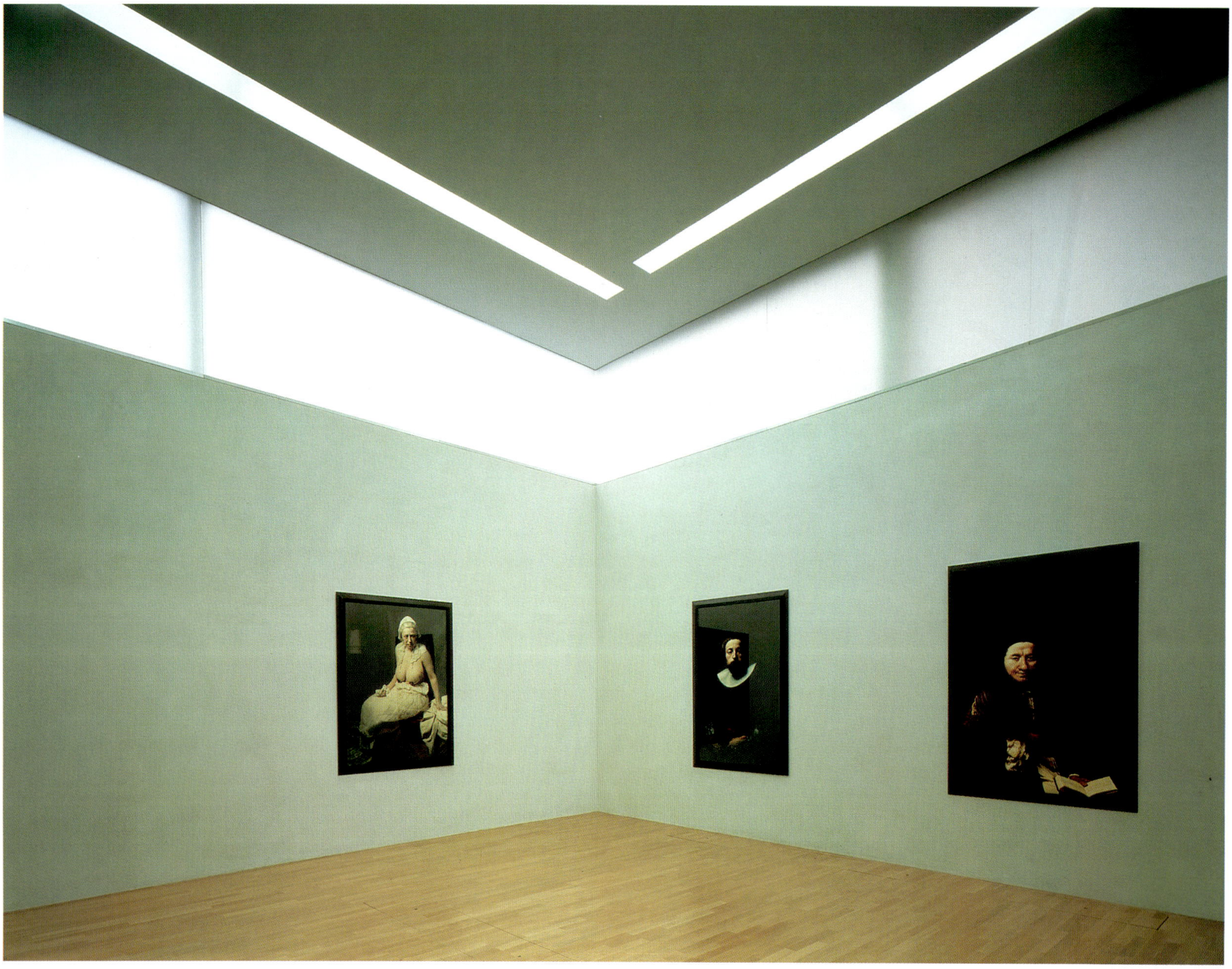

The natural lighting of the spaces is enhanced by a continuous band of sanded glass at the top of the walls. Here, the room devoted to Cindy Sherman.

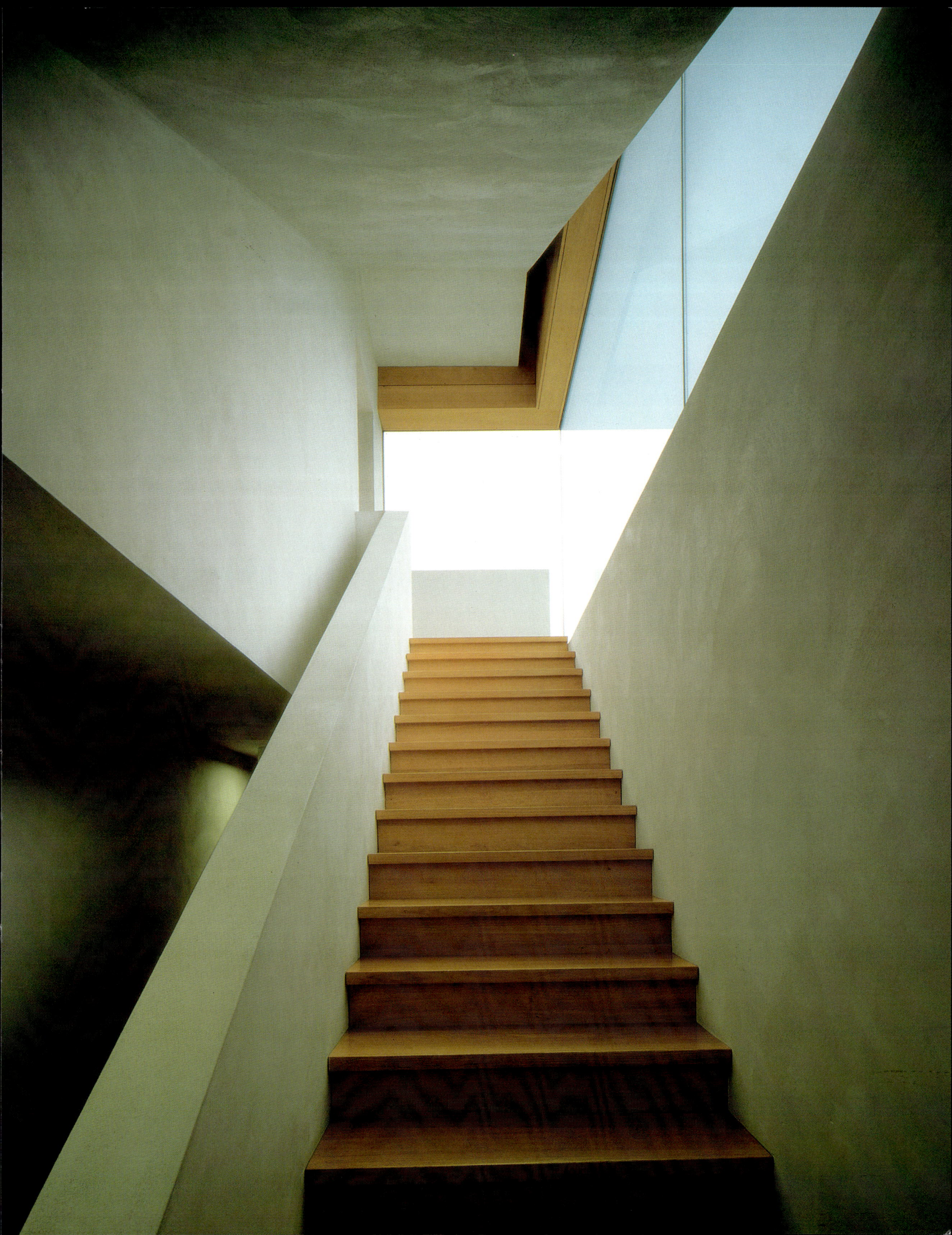

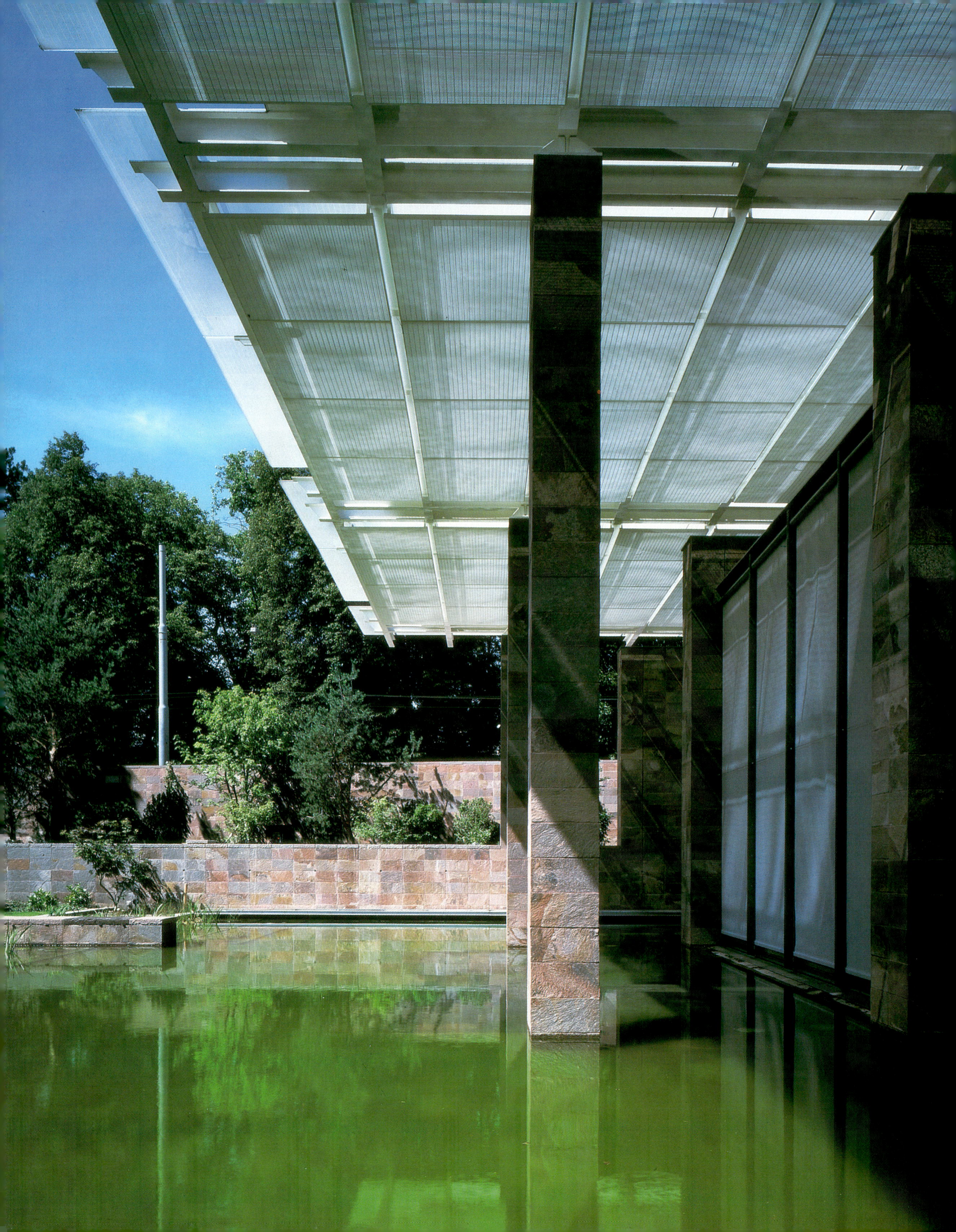

Renzo Piano

Fondation Beyeler

Basel, Switzerland

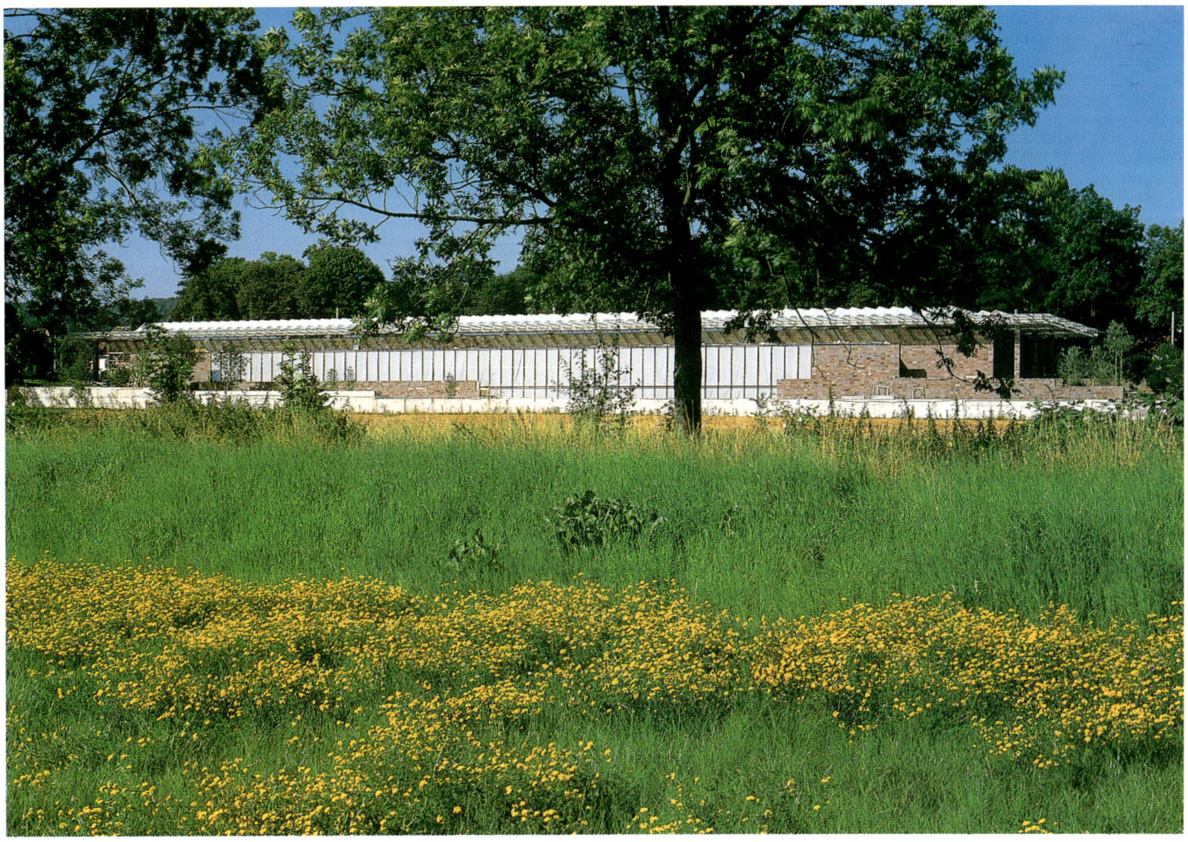

Art as an expression of "Joie de vivre": theme of the inaugural exhibition of this new museum of contemporary art and the credo of its founders, Hildy and Ernst Beyeler. Creative work is in keeping with a sort of natural harmony, which Piano transcribed in this oblong building replete with transparency, opening upon views of the aquatic garden and the surrounding park.

Over the last fifty years, the art dealers Hildy and Ernst Beyeler from Basel have amassed an impressive art collection comprised of works they simply could not part with. Their gallery's success has gained international recognition, holding exhibitions as early as 1940. Due to their active involvement in the arts, they were able to develop close ties with important artists of this century, acquiring some of their best works including *Improvisation 10*, a major work by Wassily Kandinsky from 1910, not to mention a group of paintings by Klee and several Picassos. With the quality and scope of this collection, offering an overall look at the modern classics and grouping some 160 paintings, all that remained was to find it a permanent home and make it accessible to the public. The project was realized in 1997 with the inauguration of the Beyeler Foundation which received a gracious welcome from the commune of Riehen near Basel. The new museum takes up a charming site in the Berower park, its administrative offices and restaurant housed in the 18th-century Berower Villa. Financed by the Foundation, the museum's design was entrusted to the Genoise architect Renzo Piano in 1991.

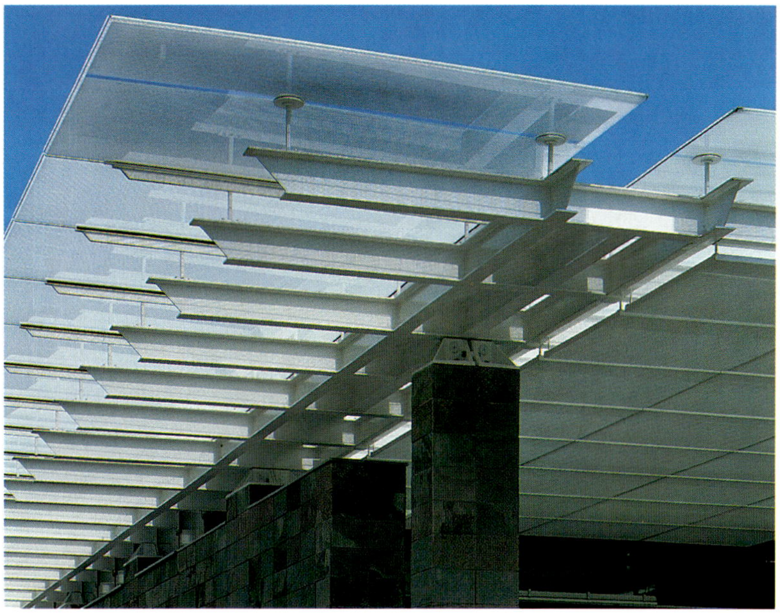

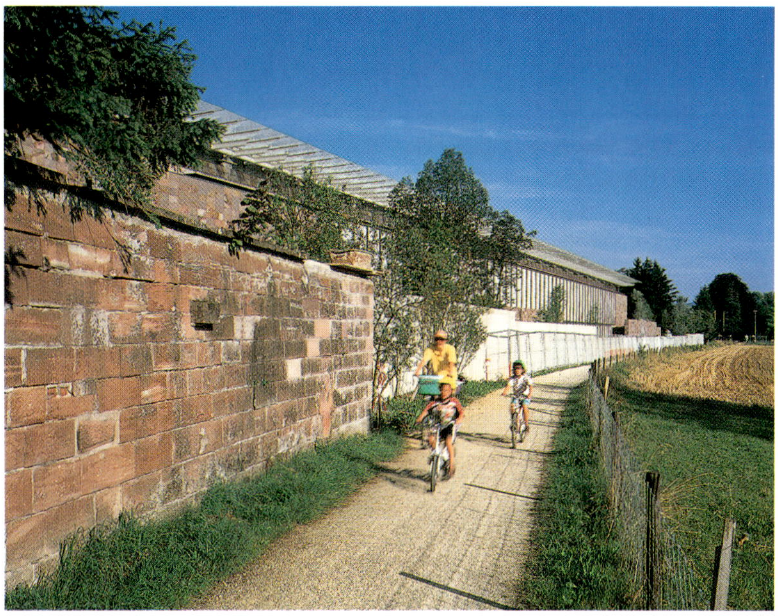

The bucolic feeling of the Beyeler Foundation site – already designated in the 18th century as a garden and transformed in the next century into an English-style garden by landscape designer Caillat – inspired Piano to use greenhouse architecture. Large glass walls and red porphyry-clad facades. Immense glass roof, with sun screens in redans articulated upon a steel structure painted white: this aerial cover allows natural light to pour into all the interior spaces.

Piano opted for a reserved style "to serve art, and not the other way round." Set in a bucolic setting, this oblong building adopts the simple elegance of a garden greenhouse. It is characterized by two striking elements: walls clad in red Patagonian porphyry and an immense aerial glass roof measuring 4,000 square meters (36,000 square feet). The interior, supported by four parallel load-bearing walls, is divided up into long bays at distances of about 7 meters (21 feet). The two glass frontal facades offer views of the English-style gardens. The side facing the street is protected by a windowless wall joining the outside wall of the library and cloakrooms. The opposite longitudinal facade houses a winter garden.

All the main exhibition halls are on the first floor and arranged perpendicularly to the bays, each hall measuring about 7 x 11 meters (21 x 34 feet) and some even larger. Here again, the architect opted for a strict simplicity: white walls with openings allowing the visitor to look from one hall to the next; light-colored French oak floors and a few rest benches in the same wood. To favor a constant dialogue with contemporary artists, a third of the first floor is reserved for itinerant exhibitions to take place alongside the permanent collection or in a space installed below for multiple uses.

Probably the strongest point of this building is its exceptional lighting. The immense glass roof, complete with sunscreens set at an angle, allows natural light to filter into the interior without resorting to homogenizing the daylight with fanlights. Furthermore, a support of three systems with artificial light sources illuminates the rooms when the daylight is insufficient. The Beyeler Foundation thus offers a new museological space to the cultural capital of Basel – or very close by – benefiting from the city's annual contribution of a third of the museum's running costs. □

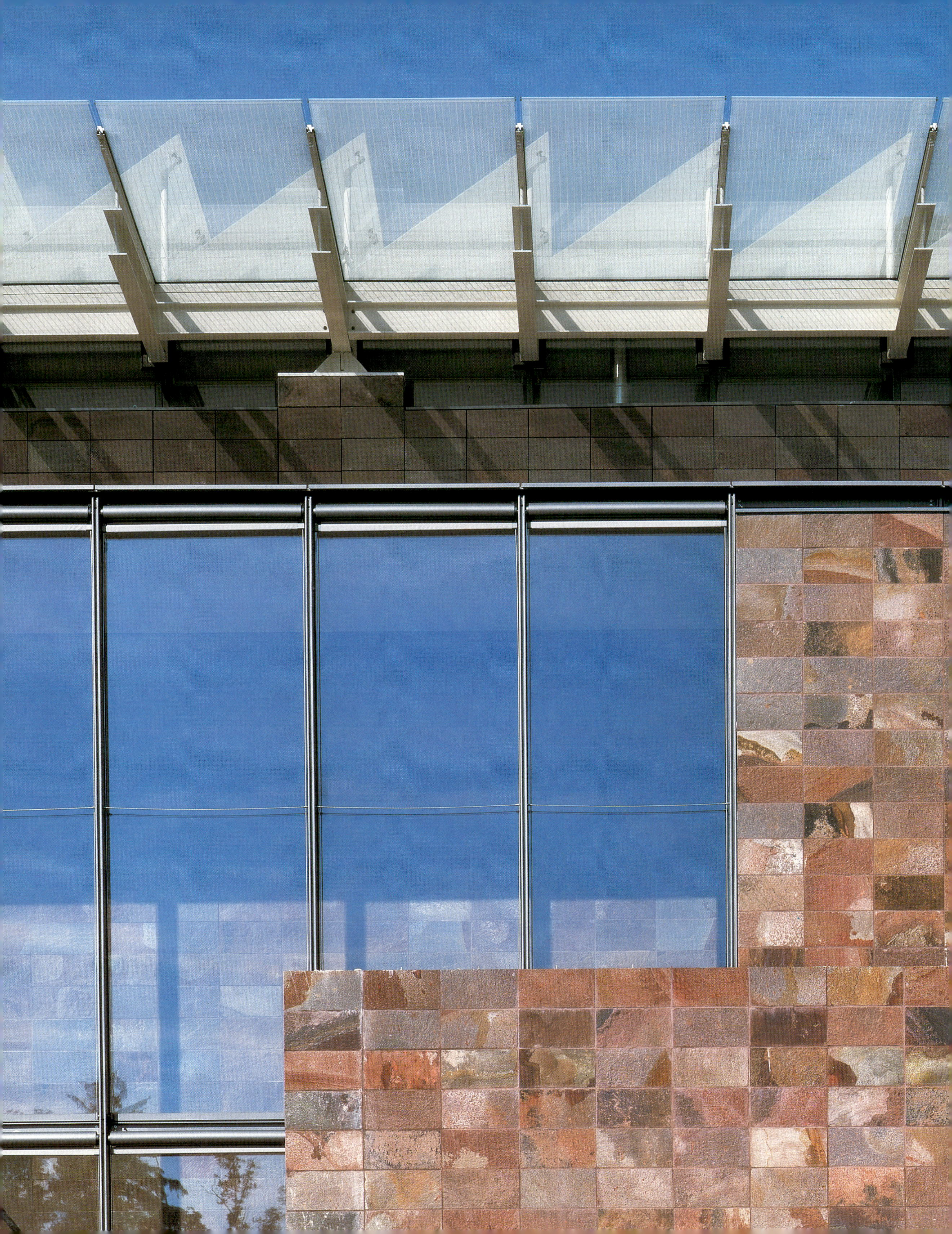

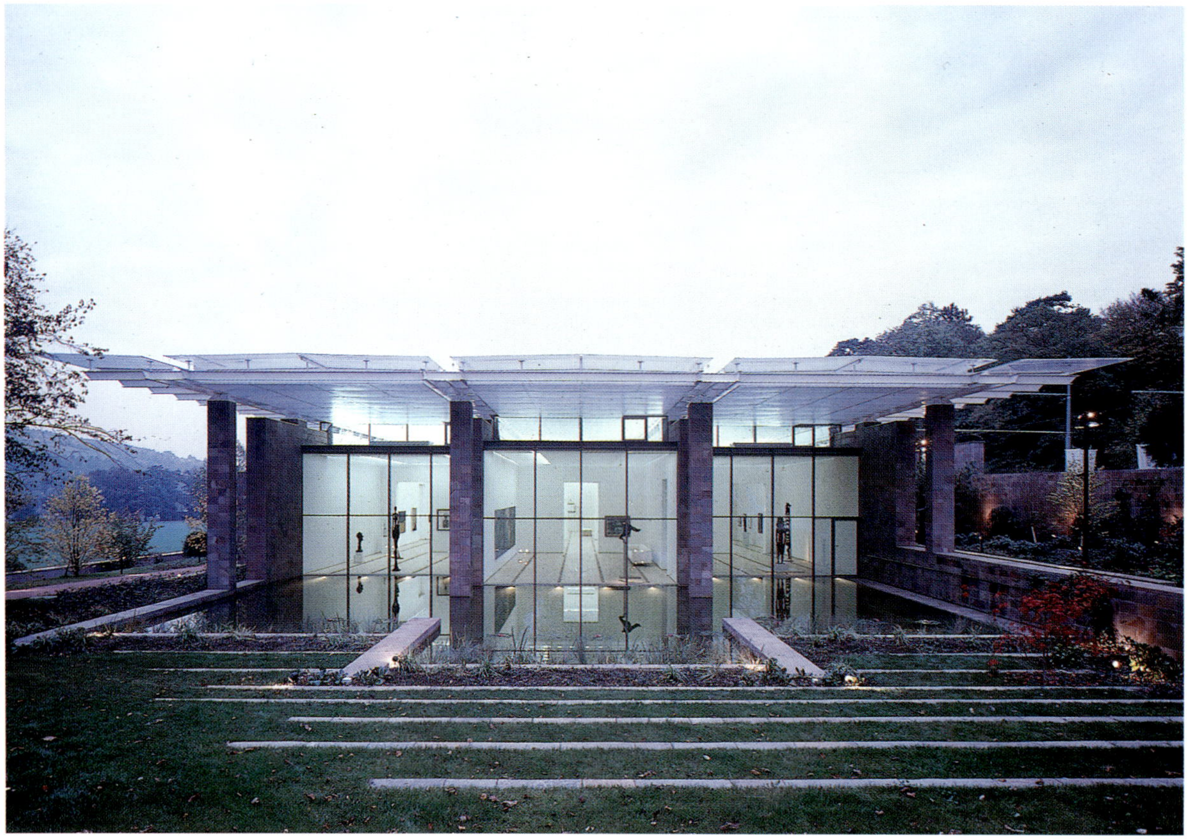

View of the museum building from the aquatic garden terraces and longitudinal section of the site and the various buildings which make up the ensemble of the Beyeler Foundation.

Opposite page

Floor plan of the museum in which the exhibition rooms are organized in a framework of parallel galleries partitioned into a series of regular quadrilaterals.

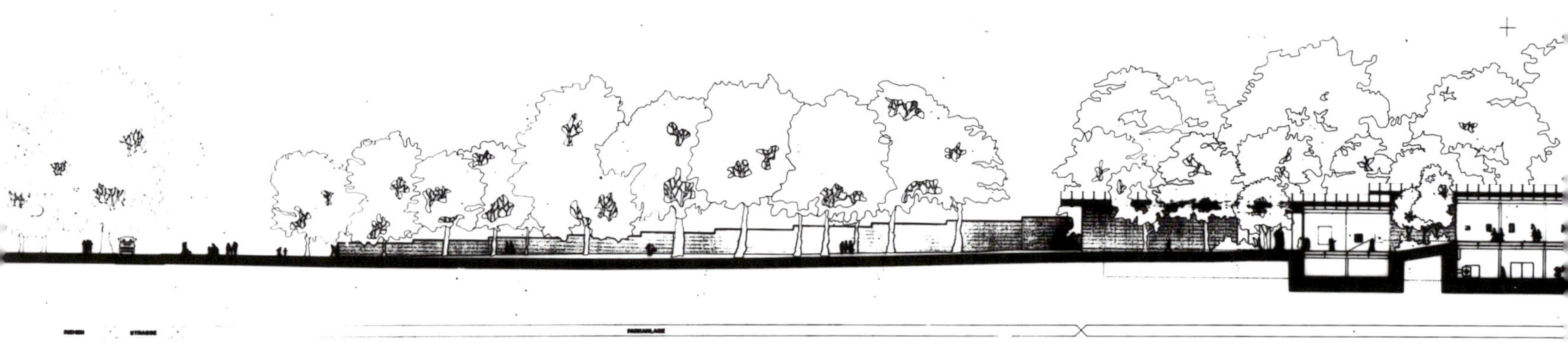

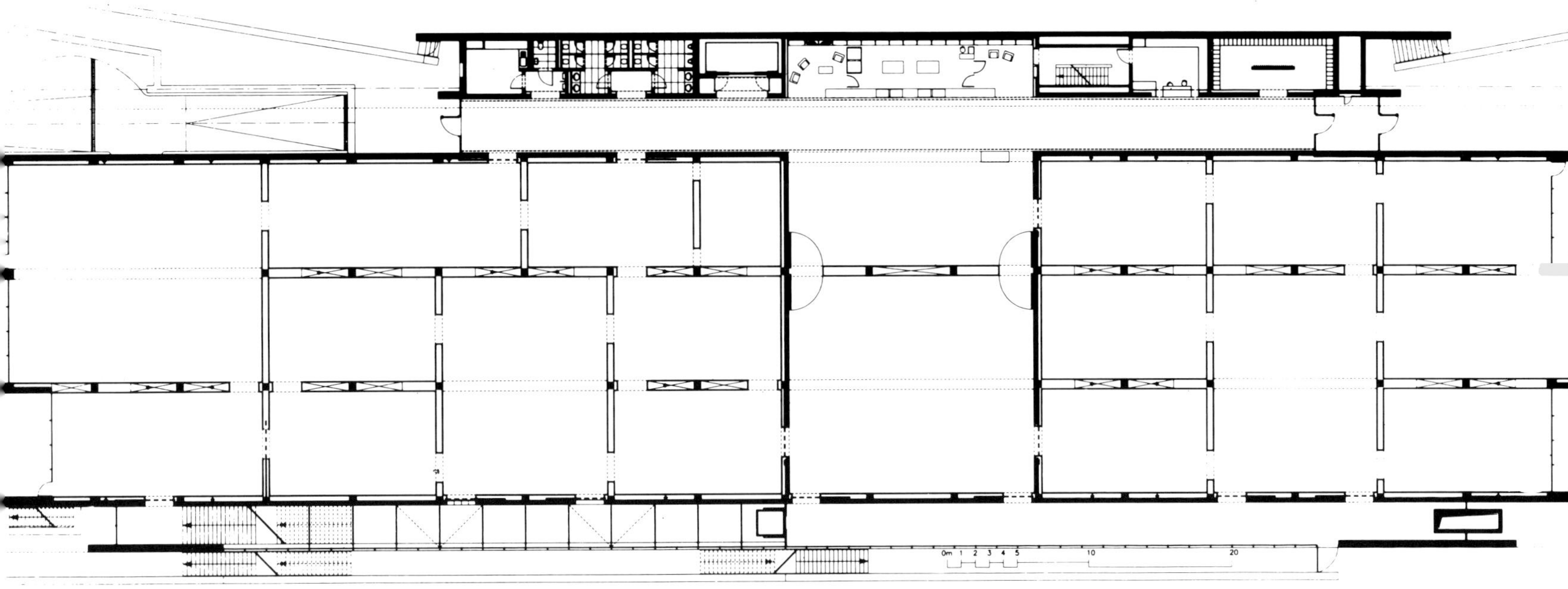

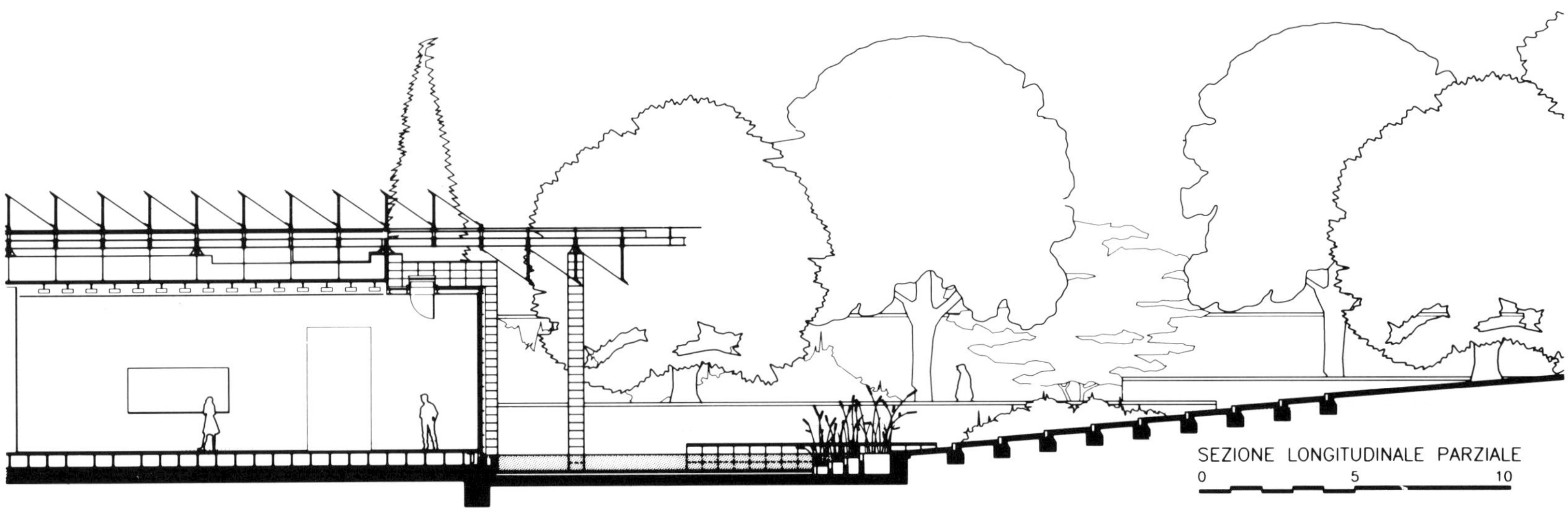
SEZIONE LONGITUDINALE PARZIALE
0 5 10

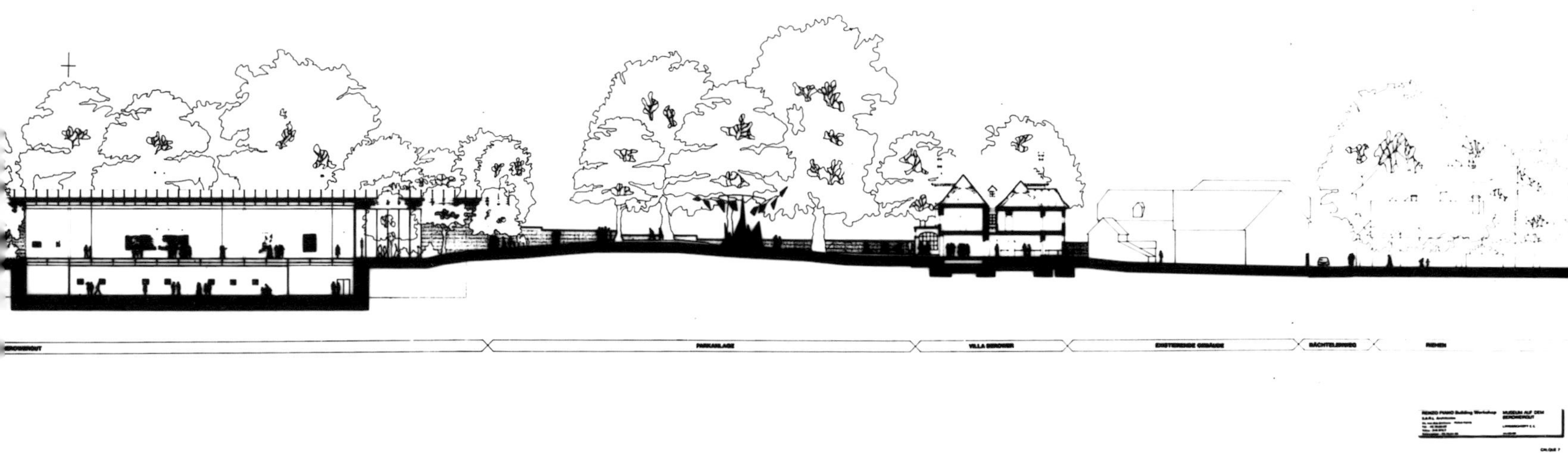

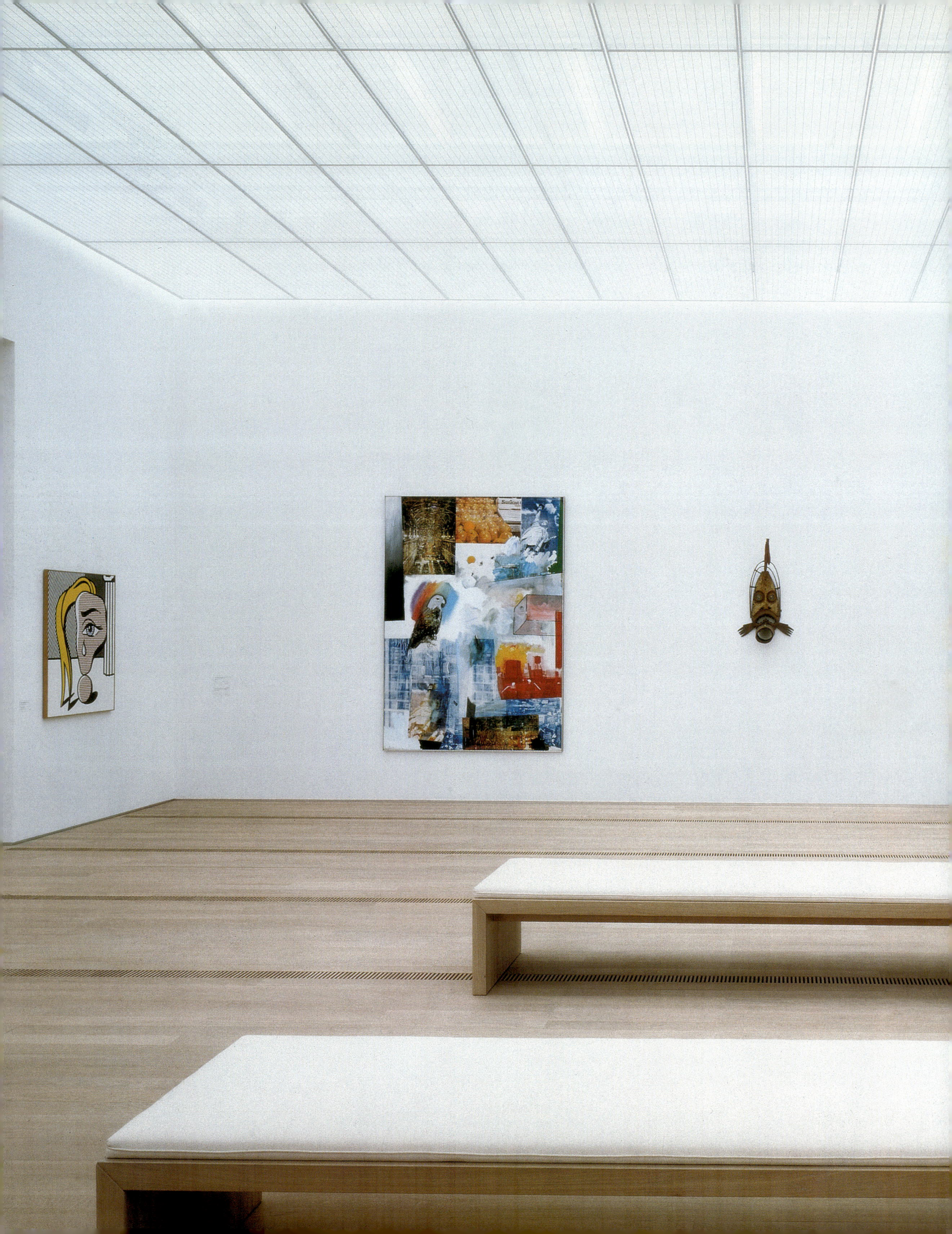

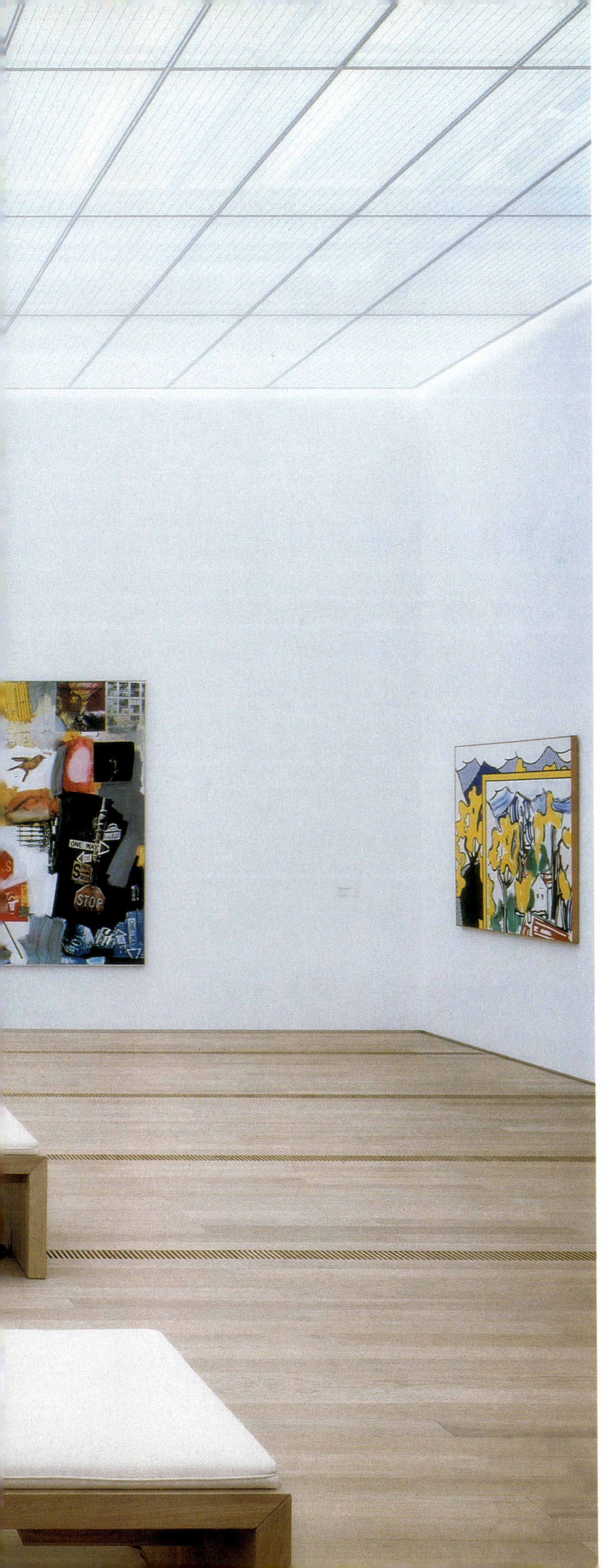

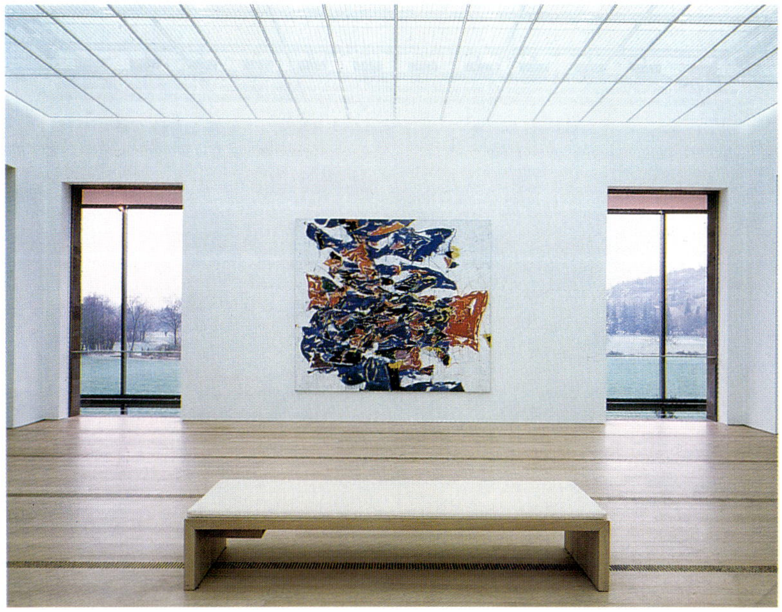

Neither discourse nor decorative or technical detail disrupt the clear serenity of the exhibition rooms. The ethnic mask, the Lichtenstein canvas and Rauschenberg pictures converse without intermediary, in a sort of natural intimacy where numerous possible relationships are formed: between the works themselves, between the paintings and the landscapes framed by the bay windows, between the artist and the visitor. All types of exchanges and encounters are possible here with the invitation of a few benches placed upon pale oak.

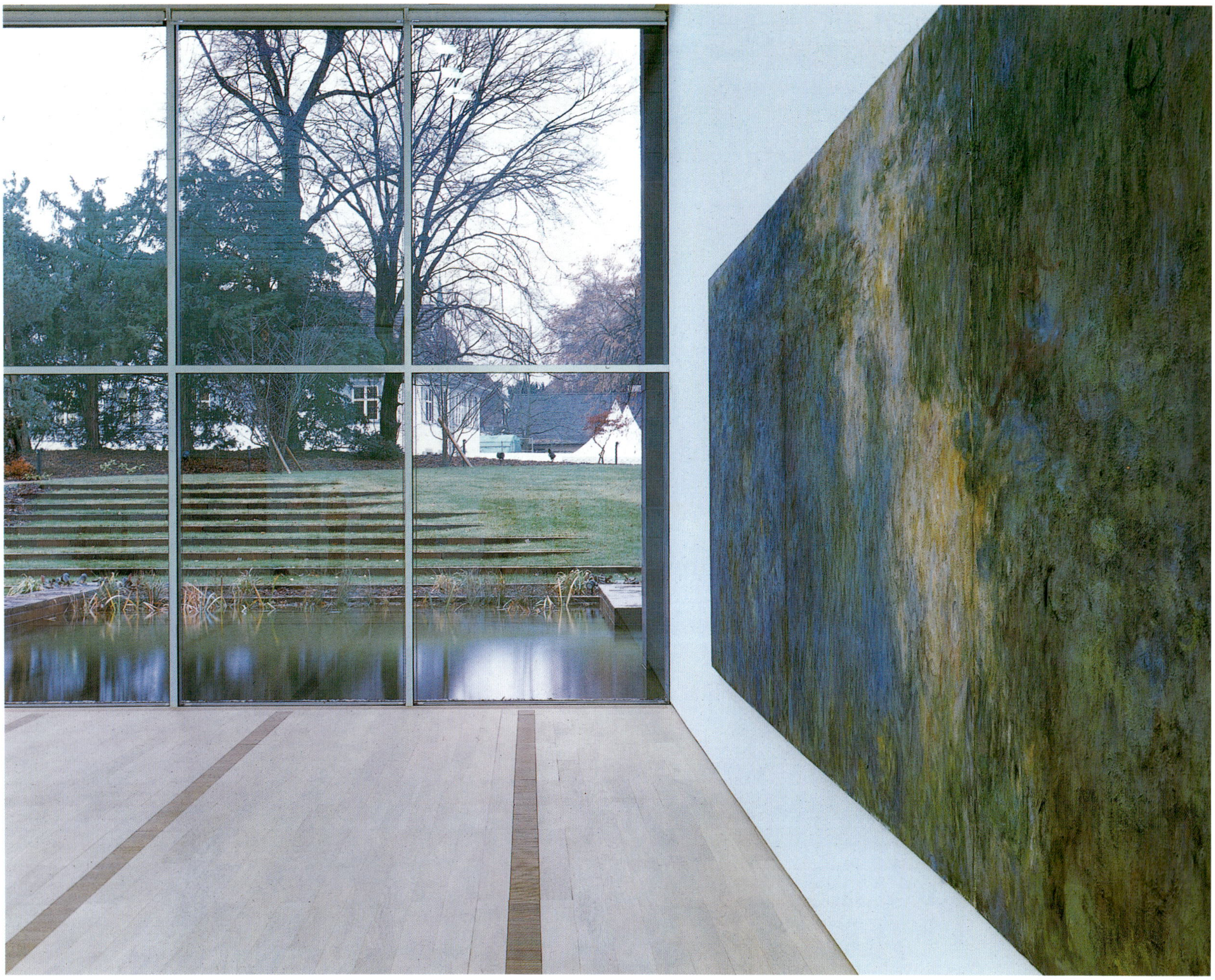

The building's transparency symbolizes the museum's continuous relationship with the exterior world. Transparency of glass facades with a view upon the Berower Villa, 18th-century residence which now houses the Foundation's restaurant and administrative offices. Transparency, as well, of the colonnades, which frame and define various "pictures" of greenery.

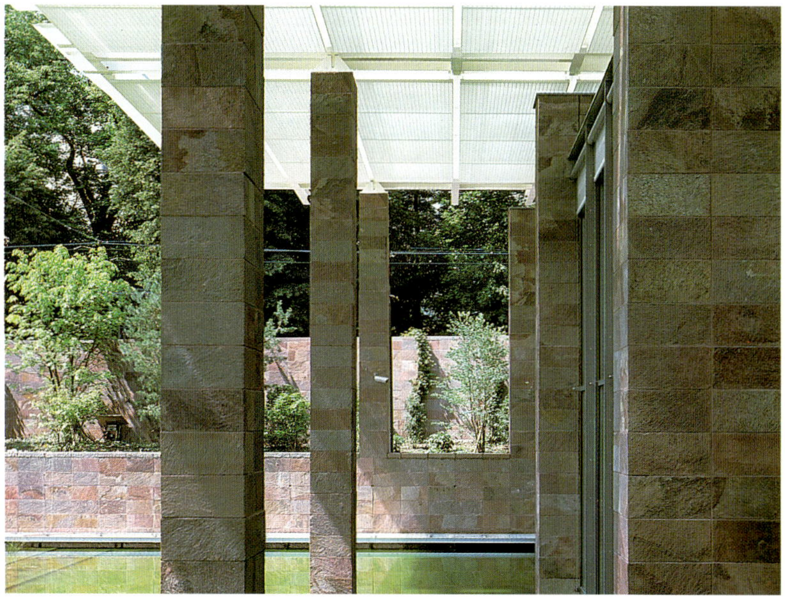

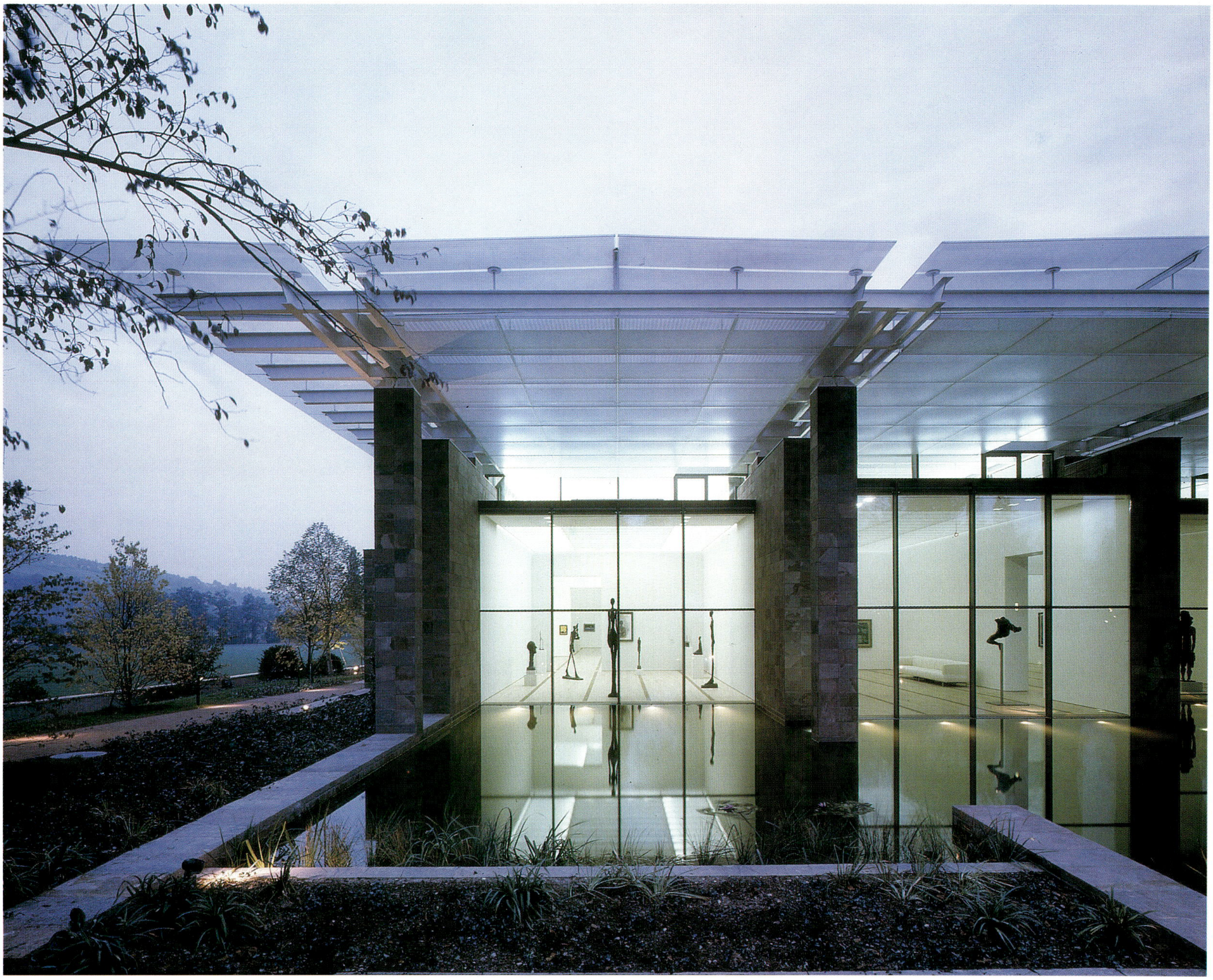

At nightfall, the values are reversed and it is the transparent edifice of the museum which in turn becomes a source of light and reflected views.

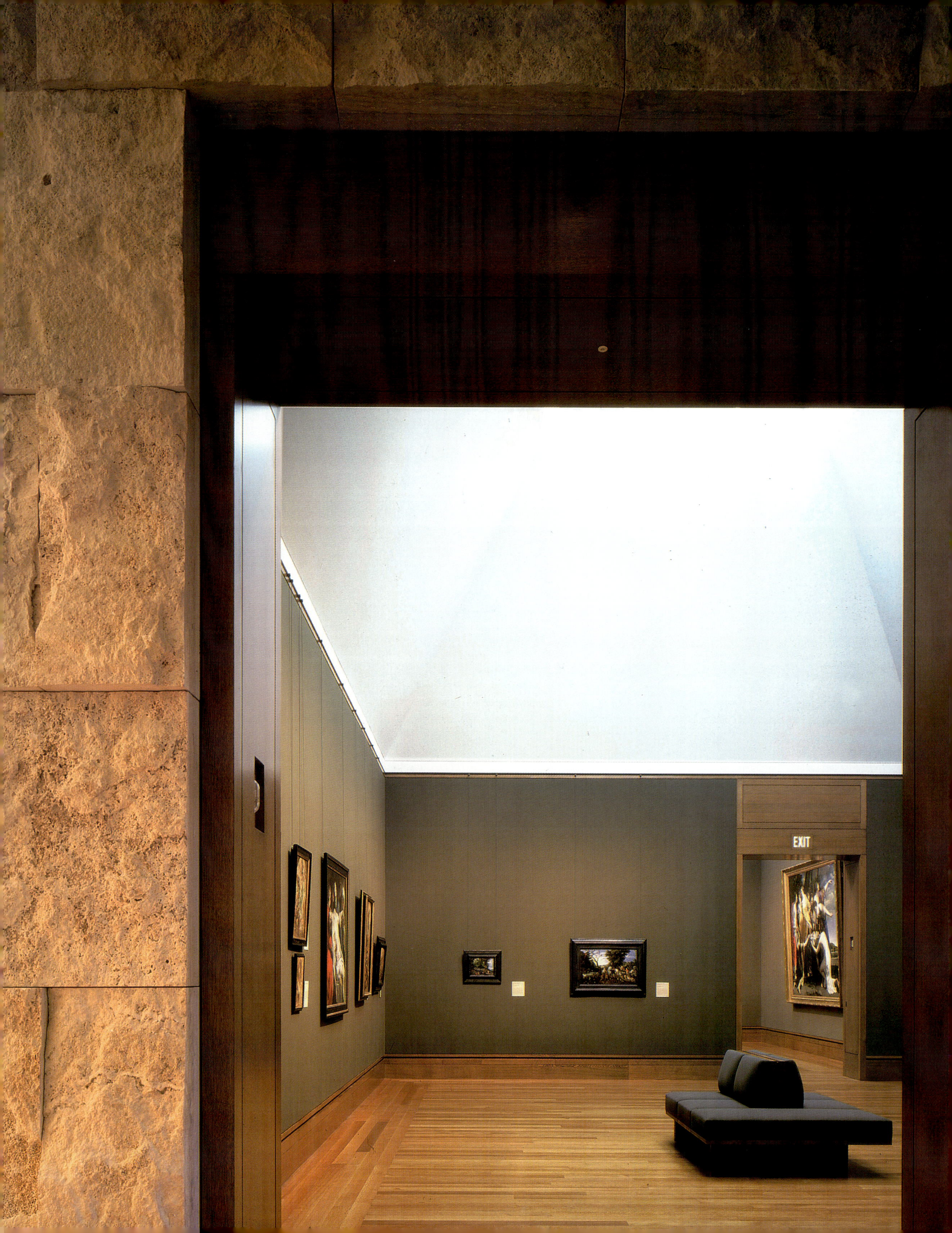
EXIT

Richard Meier

Getty Museum

Los Angeles, United States

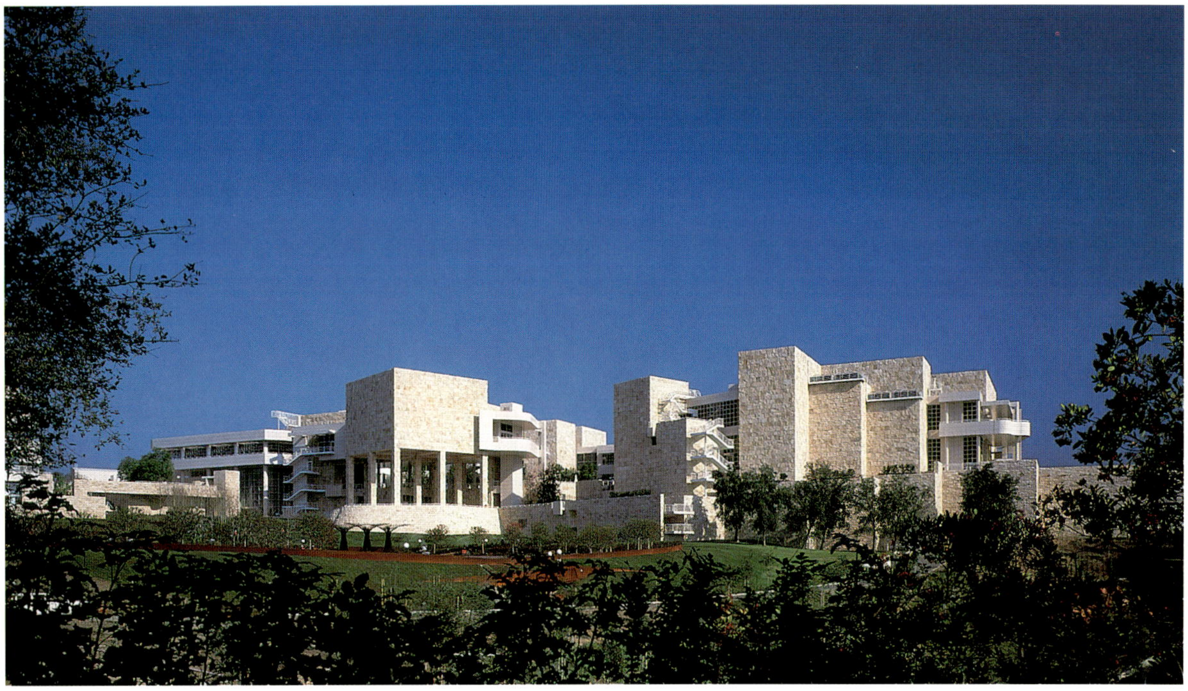

Over the past fifteen years, museum architecture has become Richard Meier's primary interest. Since the High Museum of Art in Atlanta, designed in 1985, numerous projects have been entrusted to him, among them the Des Moines Art Center in the state of Iowa, the Contemporary Art Center of Barcelona, the Museum of Decorative Arts and the Museum of Ethnology and Anthropology in Frankfurt. And finally the Getty Center, an immense complex erected upon a hilltop overlooking Los Angeles like a great white acropolis sparkling with light. For Meier, "light is the very symbol of the architecture of a museum, which must physically and metaphysically irradiate."

Opposite page
Detail of an exhibition room framed by stone facades: travertine, a pale stone, chosen for its exceptional light-reflecting quality.

The establishment of the Getty Center in Los Angeles follows in the natural evolution of the Getty Foundation. This Foundation, created in 1982, carried through the will of oil magnate John Paul Getty, who had amassed an impressive art collection during his lifetime comprised of works from Antiquity, the Renaissance and the French 17th and 18th centuries.

The new complex groups the main departments of the Foundation in one location and, most notably, houses its collection of works up to 1900 from its well-known museum in Malibu – a majestic replica of a Roman villa from Herculanum – now entirely dedicated to the classics of Antiquity. The institution provokes the admiration and envy of curators and museum directors worldwide as the funds of the Getty Oil Corporation allow it to have an impressive, if not an astronomical acquisition budget.

In 1984 the Getty Foundation contracted architect Richard Meier to design what was considered "the commission of the century." Everything about the project was exceptional, the budget being, of course, phenomenal and the designated site, extraordinary, as it covers 150 acres on top of a hill overlooking the city and the San Diego freeway, just as it plunges into the Santa Monica mountains. The overall complex, like a great white acropolis, is based on a triangular floor plan with its southern point joining the terminal of the

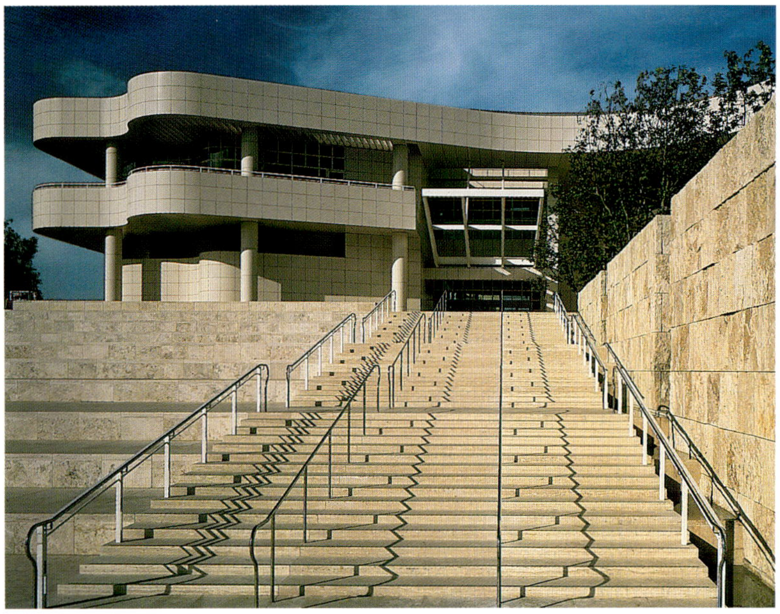

shuttle that leads to the gigantic parking lot built at the foot of the hill. Here visitors are requested to leave their vehicles.

A monumental staircase leads up to the museum's main entrance. A rotunda in the shape of a great cylindrical hall is the strategic focus of this architectural ensemble. Six buildings house respectively, the museum – the largest building by far, the administration, the research center, the library, the auditorium and a restaurant. The whole evolves like a suite of two or three-storey buildings (some have several underground levels) organized in geometric variations around a cube or cylinder.

The relative dissimilarity of the structure is reconciled by the spectacular treatment of the facades: aluminum enameled panels of the walls and columns, the frame of the picture windows, and the beautiful pale stone all participate in forming a grille motif.

The use of stone is a central element to Richard Meier's concept, which came to fruition during his numerous fact finding trips to Rome. The travertine cladding – the same stones as the Coliseum – establishes a clear link between the Getty Center and Rome. Cut in large blocks, the stones clad the concrete structure of the building, giving it an impression of sturdiness, of timelessness. They also highlight the exceptional quality of the California light which had left such an impression on Meier during his first visit to Los Angeles.

The natural setting plays as much a part of this grandiose construction as the architectural concept itself. This explains the great care given to the fountains and gardens that dot the grounds.

Unfortunately, the cacti garden suffers from a too rigid design and the oak trees fall short of expectations. With time, however, the vegetation will soon integrate itself into the environment and Californians will grow accustomed to

Detail of the monumental staircase leading up to the main entrance of the museum.

Site elevation showing the layout of the various Getty Center buildings among which the museum edifice appears as the most spectacular and imposing.
1. Auditorium
2. Getty Information Institute/Getty Conservation Institute
3. Getty Museum

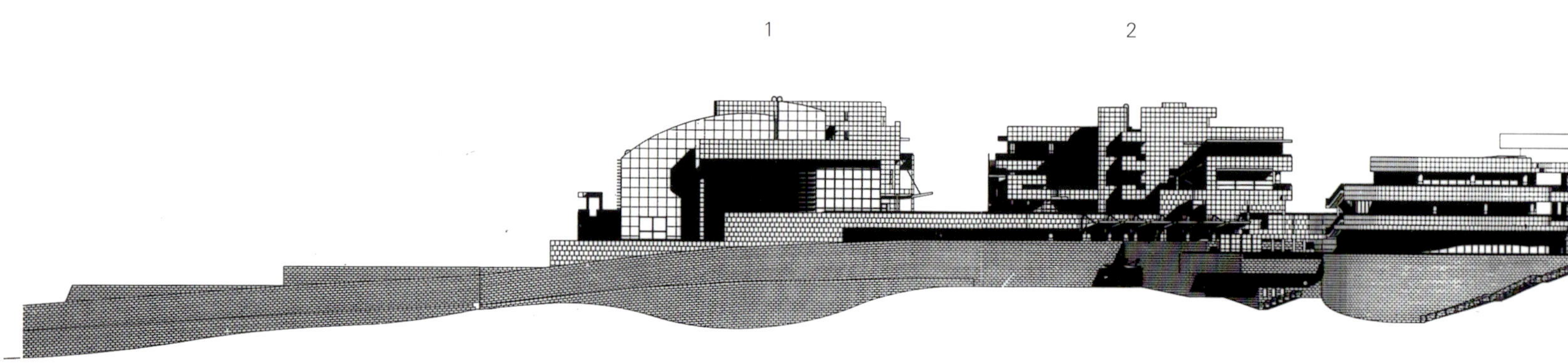

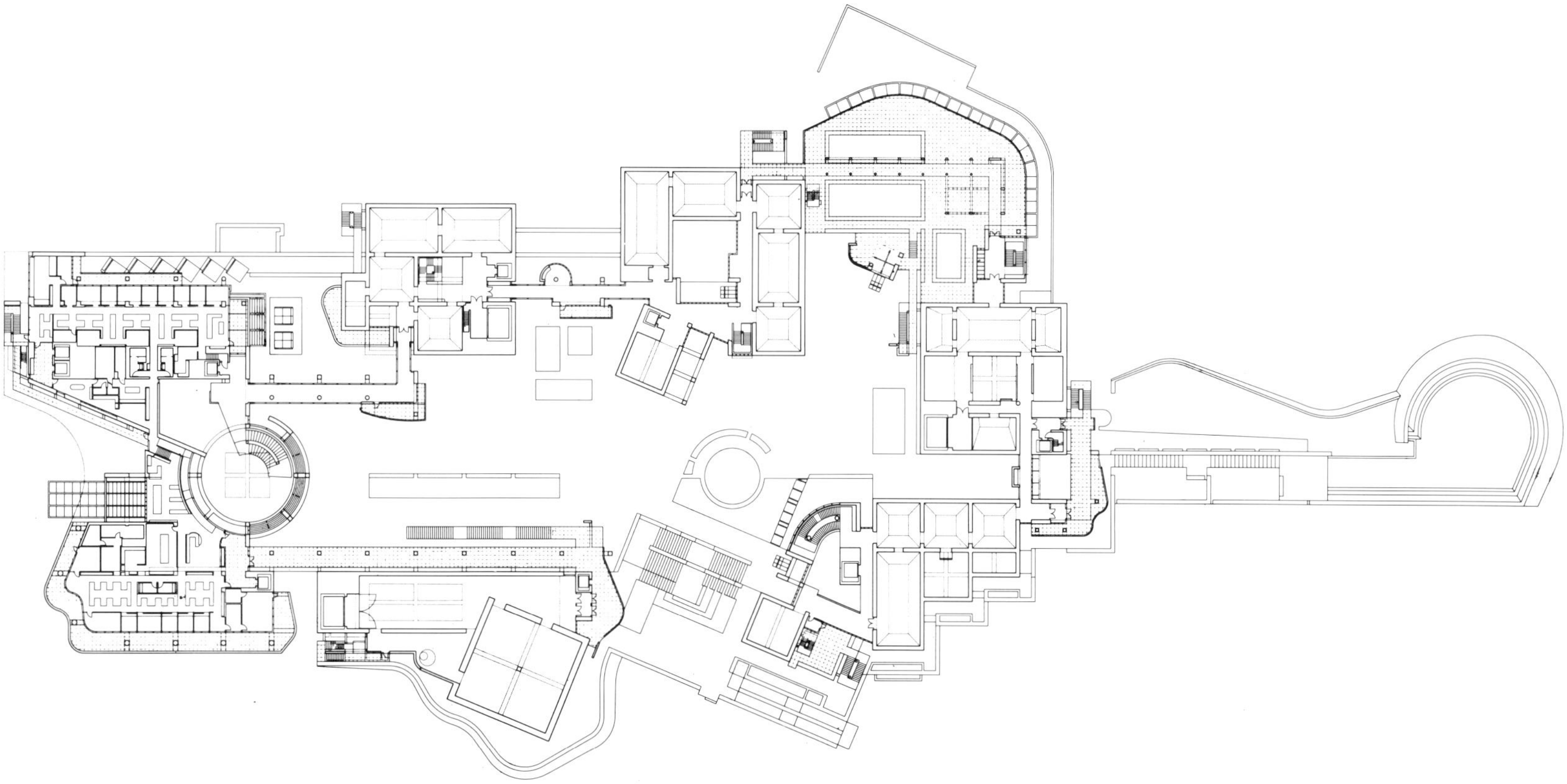

this new acropolis, seen by some critics as too arrogant and detached from the city and its cultural needs.

Nevertheless, since its opening in December 1997, the Getty Center has had an average of 6,000 visitors a day, the difficulty of finding a parking spot in its seven-storey garage being just one measure of its success. □

Site plan of the Getty Museum.

3

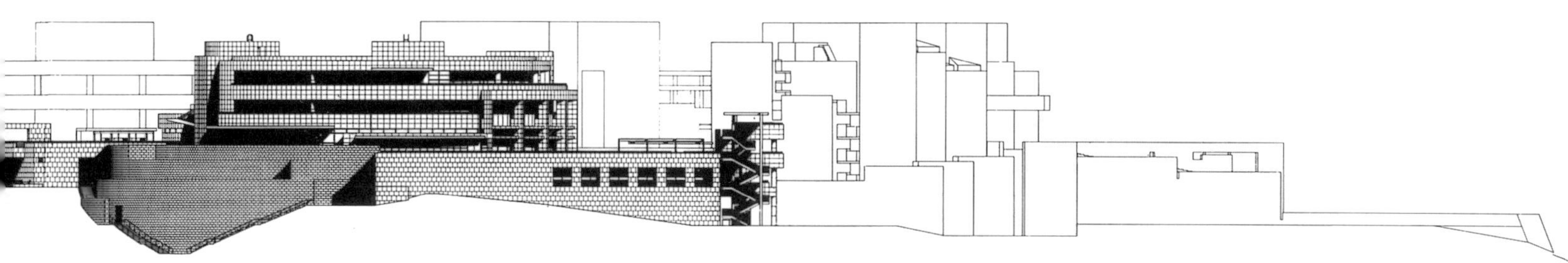

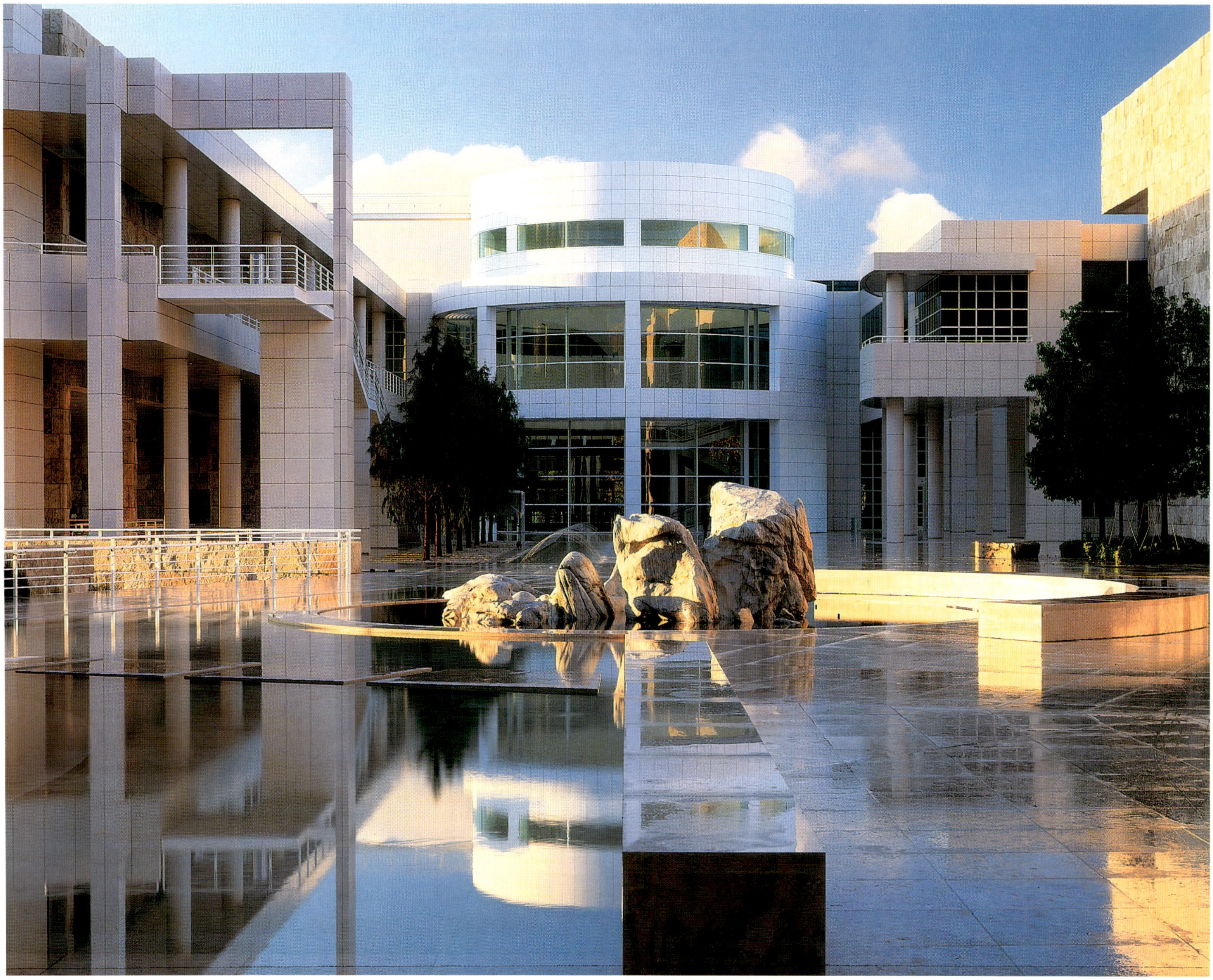

Another of Meier's preoccupations, and a constant in his museographic realizations: the necessity to establish a dialogue between interior spaces and exterior landscape, between art and nature. The Getty Center ensemble is punctuated with gardens and the museum rotunda communicates with a tree-lined patio freshened by basins and a fountain.

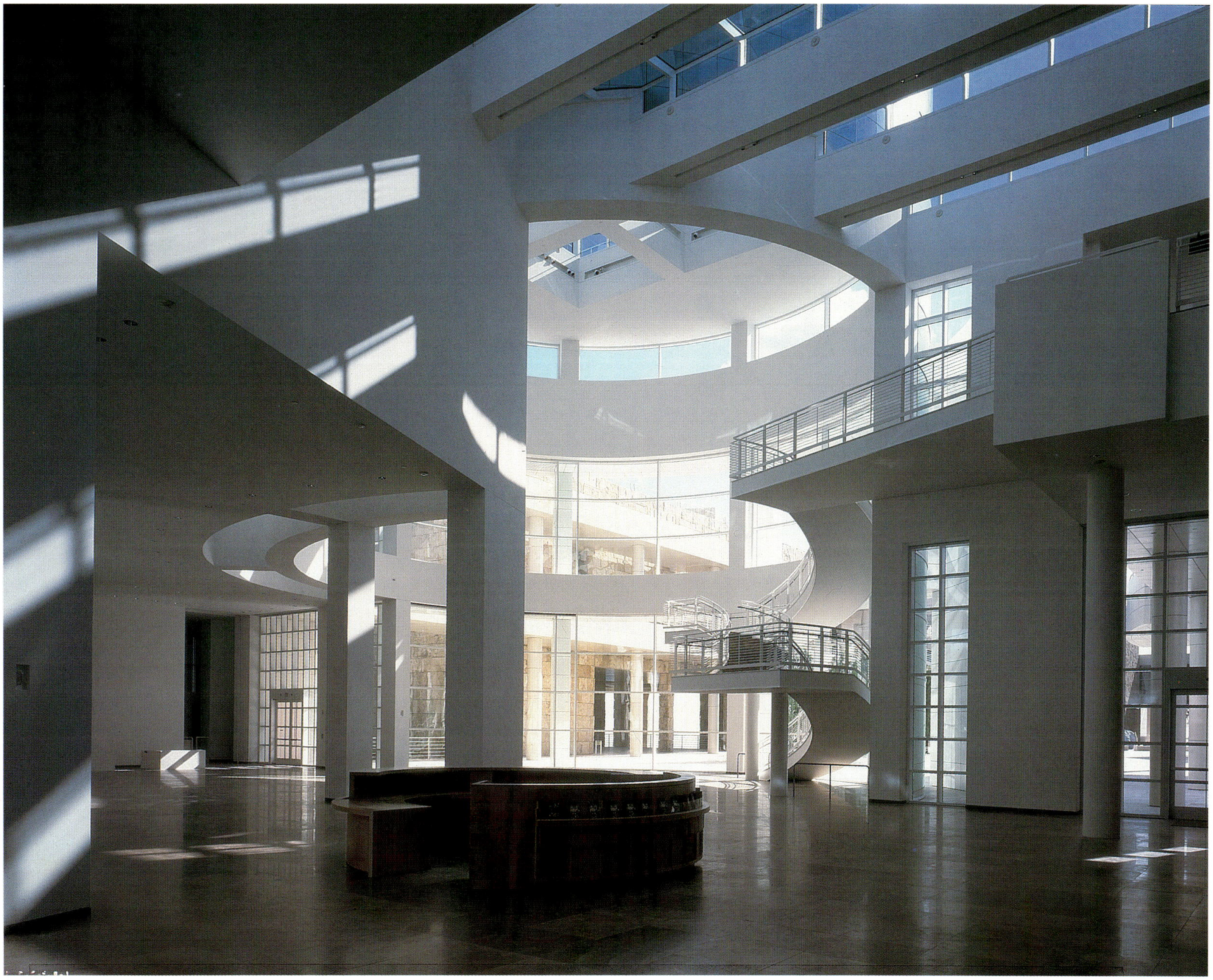

Interior view of the museum's main hall: a vast rotunda, built like a well of light, redistributing and refracting the California sun.

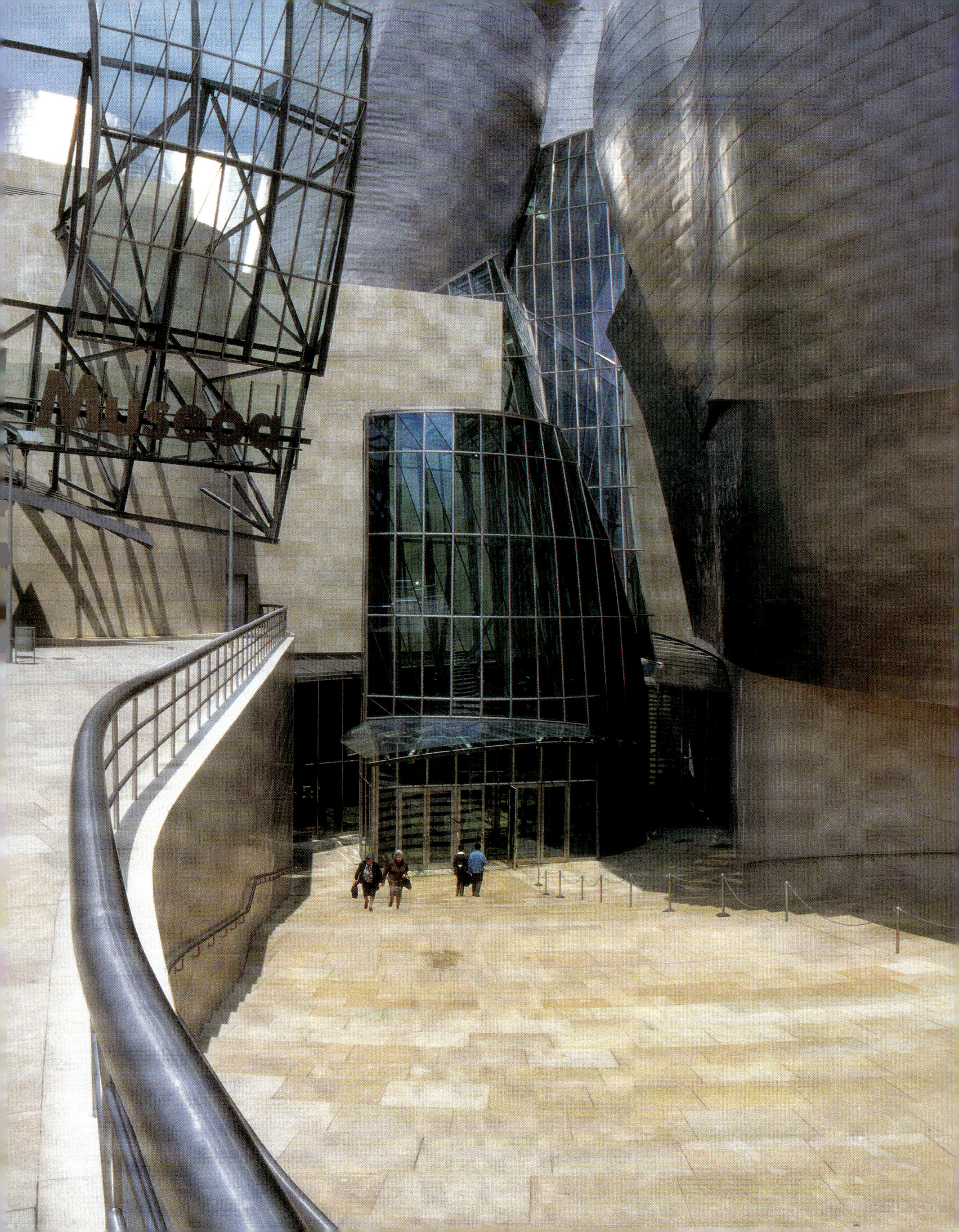
Museoa

Frank O. Gehry

Guggenheim Museoa

Bilbao, Spain

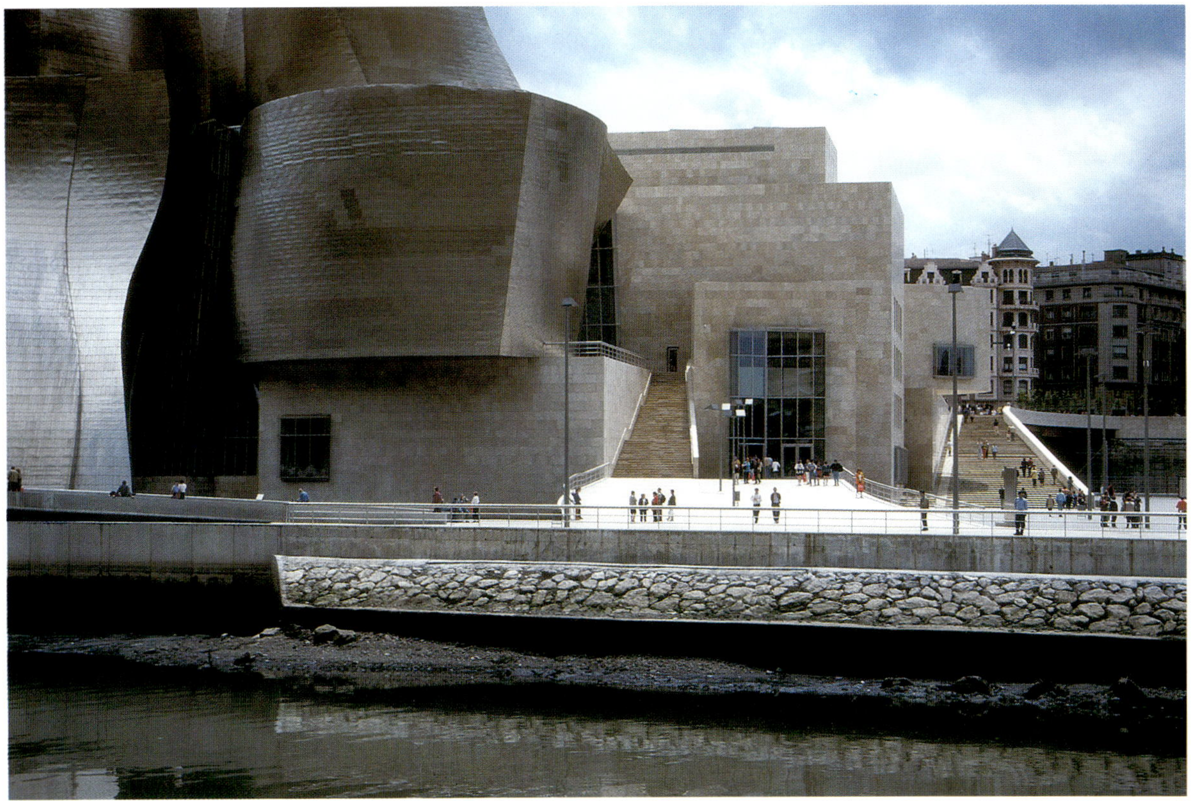

The Guggenheim Museum, an enormous, unusual object, paradoxically reinforces the urbanity of its surroundings by the dialogue it creates between city and river.

Opposite page
One enters the museum after a long descent between walls of titanium, stone and glass.

The Solomon R. Guggenheim Museum of New York is a wealthy, powerful institution with one of the most formidable collections of 20th century art. Since the late 1980's, its director Thomas Krens has embarked on an ambitious expansion program with the aim of making the museum's collection more visible. Initially the museum was extended, followed by the opening of a new building in SoHo.

Following the trend of globalization, however, Thomas Krens's ambitions likewise have expanded. The next most obvious and necessary step was to establish a new foothold in Europe. To avoid any friction with major European institutions – Paris or London were out of the question as both the Tate Gallery and the Pompidou Center are respected colleagues – the Guggenheim looked for a more peripheral location with a different appeal. The Austrian city of Salzburg was first seriously considered, its summer festival giving it an international appeal. But shortly after Hollein won the architectural competition, the Guggenheim suddenly turned elsewhere, finding new interest in the Basque city of Bilbao. While it is hard to say who discovered who, negotiations led to an agreement that was quickly signed whereby the city of Bilbao would finance the museum's construction and the

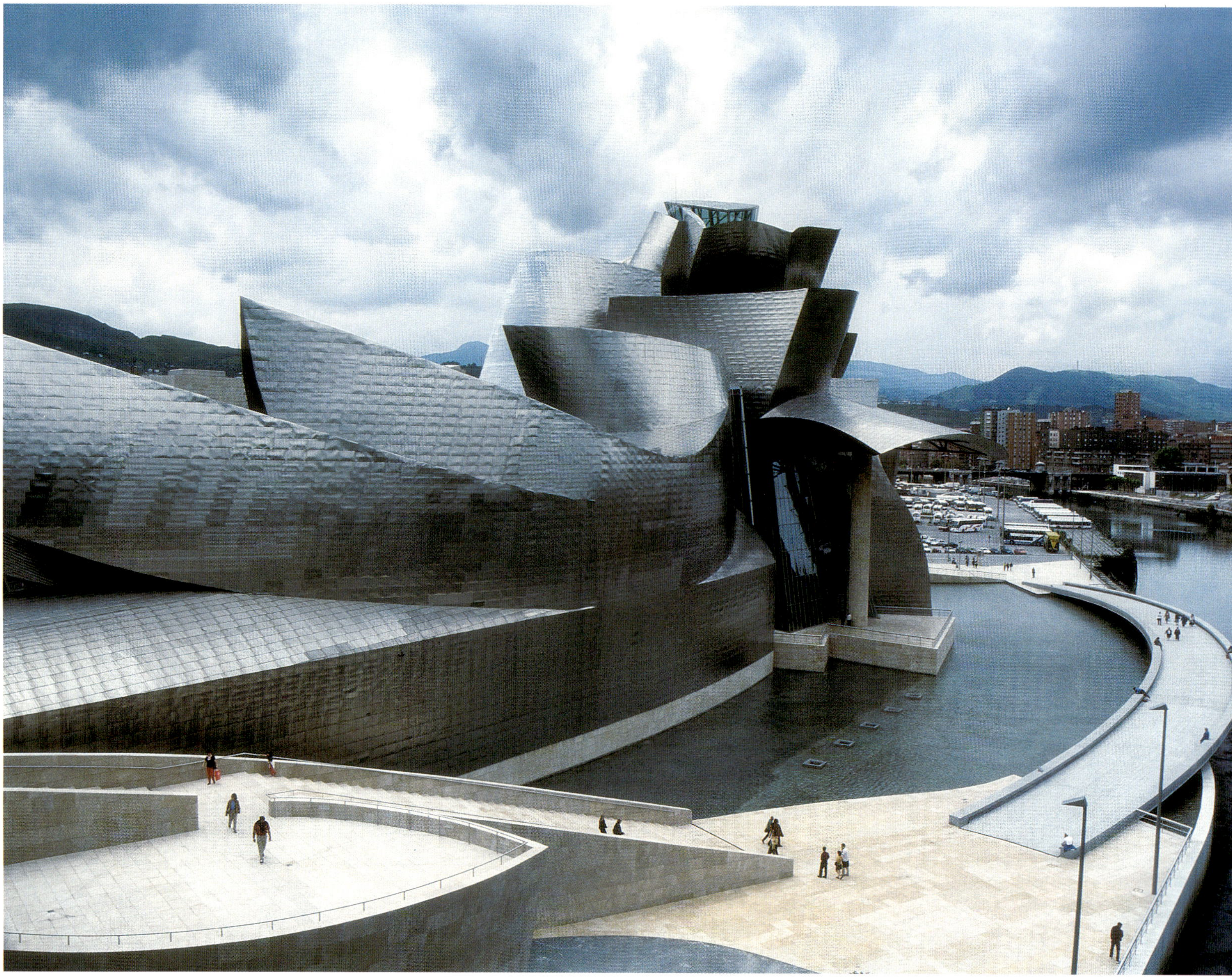

View from the bridge:
flowing and sharp forms,
an overhanging footbridge
and a man-made lake
make up the transition
from the aquatic world to
solid ground.

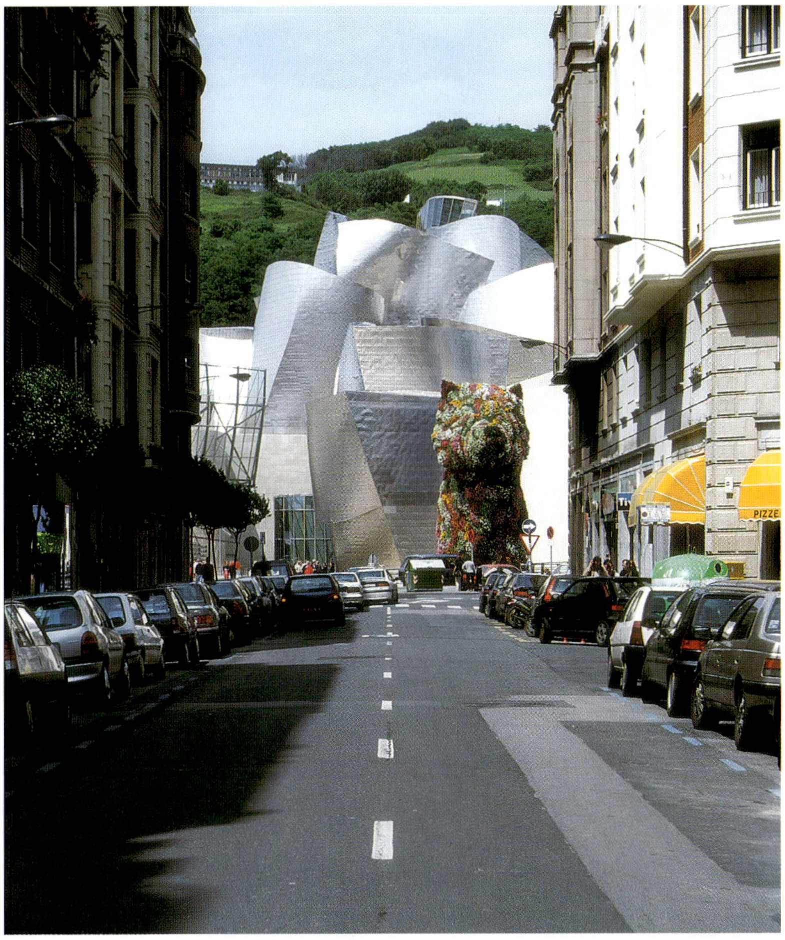

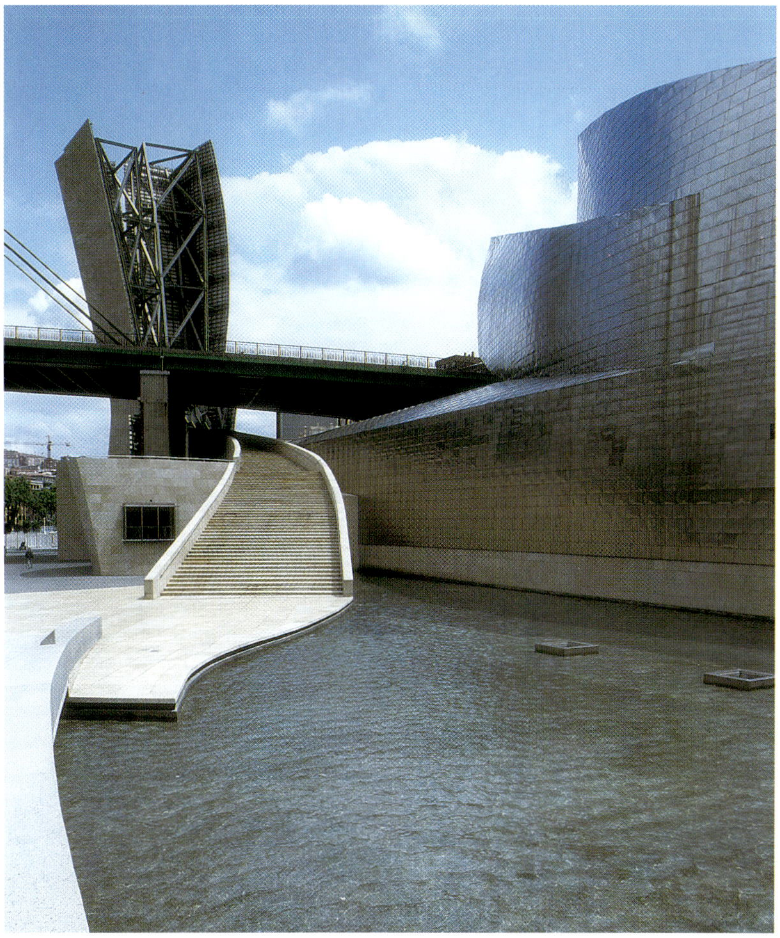

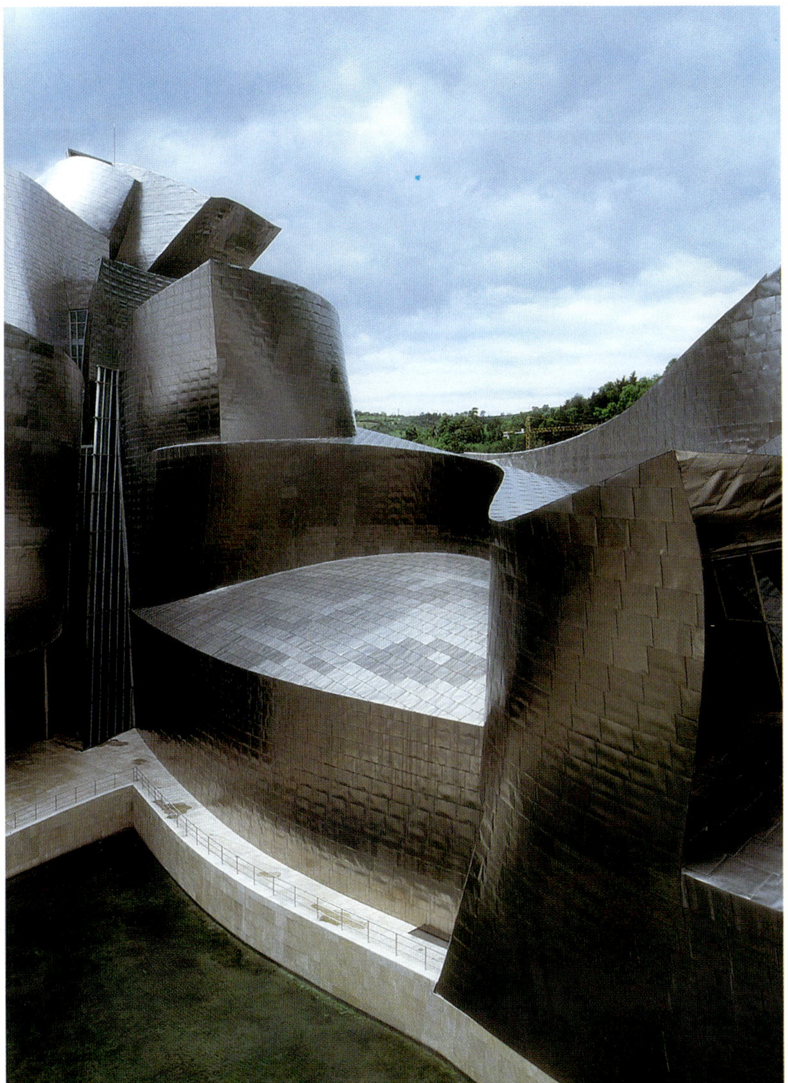

View from the city: a shiny mass guarded by Jef Koons' flowered dog.

View from the river bank: a stone stairway leads up to the tower and the existing bridge.

View from the bridge: an entanglement of perfectly controlled, fluid forms.

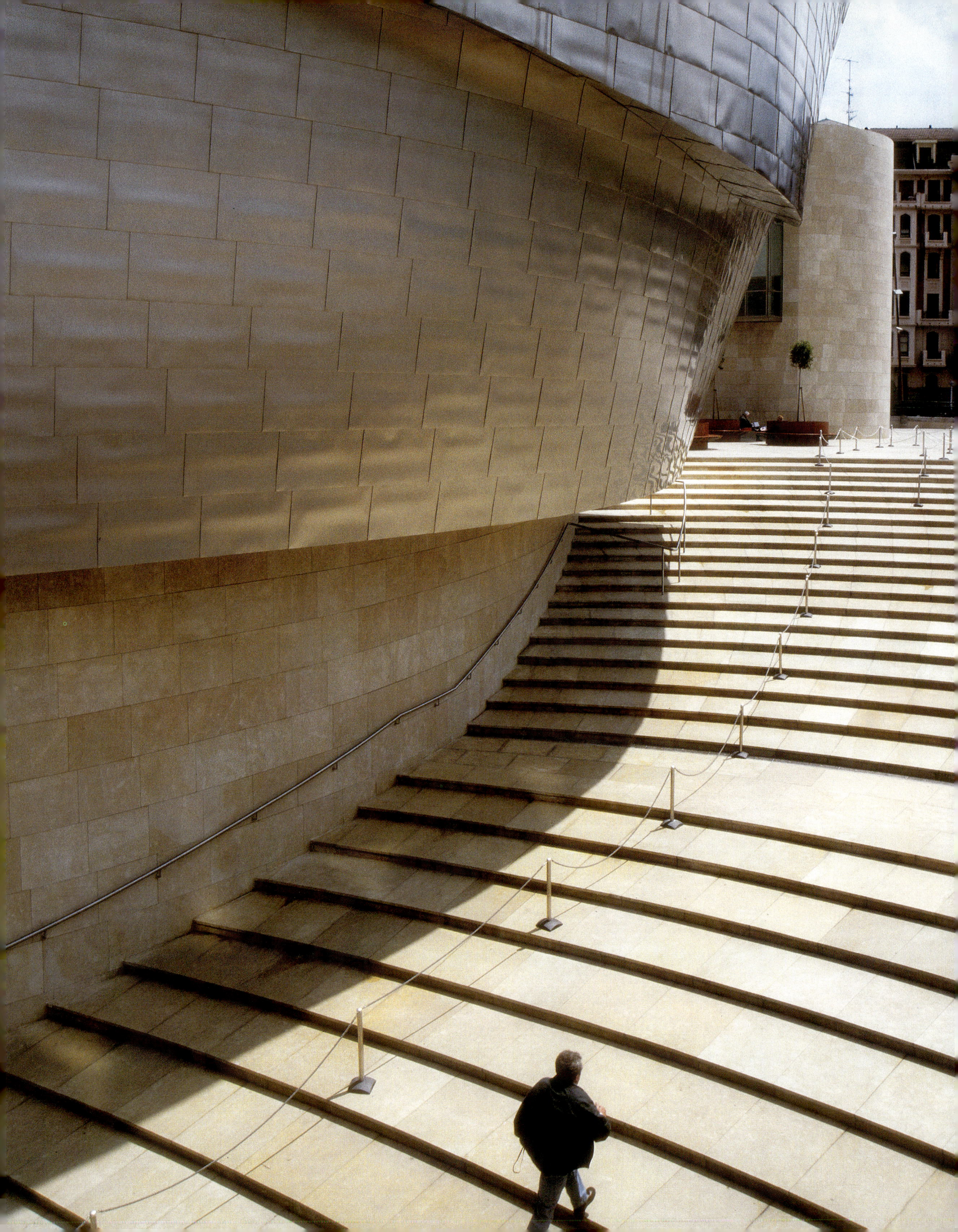

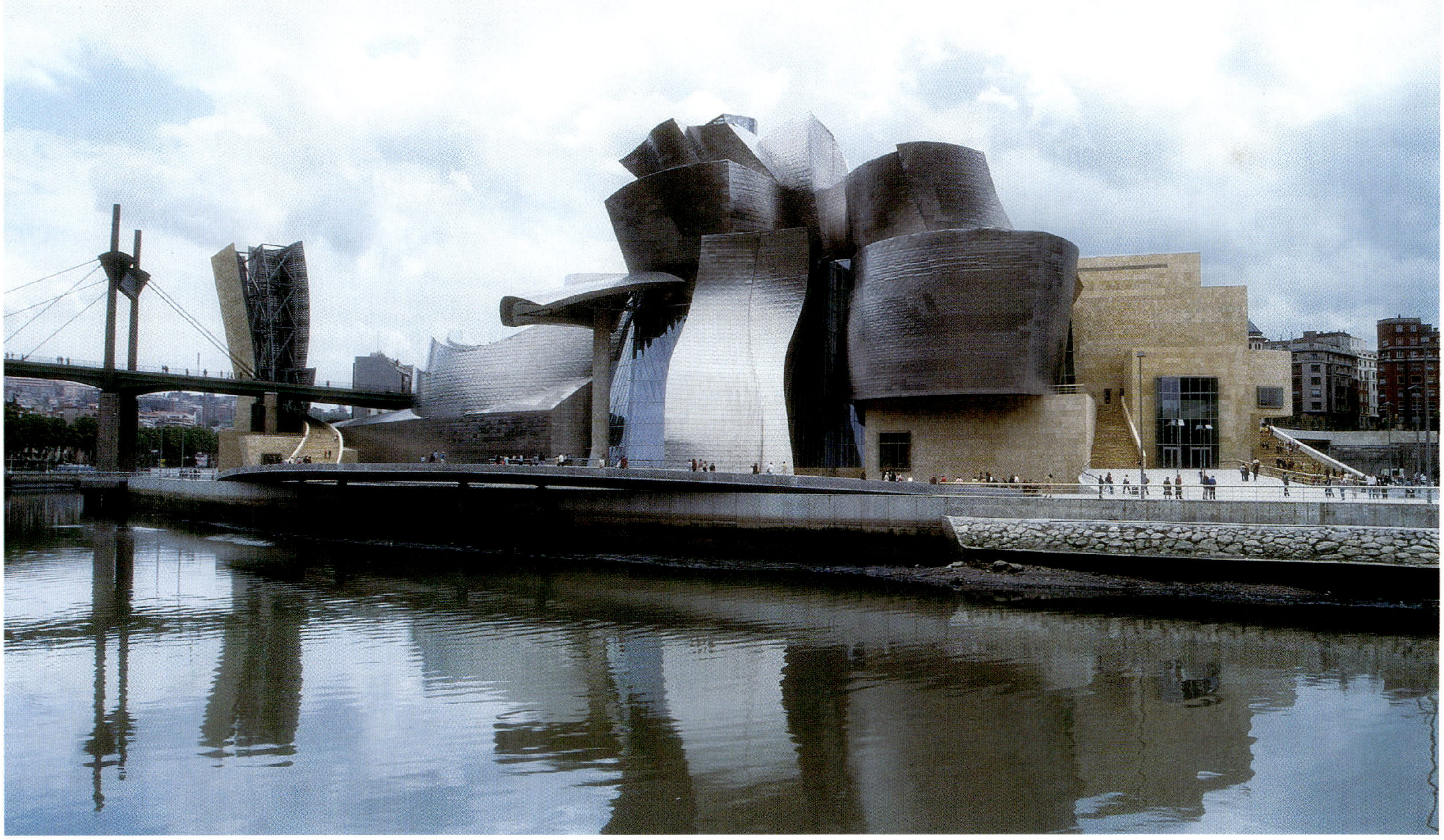

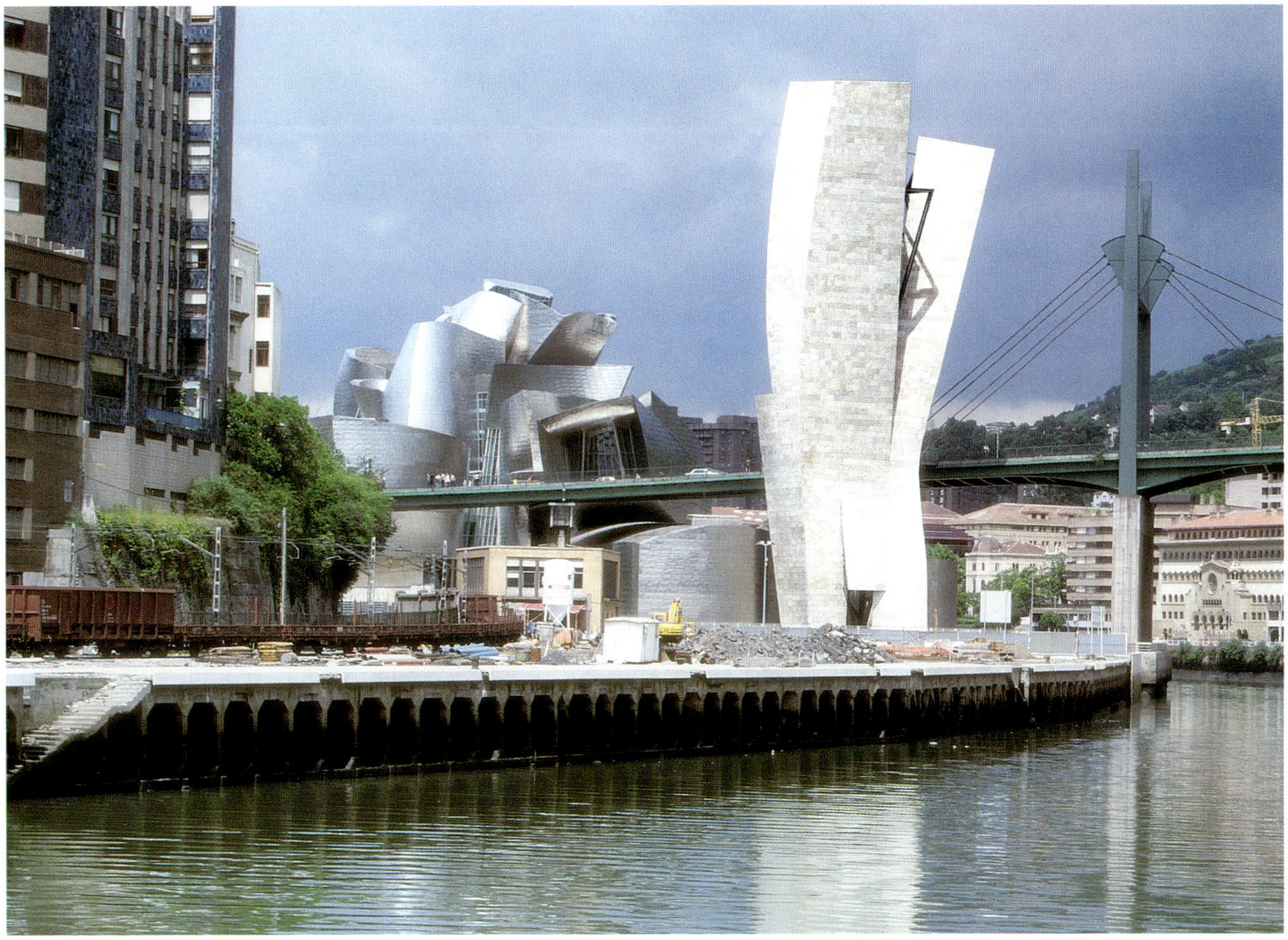

View of the ensemble from the opposite bank of the river: the long metal tongue slips under the existing bridge and rises again in the form of a tower which acts as a signal.

View from the Calatrava footbridge upstream: the building absorbs the entire urban landscape and traces of the industrial landscape.

Opposite page
The stairway of the museum entrance: a round, shiny, cantilevered form leans out over the wide stone steps.

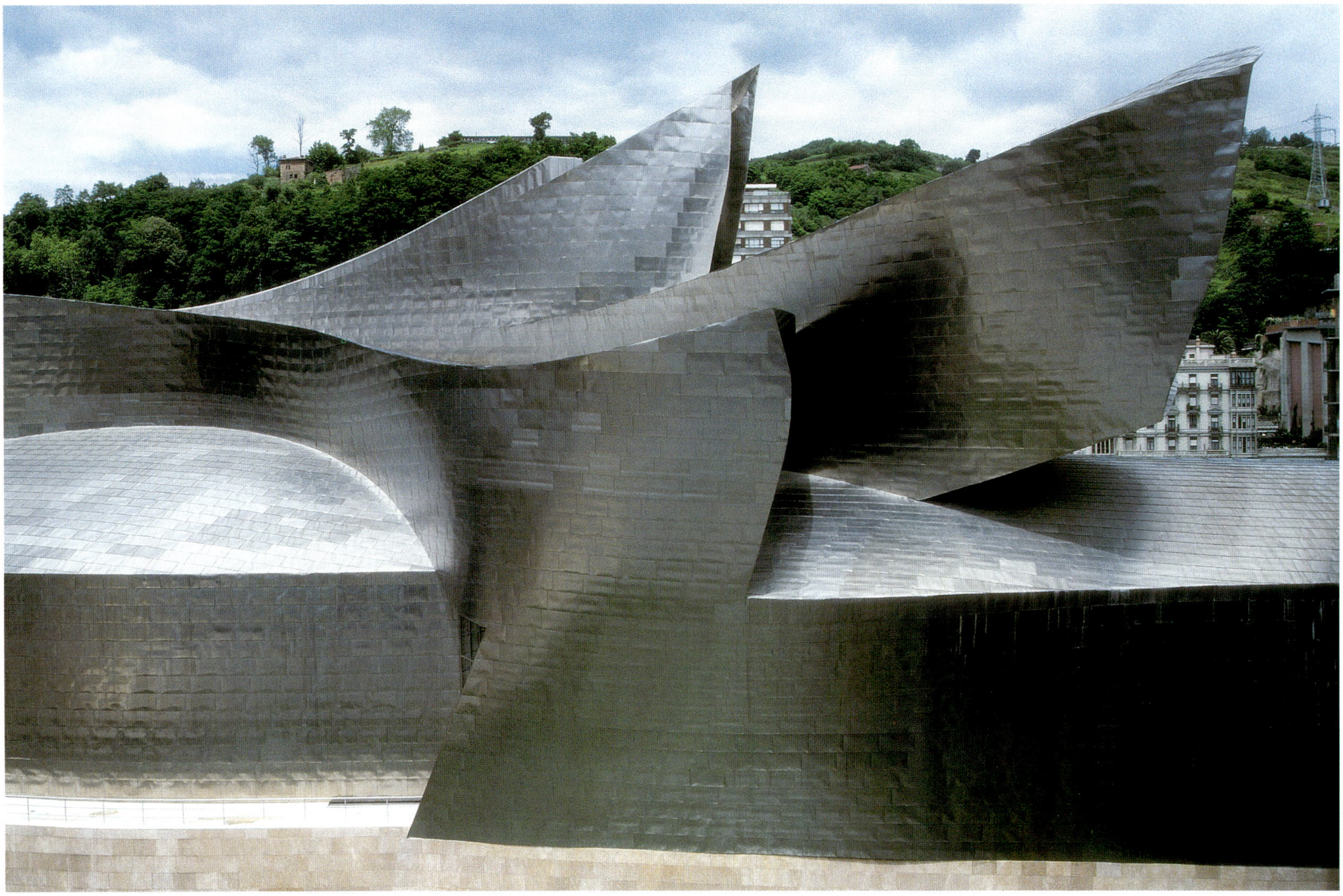

Stems, seagull wings, full sails, the building moves through a complete repertory of marine metaphores.

Guggenheim would supply its management, provide the basic collection and organize future exhibitions.

With Frank Lloyd Wright as the architect of the Guggenheim Museum in New York, it seemed only natural for the new "Guggenheim" to express the same architectural ambition. For Bilbao, Thomas Krens had to choose between the Vienna-based Coop Himmelb(l)au, Arata Isozaki who had been very successful with his design of the entrance hall of the Guggenheim's SoHo building in lower Manhattan or Frank O. Gehry. After a long selection process, Krens commissioned Gehry.

Gehry's first hurdle was to persuade his clients to abandon the original site, which lacked any outstanding features, in favor of a location along the river Nervion. The new site took up an abandoned industrial section of the city and had the advantage of being closer to the center. Following in the same spirit as the museum holding the Weisman collection in Minneapolis, Gehry proceeded to design a masterpiece. While "masterpiece" may seem somewhat exaggerated, it is the only word that comes to mind, and not without reason.

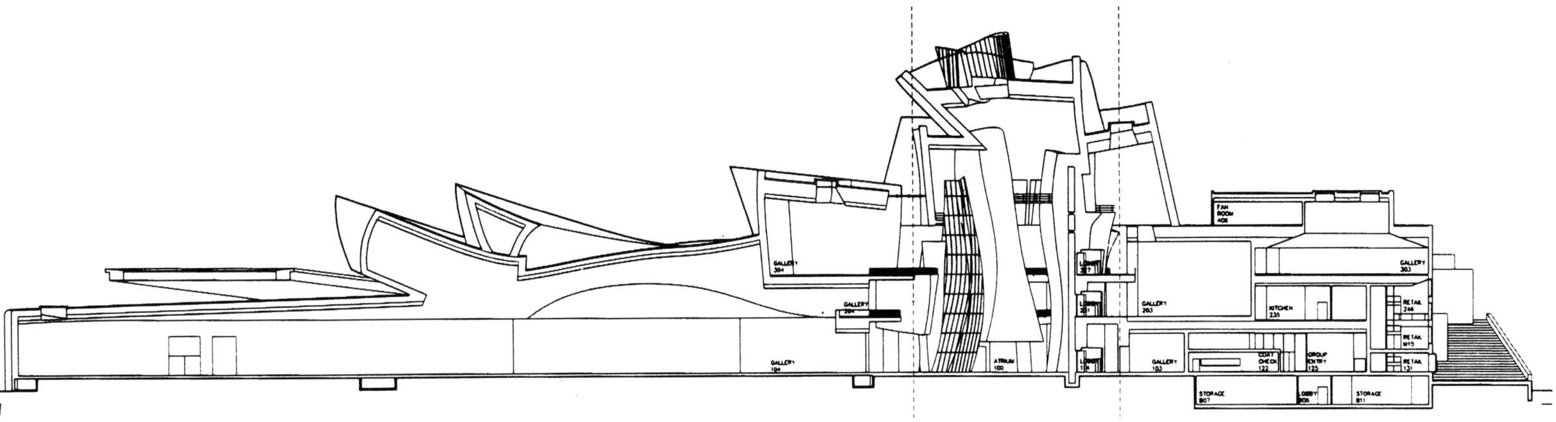

Section AA

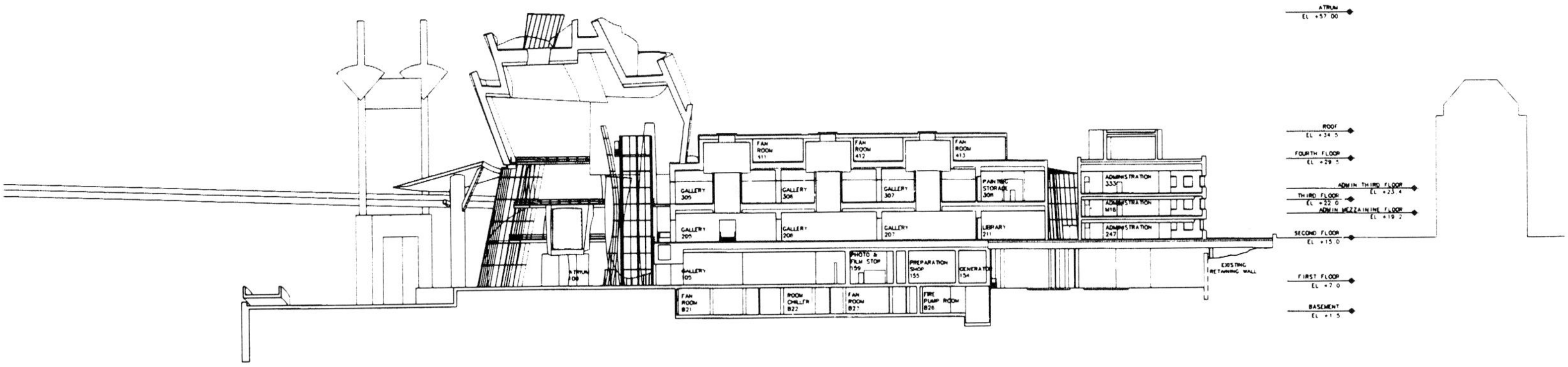

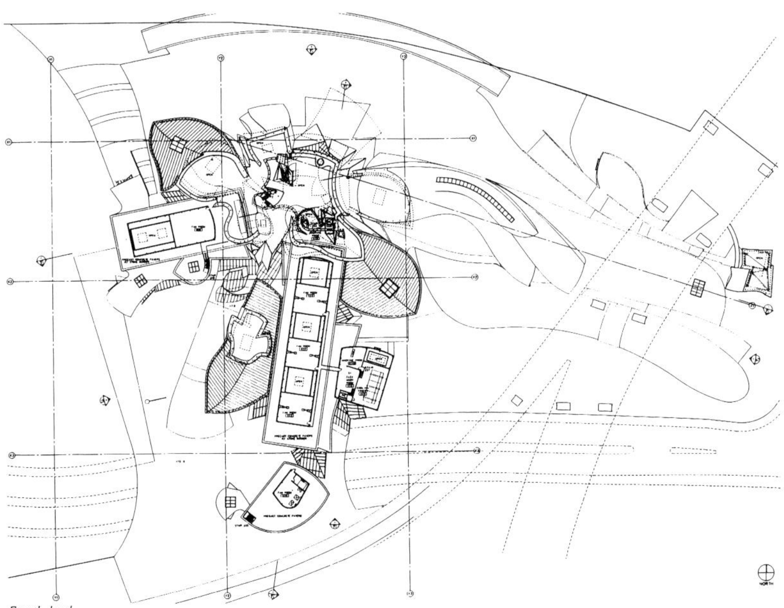

Fourth level

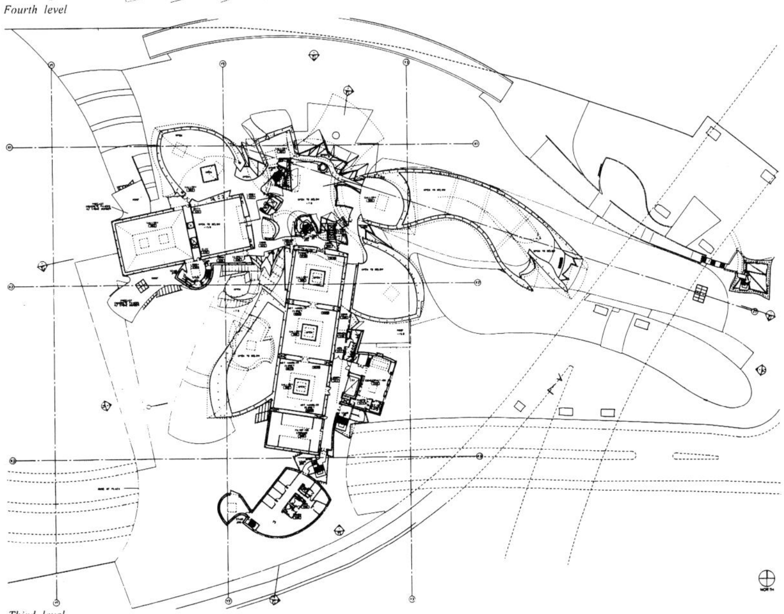

Third level

South-east/north-west longitudinal section.
North-east/south-west cross section.

The plan is centered around the entrance atrium. Galleries and spaces are distributed in a centrifugal pattern: an expressionist basilica.

Following pages
Hills and their greenery, the city and its buildings, containers, the railroad: the building absorbs and reconciles these disparate elements.

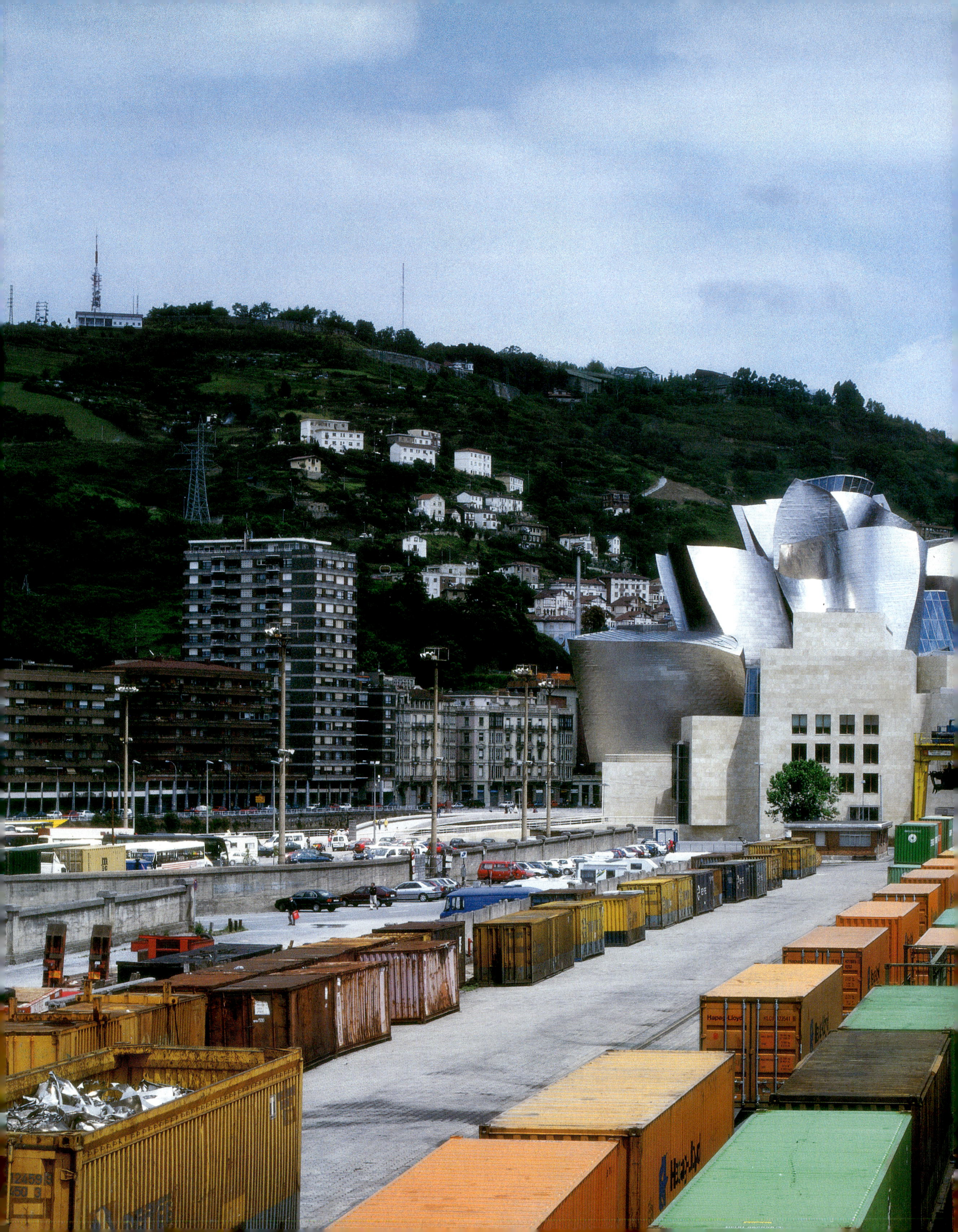

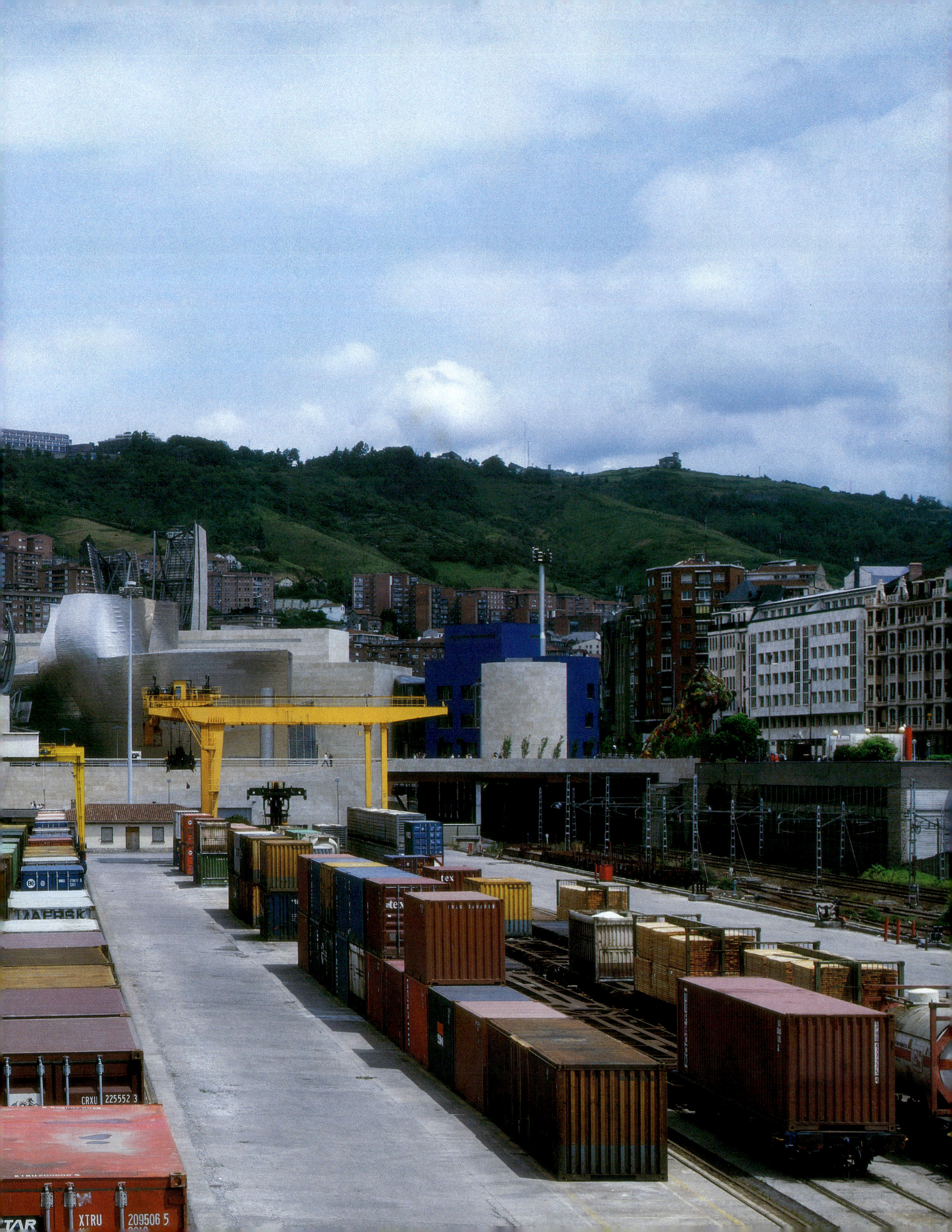
CRXU 225552 3
XTRU 209506 5

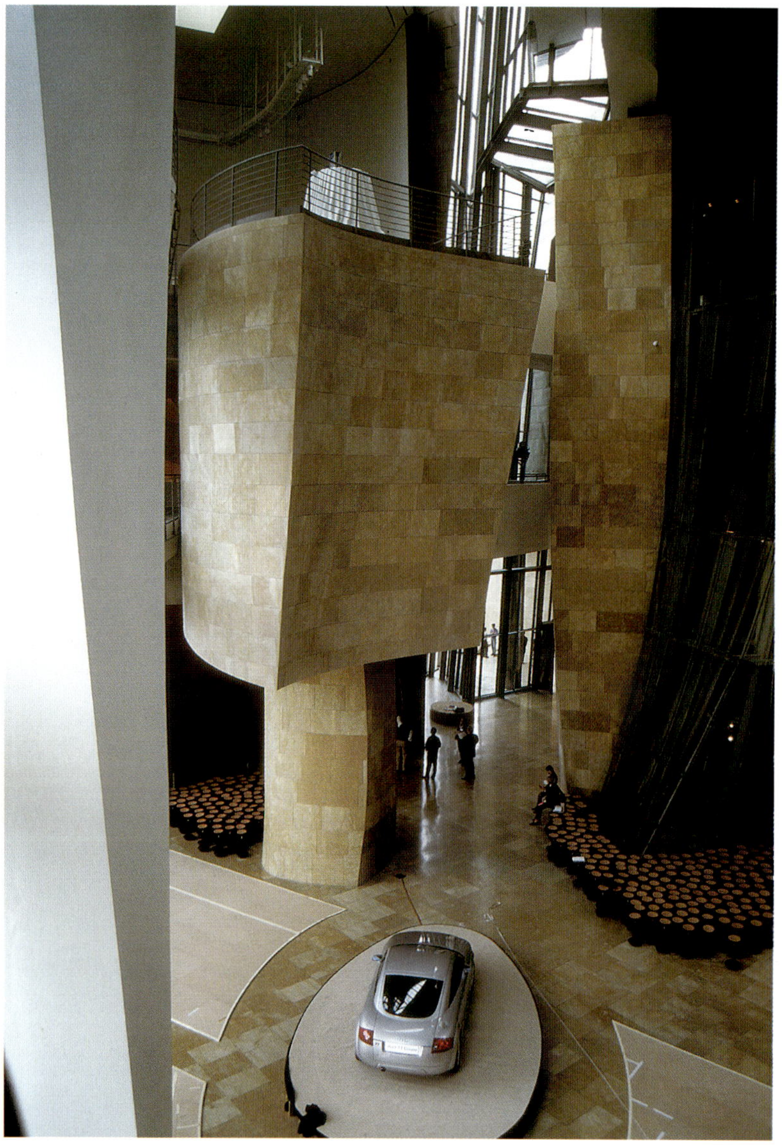

The atrium (or should one say the choir?) and its tendrilled structures sheathed in stone, metal and glass: the edifice is reversible.

Opposite page
Low-angle shot towards the light (divine).

First, let us look at the urban aspect. Despite a drop in the terrain relative to the surrounding neighborhood, the museum fits in surprisingly well with the adjacent turn-of-the-century, six-storey buildings. One could almost call the setting Parisian! From the opposite bank and from the bridges, the museum's striking outline reconciles the industrial landscape with the city; its outlandish appearance succeeds in appeasing the landscape, providing a good transition between the river and the urban houses. With a touch of humor, it even incorporates the bridge that crosses the site.

The Guggenheim underscores with conviction Gehry's formal freedom and the development of his command of a vocabulary that is reminiscent of the paper cuts by Matisse – on a monumental scale. The double curves, the protrusions, the projections in the shape of a prow, the breaks and the humps follow and oppose each other in a well-orchestrated movement. The picture would not be complete, however, without mentioning the materials that shimmer under the contrasted Basque sky. Everything concurs to enthrall the visitor: the alternating glow of titanium, the shine of stones, the radiance of the cobalt marking the entrance, the reflection of the windows – windows that enable the viewer to look deep into the building.

A centrifugal floor plan around the heart – or should we call this a transept? – controls both horizontal and vertical circulation within the edifice as the two pass through elevated structures offering dramatic overviews. The light penetrates through a complex design of openings around the upper volumes encompassing the gigantic atrium open to the sky and river. Mention should also be made of Gehry's use of the most up-to-date techniques: an almost unpalatable twisted metallic structure, doubly curved volumes that were designed with the help of the "Katia" software of the Dassault corporation, titanium used with a maniacal precision and, in a more general sense, the overall perfection of the work. The Basque, aware of the importance of the project, left nothing to chance

The Guggenheim is an exceptional building that has already entered into history. A "modern cathedral," it flaunts all references and begs to become a cliché. It has even put a stop to the age-old quarrel between the contents and the container by offering, for once, an appropriate setting. Asked whether the height of the exhibition walls favored large works, Gehry replied – indicating with his fingers – that a small Klee would fit in just fine. He then added that, "of course, not every one is like Klee!" □

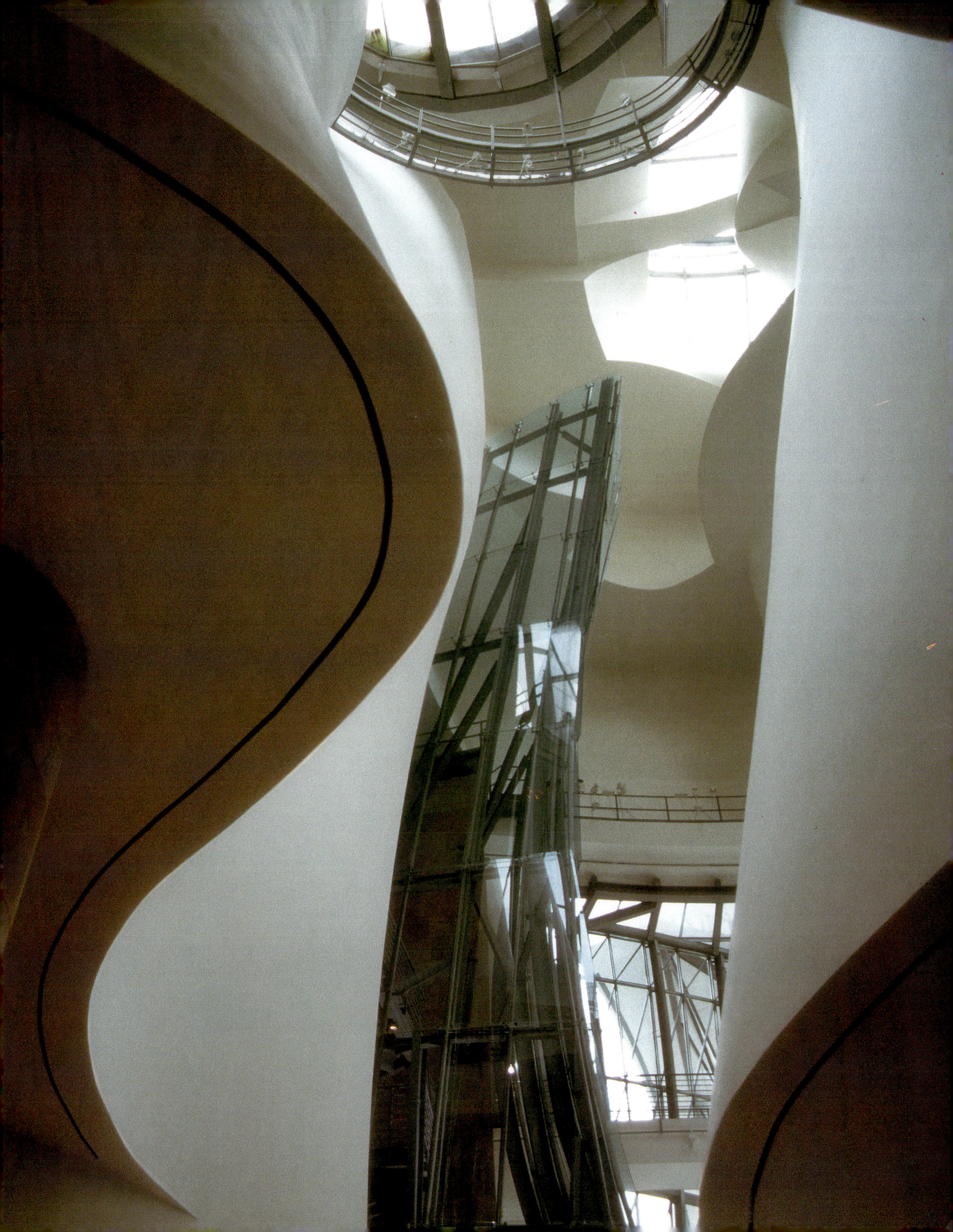

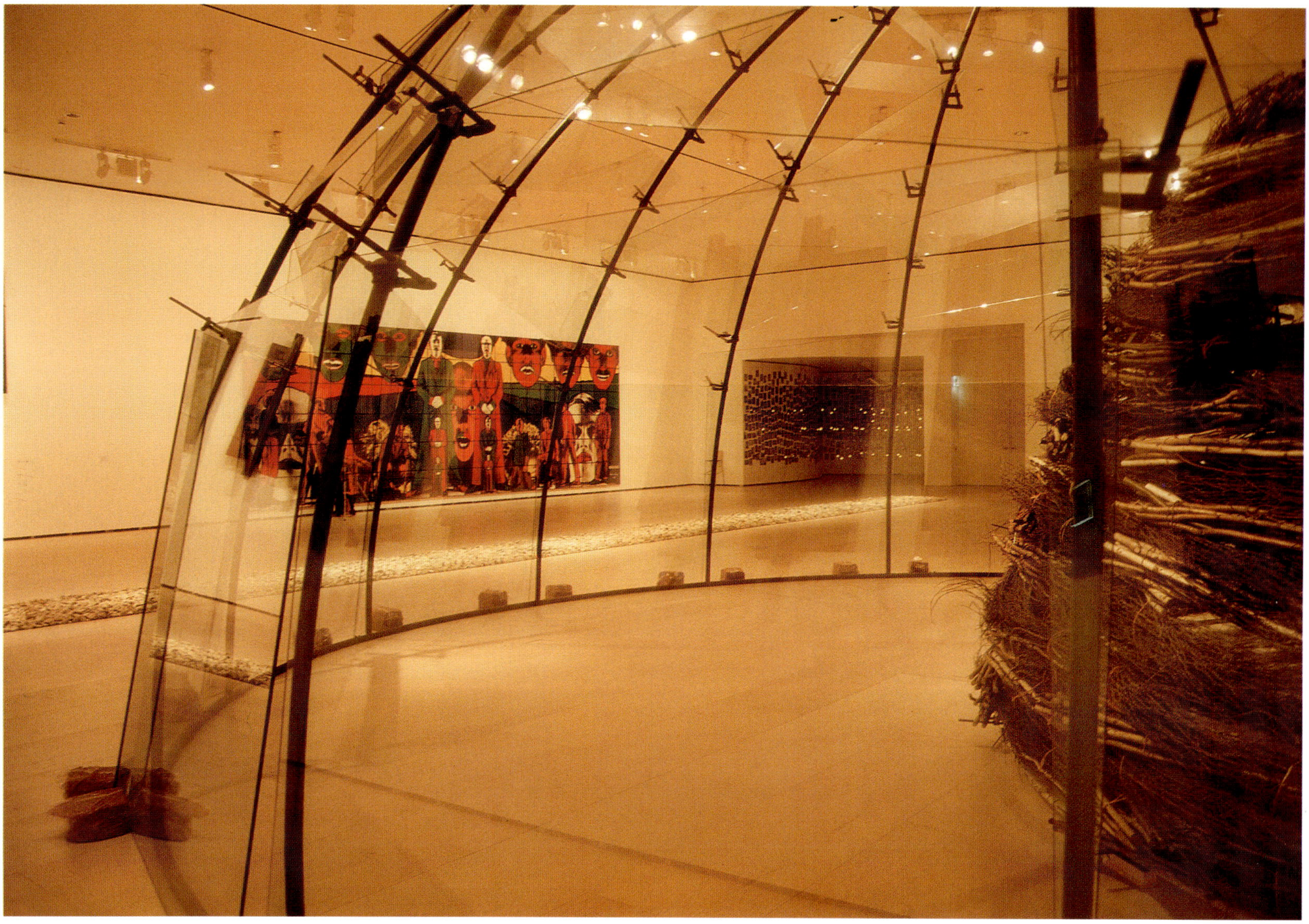

The contemporary European collection room: in the foreground, an igloo by Mario Merz, on the floor, an alignment of stones by Richard Long, on the wall, a work by Gilbert & George and at the far end, Christian Boltanski's chapel.

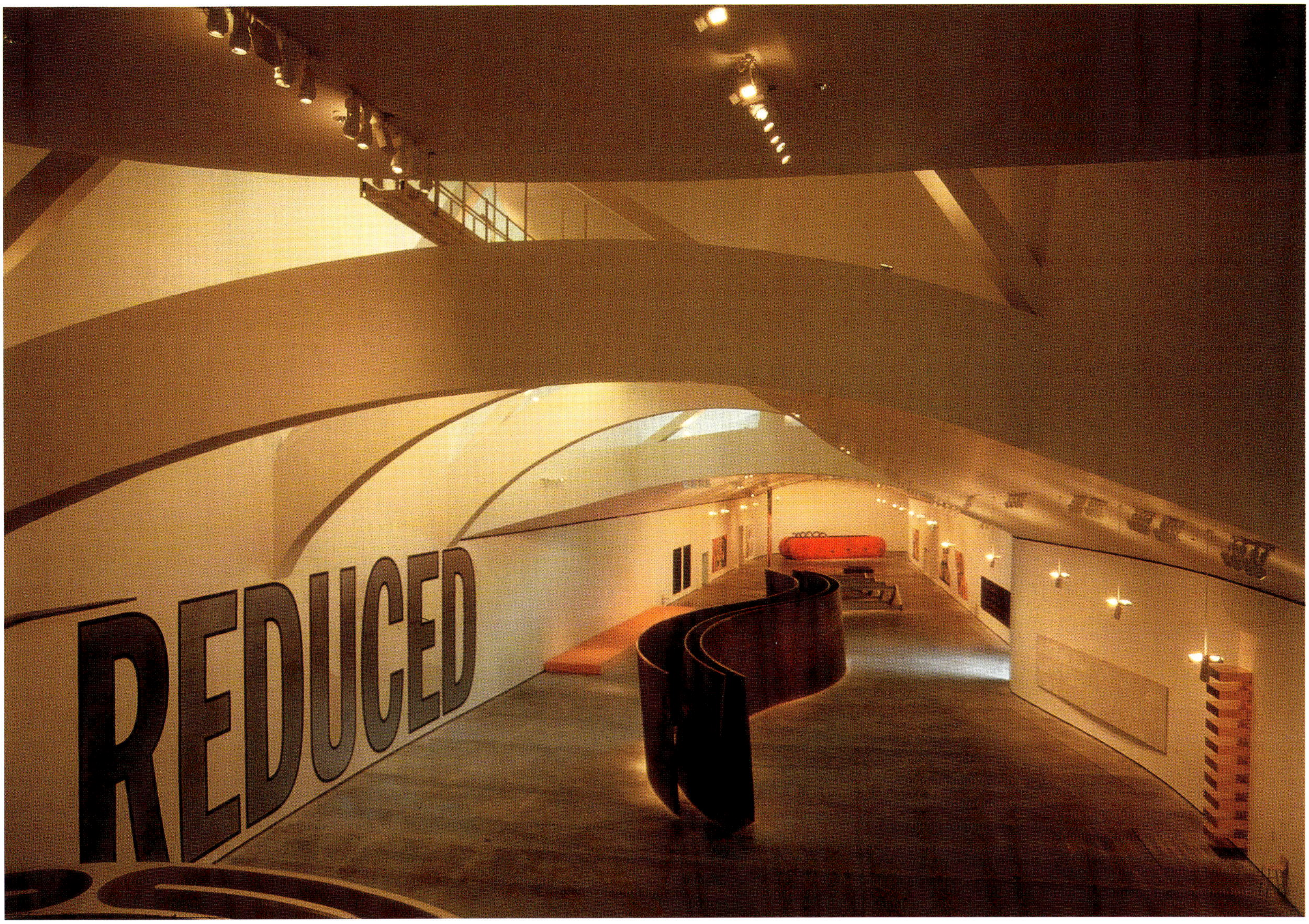

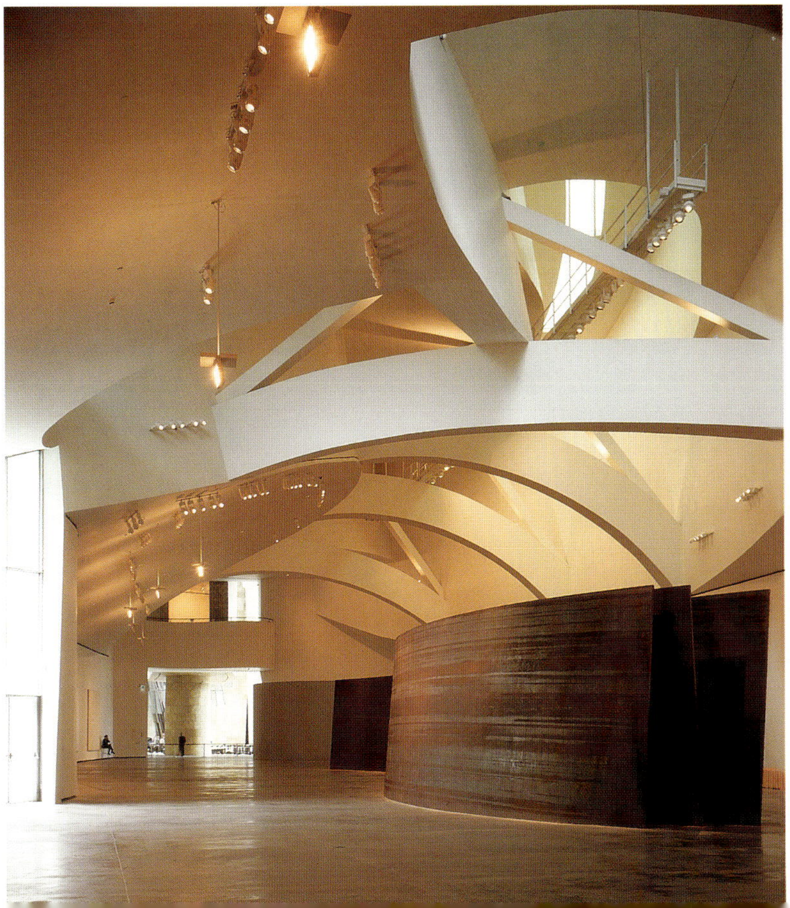

Two views of the great vaulted nave, where part of the contemporary American collection is shown: Richard Serra, Claes Oldenburg, Robert Morris, Dan Flavin...

Biographies

AMADO ROSER & DOMENECH LLUIS

AMADO Roser

Born in Barcelona, 1944.
Graduated from ETSAB (Escuela Tecnica Superior de Architectura de Barcelona) in 1968. Specialized in the restoration of historical buildings at the Colegio de Arquitectos (1980).
In partnership with Lluis Domenech since 1974.

DOMENECH Lluis

Born in Barcelona, 1940. Grandson of architect Domenech i Montaner.
Graduated from ETSAB in 1964.
Specialized in the restoration of historical buildings at the Colegio de Arquitectos (1980).
Director of the Barcelona Museums (1983-1986).

DOMENECH Ramon

Born in Lleida, 1944.
Graduated from EINA (1970).
Lectured on the restoration of historical buildings at the Technical School of Architecture of Barcelona (1990) and at the Colegio d'Aparelladors i Arquitectes Tecnics de Barcelone (1994).

Major Works:
Barcelona: restoration of the Paseo de Picasso (1981-1983); Central Health Laboratory for Catalonia (1983); Carburos Metalicos offices (1990); Antoni Tapiès Foundation (1987-1990); offices and stores for Honda (1992).

BRUNO Andrea

Born in Turin, 1931.
Graduated from the Politecnico of Turin (1956).
Worked between his two offices in Turin and Paris. Numerous missions as expert consultant in Afghanistan (1960-1995) and Iraq (1964-1972). Consultant to Unesco in Afghanistan, Algeria, Cyprus and Bahrain. Lecturer at the Politecnico of Turin (1976-1990) and at the Politecnico of Milan since 1991. Director of the Research Center for the Conservation of Urban and Architectural Heritage at the catholic University of Louvain. Winner of the Europa Nostra Prize in 1993 and 1995.

Major Works
Restorations
Afghanistan: Abdur-Razaq mausoleum in Ghazni (1960-1965); minaret of the Jam Valley (1974-1978); citadel at Herat (1976-1980). Italy, Turin: Castello di Rivoli (1961-1995); Palazzo Madama (1963-1994) and Palazzo Carignano (1980-1985); conversion of the Istituto di Riposo per la Vecchiaia into the information center of the Universita Polytecnico di Piemonte. Rome: Antonina column (1985); dungeon (1971); medieval house (1972). Avigliano: Palace of the Ducs of Savoy (1993).
Architecture
Baghdad: Italian Institute for Architecture and Restoration (1969). Kabul: Italian Embassy (1973). Rivoli: housing complex (1971). Vignale Monferrato: multipurpose hall (1979); Italgas Center (1988). Archeological Museum of Mâa in Cyprus (1989). Houses in Ivrea (1959), Moncalieri (1969), Chieri (1988), Romano Canavese (1973), house with artist's studio in Turin (1974).

Work in Progress
Turin: Museo regionale delle scienze naturale in the former San Giovanni Hospital. Corte, Corsica: musée de la Corse. Tarragona, Spain: restoration of the amphitheater. Paris: renovation of the Conservatoire des Arts et Métiers de Paris. Nîmes: Université bipolaire Montpellier.

FOSTER Norman

Born in England, 1935.
Graduated from the University of Manchester School of Architecture. PhD in architecture from Yale (1963). Created "Team 4" with his wife Wendy Cheesman, Richard Rogers and George Wolton. In 1967 opened Foster Associates in London. Gold Medal RIBA (1983).

Major Works
Cornwall: Creek Vean House with Rogers (1964-1966). Cosham, Hampshire: IBM Pilot Head Office (1970-1971). Ipswich: Willis Faber & Dumas offices (1973-1975). Sainsbury: Centre for Visual Arts and the Crescent Wing (1976-1977). Hong Kong: Hong Kong and Shangai Banking Corporation headquarters (1981-1986). Nîmes: Carré d'Art (1987-1993). London: Sackler Gallery of the Royal Academy of Arts (1989-1991). Duisburg, Germany : Micro-Electronic Park (1990-1996). Fréjus, France: Lycée Albert Camus (1992-1993). Cambridge School of Law (1993-1995). Bordeaux: EDF regional headquarters (1993-1996). Frankfurt: Commerzbank headquarters (1994-1997). Berlin: new federal parliament building, under construction.

GEHRY Frank O.

Born in Toronto, Canada, 1929.
Graduated from University of Southern California (1954).
Founded Frank O. Gehry Associates in 1962. Elected a Fellow of the American Institute of Architects in 1974. Lives and works in Los Angeles. Lecturer at the University of Southern California, at the University of California at Los Angeles, at Yale and Harvard. Winner of the Pritzker Prize in 1989.

Major Works
Malibu: the Ron Davis studio, (1970-1972). Hollywood: Hollywood Bowl (1970-1982). Santa Monica: Santa Monica Place (1973-1980), the Gehry House (1979-1987). Columbia: Main office for the Rouse Company (1974). Beverly Hills: Wosk Residence (1982). Los Angeles: California Aerospace Museum (1982-1984); Walt Disney Concert Hall (1989). Venice: the Norton House (1983). Minnesota: the Winton's Guest House in Wayzata (1984-1986); Minnesota University Museum of Art (1990); Brentwood: the Schnabel House (1986); Kobe, Japan: the Fish Dance restaurant (1986-1989). Weil am Rhein, Germany: Vitra Museum (1989). Bilbao: the Guggenheim Museum Bilbao (1997).

HERZOG & DE MEURON

Both born in Basel, 1950.
Graduated from Zurich's Eidgenössische Technische Hochschule (1975) where they followed Aldo Rossi and Dolf Schnebli's courses.
In 1977, assistants to Dolf Schnebli at Zurich's ETH. In 1983 Herzog was a visiting professor at Cornell University in Ithaca, at Harvard in 1989 and at Tulane University in New Orleans in 1991. Herzog & de Meuron became partners with Rémy Zaugg, and since 1992 with Harry Gugger and Christine Binswanger. Berlin Akademie der Künste Prize in 1987.

Major Works
Oberwil, Switzerland: the Blue House (1979-1980). Tavole, Italy: the Stone House (1985-1988). Munich: the Goetz Gallery (1991-1992). France: the Antipode campus for the University of Bourgogne (1991-1992). London: extension of the Tate Gallery. Basel: building on Helbelstrasse (1984-1988); housing project along a wall of the Schützenmattstrasse (1987-1988); the Schwitter Building (1987-1988); Suva (1988-1993); Basel train station (1992-1995).

HOLL Steven

Born in Bremerton, United States, 1947.
Studied in Rome and at the London Architectural Association (1976).
Founded his own firm in New York in 1976. Lecturer at the University of Washington, at the University of Syracuse and at Columbia since 1981. National Honor Award from the American Institute of Architects (1992).

Major Works
Seaside, Florida: the Hybrid building (1984-1988). Fukuoka, Japan: appartment complex Void Space/Hinged Space (1989-1991). Dallas: the Stretto House (1989-1992). Makuhari, Japan: housing complex (1992-1997). New York: Storefront gallery (1994). Helsinki: Museum of Contemporary Art (1993-1997). Seattle: the Saint-Ignacio chapel at the University of Seattle (1995-1997).

IBOS & VITART

IBOS Jean-Marc

Born in Saint-Cloud, 1957.

VITART Myrto

Born in Paris, 1955.
Partners of the Agence Jean Nouvel & Associés (1985-1989). Founded their own firm in 1989. Winners of the Triangle de la Folie competition in La Défense, Paris (1989). Visiting professors at the Ecole spéciale d'architecture de Paris (1994-1995).

Works
Nîmes: Némausus housing (Jean-Marc Ibos and Jean Nouvel, 1987). Saint-Herblain: Onyx Cultural Center and the Atlantis parking (Myrto Vitart and Jean Nouvel in partnership with Barto & Barto, 1988). Lille: renovation and extension of the Palace of the Palais des Beaux-Arts (1990-1997).

ITO Toyo

Born in Seoul, 1941.
Graduated from the University of Tokyo (1965).
Worked in Kiyonori Kikutake's firm until 1969. Founded his own firm in 1971 named Toyo Ito Architect & Associates in 1979.

Major Works
Nagano: U House (1976) and the D Hotel (1977). Nagoya: PMT House (1978). Tokyo: Silver Hut residence (1984). Yokohama: the Tower of Wind, Kanagawa (1986). Frankfurt: playground in Eckenheim (1988-1991). Brussels: the Pao 2 housing complex for Tokyo Nomad Woman (1989). Kumamoto: Municipal Museum of Yatsushiro (1989-1991); old people's home (1992-1994). Yatsushiroon Kyushu island fire station (1992-1995). Nagano, Shimasuwa-machi: Shimasuwa Lake Suwa Museum (1990-1993).

JUDD Donald

Born in Excelsior Springs, Missouri, 1928. Died in Ayala de Chinati, Texas, 1994.
Graduated in art history from Columbia University (1962).
First personal exhibition at the Panoras Gallery, New York, 1957. Art critic at *Art News, Arts Magazine* and *Art International* (1959-1965). In 1971, moved first to Marfa then to Ayala de Chinati, Texas. In 1975, the National Gallery of Canada published the *Catalogue raisonné of the painted work,* objects and sculpted wood (1960-1974). The New York University Press published the *Complete Writing* (1959-1975) which will be followed a second volume (1975-1986), published by the Dutch Van Abbe museum in 1987. Donald Judd inaugurated the Chinati Foundation in 1986.

MEIER Richard

Born in Newark, New Jersey, 1934.
Graduated from Cornell University in Ithaca, New York (1957).
Member of the American Institute of Architects. Established in New York. In 1959, worked for Davis, Brody & Wisniewski, then in 1960, for Skidmore, Owings & Merrill and from 1961 to 1963 for Marcel Breuer on the Whitney Museum project. Associate

professor of architecture at Yale University in 1975. Winner of the Pritzker Prize, 1984. Royal Gold Medal of the RIBA in 1989. Honored Commandeur des Arts et des Lettres in 1992. Elected member of the American Academy of Arts and Sciences in 1995; AIA Gold Medal in 1997.

Major Works
Private homes: House in Essex Fells, New Jersey. New York: Frank Stella's studio (1965); Darien, Connecticut: the Smith House (1967); Harbor Springs, Michigan: the Douglas House (1973); Malibu: the Ackerberg House; Harding Township, New Jersey: the Grotta House (1984).

Architectural Projects
New York: Bronx Development Center (1970). New Harmony, Indiana: the Atheneum (1975-1979). Frankfurt: Frankfurt Museum of Decorative Arts (1979). Atlanta: High Museum of Art (1980). Los Angeles: the Getty Center (1985-1992). The Hague: City Hall and Central Library (1985-1994). Ulm, Germany: Cultural and Administrative Center (1985-1993). Barcelona: Museum of Contemporary Art (1988-1995). Schwendi, Germany: Weishaupt Forum (1992). Houston, Texas: Compaq Computers headquarters (1994).

MONEO Jose Rafael

Born in Tudela, Spain, 1937.
Worked with Francisco Serenz de Oiza in Madrid and later with Jorn Utzon in Denmark. Winner of the Rome Scholarship in 1967. Lecturer at the ETSA Barcelona (1970-1980), then at the ETSA Madrid (1980-1985). Senior member of the Graduate School of Design at Harvard (1985-1990).

Major Works
Madrid: Bankinter building (1976). Logrono: City Hall (1981). Merida, Archeological Museum (1986). Seville: the Prevision building (1988). Barcelona: auditorium (1988). San Sebastien: Kursaal (1990). Venice: Lido (1991). Madrid: refurbishing of the Villahermoso Palace (1991); Atocha train station (1992). Palma de Majorca: Fundacio Mirò (1992). Davies Museum in Massachusetts (1993). Stockholm: Museum of Modern Art and Architecture (1998).

OMA - KOOLHAAS REM

KOOLHAAS Rem

Born in Rotterdam, 1944.
Journalist, scriptwriter.
Studied at the London Architectural Association (1968-1972). Reciptient of a grant to study in the United States in 1972.
Worked with Oswald-Mathias Ungers at Cornell University in 1972-1973, then with Peter Eisenman at the Institute for Architecture and Urban Studies in New York.
In London, 1975, together with architects Madelon Vriesendorp, Elia and Zoé Zenghelis, he founded OMA, Office for Metropolitan Architecture.
In 1978, published Delirious New York and in 1979 organized a retrospective for New York architect Wallace Harrison, "Beyond good or bad", at the IAUS.
In 1980 opened a firm in Rotterdam. Visiting fellow at the IAUS until 1979. Lecturer at Columbia, UCLA and at the Architectural Association. Since 1990, professor at Harvard.

Major Works
Holland: The Hague: National Dance Theater (1987); Rotterdam: bus terminal (1987), Patiovilla (1988), Kunsthal Rotterdam (1991); Gröningen: Brink buildings (1988); Amersfoort: RWA studios (1990); Amsterdam: Bysantium offices and stores (1991); Utrecht: Educatorium of Utrecht University (1997). France: Saint-Cloud, villa Dall'Ava (1991); Euralille and Lille-Grand-Palais; villa in Bordeaux (1998). Furka Pass, Switzerland: Furkablick hotel (1990). Fukuoka, Japan: Nexus complex (1991).
Work in Progress
Seoul: University Museum. Geneva: Human Rights building. Utrecht: Business Center. Berlin: Dutch Embassy. Bangkok: Hyperbuilding.

PEI Ieoh Ming

Born in Guangzhou, China, 1917.
Master of Architecture (1942), PhD from Harvard (1946).
Founded I.M. Pei & Associates in 1955. 1979 AIA Gold Medalist. 1983 Pritzker Prize. 1989 Imperial Prize, Japan.

Major Works
Boulder, Colorado: National Center for Atmospheric Research (1961-1967), 50 air traffic control towers for the Federal Aviation Agency (1962-1970). Boston: John F. Kennedy Library (1965-1979). Washington DC: National Gallery of Art (1968-1978). Hong Kong: Bank of China tower (1982-1989). Paris: Grand Louvre (1983-1993). Cleveland: Rock and Roll Hall of Fame (1993-1995).

PIANO Renzo

Born in Genoa, 1937.
Graduated from the Politecnico of Milan (1964).
Assistant to Marco Zanuso and Gino Valle. Worked in Milan and in London (1964-1970). In 1970 began a partnership with Richard Rogers which lasted until 1976. Collaborated with Peter Rice. In 1980 opened offices in Paris and Genoa.

Major Works
Paris: Centre National d'Art Moderne Georges Pompidou with Richard Rogers (1971-1978). Houston: Ménil Foundation (1982-1986). Bari, Italy: San Nicola Stadium (1987-1990). Charenton-le-Pont, Paris: shopping center Bercy 2 (1987-1990). Osaka, Japan: Kansai international airport (1990-1994). Nouméa, New Caledonia: Jean-Marie Tjibaou Cultural Center (1993-1998). Amsterdam: National Science and Technology Center (1996-1997). Riehen, Switzerland: Beyeler Foundation (1996-1997).

ROSSI Aldo

Born in Milan, 1931. Died in 1997. Graduated from the Politecnico of Milan in 1959.
Collaborated to the review Casabella Continuita from 1955 to 1964. In 1966 published *L'architettura della citta*. Lecturer at the University of Palermo (1970), at the Politecnico of Milan (1972/73), at Zurich's polytechnic, at Yale, Harvard and at the Institute for Architecture of New York. 1990 Pritzker Prize.

Major Works
Milan: housing complex in the Gallaratese neighborhood (1973). Modena: San Cataldo cemetery with Gianni Braghieri (1971). Venice: Teatro del Mondo (1979). Berlin: appartments on Rauchstrasse (1983), housing complex for the Internationale Bauausstellung (1984-87). Parma: Centro Torri (1985-88). Miami: University of Miami School of Architecture (1986). Toronto: Toronto Lighthouse Theater with Morris Adjimi (1988). Fukuoka, Japan: Il Palazzo hotel (1989). Maastricht: Bonnefanten Museum (1997).

SIZA Vieira Alvaro

Born near Porto, Portugal, 1933.
Studied architecture at the ESBAP, (Escuela Superior de Architectura de Porto), 1949-1955.
In 1988, Gold Medalist at the Colegio dos Arquitectos of Madrid and the Alvar Aalto Foundation; Prince of Wales Prize; Mies Van der Rohe Prize. 1992 Pritzker Prize. 1994 Premio Nacional de Arquitectura.

Major Works
Leça da Palmeira, Portugal: Boa Nova restaurant (1963). Matosinhos: collective housing (1968). Porto: Sao Victor and Bouça; New School of Architecture (1993). Evora: Quinta da Malagueira (1977). Lamego: Oliveira de Azemeis Bank (1974); Vila do Conde (1986); Sines Cultural Center (1985). Setubal: 'Normal' school (1992). Aveiro: Aveiro University Library (1993). Berlin: appartment complex in Kreuzberg (1979-1988). The Hague, Holland: housing in Schilderswijk Ward (1988). Madrid: La Defensa Cultural Center (1988). Marco de Canavezes: Church and Parish (1990). Santiago de Compostella: Museum of Contemporary Art (1993-1997).

MICHAEL WILFORD & PARTNERS

STIRLING James

Born in Glasgow, 1926.
Graduated from the University of Liverpool (1950).
Worked with Lyons, Israel and Ellis (1953-1956). Opened his own firm in 1956. Partnership with James Gowan (1963), then with Michael Wilford (1971). 1980 Gold Medal RIBA. 1981 Pritzker Prize.

WILFORD Michael

Born in Surrey, 1938.
Studied at the Northern Polytechnic School of Architecture in London (1955-1962).

Major Works
James Sirling: Leicester: University of Leicester with James Gowan (1959-1963). Cambridge: University of Cambridge (1964-1967). Haslemere: Olivetti Training School (1969-1972).
James Stirling & Michael Wilford: Stuttgart: Staatsgalerie (1979-1983). Houston: extension of the School of Architecture of Rice University (1979-1981). London: the Clore Gallery, Tate Gallery extension (1980-1985).

Bibliography

General bibliography

ALLÉGRET Laurence, *Les Musées,* Electa Moniteur, Paris, 1987. Tome II, Paris, 1992.
DAVIS Douglas, *The Museum transformed*, Abbeville Publishers, New York, 1990.
KLOTZ Heinrich & KRAUSE Waltrand, *Neue Museumsbauten in der Bundesrepublik Deutschland*, Francfort, 1985.
LACOUTURE Jean, *Les Musées en chantier*, Réunion des musées nationaux, Paris, 1991.
MONTANER Josep Maria and OLIVERAS Jordi, *los Museos de la ultima generacion*, Gustavo Gili, Barcelona, 1986.
MONTANER Josep Maria, *Nuevos Museos : Espacios para el este y la cultura*, Gustavo Gili, Barcelona, 1990.
SCHUBERT Hannelore, *Moderner Museumsbau : Deutschland, Österreich, Schweiz*, DVA, Stuttgart, 1986.

El Arquitecto y el Museo, Colegio oficial de arquitectos de Andalucia occidental, 1990.
The Museum of Modern Art, Gunma, Arata Isozaki, Phaidon, London, 1996.
Nouveaux musées, le musée en mouvement, ADAC, 1990.

Monographs

BUCHANAN Peter, *Renzo Piano : Complete Works*, 3 volumes, Phaidon, London, 1997.
FERLENGA Alberto, *Aldo Rossi : Opera Completa, 1957-1996*, 3 volumes, Electa, Milan, 1996.
GILI Gustavo, *Alvaro Siza : Works & Projects 1954-1992*, Barcelona, 1993.
JODIDIO Philip, *Sir Norman Foster*, Benedikt Taschen, Cologne, 1997.
JODIDIO Philip, *Richard Meier*, Benedikt Benedikt Taschen, Cologne, 1995.
LUCAN Jacques, *OMA-Rem Koolhaas*, Electa/Moniteur, 1990.
MARK Gerhard, *Herzog & de Meuron*, 2 volumes, Birkhäuser, Zürich, 1996.
MORRIS Adjimi, *Aldo Rossi : Architecture 1981-1991*, New York, 1991.
OMA/Rem KOOLHAAS et Bruce MAU, *S, M, L, XL.*, 010 Publishers/The Monacelli Press, 1995. Benedikt Taschen, 1997.
PIANO Renzo, *Carnet de travail*, Seuil, Paris, 1997.
ROULET Sophie & SOULIÉ Sophie, *Toyo Ito*, Ed. du Moniteur, Paris, 1991.
WANG Wilfried, *Herzog & de Meuron,* Artemis, Zürich, 1994.

Alvaro Siza 1954-1995, 2 volumes, Blau, Lisboa, 1995.
Alvaro Siza 1958-1994, El Croquis, n°68/69, Barcelona, 1994.
FRANK GEHRY, Electa, Milan, 1998.
FRANK GEHRY, Global Architecture n°10, A.D.A., TOKYO.
FRANK GEHRY, El Croquis n°74/75, Barcelona, 1995.
Frank Gehry, Museo Guggenheim Bilbao, El Croquis n°88/89, Barcelona, 1998.
Herzog & de Meuron, El Croquis n°84, Barcelona, 1997.
James Stirling : Die neue Staatsgalerie Stuttgart, Verlag Gerd Hatje, Stuttgart, 1984.
James Stirling : Buildings and Projects 1950-1974, Thames & Hudson, London, 1996.
James Stirling, Michael Wilford & Associates : Buildings and Projects 1975-1992, Thames & Hudson, London, 1996.
José Rafael Moneo, El Croquis n°64, Barcelona, 1997.
Making architecture. The Getty Center, Thames & Hudson, London, 1997.
Norman Foster : Buildings and Projects 1964-1989, 4 volumes, Watermark, Hong Kong, 1989.
Oltre il restauro. Progetti e realizzazioni di Andrea Bruno (1960-1995), Lybra Immagine, Milan, 1996.
Steven Holl, Global Architecture n°11, A.D.A., Tokyo.
Steven Holl, El Croquis n°78, Barcelona, 1996. Et aussi : *Steven Holl : Musée Knut Hamsun à Hamaroy, Norvège*, El Croquis " Worldsmundos " (I), n°88/89, Barcelona, 1998.
Toyo Ito, El Croquis n°71, Barcelona, 1995.

Photo credits

Pages 8 to 17: photos Fessy
Pages 18 to 23: photos Tate Gallery Publishing Limited
Pages 24 à 31: Museo d'Arte Contemporanea (Castello di Rivoli) and Andrea Bruno archives.
Pages 32 to 39: Fundació Antoni Tàpies archives
Pages 40 to 51, 143 à 157 and back cover: photos AD.OB Design
Pages 52 to 57: photos Foster and Partners, James H Morris
Pages 58 to 65: photos Hans Werlemann
Pages 66 to 73, 102 to 111: photos Duccio Malagamba
Pages 74 to 85: photos Timothy Hursley
Pages 86 to 93: photos Tomio Ohashi, Naoya Hatakeyama
Pages 94 to 101: photos KMS - Kim Zwarts
Page 112 to 121: photos Philippe Ruault
Pages 122 to 127: photos Margarita Spillutinni
Pages 128 to 137 and front cover: photos Christian Richter
Pages 138 to 143: photos Scott Frances/Esto Photographics Inc

Printed and bound in Great Britain by
Butler & Tanner Ltd, Frome and London